NFoss

# Child Abuse and Neglect

## The Family and the Community

edited by
**Ray E. Helfer**
and
**C. Henry Kempe**
preface by
**Walter F. Mondale**

**Ballinger Publishing Company** ● **Cambridge, Mass.**
*A Subsidiary of J.B. Lippincott Company*

The editors dedicate this book to the more than 3,000 families who, over the past twenty years, have allowed us to work with them and thereby taught us how to help others.

International Standard Book Number: 0-88410-217-3

Library of Congress Catalog Card Number: 76-8891

Printed in the United States of America

**Library of Congress Cataloging in Publication Data**

Main entry under title:

Child abuse and neglect.

    1. Child abuse—Addresses, essays, lectures. 2. Family psychotherapy—Addresses, essays, lectures. 3. Violence—Addresses, essays, lectures. I. Helfer, Ray E. II. Kempe, C. Henry, 1922–HV713.C382     362.7'1
76-8891                            ISBN 0-88410-217-3

# ✳ Contents

*v*

# ❄ List of Figures

*ix*

# ✻  List of Tables

*xi*

 **Preface**

This important compilation of the most current approaches and ideas in the field of child abuse and neglect promises to take its place along with *The Battered Child* and *Helping the Battered Child and His Family* as an essential resource for those interested in learning about and attempting to resolve a critical national problem.

The editors' previous work in the field—through writing and through the National Center for the Prevention and Treatment of Child Abuse and Neglect in Denver—has provided our country with the most important, fundamental insights into child abuse and neglect. The identification of the "battered child" syndrome, the development of the multidisciplinary approach to treatment, the emphasis on the concept of prevention are all contributions of inestimable value to the thousands of children and families affected by child abuse and neglect in this country.

The work of this Center also served as both an inspiration and an educational tool for the Committee on Labor and Public Welfare in the process of its hearings and development of federal legislation. Although we have made significant progress through the legislation enacted, I still believe strongly in the need for projects such as the Denver Center to sustain the awareness of and commitment to the tragically abused and neglected children in this country.

It may be many years before we are able to effectively prevent and treat child abuse and neglect. We must, however, assure that these children are not abandoned by society. I am confident that this book will make an invaluable contribution toward that goal.

Walter F. Mondale
United States Senate

# ✳ Foreword

As more is learned about child abuse and neglect, it becomes increasingly evident that the plight of children in contemporary society is alarming. Even more concerning, this plight is apparently becoming worse. The sheer repugnance of the signs of physical abuse draws deeply upon the compassion and composure of all sensitive people, including those whose professional training and experience has enabled them to be somewhat more objective and yet empathetic about such human dynamics. The insidious and perhaps more pernicious phenomenon of intentional or inadvertent neglect of a child's physical, affective, and cognitive needs may in fact be even greater, albeit less dramatic. The loss to our society and the individual tragedy of the unknowing and innocent victim is often irreparable.

Child abuse and neglect represent a societal symptom suggesting that children, much as other resources, are both plentiful and expendable. It is unfortunate that extremes of violent and negligent parenting must be cited in order to get the public's attention focused on a resource upon which we spend less than 10 percent of our GNP, yet which represents 40 percent of our population and 100 percent of our future—our children. By increasing the visibility and understanding of child abuse and neglect, it is hoped that a more general concern for the welfare of our nation's children will be advanced.

A raised consciousness and concomitant greater responsibility for our children's cause promises to provide a more just share of inalienable rights to this nonvoting but extraordinarily important ingredient in the nation's present hope and future destiny. Indeed, at the federal, state, and local levels, all citizens are now much more aware of the issues surrounding child abuse and neglect.

The past several years of legislation, research, and service demonstration projects sponsored under a wide variety of public and private auspices have helped. Without exploiting these highly vulnerable victims, it is important to be an outspoken advocate for children and to declare a renewed dedication to their universal welfare in this 200th year of our nation's existence. Child advocacy is a prime reason for the existence of the Office of Child Development in the U.S. Department of Health, Education, and Welfare; its multiple efforts in behalf of abused and neglected children and their families give ample testimony to the depth and breadth of the federal government's commitment to alleviating this problem and promoting optimum child growth and development.

In a world society, wherein the fundamental socializing agencies and institutions (such as the family itself) are undergoing radical changes in composition and function, it is even more urgent that informed, balanced, and current sources of the state of the art and science about such pressing issues be made available. This encyclopedic text is a most timely and appropriate collection of authoritative and cogent statements about child abuse and neglect, presented from an interdisciplinary and ecological perspective.

It is noteworthy that two of the prime pioneers in this field, whose research and skills in the clinical aspects of child abuse and neglect have earned for them an undisputed claim as champions of children, have gone somewhat beyond the children themselves and have now turned their expertise toward understanding the highly complex related factors in the family and the community. This broader treatment of the problem, especially the encouraging section addressing early identification and prevention, is most enlightening and relevant.

It is a distinct honor and pleasure to contribute the foreword to this next milestone in a series of definitive books edited by two esteemed colleagues. Furthermore, I would feel remiss if I failed to gratefully acknowledge the pervasive and salutory influence of Drs. Ruth and C. Henry Kempe on the personal and professional lives of my wife and me as we have collaborated during this past decade in behalf of abused and neglected children and their families.

John H. Meier, Ph.D.
Director, U.S. Office of Child Development
and Chief, U.S. Children's Bureau,
Department of Health, Education
and Welfare

# ✳ Introduction

The last major outbreak of poliomyelitis in the United States occured in 1959. During that epidemic 5,500 children were affected. This came four years *after* polio vaccine had been shown to be very effective in the prevention of this paralytic disease. The public was outraged; "Why hadn't something been done?" While the "city fathers" in one large city argued about appropriating funds to immunize the masses, approximately 60 children developed paralysis. After considerable debate as to the merits and ethics of mass immunization, the decision was made, the money allocated, and one million people were immunized. The epidemic came under prompt control.

In 1975 there were approximately 550,000 cases of suspected child abuse and neglect reported in the United States. (The Department of Health, Education, and Welfare estimates the actual number to be over a million.) This came some four years after certain treatment programs had been shown to be helpful in reducing the devastating effect of this problem. The general public was not outraged; only a few voices were heard. Most "city fathers" were not even debating the merits of implementing a communitywide treatment program. Approximately *1 percent* of American children are reported to be abused or neglected each year. Considering the number of unreported cases, especially the siblings of those who were reported, the total percentage of those actually abused or neglected is no doubt higher.

The effects of child abuse and neglect are cumulative. Once the developmental process of a child is insulted or arrested by bizzare child rearing pattern, the scars remain. One should not be surprised, then, to find that the large majority of delinquent adolescents indicate that they were abused as children; little wonder that 25 percent of a group of 250 women who had just delivered their babies and were not known to have been abused, responded "I agree" to the query, "When I was a child my parents used severe physical punishment on me or one of my siblings."

In the first edition of *The Battered Child* (University of Chicago Press, 1968) there is this statement: "This upper limit for the year ending October 1965, was between 2.53 to 4.07 million (cases) for a population of about 190 million, or about 13.3 to 21.4 incidents per 1,000 persons." The results of this survey were, for the most part, discounted. Child abuse and neglect is eroding every aspect of our society. The problem presents itself in a variety of ways, from the severely battered infant to the runaway adolescent who cannot tolerate the abuse any longer. It is ever with us. The end results are teenagers and young adults who are ill prepared to function with their peers, much less raise our next generation.

There is no strata of our society currently giving the problem of abuse and neglect the attention it demands. Violence is glorified rather than abhored on television; schools teach basket weaving rather than child and family development; over $120 billion are spent to defend against a threat from without while our families, the core of our society, are being eroded with the cancer of abnormal rearing practices. Parenting practices in our society are likened to the great tree, standing erect, shielding us from the sun, only to fall one day from internal decay.

Those who are recognizing the seriousness of this problem are growing. Some "city fathers" are beginning to pay attention. Our children are fortunate that Senator Walter Mondale and his colleagues, and a few other key city and state leaders are among them. There is cause for some optimism. Like an eternally optimistic 5-year-old who ran to his mother and said, "Mommy, I have good news and bad news!" "Better give me the good news first," was her reply. "Most of my dirties went into the toilet."

We too have good news. Our government is beginning to take heed. The Office of Child Development is giving major emphasis to the problems of abuse and neglect. The psychodynamics are better understood; treatment innovations are under way all over the country; community programs are growing; and most important, helping people are talking to each other. We are beginning to think about early recognition and prevention.

The great majority of these families can be helped, but a few cannot. When the latter occurs it must be admitted and the children saved from this never-ending cycle by permanent removal, adoption and retraining. Special recognition should be given to the Robert Wood Johnson Foundation, the Grant Foundation, the Kaiser Family Foundation and Commonwealth Fund for their support.

This book is the third in a series of edited manuscripts, the purpose of which is to bring to the attention of the public the current "state of the art" in the field of helping families caught up in the cycle of abuse. *The Battered Child* (published in 1968 by the University of Chicago Press) presented the knowledge in the field at that time, particularly as it pertained to the medical, social, and psychodynamic aspect of the problem. Much of this information is still of fundamental importance; for this reason this book was updated and a second edition published in 1974.

Between the years 1968 and 1972 considerable information was obtained to better understand ways in which these families could be helped. The second book, *Helping the Battered Child and His Family* (published by J.B. Lippincott in 1972) drew attention to those therapeutic advances.

Four more years have passed, and now thousands of lay and professional individuals have become interested. New information and methods are available. For the first time the editors found it difficult to determine which of the many excellent writers and programs to bring to the public's attention. Reducing the manuscript to a reasonable size was difficult—a problem not encountered in the previous books.

The major purpose of this volume is to help the thousands of individuals now working in the field of child abuse and neglect to implement effective, efficient, and coordinated programs of family assessment, treatment, and learning, both in this country and abroad. *Child Abuse and Neglect: The Family and the Community* is divided into six sections:

Part I     —Dysfunction in Family Interaction
Part II    —Assessing Family Pathology
Part III   —Family Oriented Therapy
Part IV    —The Community
Part V     —The Family and the Law
Part VI    —Early Recognition and Prevention of Potential Problems with
             Family Interaction

The term "the battered child" has been dropped. When coined fifteen years ago, its purpose was to gain the attention of both physicians and the public. We feel, now, that enough progress has been made to move on to a more inclusive phrase—child abuse and neglect. The problem is clearly not just one of *physical* battering. Save for the children who are killed or endure permanent brain damage (and these remain a prime concern), the most devastating aspect of abuse and neglect is the permanent adverse effects on the developmental process and the child's emotional well-being.

As in the previous publication, the editors see this endeavor as coming at a time of transition. At this time we must take what is known in this field and weave those ideas and techniques into a smoothly functioning, long term treatment and remedial program for families. This will require extensive efforts on the part of every community in the country. Our next book will, hopefully, begin where this one leaves off—with the developing skills of early prediction and prevention. Prevention is not far away, given the right amount of effort and priority setting by all those concerned with this field.

The editors have refrained from imposing too many of their stylistic preferences on the contributors because this results in the inevitable loss of individuality. We have added certain concepts, appropriately identified, and asked others for commentaries where this was thought to be helpful. A companion book, also published by Ballinger, will give more emphasis to the abused and neglected *child.* This is entitled, *"The Abused Child: A Multidisciplinary Approach to Developmental Issues and Treatment,"* and is edited by Dr. Harold Martin.

The task is to give our children at least as high a priority as our air, our water or our energy. Even the strongest advocate for our ecology would agree that our children deserve equal ranking.


We urge you to become advocates for young children today, for they are indeed our nation's hope for tomorrow.

Ray E. Helfer
C. Henry Kempe
1976

**Part I**

# Dysfunction in Family Interaction

# ✳ Introduction

Violence, when it permeates a family, is devastating, and its consequences appear endless. All members of the family are affected by the emotional and developmental insults, if not by actual physical abuse. Millions of children are brought up in a "world of abnormal rearing" (WAR). The psychological injuries sustained during this WAR are carried into adulthood and transmitted like some insidious genetic disease to their children. We anticipate impairment rather than improvement in the parenting competence of a great number of children in the next generation unless we can intervene and provide help to break the cycle.

Chapter One presents Dr. Brandt Steele's concepts on violence in the family. He sees violence as undermining the very psychological stability of every family member. Part One ends with a presentation by Drs. Ounsted and Lynch, a psychiatrist and pediatrician, who view the problems of family violence from a different global perspective. Also included in this section are some of the newer concepts relating to the attachment or bonding of a mother to her newborn infant. This attachment has been studied for years in animals but its importance in humans was given little consideration until Drs. Kennell and Klaus began their work ten years ago. There is little question that their findings have significant implications relating to the field of child abuse and neglect.

The effects of child abuse and neglect on the early developmental process of these children is discussed in Chapter Three by Drs. Helfer, McKinney, and Kempe. What really happens to a growing, developing child when this sequence of events is interrupted or frozen? Their conclusions are frightening.

Ray E. Helfer
C. Henry Kempe

Chapter One

# Violence Within the Family

Brandt F. Steele

"To the infant its nursery is the world. The first ideas of the human race are its particular conceptions of its nurse and mother; and the origin and history of all its notions may be traced to its animals wants, to the light that breaks in from its window, and to the few objects in the immediate neighborhood of the cradle and hearth."

—Thomas C. Upham, 1852[1]

Combining "violence" and "family" in the title may seem like a paradox, or even shock people who are unfamiliar with some aspects of human behavior. "Violence" is destructive, dangerous, and frightening, while "family" means the human environment where there is love, safety, warmth, the opportunity to grow, and a sanctuary to seek when all else in the world goes awry. True, most families do fulfill this ideal of nurturance; but many do not. Nevertheless, the family has always been and still remains the central, basic structure of society; and the constant growth of human populations indicates its adaptative survival value, despite the concomitant presence of violence in its midst.

Violence has always been part of the human condition, a recurring aspect of human life since time immemorial. Much of what we call history is a chronicle of the recurrent wars of conquest and rebellion which have always been involved in the creation of new governments and states. Such violence has existed on the broadest cultural, ethnic, and religious bases and has filtered down through smaller units of society into territorial and economic struggles and vendettas between tribes, clans, and families.

*Special recognition is given to the Grant Foundation for the support given to the work of Dr. Steele.

3

Throughout history the well known motives of the search for power, position, and possessions, and prestige, and the powerful drives of envy and jealousy have led to violent behaviors.[2] These particular patterns seem to be recurrent, not only in the broad area of international relations, but also in the wars of colonization and rebellion.[3] Thus it is not surprising to find similar patterns of violence occurring within the family. In the relationships among family members the same conflicts may arise over problems of recognition, material supplies, and questions of loyalty, control, and sexual fidelity. Violence may be used to resolve such conflicts.

## FAMILY VIOLENCE

Violence has been part of the lives of families and of individuals since the very beginning. In the familiar biblical story of creation and the life of early man we find murder in the form of brother killing brother. According to this story the Lord did not respect Cain for his offering but did respect that given by the younger brother, Abel. Cain became angry because the Lord did not sympathize with him, but instead scolded him; and following this, "Cain rose up against Abel his brother and slew him." The evident themes of rivalry, need for approval, and resentment because of lack of appreciation and respect are even today familiar to us as emotional precipitants of aggression.

A somewhat analogous story is told in the myth of the founding of ancient Rome by the wolf-suckled twins Romulus and Remus. After they had decided upon the site of the future city they were to govern, Remus is said to have ridiculed Romulus's strength and authority, whereupon Romulus turned upon his twin and killed him. The classic Greek myth of Oedipus tells of patricide, filicide, fratricide, and multiple suicides in three generations of one family. Such emotional states continue to be motivations for violence in the family as we have known it all through recorded history.

Agrippina, the mother of Nero, poisoned her second husband, the Emperor Claudius, in order to ensure the succession of her son. Later Nero had his mother, Agrippina, murdered, and also killed his first wife, Octavia, in order to marry Poppaea. He later killed Poppaea by kicking her in the stomach while she was pregnant. Also out of fear of challenge to his power he killed Brittanicus, the son of Claudius. Cesare Borgia arranged for the murder of his brother-in-law whom he felt to be a dangerous political rival. King Henry VIII of England had two of his wives beheaded. One cannot help being impressed by the amount of intrafamilial violence that seems to be part of the human condition. Parents kill children, children kill parents, spouses kill each other, children kill each other, and paramours and in-laws are common victims.

### Homicide

If we take the act of homicide as a paradigm of violence we find it is mostly a family matter. Many people find it hard to believe that murder is essentially a behavior acted out predominantly within the confines of kinship, but it is true nevertheless. Year after year, statistics show that the great majority of murderers and their victims are blood relatives, relatives by marriage, or close friends or acquaintances well known to each other. Only a minority of murders occur between strangers, roughly 25 percent or less.

The most accurate statistics we have on violence are those published annually by the Federal Bureau of Investigation. In 1973, 17,123 cases of murder were analyzed.[4] Out of this total, 13.7 percent were spouse killing spouse, 3.3 percent parent killing child, 8.7 percent were other family killings, 7.2 percent were romantic triangles and lovers' quarrels, and 42 percent were "other arguments." Only 24.9 percent were known or suspected felony murders. ("Felony murders" in uniform crime reporting are defined as those killings resulting from robbery, burglary, sex motives, gangland and institutional slayings, and all other felonious activities.)

Much more common than actual murder (cases in which the victim dies) is the violent crime classified as "aggravated assault," which is defined as "an unlawful attack by one person upon another for the purpose of inflicting severe bodily injury, usually accompanied by the use of a weapon or other means likely to produce death or serious bodily harm."[4] This is much more common than actual murder; the FBI estimated 416,270 aggravated assaults in the nation in 1973. The chief difference between murder and aggravated assault is the victims in the latter instances did not die, and were presumably the objects of less severe attack. In other respects the two crimes are quite alike, the FBI stating that "most aggravated assaults occur within the family unit and among neighbors or acquaintances. The victim-offender relationship as well as the nature of the attack make this crime similar to murder."

A further indication of the prevalence of violence in family situations is the fact that in 1963, 26 percent of assaults on law enforcement officers, while 13 percent of deaths among them occurred when the officers were answering disturbance calls.[5] "Disturbance calls" is the category largely composed of requests to interfere in domestic quarrels. Police officers in general believe involvement in situations of domestic fighting is one of the most dangerous of their duties.

The data from the United States are not unique. Other nations comprising western civilization have similar statistics, although their total amount of crime may be much lower than that of the United States. Comparable patterns may also be found in other quite different cultures; for instance, Bohannan[6], in studying native African homicide and suicide, found that murder occurred predominantly among kinsmen, although their patterns of kinship are quite different from those of more developed nations. That this is not entirely a matter of ethnic or cultural difference is suggested by Wolfgang's findings in his study of homicide in the black population of Philadelphia.[7] There, too, murder most commonly involved family members and close acquaintances.

Statistical details of intrafamilial homicide are not often published. However, Bard quotes the following figures from the Police Department of New York City for the year 1965.[8] In that year, husbands killed 40 wives and wives killed 17 husbands; seven brothers were slain by their brothers and two sisters killed their sisters; eleven sons and thirteen daughters were murdered by their mothers, and five sons and one daughter by their fathers. In less than 20 percent of all the homicides reported that year were victim and attacker complete strangers.

These figures indicate only the amount of violent crime within the family that comes to public notice. The statistics do not cover an enormous amount of the interpersonal actions within families which involve some degree of violence involving physical attack, nor do they describe the enormous amount of emotional violence directly released upon family members including children. There is no reference to the question of child abuse and none to the problem of child neglect. Fully 460 of the murder victims reported by the FBI in 1973 were recorded as being under age five—approximately 2.7 percent of the total. Obviously this is an inaccurate figure, as it is well known that many cases of death in infants are listed as the result of accidents or various diseases rather than due to inflicted injury, and hence do not come within the purview of crime statistics. Actually, it is estimated conservatively that approximately 2,000 children die each year in the United States of injuries inflicted by their caretakers; another 60,000 are injured by their parents or other caretakers but do not die. And probably ten times as many children suffer from the damage caused by emotional violence and neglect.

## ORIGINS OF VIOLENCE

The occurrence of violence throughout history in all levels of society from the largest national groups down to the smallest family units inevitably leads to the question "Why?" Attempts to answer this question have lead to considerable arguments among ethologists, sociologists, psychiatrists, and others about whether or not man has an "instinct of aggression" or an "innate aggressive or destructive drive" that would account for this recurrent behavior. We cannot enter into the theoretical discussion of this unanswered problem at this time. Suffice it to say that human beings universally reveal an obvious capacity to behave aggressively, and at times to escalate aggression to the point we call violence.

Trying to find causes or explanations that will account for the appearance of the more extreme forms of this behavior leads us into a complex field of interacting factors which can be grouped under four main categories—namely, biological, psychological, sociological, and cultural. Under biological factors can be included the normal anatomical structures and biochemical physiological functions that enable human beings to respond to stress or to perceived danger by what W.B. Cannon called the "fight-flight" response.[9] This phenomenon is certainly an adaptive mechanism which has had survival value for the human race. But despite its universal presence, the "fight-flight" response is a rather gross automatic primitive mechanism; it is not adequate to explain the sophisticated patterns in which human violence is expressed, especially in the form we know as child abuse.

There are studies that have shown an association of the male sex hormone androgen with aggression, higher levels of the hormone being correlated with increased aggressive behavior. It is also known that aggressive behavior of male animals can be significantly reduced by castration or by the administration of female sex hormones.[10] On the other hand, there are many men with normal androgen levels, as well as those with endocrine disease characterized by low androgen levels, who have been involved in actions of violence and abuse. Furthermore, women without excess androgen and with quite normal estrogen levels can be similarly aggressive. Thus theories of hormonal causes of violence cannot be called upon as adequate to explain violent abusive behavior, except as possibly enhancing elements that might work through some effect on certain brain structures.

Violent behavior in some instances is related to specific brain tumors and to foci of abnormal neuronal discharge in certain brain tissues, especially in the limbic system.[11] Such epysodic discontrol and seizurelike states due to organic brain disease or epileptiform discharges of unknown cause warrant careful diagnosis and treatment. Yet they are comparatively rare, and cannot in any way account for the great bulk of violent, abusive behavior we too commonly see.

A decade ago a new element was added to the list of possible causes of violent behavior. It was discovered that a significant number of men with criminal records in a maximum security mental hospital had a chromosome abnormality of 47,XYY.[12] Further studies have shown there is indeed an increased frequency of the XYY genotype in males in penal institutions and in hospitals for mentally disturbed criminals. These men often shown a combination of antisocial behavior, increased height, and psychiatric illness or mental deficiency.[13,14] But the picture is not quite as definite as it seemed at first. Although it seems clear that the incidence of XYY abnormality may be several times as frequent in institutional populations as it is among the general public, it is also now known that many males with 47,XYY are living perfectly normal lives in society. There is also the finding, when compared to inmates with normal 46,XY genotypes, that the 47,XYY offenders were not uncontrollably aggressive, and that their histories indicated more crimes against property rather than persons.[12]

While the chromosome abnormality may have an adverse affect on the growth or function of some elements in the central nervous system, there is no evidence of a one-to-one relationship between this uncommon genetic deviant and violence in general. Other explanations must be sought for the great majority of violent males who do not have this chromosomal variant, and of course for women who cannot possibly have the abnormality, but nevertheless behave with great violence. Further, while statistics show greater amounts of violence, including the phenomena of child abuse and neglect among lower socioeconomic groups and in ghettos, no correlation can be shown between the incidence of 47,XYY and socioeconomic level.[15]

In general, men show more aggressive behavior and violence than women. More men murder their wives than wives kill husbands, and violent crimes in general are committed by men more often than by women. Boys significantly outnumber girls in delinquent behavior involving violence, although there is presently a trend toward equality. Women infrequently physically abuse their husbands, but the beating of wives by husbands is a common occurrence, one that has been accepted rather too nonchalantly by the general public and by the judicial system, and sometimes by the wives themselves. Such wife beating may be influenced to some extent by males having greater muscle mass and strength, but long-lasting sociocultural patterns seem more likely explanations.

Persisting through centuries have been residual variations of the ancient Roman concept of "manus," the power of the husband over the person and property of his wife, which gave him the right to punish, kill, or sell her. More recently, with the increasing effectiveness of the women's rights movements, relative disregard of this common pattern of violence has been replaced by realistic attempts to correct it. In London, for instance, women finding it difficult to get protection through normal legal channels have established shelters where abused wives can go with their children to find sanctuary, and they have organized to instigate changes in the law and obtain the right of better social benefits (e.g., Chiswick Women's aid).[16] Similar places of safety for beaten wives are being created in other countries, including the United States.

When we come to the problem of intrafamilial violence expressed in the form of child abuse we find no consistent gender-linked difference between men and women. Various studies of child abuse report different statistics on the incidence of men and women who abuse their offspring, some showing a very high proportion of women, others showing a high proportion of men, and some showing approximately equal numbers. The marked differences reported seem more related to the population studied, and to other factors such as the time a child was exposed to the abusive caretaker, rather than to any specific differences in the abusive potential of males and females. Our own studies have indicated that both abusive men and women have very similar attitudes toward children, sharing the same patterns of child rearing and the same concepts of how parents should behave. There is thus a kind of collaboration between the parents, regardless of which one may be doing the actual abusing.

Infanticide is much more commonly accomplished by mothers than fathers. In some instances the act may be closely related to emotional disturbances in the mother associated with pregnancy or a postpartum psychosis. In most instances, however, mothers kill babies for reasons not directly sex linked, but which are quite similar to those of fathers and which can be correlated with serious mental disease, cultural beliefs, or social stress. Children may die as a result of repeated or severe abuse, but in most cases death is an "accidental," unplanned result of punishment. The parents have a desire for a living child who will behave better and be more rewarding; death is not intended.

Quite different is the planned or purposeful killing of an infant by someone for whom the infant has become part of a psychotic delusional system and must therefore be done away with. Direct murder of children is usually accomplished by a psychotic relative or close acquaintance. Illegitimate, unwanted babies, or babies believed to be abnormal because of physical defects, or being twins, may be killed by strangulation, smothering, or abandonment. Although this is usually done by women, it is much more related to problems of social opprobrium and cultural superstition than it is directly sex linked.

### Psychosocial and Cultural Factors

When we try to describe the relationship of cultural, social, and psychological factors to the development and expression of violence in general, and of child neglect and abuse in particular, we encounter a tangled web of interacting elements. In an effort to separate out and delineate specific principles and influences, various investigators have followed their own biases and described the observed behaviors too exclusively through the eyes of their own disciplines, overemphasizing some elements to the neglect of others.[17,18] Unfortunately, much misunderstanding has resulted. Some sociologists object strongly to the "psychopathological model" of child abuse, while some psychiatrists and psychologists feel that the unique psychological patterns of abusive parents have been unnecessarily disregarded by the accent placed on social and economic forces.

The cultural, sociological, and psychological points of view are certainly not mutually exclusive or contradictory, but rather describe different and usually overlapping approaches to the same problems.[19] Taken together they can fully describe the functioning of a specific individual as a member of his family and within the social and cultural patterns through which the family operates. The interaction of these factors is nicely described by Erikson in his writings on the development of basic trust.

> Parents must not only have certain ways of guiding by prohibition and permission; they must also be able to represent to the child a deep, an almost somatic conviction that there is meaning to what they are doing. In this sense a traditional system of child care can be said to be a factor making for trust, even where certain items of that tradition, taken singly, may seem irrational or unnecessarily cruel. Here much depends on whether such items are inflicted on the child by the parent in the firm traditional belief that this is the only way to do things, or whether the parent misuses his administration of the baby and the child in order to work off anger, alleviate fear, or win an argument, with the child or with somebody else (mother-in-law, doctor, or priest).[20]

Anthropologist Margaret Mead described the effects of culturally different types of child rearing observed in two tribes in New Guinea.[21] The Arapesh are extremely kind to children, quickly responding to all the needs of infants and small children, and sharing the care of children among many extended family members. From infancy on, members of this tribe feel quite secure and turn with confidence to other tribal members; they are very peaceful, and possibly almost too passive. A nearly opposite type of child rearing is practiced by the Mundugumor. In this culture infants are treated in ways which repeatedly stimulate frustration and rage. For instance, suckling babies are pulled off the breast and are not allowed to start nursing again until thoroughly enraged. Later on the children are encouraged to express anger and violence freely in their daily interactions with their peers and with adults. Not surprisingly, the adults of this tribe tend to be rather angry, violent, and cannibalistic.

Sociologists have repeatedly observed that the experience of growing up in the violent atmosphere of an inner city ghetto can produce adults prone to violent behavior, showing the effect of early experience on later behavior in a way somewhat analogous to that observed by Mead among the Mundugumor. Persons found guilty of various kinds of antisocial behavior, including criminal violence, show a statistically highly significant preponderance of those who have grown up in poverty, especially in the crowded inner city environment. There can be no question about such environmental stresses having a profound effect upon patterns of behavior, and upon the development of specific character structure.

Poignant documentation of these experiences is seen in such autobiographical accounts of childhood as Claude Brown's "Manchild in the Promised Land."[22] There is a tragic, lasting impact of such early life training in a violent subculture: it is useful and adaptive to be violent. As Claude Brown says, "This was how it was supposed to be, because this was what we had come up under." Yet, such experience is not confined to being in a subculture like that of Harlem. Children may be similarly affected by growing up in a family where great violence is expressed in the privacy of the home in an otherwise peaceful neighborhood. Statistics show a significantly higher incidence of child abuse and neglect reported from lower socioeconomic groups, and it has been assumed by some sociologists[23] that growing up in the ghetto with the deprivations of poverty and poor education are the chief and almost sufficient causes of abusive parental behavior.

Growing up in a family plagued by poverty can lead to devastating deprivations of the adequate materials for living; insufficient food, clothing, and shelter can result in physical and intellectual deficits in the developing child. This is different from the neglect due to parental disregard of needs of offspring which can occur within a poverty stricken environment or quite independently of it. There may also be a deprivation of educational possibilities, which prevents the development of competitive skills and in this way perpetuates deprivation. More subtle but possible of greater importance is the lack of adequate pleasure or reward in living. Insufficient pleasure in the presence of other material deprivations leads to unbearable frustration and anger, especially if the longed-for material things that are lacking are within sight in the possession of other more fortunate people and therefore within reach.

Such frustration and temptation easily leads to attempts to take what is desired, even to the use of violent means to get it. The deprived person is doing as an individual what tribes and nations have always done—just as the "have not" nations of the Third World are at present expressing violence toward those nations and cultures which are more financially successful and have higher standards of living. Economic deprivation and social and ethnic discrimination have been a cause for conflict since ancient times. The Trojan wars were probably instigated more by the economic concerns of Greek merchants than because of the romantic triangles of beautiful Helen, which Homer accented in the Iliad.

Because the deprivations and stresses of low socioeconomic status are so obviously influential in the conduct of the lives of those who live within its restrictions, it is tempting to think of these factors as primary or almost exclusive causes of criminality, violence, and other forms of antisocial action. Yet such explanations seem much too simplistic, and several facts cast great doubt on such assumptions. Well educated people whose lives have been spent in affluence, living in comfortable suburbs can also be involved in crime and violence and in child abuse in particular. They may not be brought to public attention as often as are the poor, and their problems, if discovered, may be dealt with much differently by courts and by the rest of society. Nevertheless they do show the same kinds of "antisocial" behavior as that seen among the poor.

Similar behavior can be shown by people who have spent their formative years in relatively quiet small towns, or in open rural environments far away from the aggression ridden atmosphere of the ghetto. Too often one hears or reads about the experience of "growing up in a ghetto" or of being a member of a lower socioeconomic class or a minority group as if these were constants, as if ghettos and lower socioeconomic groups were homogeneous masses, all of whose members had identical experience and ended up living the same way. This, of course, is far from true. The majority of people, probably three-fourths, who grow up in poverty in an inner city environment do not become violent or involved in criminal behavior, and probably even a higher percentage of them do not abuse and neglect their children.

The reasons for these differences have been inadequately investigated and are poorly understood. It should not be forgotten that out of such environments have also come many individuals, black and white, who have made enormous contributions to science, literature, music, drama, dance, politics, and social welfare. Human compassion, intelligence, kindness, and loving care of children are not the sole prerogatives of the educated or the well-to-do; in fact it would probably be easy to accumulate data indicating the poor exhibit such qualities more often than their richer brethren.

Information on the subject is meager, but there is a suggestion that upward social movement does not of itself alleviate child abuse. For example, the National Society for Prevention of Cruelty to Children in England noted that when families were moved from row house slums to new, nearby comfortable flats in high rise buildings, the incidence of neglect and abuse of children increased.[24] This was apparently related to increased isolation and less free mobility and more difficult access to neighborhood amenities.

Financial problems are a common cause of conflict within the family, beginning with discussion and leading on to argument and eventually to verbal and physical violence. Abuse and neglect of children may be precipitated when parents become overwhelmed by such crises. Yet, everyone who has been involved in individual, group, or family therapy knows such conflicts and violent results can occur in all socioeconomic levels, from the most poverty stricken to the most well-to-do. Unemployment is a common source of financial problems, but it also has other devastating affects on the family beyond the direct influence of less money. Job loss is often an unbearable insult to an already fragile sense of self-esteem and pride, leaving the parent with a sense of failure and anger toward both individuals and organizations. Such anger can be redirected toward spouse or children when they fail to restore the self-respect of the parent or even criticize the parental failure to provide. Abuse can easily occur in this setting.

Parents whose cognitive functions are dulled by the overuse of alcohol or other drugs are obviously unable to care well for their children, inevitably disregard the children's needs, and produce a typical picture of neglect. The chronic use of alcohol and the taking of hallucinogenic drugs can cause severe distortion of mental functioning with delusional thinking and the lowering of the threshold for the release of violence in many forms, including child abuse, homicide, and suicide. These addictions, of course, can also disrupt family living through causing job loss and financial disaster. In the case loads of some facilities, the incidence of alcoholism among abusive parents is as high as 40 to 50 percent, but in other study populations the incidence is minor (no more than 5 to 10 percent), which is not greatly different from the general population. The contribution made by alcoholism and drug abuse to the problems of violence and maltreatment of children cannot be doubted. On the other hand, we have been impressed by the amount of child abuse we have seen in families who are total abstainers because of firm religious beliefs or other convictions.

## FAMILY STRUCTURE

Some sociologists express concern over what may be a change in the basic patterns of family organization occurring in recent decades. The change most often noted is the dissolution of the "extended family," resulting from increased mobility and geographical separation of family members, and more recently from social, cultural, or idealogical pressures for younger generations to become independent and live separately from their relatives. The lack of extended family is thought to diminish the transmission of traditional values and modes of living, thereby contributing to problems of poor child rearing and child abuse as well as to the alienation and patterns of violence in young people. This association of child abuse with lack of extended family seems to receive support from the histories of a large proportion of abusive, neglecting parents who describe high degrees of alienation from their families, and lack any close ties with their own parents or other relatives that could provide support and help in times of stress.

The problem, however, is not quite as simple as it looks. In the first place, if we assume the extended family did exist in the past as commonly and effectively as it is assumed by sociologists and historians, then we are faced with the fact of child abuse being just as common in those times as it is now. Second, at the present time we see parents, grandparents, and other relatives living in the same neighborhood, next door, or even in the same household, and in such situations abuse can occur and apparently be escalated by interactions with members of the extended family. We know of many instances in which grandparents not only condoned maltreatment of children but actually encouraged parents to use more frequent, more severe methods of discipline on their offspring.

We also see parents, all of whose relatives are far away in different states, and with whom there is little contact, either by visit, letter, or phone, and yet their child rearing abilities are beyond reproach. As a rule these parents who do extremely well with their children despite few family contacts had good relationships with their own parents in their earliest years, are socially comfortable, and have been able to find friends and rewarding contacts of all kinds in their new environment. Occasionally one sees parents who are doing well with their children precisely because they *are* separated from other relatives with whom contact would be unhappy and disrupting.

There is no one-to-one relationship between the presence or absence of an extended family and the occurrence of child abuse. Rather, a most important concept to be considered is not whether the parents have contact with an extended family in either the geographical or emotional sense, but rather the quality of the emotional relationship with family members which the parents had during their earliest period of development. Often the alienation is the result of early childhood experience with parents who were excessively critical, punitive, unrewarding people and therefore not good prospects for a continuing relationship.

### Child Abuse

During the past fifteen years of working with parents who neglect or abuse their children we have been led to the conviction that the basic ingredients of this behavior have their origin in the very earliest part of the parent's life, and predominantly in relation to the lack of "empathic mothering," combined with early demand and control.[25,26] Repeatedly we have found the most common element in their lives to be the history of having been significantly deprived or neglected, with or without physical abuse, in their own earliest years. This one finding is more nearly universal in the population of parents who maltreat their babies than any other single factor such as socioeconomic status, living conditions, race, religion, education, psychiatric state, cultural milieu, or family structure.

The term "lack of empathic mothering" is used to describe a variety of less than ideal responses of the caretaker (usually the mother) to the infant. It often begins in the perinatal period with insufficient bonding and poor development of mother-infant attachment, and is evidenced in the ensuing months by insufficient awareness of, or response to, the infant's state, needs, and abilities. The interaction is oriented much more to the needs and satisfaction of the caretaker than to what is most appropriate for the physical well-being and emotional development of the child.

Under these circumstances it is impossible for the infant to develop what Benedek[27] calls "confidence" and Erikson[28] describes as "basic trust." Unless there are significantly remedial experiences the child will never feel quite safe in the world or trust other people to be reasonably good or helpful. There is also a persistent residual feeling of emptiness and yearning to be cared for and cared about which appears in later life as "excessive dependency." As the child grows, the parent typically expects too much too soon in the way of behavioral responses to the caretaker's needs and commands. Inevitably the infant fails to meet the excessive expectations and is verbally criticized, physically punished, and emotionally rejected. As a consequence the child is left with a sense of failure, low self-esteem, and a beginning tendency to believe in the use of physical attack to solve problems. There may also be the beginning of patterns of either being unduly compliant and submissive or being too negativistic and aggressive.

The early life experience briefly described above is reproduced in the parenting behavior of the grownup maltreated child. When men and women become parents, two kinds of memories are activated, often largely unconscious: the memories of what it was like to be a child, and the recollections of how one's parents cared for one in the earliest years. From these two sources the main patterns of child rearing will be derived.[29] This is a normal mechanism; all parents tend to follow their own parents' style of child rearing. If one's early life was unfortunately beset by neglect and abuse, then one is likely to repeat it, and treat one's offspring as one was treated. Thus we see the tragic recurrence of abuse and neglect in generation after generation. A parent's propensity for abuse is commonly supported or enhanced by a corresponding tendency in the spouse. Those who have been maltreated in childhood have an almost uncanny ability to find and to marry someone with a similar background and similar ideas about child rearing. Thus the abuse or neglect of offspring can often be an unconscious collusion or cooperation between the parents, even though only one of them is the active agent.

It is largely accepted that the fundamental patterns of behavior and of language are learned by the growing child in the first three years of life, in his own home, from the examples and precepts of his caretakers. Only later does he leave the home, go out into the neighborhood, and learn the general patterns of his culture from its other members. The lessons learned in these first three years seem to be the most permanent, and they also tend to influence all later acquisitions of knowledge and behavior. The process of learning is described in different ways by different disciplines, and can be understood as variations of conditioning, imitation, cognitive learning, social learning, identification, and so forth.

Whatever theoretical framework is used to understand the child's development there is ample evidence the parental patterns have been absorbed and well integrated into the child's developing psyche very early in life. We see an unbroken line of the repetition of parental abuse from childhood into adult years. For example, Johnny, a four-and-one-half-year-old boy whose mother had shaken, choked, and bruised him in infancy because of unsatisfactory behavior was found to have choked and shaken his two-year-old sister, Mary, when she failed to do something he requested. When asked by his mother why he did this, he responded simply and directly, "Mommy, that's what you used to do to me." An eleven-year-old boy, Manuel, who had been repeatedly whipped and beaten by his father since his earliest years was left to babysit with a niece. Upon the family's return it was found he had punished the girl severely for persistent crying, producing significant bruising. Upon discovering this fact the boy's father said, "Manuel needs a good beating for this"—an act which would, of course, reinforce the abuse pattern.

Steve, a nineteen-year-old young man, began living with a girl he had known earlier in school, and who had a child now 18 months old, by another man. Both he and the mother decided the baby was "spoiled" as a result of having followed the "foolish advice in some crazy baby book," which said spanking was not necessary. After talking this over they decided to "bring the baby up like they had been brought up." With her approval he started spanking the baby and within a few weeks the baby was brought to the hospital with serious body bruises, brain injury, and blindness. This young man had suffered mild physical abuse and considerable emotional deprivation during his life. He expressed clearly the mixture of attitudes which abusive parents have towards small children, saying, "Children are precious and I love them," then adding a few sentences later, "Baby's butts are built to be busted." This latter colorful statement links two important residues of his earlier years. The first is, "I was spanked regularly, twice a day," the second is, "of course I deserved it, I was always a bad kid, I never did what anybody wanted me to." These three examples show how deeply embedded the pattern of abuse can be and also indicate the strong sense of rightness, if not righteousness, with which behaviors learned from parents can be repeated.

The staying power of the patterns acquired in earliest years in the family environment is remarkable. This is true not only of language and styles of parenting but of many other things, such as religious beliefs, moral attitudes, political affiliations, and national loyalty. Later, this early family-established core can be elaborated, enhanced or sometimes altered by experience and learning gained in the larger cultural milieu.

Claude Brown writes with painful clarity of the mutually reinforcing interaction between family and culture in relation to violence.[22] He describes running home as a child to avoid getting beaten up by two boys who were "messing" with him. His father met him at the door, and told him if he was running away from the boys to avoid being messed with, that he himself would start messing with Claude. Claude remonstrated there were two boys, both bigger than himself, and they could hit harder than he could. Dad replied, "You think they can hit harder than I can hit?" then added, "Damn right I can hit harder than they can. And if you come in here you're going to get hit by me." Claude's mother intervened, taking him into the house, despite Dad's saying she was pampering him. "I went in and I laid down. I just got sicker until I went downstairs. They really did kick my ass. But it was all right. I didn't feel sick any more."

Claude Brown describes two things about his father than used to scare him; the scar on his neck and his knife. He felt it was because of the scar on his neck that he carried the knife; he was never going to get caught without it again. Brown implies that he had always had the impression of his father as someone who believed in fighting and was always ready to fight. In this vignette he aligns himself with his father and is ashamed to run away from a fight, and yet is also unable to accept the protection which his mother tried to give him. His father's attitude was echoed by the Harlem subculture of that time, described as "The little boys in the neighborhood whom the adults respected were the little boys who didn't let anybody mess with them."

### Early Childhood and Physical Punishment

The question of whether the earlier family experience or the later cultural environment is the more potent influence toward subsequent violent behavior has not been answered definitely. Although there are doubtless many exceptions to any general rule, we feel strongly the early interaction of child and parent involving neglect or abuse is the more essential element. Of several siblings in one family, the one who has suffered the most maltreatment is most likely to have later trouble than his less traumatized siblings, although all have lived in the same culture. As noted above, the great majority of those who grow up amidst the culture of inner city violence do not become antisocial; there is some evidence suggesting their early family experience was without significant abuse or neglect. Men who are trained and rewarded for violence and killing, as they are in the subculture of the armed services, do not as a rule continue to be violent in civilian life. Possibly the violent behavior would be maintained only by those in whom this training in violence falls upon the fertile ground provided by early childhood maltreatment.

The family is the channel through which cultural and subcultural patterns of aggression may be used in child rearing practices and transmitted by parents to their offspring. There are also other factors besides familial and subcultural violence that can contribute to the problem of child abuse. Throughout history children have been loved, cherished, and highly valued as individuals by their parents. On the other hand, there has been at the same time a strong traditional belief that children were the property of parents, who had the exclusive right to deal with their offspring as they saw fit. In ancient Rome by the legal right of *patria potestas,* the father had absolute authority over his children and could, if he wished, sell them, expose them, kill them, eat them, or otherwise dispose of them in any way.

Efforts to establish the rights of children are fairly recent; and they are making headway only with great difficulty. Those who work in the field of child protection are well aware of the almost insurmountable obstacles often presented by parents and by the legal system when attempts are made to intervene in a family's destructive style of child rearing. In addition to the legal concept of children as the property of parents, there is the biologically determined long period of infancy in the human species, which provides opportunity for the parents to exercise control over the basic developmental processes. The infant is in a sense at the mercy of whatever ideas about child rearing the parents may have, and his psychological development will be molded accordingly, producing effects that last into later life.

Relevant to child abuse there is a prevalent belief in our western Judeo-Christian culture that infants are easily spoiled, and may have an innate tendency to be stubborn and willful, or are even born with "original sin." Accompanying this is the belief in physical punishment as the most appropriate means of counteracting such nefarious tendencies. Many abusive parents quote passages from the Bible to justify their punitive actions. Typical examples are: "He that spareth his rod hateth his son: but he that loveth him chasteneth him betimes" (Proverbs 13:24); and "Withhold not correction from the child: for if thou beatest him with the rod, he shall not die. Thou shalt beat him with the rod, and shalt deliver his soul from hell" (Proverbs 23:13–14). In addition to this righteous, religiously based conviction of the usefulness or necessity of punishment, there is a strong belief in punishment as a valuable ingredient of the educational process. There is an unbroken record of the use of whipping, beating, and other punishments in our schools, from the time of the earliest records from Sumer in 2800 B.C.[30] up to the present time. Only three states— Massachusetts, New Jersey, and Maryland—have legally abolished corporal punishment in the schools, and a recent Supreme Court decision has refused to remove the right of local school systems to continue this practice. The traditional practice of caning in the British type of public school, although criticized in some quarters, has also been considered to be a desirable, even admirable, educational ritual.[31]

Physical punishment in the service of education is, of course, not confined to the school system but can exist in equal or greater degree in the privacy of the family home during the earliest years of a child's life. To a large extent the physical injuries diagnosed as child abuse have been inflicted by caretakers in an effort to make the child cease bad behavior and start good behavior, although it is obvious that parental zeal and anger have been carried much too far for the child's good. The belief in the value of punishment and the transmission of punitive patterns from generation to generation is nicely pictured in a letter written by King Henry IV of France to the woman in charge of the nursery where the infant Dauphin, who would later be Louis XIII, was being raised. "I have a complaint to make: you do not send word that you have whipped my son. I wish and command you to whip him every time that he is obstinate or misbehaves, knowing well for myself that there is nothing in the world which will be better for him than that. I know it from experience, having myself profited, for when I was his age I was often whipped. That is why I want you to whip him and to make him understand why."[32]

The use of physical punishment to change behavior is not entirely irrational. The stimulus of physical pain undeniably alters the behavior of the individual upon whom it is inflicted. This is an observable fact, which can be confirmed by any parent who uses spanking for discipline of his children, or by any experimental psychologist who has worked to modify the behavior of rats or other experimental animals. However, because of the highly developed symbolic functions of the human mind, the modification of human behavior by painful punishment is not a simple matter. Certainly, "the burnt child fears the fire" and the good result of future avoidance of fire has been accomplished.

But something else usually happens in a family where the child is well cared for: the burnt child can turn to the caretaker for comfort, mother can "kiss it and make it all better." The situation is different if pain is inflicted by the parent rather than an inanimate object, particularly if the painful punishment is accompanied by an angry voice and facial expression. The hurt child then tends to fear the pain-causing parent as well as learn to avoid the act that led to punishment. This creates complexity for the child; he must look for protection and nurturence from the same person who causes pain and whom he fears. The ensuing intrapsychic conflict, with its accompanying burden of anxiety, can be at least partially resolved by the use of a defensive mechanism known as "identification with the agressor." The child psychologically protects himself from fear and anxiety by assuming the role of being the aggressor rather than the victim and he begins to believe in the adaptive value of authoritative patterns of attacking and hurting. Insofar as this is associated with punishing children while disregarding their needs, we see one of the earliest and most potent mechanisms related to the development of patterns of maltreatment of children and how they pass from generation to generation.

It is not only the actual amount of painful punishment that affects the child but also the inevitable accompaniments of diminished love and approval as well as increased criticism and verbal attack. This emotional abuse and lack of empathic understanding is probably more important in causing later character difficulties than the simple fact of painful punishment or injury. The serious injuries we see in abused children are, except in the case of serious head injuries, more useful as indicators of serious family trouble than they are specific signs of damage to future development. Many normally reared children have had accidentally caused injuries and fractures of serious degree without having their subsequent development significantly impaired. In the situation of abuse and neglect it is not only the pain of the injury but the inability of the child to have confidence in getting comfort, care, and love that creates the permanent damage.

Thus we see emotionally neglected children who have not been physically injured showing many of the same signs of distorted development as other children in the family who have been bodily hurt. We have often seen children who have been cruelly beaten by their fathers who feel more distressed by their mother's failure to protect them than by their father's severely hurting them. The difficulty involved in the child expecting punishment from the ones to whom he turns for protection and the inability to get comfort is clearly pictured in the vignette above quoted from Claude Brown. Equally clear is how the primary identification with the aggressive, uncaring parent can be reinforced and perpetuated by experience in the social and subcultural milieu.

As far as the value of punishment in developing proper behavior is concerned, considerable doubt has been cast upon the effectiveness of punishing children for excessively dependent or aggressive behavior. For instance, Kohlberg[33] states:

> Direct training and physical types of punishment may be effective in producing short run situational conformity but do not directly produce general internalized habits of moral character carried into later life, carried outside home, or carried into permissive situations.

There is also evidence that children punished for excessive dependent behavior or for unduly aggressive acts show increased dependency and aggressive behavior later, thus indicating that punishment does not in the long run correct the behavior it is designed to improve.[34]

### Late Effects of Abuse

Many maltreated children, helped by the influence of more beneficial experience both in early years and later life, grow up to be essentially normal citizens and average parents. But there is ample evidence of less desirable late effects of the early childhood experience. Children who have been abused and neglected provide the pool from which the next generation of neglecting, abusive parents are derived. We have repeatedly noted that nearly all those caretakers who maltreat their children give a history of similar treatment in their own earliest years, and the cases cited above indicate how early in life the pattern may become manifest. There is also evidence that abuse and neglect have a profound effect on behaviors other than parenting in later years. Exposure to excessive physical aggression and emotional deprivation in early life has an impact on psychic development so as to provide a matrix that can be modified by later experience into several varieties of antisocial and violent behavior.

Aichorn, fifty years ago, was one of the first investigators to draw attention to the importance of the family background in juvenile delinquents.[35] He noted that delinquency was not just the result of the youngster's being in bad company and running around on the streets, but was also significantly related to the earliest emotional relationships the child had had with his parents. Twenty years later, Bender began publishing a series of studies of over 5,000 children under age thirteen with "psychopathic disorders," who were aggressive, disturbed, delinquent, and antisocial.[36,37,38] She described these behaviors as due primarily to "distortions in personality development in children who in earliest childhood or infancy were grossly deprived, neglected, abused, and traumatized by adults who were themselves disturbed or inadequate, thus giving the child only a pathological pattern for identification." Bender was not unaware of other contributing factors including cultural ideologies and variable standards of minority groups in lower socioeconomic status.

The Gluecks, in their very exhaustive study of juvenile delinquency,[39] reported that in comparison to parents of nondelinquents the parents of delinquents showed more lax, unkind, inconsistent discipline, with far greater resort to physical punishment. Several years ago Weston interviewed 100 juvenile offenders in Philadelphia and found a history of neglect and abuse in 82 of these young people, as well as a recollection of being knocked unconscious by one or the other parent in 43 of them.[40]

More recently my colleague, Joan Hopkins, interviewed 200 youngsters soon after they were picked up by the police for the first time and brought to a juvenile detention center.[41] This was the sole facility in that county for the reception of juvenile offenders. The county population includes members of all socioeconomic classes and living conditions vary from crowded, slumlike areas to wealthy suburbs and rural ranches. Of 100 juveniles whose statements could not be confirmed, 72 told of abuse and neglect before school age. Of the other 100 juveniles, whose statements were confirmed by parents or other reliable sources, 84 had a history of neglect or abuse at home before age six, and 92 of them had been maltreated in the year and a half previous to this first pickup. The great majority of families in both groups were intact, and very few of the children came from an environment that in any way resembled the crowded inner city milieu of poverty and violence from which the usual statistics on delinquency are derived.

Data of another type also support this association of early abuse with later delinquent behavior. The family records of 5,000 children who were reported as abused or neglected in eight New York counties over a one-year period (1952–53) were rechecked a dozen or more years later. Grouping together the records from all eight counties it was found that 19 percent of the children were later reported as delinquent or in need of supervision, and if the siblings of the index case were added, the percentage increased to 35. In Monroe county, which had the most complete records, the corresponding figures were 30 percent and 62 percent.[42]

The association of aggressive, antisocial behavior in youth with early experiences of neglect and abuse is not surprising. As noted before, children learn from their parents by imitation and identification. The taking over into the child's mind of parental standards of conduct is the basis of what we call the conscience or superego, which later directs behavior with a sense of rightness. The basic intrafamilial determinant of moral standards and behavior can be reinforced by later cultural and social experience; and this can happen whether the basic patterns are either culturally syntonic or deviant.

Parent-child interactions in maltreatment have in another way the effect of predisposing the child to later delinquent behavior. The parental admonition of "don't do what you think or want, do as I tell you" creates temporary obedience but deprives the child of developing healthy internal controls, and he remains unduly vulnerable to outside suggestion. Then, in adolescence, the common tendency to rebel against parents cannot be counteracted by adequate internal standards but is instead reinforced by the antisocial deviant behavior suggested by "bad companions." The very methods used by the parents to establish rigid control over the child's behavior has resulted in the opposite effect of making him unduly susceptible to being led astray by the exciting temptation of other antisocial companions.

Johnson and Szurek point out that juvenile delinquents tend to have what are described as "superego lacunae," which result from the either open or unconscious aiding and abetting of delinquent behavior by the parents themselves.[43] A simple, clear example of this mechanism was seen in one of the families we studied. The older sister of a child who had been severely abused came home one afternoon with a gold watch that she had stolen at school. She gave it as a present to her mother, who responded, "Oh thank you—this is wonderful. It means you love me."

### Homicide

The most extreme form of delinquency is, of course, murder. In children who kill or who attempt murderous aggression, Bender says the most common factor is "the child's tendency to identify himself with aggressive parents, and pattern after their behavior."[36] King reports on nine youths who had committed homicide at about age fourteen.[44] As children they had been subjected to beatings, usually more so than their siblings. At the time of the homicide most of their homes were intact, although some of the fathers had had episodic desertion. Of interest is the evidence these youngsters showed of poor cognitive development, especially in the form of poor language skills. These are deficits often noted in young children who have been abused and neglected even though they have not had head injuries.[45] Another study, by Russell, of fifteen murders committed by juvenile boys indicated "All of the murders had their roots in the frustrations attendant to maternal deprivation with faulty human conditioning in the earliest periods of life."[46] Easson reported eight cases of murderous assault and murder by children and adolescents "all from socially acceptable normal family homes. . . . All cases demonstrate that one or both parents had fostered and had condoned murderous assault."[47]

Following the theme of murder's being the epitome of violence, we find that in adults there is again a demonstrable association between homicide and maltreatment in early childhood. Duncan et al. found "among six prisoners convicted of first degree murder, remorseless physical brutality at the hands of the parents had been a constant experience for four of them." They had learned to behave like their brutal aggressors. The other two prisoners had been psychotic at the time of the murder, but had not been treated with such gross brutality.[48] Four men who murdered for "no good reason," studied by Satten et al., all had a history characterized by extreme parental violence and early severe emotional deprivation.[49] A larger study was done by Tanay of 53 murderers, none of whom had committed homicide as part of another crime. In 35 of 41 in whom the history was available there had been severe corporal punishment during their developmental years. Only 15 percent of this group of homicides was with strangers, and 58 percent of them actually occurred in the home.[50]

We have come full circle: violence does breed violence.[51,52] We began with violence in the form of murder as essentially a family matter, and we have followed the thread of intrafamilial violence in the form of maltreatment of children through to the production of another generation of violence, which again expresses itself in homicide in the family. At the risk of seeming to neglect all the cultural, social, and economic factors that make enormous contributions to patterns of violence, we wish to express our conviction that *the maltreatment of children is the most prevalent common denominator in the production of such patterns.*

Margaret Mead has asked,

How do human societies teach their children not to commit murder—that is, not to kill in forbidden ways? We know of no human society that does not distinguish between a permissible and impermissible killing. To kill a human being in forbidden ways is *murder*; to kill the trespasser, the enemy, is approved, or even enjoined. But most human children do not have demonstrations during childhood of the distinctions between murder and the enjoined approved brave killing of other human beings. How do they learn?[53]

We would answer that the children learn in their earliest years from the treatment they receive at the hands of their caretakers. Children raised with adequate empathic understanding and love, as well as kindly discipline, without neglect and abuse, will not be the ones who do the impermissible killing. Those who have been the unfortunate recipients of maltreatment become vulnerable to all the aggression-promoting factors present in their social milieu and culture, particularly those channeled to them by their own caretakers.

## SUMMARY

Human violence in general, and its expression within the family, particularly in the form of child abuse and neglect, are patterns of behavioral discharge resulting from the interaction of many complex biological, psychological, social, and cultural factors. The single most common element in the lives of violent or abusive adults is the experience of being neglected or abused to some degree by caretakers during their earliest years. Such experience starts the developing child along a path that predisposes him to use aggression as a means of problem solving, accompanied by lack of empathy for other humans, a diminished ability and impoverished repertoire to cope with stress, and a vulnerability to the examples of agression and violence presented by society and culture.

The establishment of this matrix of character structure in the earliest years of life accounts for the tragic repetition of the pattern of child abuse and neglect in generation after generation. It also sets the stage for the ramifications of aggression and violence into other antisocial behaviors, which surface in adolescence and adulthood.

## Chapter Two

# Parent-Infant Bonding

John Kennell, Diana Voos, and Marshall Klaus

## THE EARLY AFFECTIONAL BOND

Other chapters in this book present alarming evidence of the dysfunction and disintegration of the family. However, problems such as child abuse are only the tip of the iceberg, as there are many other indices such as the rapidly increasing divorce rate that appear to reflect the weakness of family bonds. Is there a general problem with the attachment bonds between family members? Are the bonds somehow weaker or different than they were a generation ago? It is appropriate to consider the available evidence about the processes that enhance and those that interfere with one of the most important of the bonds between family members, the attachment of a parent to his or her infant. As we consider what is known about parent-to-infant attachment we may gain a better understanding about how bonds are formed between other family members.

Early in life the infant develops an attachment to one individual, most often the mother. Throughout his lifetime the strength and character of this attachment will influence the quality of all future bonds to other individuals. An attachment can be defined as an affectional bond between two individuals that endures through time and space and serves to join them emotionally. Significant attachments are such unique relationships that it is not unusual for an individual to have fewer than ten throughout his lifetime. It is useful to differentiate human attachments according to the individuals involved so that we may focus on the specific characteristics and functions of one relationship before we return to a consideration of the whole family.

Perhaps the strongest of these affectional ties in the human is that of the mother to her child. Why are mothers willing to make the sacrifices necessary to care for an infant day after day? How do they develop such a powerful bond to these tiny infants who at first sleep for hours on end and only awaken to cry, eat, burp, soil, and fall asleep again? What is the process by which this relationship develops?

Although the development of the attachment of an infant to his mother has been widely investigated in the past three decades, beginning with the publications of Bowlby[1] and Spitz[2], the tie in the opposite direction, from a mother to her infant, has only recently been the focus of study. More recent still has been the interest in the father and his relationship to his newborn child. Nonetheless, studies and observations from a variety of sources now make it possible to fit together a tentative model of how affectional bonds between the human mother and her infant develop. It is also possible to identify factors that may alter or distort this process either temporarily or permanently.

## ANIMAL BEHAVIOR PERTINENT TO THE HUMAN MOTHER AND FATHER

Animal models have provided a valuable starting point for studies of mother to infant and father to infant interaction and attachment. They have suggested important variables for studies of the behavior of human mothers and fathers.

### Species Specific Behavior

The observations of species specific maternal behavior patterns (such as nesting, exploring, grooming, and retrieving) which have been noted in animal mothers before and immediately after birth have been very useful. They have demonstrated that nature has not left the survival of the species to chance, but has provided intricate mechanisms that trigger maternal behavior in females during and after delivery, thus insuring the care of the young.

Detailed observations of the events surrounding delivery in a large number of animals have shown a species specific sequence of maternal behavior which is repeated over and over again. For example, the events during parturition in the domestic cat are similar throughout the world. Toward the end of her pregnancy, the activity of the female markedly decreases. She selects a warm, dark place for a birth site, usually away from humans. During parturition the female cat usually licks both herself and the neonates. Invariable, she licks the posterior part of her body, especially the vaginal area, and this often leads her to lick the kitten immediately after birth.

After the birth of the last kitten and the placenta and membranes have been eaten, the female usually lies down, encircling her kittens, and rests with them for about twelve hours. While lying with the kittens, she licks them, stimulating them to nurse. This may begin as early as a half-hour after birth, and typically before the end of the twelve-hour resting period. For the first few days, the mother remains with her litter, leaving them only once every few hours to feed.

The elk and moose, although closely related species, exhibit very different patterns of maternal behavior. However, within each species the sequence of maternal behavior is the same.

### Maternal Sensitive Period

In some animals, separation shortly after delivery, during what might be termed the maternal sensitive period, may result in the mother's refusal to accept and care for her offspring when the two are reunited. If separation occurs a few days later for a similar period of time, the normal mothering behavior will be resumed when the pair are brought together again. This phenomenon is most dramatic in the goat. If the newborn kid is separated from the mother during the first five to ten minutes and the two are reunited, the mother goat will kick and butt the infant and refuse to allow it to nurse. Interestingly, if the newborn kid remains, or a strange infant is introduced to the mother during the first five-minute period, the dam will nurse and care for either infant in the succeeding days and weeks.

Meier[3] observed the mother's acceptance of her newborn after surgical delivery in monkeys reared in the wild (feral) and those reared in the laboratory. In this study, mothers were delivered surgically and separated from their infants for two hours. Although mothers with normal deliveries immediately accepted their infants, none of the laboratory monkeys delivered by caesarean section accepted their infants by the third day after delivery. However, four out of seven feral monkeys reared under natural circumstances, accepted their c-section delivered infants on the first day, and the remaining four accepted theirs by the second day.

Sackett and Rupenthal[4] suggested an explanation for the different behaviors by feral and laboratory reared monkeys. Lab-reared monkeys were "motherless monkeys" reared in cages without their own mothers. Feral monkeys were typically captured after being reared by their own mothers. They indicated that this may be a second generation effect of inadequate mothering in laboratory monkeys whose maternal behavior is more easily extinguished under stress. Do these observations in animals have implications for the human situation where (1) mothers have been separated from their babies following hospital delivery for a few hours with a full term infant or for weeks with a premature, (2) where a mother has had a general anesthesia during delivery, or (3) where she has been ill or has required special monitoring?

## PREGNANCY AND POST PARTUM PERIOD

### Early Pregnancy

For most women, pregnancy is a time of change and of strong emotions which are sometimes positive, other times negative, and frequently ambivalent.

During pregnancy, a woman experiences the physical and emotional changes within herself as well as the growth of the fetus in her uterus. How she feels about these changes will vary widely according to whether the pregnancy was planned, whether she is married, whether she is living with the father, whether she has other children, whether she is working or wants to work, her memories of her childhood, and how she feels about her parents.

Prenatal interviews with women during their first pregnancy have uncovered anxiety which has often seemed to be of pathological proportions. Brazelton has clarified the importance of the psychological changes and turmoil that occur during pregnancy for the subsequent development of attachment to the new infant. He considers the turbulent, emotional changes during pregnancy as "readying the circuits for new attachments." He believes "that the emotional turmoil of pregnancy and the neonatal period can be seen as a positive force for the mother's adjustment for the possibility of providing a more individualized environment for the infant."[5] Some of the steps important in attachment are:

1. Planning the pregnancy
2. Confirming the pregnancy
3. Accepting the pregnancy
4. Fetal movement
5. Accepting the fetus as an individual
6. Birth
7. Seeing the baby
8. Touching the baby
9. Caretaking

Caplan[6] considers pregnancy to be a developmental crisis involving two particular adaptive tasks for the mother. The first is the identification of the fetus as an "integral part of herself" and the second is awareness of the fetus as a separate individual. The second stage is usually initiated with the sensation of fetal movement (quickening), which is a remarkably powerful event. During the period following quickening, the woman must begin to change her concept of the fetus from a part of herself to a living baby who will soon be a separate individual. Bibring et al.[7] believe that this realization prepares the woman for delivery and physical separation from her child. This preparedness lays the foundation for a relationship to the child.

After quickening, a woman will usually begin to have fantasies about what the baby will be like, attributing personality characteristics to the infant and developing a sense of attachment and value toward him or her. She will develop a mental image of the neonate as being a particular sex, having a certain color of hair, eyes, and shape of nose. After sensing fetal movement further acceptance of the pregnancy and marked changes in attitude toward the fetus may be observed. Unplanned, and originally unwanted infants may seem more acceptable. There will usually be some outward evidence of the mother's preparation for the infant, such as the purchase of clothes or a crib, the selection of a name, and the rearrangement of space to accommodate a baby.

Any stress (such as moving to a new geographic area, marital infidelity, death of a close friend or relative, previous abortions, or loss of previous children) that leaves the mother feeling unloved or unsupported or causes her concern about the health and survival of her baby or herself may delay preparation for the infant and retard bond formation. In her study of child abuse, Margaret Lynch[8] has identified six factors that were strikingly overrepresented in the history of abused children when compared with their unabused siblings. These factors included an abnormal pregnancy, an abnormal labor or delivery, neonatal separation, other separations in the first six months, illnesses in the infant during the first year of life, and illness in the mother during the first year of life. Lynch concludes that "treatment of parents during the pregnancy, the perinatal period, and early infancy may well be fruitful in the prevention of child abuse," and, we might add, other serious behavioral disturbances (see Tables 2–1, 2–2, 2–3).

After the first trimester, behaviors suggesting rejection of the pregnancy include the mother's preoccupation with her physical appearance, with negative self-perception, excessive emotional withdrawal or mood swings, excessive physical complaints, absence of any response to quickening, or lack of any preparatory behavior during the last trimester. Brazelton[5] suggests that prospective fathers go through an upheaval similar to that of the mothers. In our lonely nuclear family structure in the United States, the young father is often the only available support for his wife. There rarely are other supportive figures nearby, such as family physicians, ministers, close friends or neighbors, who can help the expectant parents.

To enable us to understand the complex events that occur during the perinatal period, we will direct our attention primarily to the mother-infant dyad. However, it is essential for us to emphasize that the father, the other siblings, and the extended family are of vital importance to this dyad.

**Table 2-1.** Frequency of Separation

|  | *Abused Children* *(25)* | *Siblings* *(35)* | *P* |
|---|---|---|---|
| Neonatal separation for 48 hr: | | | |
| Yes . . . . . . . . . . . . . . . . . . | 10 | 2 | <0.01 |
| No . . . . . . . . . . . . . . . . . . | 15 | 33 | |
| Other separations in first 6 mos: | | | |
| Yes . . . . . . . . . . . . . . . . . . | 9 | 2 | <0.01 |
| No . . . . . . . . . . . . . . . . . . | 16 | 33 | |

From M. A. Lynch, "Ill-Health and Child Abuse," *The Lancet,* August 16, 1975.

**Table 2-2.** Abnormalities of Pregnancy and Delivery

|  | Abused Children (25) | Siblings (35) | P |
|---|---|---|---|
| Pregnancy: |  |  |  |
| Abnormal . . . . . . . . . . . . . | 15 | 7 | <0.01 |
| Normal . . . . . . . . . . . . . . | 10 | 28 |  |
| Hospital admission during pregnancy: |  |  |  |
| Yes . . . . . . . . . . . . . . . . | 10 | 3 | <0.01 |
| No . . . . . . . . . . . . . . . . | 15 | 32 |  |
| Labour/delivery: |  |  |  |
| Abnormal . . . . . . . . . . . . | 12 | 2 | <0.01 |
| Normal . . . . . . . . . . . . . . | 13 | 33 |  |

From M. A. Lynch, "Ill-Health and Child Abuse," *The Lancet,* August 16, 1975.

**Table 2-3.** Illnesses in Abused Child and Siblings and in Mother During Child's First Year of Life

|  | Abused Children (25) | Siblings (35) | P |
|---|---|---|---|
| Childhood illness: |  |  |  |
| Yes . . . . . . . . . . . . . . . . | 15 | 3 | <0.01 |
| No . . . . . . . . . . . . . . . . | 10 | 32 |  |
| Maternal illness: |  |  |  |
| Yes . . . . . . . . . . . . . . . . | 12 | 2 | <0.01 |
| No . . . . . . . . . . . . . . . . | 13 | 33 |  |

From M. A. Lynch, "Ill-Health and Child Abuse," *The Lancet,* August 16, 1975.

### Delivery

To better understand the attitude and behavior of mothers as well as mother-infant interaction in the first hours and days of life, it is helpful to consider the effects of various delivery procedures and anesthetic interventions. The information available about this period suggests that mothers who remain relaxed during labor, and who cooperate and have good rapport with those caring for them, are more apt to be pleased with their infants at first sight (Newton and Newton[9]). The effects of anesthesia, cesarean section, and amnesic drugs on attachment and mothering behavior have not been studied systematically.

Throughout the United States prospective parents have shown an increased interest in the quality of their childbirth experience. There have been strong objections to the impersonal and medically oriented delivery in the hospital, where the woman loses all control over the events of her labor and delivery and where her husband may have only a limited role to play. The enthusiastic increase in prepared childbirth has led to discussions about how best to achieve a childbirth experience that is safe and will accommodate the wishes of the prospective parents.

Study of home deliveries have begun in California by means of videotapes and discussions with a perceptive midwife, Raven Lang[10], who has made naturalistic observations during 52 deliveries. In contrast to a woman who gives birth in the hospital, a woman delivering at home, aided by this midwife, appears to be in control. She chooses the location of the birth as well as the close friends who will be present to share this experience with her. She is an active participant during her labor and delivery rather than a passive patient. Immediately after delivery, she appears to be in a remarkable state of ecstacy, which is called ecstasis. In fact many mothers have reported that they had sensations similar to orgasm at the time of delivery.

The exuberance is contagious and the observers share the festive mood of unreserved elation after the delivery. They offer congratulations and provide grooming and other comforts to the mother. The observers show intense interest in the infant, expecially in the first fifteen to twenty minutes of life. The friends who have witnessed the child's birth have been reported to be more closely attached to the child than other family friends who had not attended the delivery. Is this a mechanism designed to enhance family bonds which has been lost in the present day hospital delivery? Although controlled studies have not yet been performed to test the effects of this experience on the mother-infant relationship, it seems clear that the conditions surrounding delivery greatly affect the mother's initial mood and interaction with her infant and her husband.

### Early Post Partum Period—Maternal-Sensitive Period

There is evidence that mothers have difficulty forming an attachment when they are separated from their babies during the first hours after delivery. Minor problems (such as slight hyperbilirubinemia, mild respiratory distress, and poor feeding) resulting in separation during this period may disturb and distort maternal affectional ties. This disturbance of mothering may last for a year or throughout childhood, even though the infant's problems were completely resolved prior to discharge.

In the first of several carefully controlled investigations involving primiparous mothers with normal full term infants, an "early and extended contact" group of fourteen mothers were given the routine contact with their babies and were also given their nude babies in bed for one hour in the first two hours after delivery and for five extra hours on each of the next three days of life. The control group of fourteen mothers received the care that is routine in most United States hospitals: a glimpse of the baby at birth, a brief contact for identification at six to eight hours, and then visits of 20–30 minutes for feedings every four hours. The groups were matched as to age and marital and socio-economic status of the mothers, and were not significantly different in the sex and weight of the infants.

To determine if the additional mother-infant contact early in life resulted in altered maternal behavior, the mothers returned to the hospital 28–32 days after delivery for three separate observations: (1) a standardized interview, (2) an observation of the mother's performance during a physical examination of her infant, and (3) a filmed study of the mother feeding her infant. There were significant differences between the two groups in all three observations. The mothers in the early and extended contact group tended to pick up the infant when it cried and to stay at home with the infant during the first month. If they did go out, the mothers in this group tended to think about their babies more often and usually returned earlier than expected.

During the physical examination, the extended contact mothers would stand and watch their infants and show more soothing behavior when their babies cried (Fig. 2–1). Figure 2–2 shows the fondling and "en face" scores for both groups of mothers during a ten-minute, one frame per second filmed feeding analyzed for 25 behaviors. Although the amount of time the mothers in each group spent looking at their babies was not significantly different, the extended contact mothers showed significantly more "en face" and fondling. Therefore, by all three measures, differences between the two groups of mothers were apparent at one month. These methods were designed to discover differences in attachment between the two groups, and not to evaluate good or bad mothering.

At one year, the two groups of mothers again showed significant differences (Kennell et al.),[11] with the extended contact mothers spending a greater percentage of time near the table assisting the physician while he examined their babies and soothing them when they cried. At two years, five mothers were selected at random from each group, and the linguistic behaviors of the two groups of mothers while speaking to their children were compared. The extended contact mothers asked twice as many questions, and used more words per proposition, fewer content words, more adjectives, and fewer commands than did the controls (Ringler et al.)[12] (see Table 2–4).

In an interesting and significant observation of fathers, Lind[13] noted that paternal caregiving in the first three months of life was markedly increased when the father was asked to undress his infant twice and to establish eye-to-eye contact with him for one hour during the first three days of life. This evidence provides strong support for the existence of a sensitive period in the first minutes and hours after birth that is important for parent-infant attachment. Four of five other recent studies in Brazil and Guatemala, where the amount of contact between a mother and her normal, full term neonate was varied, also support this concept.

**Figure 2–1.** Scored Observations of the Mother Made During a Physical Examination of Her Infant at One Month

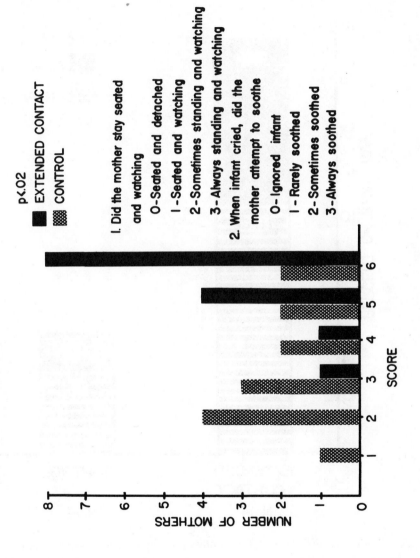

p<.02

■ EXTENDED CONTACT
▨ CONTROL

I. Did the mother stay seated and watching
  0 – Seated and detached
  1 – Seated and watching
  2 – Sometimes standing and watching
  3 – Always standing and watching

2. When infant cried, did the mother attempt to soothe
  0 – Ignored infant
  1 – Rarely soothed
  2 – Sometimes soothed
  3 – Always soothed

NUMBER OF MOTHERS

SCORE

**Figure 2-2.** Filmed Feeding Analysis at One Month, Showing the Percentage of "En Face" and Fondling Times in Mothers Given Extended Contact with Their Infants and in the Control Group

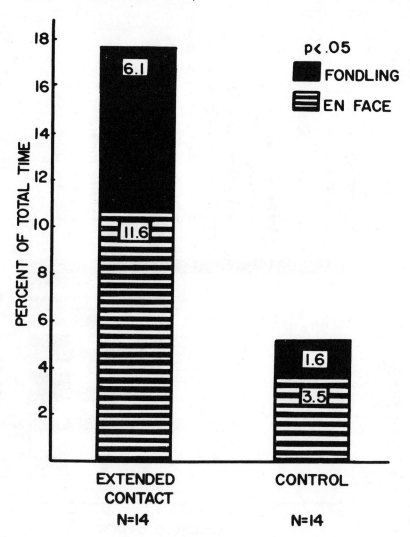

Studies of the effects of rooming-in at the hospital have also indicated the importance of the early postnatal period. When rooming-in was instituted a number of years ago, an increase in breast feeding and a reduction in anxious phone calls was found.[14] In Sweden, mothers randomly assigned to rooming-in arrangements were more confident, felt more competent in caregiving, and thought they would need less help in caring for their infants at home than nonrooming-in mothers. They also appeared to be more sensitive to the crying of their own infants than were mothers who did not have the rooming-in experience.[15] This suggests that close continual contact after birth may be important in encouraging more relaxed maternal behavior.

**Table 2–4.** Characteristics of Mother-to-Child Speech at 1 and 2 Years

| | One year | | Two years | |
|---|---|---|---|---|
| | *Extended* | | *Extended* | |
| *Measure* | *contact* | *Control* | *contact* | *Control* |
| Number of words per proposition | 3.43 | 4.34 | 4.62* | 3.66 |
| Mean utterance length | 2.5 | 2.7 | 3.9 | 3.1 |
| Percentage of | | | | |
| Adjectives/all words | 0.20 | 0.10 | 16.00† | 12.00 |
| Content words/all words | 62.40 | 57.60 | 48.00 | 62.00† |
| Questions/sentences | 10.40 | 25.20 | 41.00* | 19.00 |
| Imperatives/sentences | 68.00 | 49.00 | 43.00 | 74.00* |
| Statements/sentences | 15.00 | 26.00* | 16.00 | 6.00 |

*p <0.05.
†p <0.02.

### Species Specific Behavior and Early Reciprocal Interaction

After delivery the mother exhibits a characteristic pattern of behavior with her newborn infant. Filmed observations show that a mother presented with her undressed, full term infant begins touching the infant's extremities with her fingertips and in less than ten minutes proceeds to encompassing, massaging palm contact on the infant's trunk (Fig. 2–3).

A strong interest in eye-to-eye contact has been expressed by mothers of both full term and premature infants. When the words of mothers who had been presented with their infants in privacy were taped, 70 percent of the statements referred to the eyes. The mothers said, "Open up your eyes so I will know that you are there"; "Let me see your eyes"; and "Show me your eyes so that I'll know that you love me." Robson[16] has suggested that eye-to-eye contact appears to elicit maternal caregiving responses. Mothers are extremely interested in looking "en face" at their infants. "En face" is defined as the position in which the mother keeps her face aligned so that her eyes are in the same vertical plane of rotation as those of her infant. (This is shown by the mother in Figure 2–4). Complementing the mother's interest in the infant's eyes is the early functional development of the infant's visual pathways.

One midwife (Raven Lang) who has made observations of home deliveries has observed that the infant quiets down when given to the mother. Almost always the mother touches the baby's skin with her fingertips starting with the face. It is always a gentle stroking motion. This occurs before the initial nursing and before delivery of the placenta. Then the baby is usually put to the breast. The infant does not suck at first, but continually licks the mother's nipple,[17] which is a powerful stimulus for prolactin secretion.

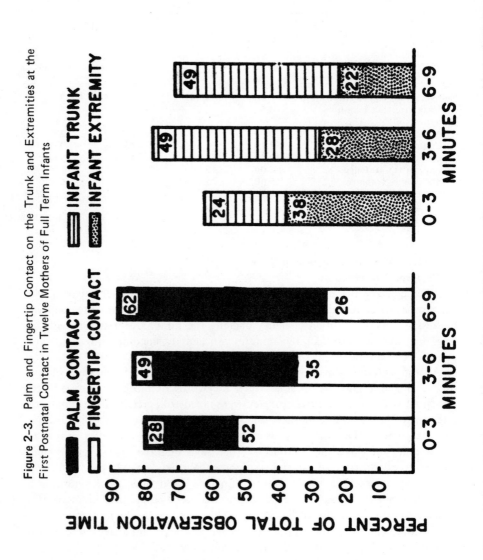

Figure 2-3. Palm and Fingertip Contact on the Trunk and Extremities at the First Postnatal Contact in Twelve Mothers of Full Term Infants

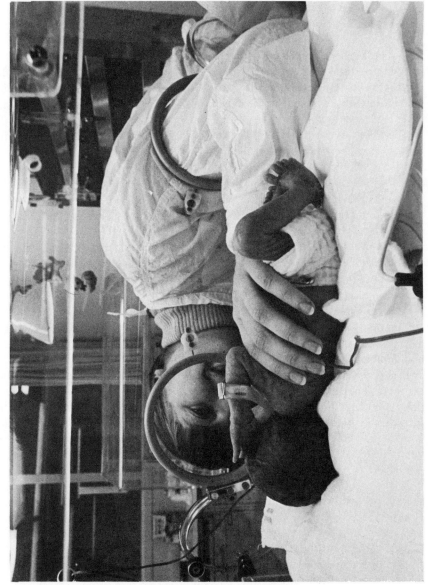

**Figure 2-4.** A Mother of a Premature Baby in the "En Face" Position

Recently, a virtual explosion of information about the states and abilities of newborn infants has contributed to our understanding of why the period immediately after birth is so important for the parent. Early observations of the competence of newborn infants indicate six separate states of consciousness in the infant, which range from deep sleep to screaming. Desmond et al.[18] observed that the infant is in state 4 for a period lasting from 45 to 60 minutes immediately following delivery. In this state the infant's eyes are wide open and he is alert, active, and able to follow during the first hour of life.[19] After this hour, the infant goes into a deep sleep for three to four hours. From the discoveries of the infant's early responsiveness to his environment we have realized why this period is particularly significant for the mother and baby. Each partner of this dyad is intimately involved with each other in an array of mutually rewarding interactions on a number of sensory levels. Their behaviors complement each other and serve to bind them together.

The infant elicits behavior from the mother that in turn is satisfying to him. And the mother brings out behaviors in the infant that in turn are rewarding to her. For example, the infant's hard crying is likely to bring the mother near and trigger her to pick him up. When she picks him up, he is likely to quiet, open his eyes, and follow. Looking at the process in the opposite direction, when the mother touches the infant's cheek, he is likely to turn his head, bringing him into contact with her nipple, which he will suck. His sucking in turn is pleasurable to both of them. The mother speaks to the baby in a high-pitched voice and infants respond more to a high-pitched voice than to lower tones. The baby has been shown to have the amazing ability to move in rhythm to words spoken to him in languages as diverse as English and Chinese.

The consistency of the mother's care during the first few days reestablishes the infants biorhythmicity which is disturbed by the shock of delivery. The mother's milk gives the baby antibodies and cells that may provide important immunologic benefits. The baby's sucking stimulates oxytocin release, which contracts the mother's uterus and leads to the expulsion of the placenta. When the infant licks the mother's nipple and areola, or nurses, the secretion of prolactin is stimulated, which increases milk production. During their early contact the mother may provide the infant with respiratory and gastrointestinal flora that protect the baby from the invasion of other organisms such as hospital strains of staphylococci. The mother also provides warmth for the infant through bodily contact.

These are only several of the interactions that may occur during the first contact between mother and newborn. Each behavior tends to trigger a number of others. However, the interactions should not be likened to a chain reaction where each link leads to only one other link in the series. Rather the effects are similar to the multitude of ever-widening rings caused by a pebble dropped into a pool. In a sense, there exists a failsafe system that is overdetermined to insure the continued proximity of mother and child.

There is an ideal opportunity for the beginning of strong attachment of the mother and father to the infant when the father is present during labor and delivery. If the mother and father have a private interlude together with the undressed baby in the first hour after birth, there is an opportunity to touch and interact with the baby. The evidence that is available at the present time suggests that the interaction of the parents with their infant, when started in the first hour, will continue in the following days and lead to increased attentiveness and interest.

A small number of studies of mothers of prematures have also focused on the possibility of a sensitive early period in the human mother. Observations at Stanford and in our own unit have been made with mothers of prematures, half of whom were permitted into the nursery in the first hours and half of whom could not come in until the twentieth day. At Case Western Reserve University, mothers who had early contact with their infants looked at them significantly more than late contact mothers during a filmed feeding at the time of discharge.

Furthermore, preliminary data on the IQs of these two groups of children at 42 months indicate that children in the early contact group scored significantly higher (mean = 99) than did children in the late contact group (mean = 85). Strikingly, a significant correlation was found between IQ at 42 months and the amount of time women looked at their babies during the one month filmed feeding (r = .71). This is consistent with our hypothesis that early contact affects aspects of maternal behavior which may have significance for the child's later development. At Stanford, when those separated from their premature babies for three to twelve weeks were compared with mothers of prematures permitted early contact with their infants, there were more divorces (five compared to one) and more infants relinquished (two compared to none) in the group of mothers with prolonged separation.[20]

Evidence that contact during this early period is not always essential for mother-infant bonding, and the establishment of satisfactory family bonds, is provided by the number of children who are well cared for and protected by their parents and the many intact families where the early attachment was minimal but later bonds between family memebers appear to be adequate. On the other hand, when there are disturbances of parent-to-infant bonds and father-mother bonds, the question may be asked, "Would the outcome have been different if parent-infant contact had occurred shortly after birth and under optimal circumstances?" Should we have particular concern about family units being formed now and in the next decades because almost every prospective parent in the present generation was separated from his or her parents in the early postpartum period?

It is not generally appreciated that in many European countries, mothers and healthy newborn babies are never separated and remain together in the hospital following delivery. In hospitals in the United States, the mother and baby usually only have interrupted contact during the post partum period in the hospital. The contact and interaction of a mother and her baby during this period (the first few days following the initial 12–24 hours), may be of great significance for the further development of the attachment bonds. Short episodes of contact may provide the only opportunity for starting an attachment in many American hospitals where separation after birth and feedings every four hours are the rule.

In the twentieth century the predominant tendency of fathers to avoid care-taking involvement with their infants has been considered a cultural, sex role phenomenon. However, the emerging studies of father-infant interaction, such as those of Lind and Parks,[21] suggest that fathers can become bonded to their babies in the early period following delivery and will then be much more involved with their care. If the father does not have an attachment to the infant and if the mother's bonds are tenuous because she has not had early and continuous contact, then the vicissitudes of life may strain the mother-infant attachment, resulting in moderate or severe consequences similar to the child abuse described by Margaret Lynch. If the infant has a neonatal illness or a series of illnesses in the first year, or if the mother herself is ill, the bonds may not be strong enough to assure the safety and well-being of the infant.

## EFFECTS OF MAJOR NEONATAL PROBLEMS

When a baby is born prematurely, or is sick or malformed, separation of the mother and the baby during the early hours is customary and there is usually a greatly decreased opportunity for the mother and the baby to interact in the first few days. During this period the mother also has turbulent emotional reactions to the production of a baby who is not healthy and normal. When the infant is born prematurely, the mother has not had time to prepare herself psychologically for the birth of the baby and her hormonal state may be quite different than in a full term delivery. All the congratulations and social and cultural rewards that come to the mother who delivers a full term baby may be muted, distorted, or absent when the baby is born with an abnormality. The parents often are hesitant to announce the birth to their friends and relatives as they would with a normal full term baby, and the response of family and friends is often restrained because of uncertainty about the nature of the problem, the outcome, and what will be best for the parents.

The mothering behavior of every mother, and her ability to endure emotional stress whether she delivers a normal or abnormal infant, is influenced by a multitude of factors (see Fig. 2–5). Some of these may be unchangeable at delivery (for example, how the mother herself was mothered as an infant, her relationship with the rest of her family, her cultural background, and her experience with previous pregnancies). Other factors may be altered, including the behavior of doctors, nurses, and other hospital personnel, the routine practices of the hospital, and whether the mother and infant are separated after birth. Distortions or disorders of mothering (such as battering, failure to thrive, parents' fears

**Figure 2-5.** Disorders of Mothering; a Hypothesis of Their Cause

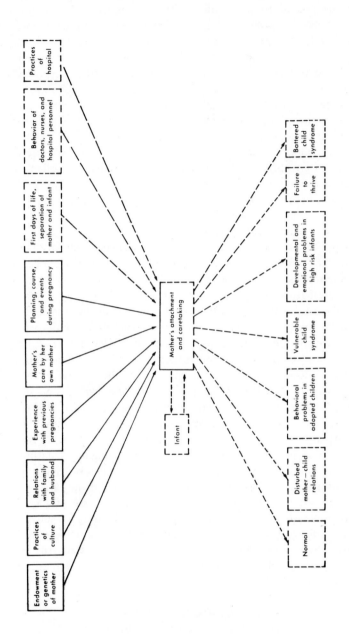

that a normal child will die prematurely, behavioral problems with an adopted child) may be related to the above influences on the mother, and a major component of these disorders may be the separation of mother and infant. The disproportionately high percentage of premature infants (Table 2–5) who return to the hospital with failure to thrive (FTT) and battering tend to support this.

Procedures that have been found to be of value with normal delivery are often eliminated or significantly altered when a baby is sick or abnormal. Some of these changes are absolutely necessary for the welfare of the baby and mother but not necessarily all. For example, we may question whether it is not even more important for the father or a close family member to be present with the mother during labor and delivery when an abnormal baby is being delivered. Then, it may be possible for the parents and the baby to be together for a short period after birth and for medications to be limited so the mother is awake and aware of what is happening at delivery.

### Premature and Sick Infants—History

The role of the mother in the high risk and premature nursery has changed greatly since the 1880s, when rooming-in was the accepted mode. The first modern neonatologist, Pierre Budin, recognized the importance of encouraging mothers of premature infants to visit and assist in the care of their infants. However, subsequent nurseries, influenced by the fear of the spread of infection, discouraged visitors and ultimately developed stringent regulations prohibiting visitors and advising limited handling of the infants. The mother of a premature infant experiences severe deprivation of contact with her infant and also faces what has been considered an acute emotional crisis. She progresses through four psychologic stages: (1) anticipatory grief, preparing herself for the infant's death, (2) acceptance of her failure to deliver a full term infant, (3) resumption of the process of relating to her infant, and (4) learning the special needs of a premature infant.

These observations were made at a time when visiting in premature nurseries was either forbidden or severely limited. It is not clear how much these stages have been influenced by the development of policies of increased visiting and parental participation in the care of premature infants. As recently as 1970, only one-third of premature nurseries allowed parents to enter. Barnett et al.[29] obtained information by questionnaires from 1444 premature nurseries. Thirty-four percent of the responding nurseries allowed mothers to visit and handle their babies. Of these nurseries, 60 percent also allowed the father to enter and touch his baby.

### Birth of an Infant with a Congenital Malformation

The birth of a baby is the culmination of his parents' best efforts and embodies their hopes for the future, so it is not surprising that the birth of an infant blighted with a malformation is a crushing blow to the parents and to

**Table 2-5.** The Effects of Separation (Many Days) on Battering and Failure to Thrive Without Organic Cause

| | *Authors* | *N* | *Number Affected* | *Percentage Affected* |
|---|---|---|---|---|
| Failure to thrive | 1. Ambuel and Harris 1963 | 100 | 27 Prematures | 27 |
| | 2. Shaheen, Alexander, Truskowsky and Barbero 1968 | 44 | 16 Prematures | 36 |
| | 3. Evans, Reinhart and Succop 1972 | 40 | 9 Prematures | 22.5 |
| | 4. Elmer and Gregg | 20 | 6 Prematures | 30 |
| Battering | 5. Skinner and Castle | 78 | 10 Prematures | 13 |
| | 6. Klein and Stern 1971 | 51 | 12 Low Birth Weight Infants | 23.5 |
| | 7. Oliver, Cox, Taylor and Baldwin 1974 | 38 | 8 Prematures | 21 |

Note: Estimates of the prematurity rate in the general population range between 5–7% (higher in the inner city area) – Ed.

everyone else who has shared in the event, and it usually alters the attachment process.

The delivery of an infant with a congenital anomaly also presents complex challenges to the physician who will care for the affected child and his family. Despite the relatively large number of infants with congenital anomalies, our understanding of how parents develop an attachment to a malformed child remains incomplete. Previous investigators agree that the child's birth often precipitates major family stress but relatively few have described the process of family adaptation during the infant's first year of live. A major advance was Solnit and Stark's[30] conceptualization of parental reactions. They emphasized that a significant aspect of adaptation is the necessity for parents to mourn the loss of the normal child they had expected. Less attention has been given to the more adaptive aspects of parental attachment to children with malformations.

The intense emotional turmoil described by parents who have given birth to a child with a congenital malformation corresponds to a period of crisis, defined as "upset in a state of equilibrium caused by a hazardous event which creates a threat, loss, or a challenge for the individual."[31,32] A crisis includes a period of impact, a rise in tension associated with stress, and finally a return to equilibrium. During such crisis periods, a person is at least temporarily unable to respond with his usual problem solving activities to solve the crisis. Roskies[33] noted a similar "birth crisis" in her observations of mothers who had given birth to children with birth defects caused by thalidomide.

In one of our studies, despite wide variations among the children's malformations and parental backgrounds, a number of surprisingly similar themes emerged from the parents' discussion of their reactions. Generally the parents could recall the events surrounding the birth and their reactions in great detail.[34] They experienced identifiable stages of emotional reactions. Although the amount of time a parent needed to deal with the issues of a specific stage varied, the sequence of stages reflected the natural course of most parents' reactions to their malformed infant.

**First Stage: Shock.**   Most parents' initial response to the news of their child's anomaly was overwhelming shock. These parents, when interviewed, report reactions and sensations indicating an abrupt disruption of their usual states of feeling. One mother said, "It was a big blow which just shattered me." One of the fathers explained, "It was as if the world had come to an end." Many parents confided that this early period was a time of irrational behavior, characterized by much crying, feelings of helplessness and occasionally an urge to flee.

**Second Stage: Disbelief (Denial).**   Many parents tried either to avoid admitting that their child had an anomaly or to cushion the tremendous blow. Each reported that he wished either to be free from the situation or deny its impact. One father graphically described his disbelief: "I found myself repeating 'It's not real'—over and over again." Other parents mentioned that the news of the baby's birth did not make sense. One admitted, "I just couldn't believe it was happening to me." Although every parent reported disbelief, the intensity of the denial varied considerably.

**Third Stage: Sadness, Anger, Anxiety.** Intense feelings of sadness and anger accompanied and followed the stage of disbelief. The most common emotional reaction was sadness. One mother reported, "I couldn't stop crying. Even after a long while I cried about it." A smaller but significant number of parents reported angry feelings. One father said, "I just wanted to kick someone." A mother reported that she was angry and "hated him [the baby] or hated myself. I was responsible." In most instances mothers feared for their babies' lives, despite strong reassurance. One mother said that she initially perceived her child as "nonhuman." "Holding him with that tube distressed me. Initially I held him only because it was the maternal thing to do." Almost all the mothers were hesitant about becoming attached to their babies.

**Fourth Stage: Equilibrium.** Parents reported a gradual lessening of both their anxiety and intense emotional reactions. As their feelings of emotional upset lessened, they noted increased comfort with their situation and confidence in their ability to care for the baby. Some parents reached equilibrium within a few weeks after the birth, while others took many months. Even at best, this adaptation continues to be incomplete. One parent reported that "tears come even yet, years after the baby's birth."

**Fifth Stage: Reorganization.** During this period parents deal with responsibility for their children's problems. Some mothers reported that they had to reassure themselves that "the baby's problems were nothing I had done." Positive long term acceptance of the child involved the parents' mutual support throughout the time after birth. Many couples have reported that they relied heavily on one another during the early period. However, in some instances the crisis of the birth separated parents. In one case, the parents blamed each other for the baby's birth. Another mother wanted to be isolated from her husband. "I don't want to see nobody. I just want to be by myself."

Despite the important similarities in parental reactions to various malformations, parents progressed through the various stages of reaction differently. Some parents did not report initial reactions of shock and emotional upset, but tended instead to intellectualize the baby's problem and focus on the facts related to the baby's condition. Other parents were not able to cope successfully with their strong emotional reactions to the birth and, as a result, did not achieve an adequate adaptation.

The crisis of the baby's birth has the potential for bringing the parents closer as a result of the mutual support and the communication required for adaptation. On the other hand, in many of the families we have studied, the baby's birth estranged the parents. The ongoing demands of the baby's care increased the isolation between some parents, particularly if they did not share the responsibility. We have used the term "asynchronous" to describe parents who progress through the different stages of adaptation at different speeds. These parents usually do not share their feelings with each other and seem to have particular difficulty in their relationships. Asynchrony often results in a temporary emotional separation of the parents and appears to be a significant factor in the high divorce rate following a major family crisis.

## PRACTICAL SUGGESTIONS

### Pregnancy, Labor, and Delivery

Until 100 years ago, events surrounding childbirth had changed little over the centuries. Elaborate customs of the society helped parents through this experience. In the last century, however, increasing emphasis has been placed on the medical and scientific aspects of delivery but less attention has been paid to the equally valid psychological considerations. A question may be raised: has the enormous improvement in medical management, which has lessened the physical dangers, contributed to a waning concern about the many other problems a mother faces during pregnancy and delivery? In 1959, Bibring[35] wrote, "What was once a crisis with carefully worked-out traditional customs of giving support to the woman passing through this crisis-period has become at this time a crisis with no mechanisms within the society for helping the woman involved in this profound change of conflict-solutions and adjustive tasks." This deficiency accounts for the development of the many support systems in our society.

The wide assortment of childbirth classes, especially those groups, such as Lamaze, which attempt to continue previous customs are good examples. These classes help the mother through the delivery period as well as aiding her in later infant and child care. They also lessen the tensions, fears, and fantasies that occur during normal pregnancies. By joining a group of mothers with whom she can talk and share her feelings, a woman can alleviate the many emotional upsets that occur during normal pregnancy. We therefore believe that these courses in which mothers—or still better, husbands and wives—participate actively have a valuable supportive role during pregnancy.

A helpful way to get acquainted with the parents during the pregnancy is to obtain a thorough family history. It is particularly important to review the health history, educational background, job and marital experiences, and fears and concerns of the parents. The following questions are suggested as possible clues to later problems. These should be included in the routine history taking.

1. How long have you lived in this immediate area?
2. Where does most of your family live?
3. How often do you see your mother or other close relatives?
4. Has anything happened to you in the past (or do you have any condition) that causes you to worry about the pregnancy or the baby?

5. What was your husband's reaction to your becoming pregnant?
6. What other responsibilities do you have outside the family?

Inquiring how the mother herself was mothered and by whom is important. Were her infancy and childhood neglected or deprived, or was her family life warm and intact? After the second trimester, the physician, nurse or social worker should look for some outward evidence of preparation for the infant; for example, purchasing clothes or a crib, or selecting a name. If preparations are not being made, this may be evidence of continuing rejection of the pregnancy.

A physician should ask a mother with a condition such as diabetes, hypertension, or heart or thyroid disease what she has heard or read about the course of an infant of a mother with this condition. How much such a mother has heard and just where she is in her comprehension of these problems must be determined. Even in very high risk situations, the odds are greatly in favor of the birth of a live baby who will ultimately be normal and healthy; therefore it is reasonable to emphasize the positive and be optimistic.

To minimize the number of unknowns for a mother while she is in the hospital, she and her husband should visit the maternity unit to see where labor and delivery will take place. She should also learn about the anesthetic (if she is to receive one), delivery routines, and all the procedures and medication she will receive before, during, and after delivery. By reducing the possibility of surprise, such advance preparation will increase confidence during labor and delivery. For an adult, just as for a child entering the hospital for surgery, the more meticulously every step and event is detailed in advance, the less the subsequent anxiety.

The mother benefits from continuing support and reassurance during her labor and delivery, whether from her husband, her mother, a midwife, or a nurse. She also must be satisfied with the arrangements that have been made to maintain her home during her hospitalization. In Holland, when mothers deliver at home, a mother's helper comes into the house at the time of delivery to take over the care of the family. She assists the midwife in delivering the infant. This gives the mother and father the freedom to concentrate on the needs of the baby and to enjoy their family.

To reduce the confusion and tension for the mother, she should labor and deliver in the same room so there will be no need to rush to a delivery room in the last minutes of labor. Once the delivery is completed and the mother has had a quick glance at the infant, she may need a few seconds to regain her composure and, in a sense, catch her breath before she proceeds to the next task—taking on the infant. This respite usually occurs while the placenta is being delivered and the mother is having any necessary suturing.

After delivery, the father, mother, and baby should have a period alone. This is usually possible only if the infant is normal and the mother is well. She should be given the baby undressed in bed and allowed to examine him completely. A heat panel easily maintains or, if need be, increases the body temperature of the infant (Fig. 2–6). Several mothers have told us of the unforgettable experience of holding their nude baby against their own bare chest and nursing. We recommend skin-to-skin contact. The father sits or stands at the side of the bed by the infant. This allows the parents and infant to become acquainted. Because the eyes are so important for both the parents and baby, we withhold the application of silver nitrate to the eyes until after this rendezvous.

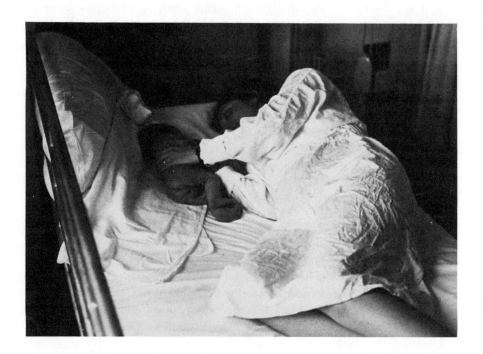

**Figure 2–6.**  A Mother and Her Infant Shortly After Birth in a Labor Room

The mother, father, and infant should be together for about 30 to 45 minutes. If the mother has had medication she and the baby often fall into a deep sleep after 10 or 15 minutes. In Guatemalan hospitals, where drugs and anesthesia are used more sparingly, mothers were usually awake after 45 minutes of privacy with their infants. The mother and father never forget this significant and stimulating shared experience. This should be a private session, with no interruptions. Affectional bonds are further consolidated in the succeeding four to five days through continued close association of baby and mother, particularly when she cares for him. Contact with the father and other children during the period of hospitalization is encouraged.

### Care of Premature or Sick Newborns

A mother should be permitted into the premature nursery as soon as she is able to maneuver easily. Mothers are told that the staff of the nursery looks forward to her visit and that her baby will make better progress once she is able to visit. When the mother makes her first visit she may become faint or dizzy when she looks at her infant, so we always have a stool nearby. A nurse stays at her side during most of the visit describing in detail the procedures that are being carried out, such as the monitoring of respirations and heart rate, the umbilical catheter, the feeding through various infusion lines, and the functioning of the incubator. Grandparents, brothers, sisters, and other relatives are encouraged to view the infant through the glass window of the nursery so that they will also begin to feel attached to the infant.

The child's health is discussed with the parents at least once a day. If critically ill, discussions should be held at least twice a day. We find out what the mother believes is going to happen or what she has read about the problem, and we move at her pace during any discussion to insure that she understands everything we say. If the mother and father are in the referring hospital, we ask the father to stand nearby so they can both hear the same message. This group communication reduces misunderstandings and usually is helpful in assuring the mother that the whole story is being told.

If there is any chance that the infant will survive, optimism is important. "We're pleased by your infant's progress. She's active and pink. We're not in the clear yet, but the outlook is good." The next day when conditions are about the same we might say, "The baby's had an excellent 24 hours. You have made a good strong baby. We're pleased that everything is remaining the same. Now that we have cared for her for another day, we can see that her condition is obviously improving." If a favorable prediction proves to be incorrect and the baby expires there is no evidence that the parents will be harmed by the early optimism. There is almost always time to prepare them before the baby actually dies. On the other hand, if the infant lives and the physician has been pessimistic, it is almost impossible for parents to become closely attached after they have prepared for the baby's death. This recommendation is contrary to many old customs and places a heavy burden on the physician. If the infant does expire, the parents will require help with the mourning period.

A mother and her infant should ideally be kept near each other in the same hospital, on the same floor. When the long term significance of early mother-infant contact is kept in mind, a modification of restrictions and territorial traditions can usually be arranged. There is need for increased emphasis on transporting mothers, before or after the birth of their infants, to the centers where their prematures will receive care. In our present transport system, where the mother usually remains in an obstetric hospital, giving the mother a chance to see and touch her infant before her baby is moved to a hospital with an intensive care unit is helpful. The house officer or the attending physician should stop in the mother's room with the transport incubator and encourage her to touch her baby and look at him closely even if he has respiratory distress and is in an oxygen hood. A comment about the baby's strength and healthy features may be long remembered and appreciated.

The father is encouraged to follow the transport team to our hospital so he can see what is happening with his baby. He uses his own transportation so that he can stay in the newborn unit for three to four hours. This extra time allows him to get to know the nurses and physicians, to find out how the infant is being treated, and to talk with the physicians in a relaxed fashion about what they expect will happen with the baby and his treatment in the succeeding days. After offering him a cup of coffee, and explaining in detail everything that is going on with his infant, he interacts with his baby. The father is thus the link between the members of his family and the hospital, carrying information back to his wife so he can let her know how the baby is doing. A Polaroid picture is taken, even when the infant is on a respirator, so that he can describe in detail to his wife how the baby is being cared for. Mothers often tell us how valuable the pictures are for keeping some contact with their infant even while being physically separated.

In overwhelming situations some parents can only assimilate a small amount of information every day. Explanations can be kept as simple as is appropriate to the situation. There is no need to discuss a wide variety of diagnostic possibilities or potential complications that may never develop. The value of touching their infant is emphasized. Studies indicate that touching their infant reduces the number of apneic episodes, increases weight gain, and hastens the infant's discharge from the unit. Parents should be allowed to call the unit 24 hours a day. This permits them to get an immediate report of the baby's status, activity, and color. Keeping a book to record parental phone calls and visits is useful in determing which mothers are likely to require additional help from a social worker or extra discussions about the health of their infant.

If a mother visits less than three times in two weeks, the probability of occurrence of a mothering disorder such as failure to thrive, battering, or giving up the baby increases (see Table 2-6). If the mother visits infrequently she should be given additional attention. Nurses must feel comfortable in reporting any worries or problems that they have about a mother or father's behavior. To accomplish this, a good working relationship between the physicians and the nurses is essential. Meetings with the nursery staff in the intensive care on a weekly basis provides an opportunity for the staff members to express their concerns and problems.

**Table 2-6.**  Visiting Frequency and Outcome in the Intensive Care Nursery

| Number | >3 visits/2 weeks 111 | <3 visits/2 weeks 38 |
|---|---|---|
| Followup | 108 | 38 |
| Disorders of Mothering | 2(1.8%) | 9(23%) $p=<.001$[a] |
| Abandoned | 1 | 1 |
| Battered | 0 | 2 |
| Failure to thrive | 0 | 5 |
| Fostered | 1 | 1 |

[a]Chi square

### The Infant with a Birth Defect

When a baby is born with a congenital defect such as a cleft lip or palate, the physician should tell the mother and father together about the problem, preferably with the baby present. He should emphasize the normal, healthy aspects of the baby, then use calm and positive statements about the near perfection of the correction that will be achieved by surgery.

How best to tell parents about their baby's birth defect is uncertain until one has had a good opportunity to listen to the parents express some of what they fear and feel. Emphasis should be placed on listening, and then explaining. Parents may need to express their wish that the baby would die or talk about the disturbing appearance of their malformed infant before they are able to become attached to him. A sensitive social worker is invaluable.

A strong feeling of guilt is common and will interfere with the parents' ability to accept the baby. The shock of the situation may deafen the parents to the explanations of the physician, so he should be sensitive to their feelings and their questions and should plan to go over his description of the baby's problem, its cause and management, two or three times during the hospital stay and at the baby's first checkups. Frequent visits of the mother with her infant, involving physical contact and caretaking whenever possible, should be arranged to counteract the mother's tendency to withdraw and withhold her full commitment to her infant.

The parents should be encouraged to talk about the baby's problem and their feelings—disappointment, sadness, anger, guilt, or inadequacy. Their communication with each other should be supported and encouraged. Whenever possible, the physician or social worker should talk to both parents together and separately. A difference in the shading of reports to one of the parents may block their communication, sometimes with harmful long term effects.

The parents' mental picture of the anomaly is often far more alarming than the actual problem. Any delay during which the parents suspect that there may be a problem greatly heightens their anxiety and causes their imaginations to run wild. Talking to both parents in the presence of the baby as soon after delivery as possible is helpful. Tranquilizers tend to blunt their responses and slows or worsens their adaptation to the problem. A small dose of Seconal at night is often helpful. Move at the parent's pace; moving too quickly runs the risk of losing the parents along the way. The parents are to be encouraged to describe how they perceive their infant. Each parent may move through the process of shock, denial, anger, guilt and adaptation at a different pace. If they are unable to talk with each other about the baby, there may be a marked disruption in their own relationship. During the process of early crisis intervention meeting several times with the parents is necessary.

Many anomalies are very frustrating not only to the parents but to the physicians and nurses as well. There is a temptation for the physician to withdraw from the parents and their infant. The many questions asked by the parent who is trying to understand the problem are often very frustrating for the physician. The parent often appears to forget and asks the same questions over and over again. The physician himself may have feelings of guilt for not having produced a healthy or intact baby for the parents. He or she may feel of no help to the mother, while actually it is with this mother that the doctor can be of most assistance. Nurses and physicians both can facilitate the attachment of parents to their malformed infant in the neonatal period and as the child grows. Knowledge about the usual course of parental reactions helps the physician take this into account in planning his interventions.

The availability of the physician and social worker throughout the child's early years puts him in a position to help with the family's adaptation. They can be sensitive to the relationship between the parents and can determine which stage of adaptation each parent has reached and check how aware each partner is of the other's progress and may be alert to evidence of any asynchrony. The advice, support and parent counselling during the baby's first year of life will be a crucial aid in maximizing the development of the child with a congenital malformation and his family.

## THE FIRST MONTH WITH THE INFANT
## AT HOME

The events of the perinatal period from the viewpoint of a new mother should be considered. She has had a strong and intimate relationship with her physician at visits of progressively increasing frequency up to the time of delivery and during her hospitalization. Suddenly these visits stop. She will usually have only one more appointment six weeks after delivery. Cut off from these contacts, a mother often feels neglected at her visits to the pediatrician, who tends to focus exclusively on the baby. In truth the pediatrician has three patients—the baby, the mother, and the father. The pediatrician needs to take a ltttle time to inquire about how the mother is doing, praising the efforts made to care for the baby and expressing empathy for the sleep they have missed and the strains experienced. Positive reinforcement of a mother's efforts is more effective than corrective and critical statements. The pediatrician's third patient, the father, needs the same attention as the mother. Time spent asking him how he is doing will usually be repaid by the increased support he will provide to his wife. Appointments for both parents to come to the office without the baby serve to get questions and problems resolved.

The affectional bonds a mother and father establish with their infant during the first days of life are crucial for his future welfare. When the bonds are solidly established, parents are motivated to learn about their baby's individual requirements and to adapt to meet his needs; they are willing to change diapers thousands of times, to respond to the baby's cries in the night, and to provide stimulation appropriate in intensity, timing, and quality. Fully developed specific ties keep parents from striking their baby who has cried for hours night after night—even when they are exhausted and alone.

Studies of mother-to-infant and father-to-infant attachment have begun to define the characteristics of the bonds of attachment. Thus far, there have been no empirical investigations of the interrelationship of attachment bonds among the individuals who make up a family. However, information from the literature and observations of many deliveries suggest that the time of delivery may be optimal for beginning new or enhancing existing attachments.

When several people attend a birth, as in the home deliveries in the Santa Cruz area described by Raven Lang, they have reported feeling a particularly strong attachment to the infant which persists throughout succeeding years. Does this special attachment provide important evolutionary mechanism to substitute caretakers for the infant during the time when maternal mortality at childbirth was commonplace? Conversely, mothers develop remarkably strong attachments to those people who attend her during delivery. It is not unusual for a mother to greet a pediatrician or obstetrician who happened to be in the delivery room only briefly, with great enthusiasm and affection, even though the physician may not remember the woman or delivery. She responds as if there were particularly strong attachment valences free to latch onto anyone nearby.

This phenomenon should be considered carefully. The father present at the delivery is essential so that the mother's attachment will be to him and the baby rather than to hospital personnel. The evidence that dysfunction of the family and the weakness of familial bonds are related to the practice of separating mother and baby after birth and excluding the husband from the labor, delivery, and postdelivery experiences is becoming most convincing. Only further research will help clarify these observations.

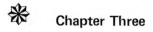 Chapter Three

# Arresting or Freezing [a]
# the Developmental Process

Ray E. Helfer, John P. McKinney, and Ruth Kempe

## SECTION ONE

### Introduction:
### Being a Kid Isn't All That Easy
### Ray E. Helfer

One Sunday afternoon I was watching my five-year-old son playing with his young friend. As they maneuvered in and out of the adult world around them, playing first behind a large bureau, under a table and then climbing the stairs, the realization of the obvious struck me. Being a little kid isn't all that easy!

With camera in hand, I followed the two children around, taking pictures of what their physical world was like. First a picture of the dog, then my son's young friend and his little sister. As they attacked the refrigerator another photo was taken. When these were developed, their world seemed rather reasonable and negotiable. The dog, the friend, the sister, and the food were all ready at hand. The remainder of the world was different—all made for adults. The top of the bureau couldn't be seen; Dad's car looked huge from his level, and sitting in the seat of the car resulted in not being able to see out of the window, except for the sky and the tops of trees. When his teenaged brother's picture was developed, I realized that five-year-olds only see their big brother's belly. When they want to see their face, the view is awesome, looking at a large silhouette against the sky.

When I showed the pictures to my five-year-old, projecting on the screen his brother's belly, I said, "David, who is that?" David said, "That's Jeff." When the silhouette of Jeff's face was projected, David asked, "Is that Jeff?" The physical

[a]See Reference "3" Chapter Four for a discussion of this term.

world is equally giantlike. The photos of the stairs to the cellar, the door from the garage to the house, the sink, stove and the like, all clearly demonstrated that the world around small children was built for big people. Growing up in a world that is made for someone twice your size is hard enough, but the first five years have other things in store for children. During this period of years a child must learn to:

| | | |
|---|---|---|
| see | walk | throw a ball |
| hear | run | trust others |
| smile | control urine | express feelings |
| roll | control bowels | begin setting priorities |
| sit | stand on one foot | make decisions |
| crawl | draw with a pencil | make friends |
| speak | color | get needs met |
| pull up | count | develop a good self-image |

and a thousand other things. Just think—the "golden years" of childhood, all there is to do is play—and learn a few little developmental tricks like talking, trusting, and feeling good about yourself. Selma Fraeberg calls these "the magic years".[1] Some developmental psychologists say the first five years are so critical that is serious deficits occur they can never be regained.

Being a little kid isn't all that easy. Postulate what happens if the people in a child's world, big as they may be, yell, scream, hit, throw, chastise and belittle the child. The results are devastating. A few examples will indicate the seriousness of what occurs when these critical years are badly handled.

1. **Children must learn to set priorities and plan ahead.** "Why plan ahead?" one mother said. "I was always disappointed. Dad never kept his word." Another commented, "Every day is like every other day. It's hard to plan ahead when I can't remember if it's Wednesday or Sunday."

2. **Children must learn to trust others.** "But people hurt you!" said one woman. "Do you have a phone?" I asked. "Who would I call?" was the response. "It's best to keep people out of your life."

3. **Children must learn to make friends.** "Do you have any friends?" I asked a young mother. "I tried that once," she replied.

"Isn't there someone who can help you out?" "Yes," another mother said. "I found a friend three weeks ago and I really like her!" (I found out later this new and only friend was her boyfriend's wife.)

4. **Children must develop a good self image.** "Did you turn the handle of the parking meter so the yellow violation sign went down?" Mrs. Enis asked her *four*-year-old daughter. "No," said the child as she hung her head. "You stupid bastard!" was the reply. "You never do anything right."

5.   **Children must learn the difference between feeling and behavior.**   "I get angry at my baby and hit her," said a mother. "Anger is a feeling and hitting is a doing," I replied. The mother was astounded. She had been reared to believe that anger and hitting was a single function.

6.   **Children must learn to express their feelings.**   "Don't you ever cry?" I asked a young mother whose son was dying after being beaten by her boyfriend.
   "I had that beaten out of me when I was little," she replied.

7.   **Children must learn to get their needs met in an acceptable manner.** One mother recently commented, "Isn't it interesting that my boyfriend beats me just like my husband used to?" "Interesting?", I replied. After asking for an incident when this happened she related the story of making her boyfriend jealous by flirting at someone else. When they got home he beat her. "At least", she commented, "that shows he likes me." Later discussion with this mother revealed that the only way she was able to get the attention of her father was to anger him to the point that he beat her. Being hit, for her, was better than being ignored.

Being a kid isn't all that easy. The adult world is hard and often cruel to a child. And yet so much has to be learned, and so little time available. Many times those who are charged with the guidance and training during these "magic years" are so badly trained themselves.

To look more objectively at these concepts a review of the literature was undertaken. This review identified a number of articles that relate to the effect of abuse and neglect on the developmental processes. As the findings of the various authors were assessed, one clear and decisive point came through—i.e., insulting or interrupting normal developmental sequences has a significant effect on this dynamic process. Its effect may be permanent if it continues for a long (as yet to be determined) period of time, or it may be temporary if only interrupted and normal process allowed to "catch up" or take place.

Medicine has known for a number of years that certain insults to a developing child will have certain effects, some temporary and some permanent. For example, a growing child who is required, because of a serious disease, to be bed-ridden for several weeks followed by health and normal growth will show on his x-rays "growth arrest lines." It is also clear that if you "bathe" a developing bone or tooth with certain drugs, the bone will be impregnated with the drug. In the case of the tooth, permanent staining may result. When a developing and growing child is given long term steroid medication, growth slows down significantly during this period.

A somewhat more intriging finding is the close relationship between the healing of burns and the feelings of the children who are burned. Medical literature states that when children with significant burns are isolated from their "people environment," the burns take longer to heal than if they are allowed to interact with certain members of their families.[2] This finding is not unexpected since a variety of human and animal studies indicate that interaction with people is necessary to stimulate the growth of a child.[3,4] The articles that appear in the medical and related literature dealing with effects of child abuse and neglect on the developmental processes of a small child indicate clearly that insults at critical points in the developmental process will, if these insults are serious and long standing, have a permanent effect.

Some of the studies of importance in this area are listed below:

1. Illingworth and Lister[5] found that if a baby is not given solid food shortly after he has learned to chew there may well be considerable difficulty in getting him to take solids later. Their concept of "critical or sensitive periods" of development is one that should be given recognition.

2. Chase and Martin[6] studied nineteen children under the age of one with a primary diagnosis of undernutrition. They found that this undernutrition was detrimental to later development, and that there was a period of rapid postnatal brain growth and cell division which they felt required maximum nutrition during these stages.

3. Elmer and Gregg[7] found in their study of 50 children that speech defects were almost universal in this group. The hypothesis is that children were emotionally and/or physically abused during critical areas of speech development.

4. Karen Peterson, from the Children's Psychiatric Hospital in Bronx, New York, reported in her article, "Contributions to an Abused Child's Unlovability: Failure in the Developmental Task and in the Mastery of Trauma"[8] that she was able to demonstrate the child's vulnerability to psychological injury. The abused child's sense of helplessness, hopelessness, worthlessness, inadequacy, shame, and guilt are delineated in his capacity to predict object reactions and to anticipate object actions.

5. Martin Cohen,[9] in the lay magazine, *Today's Health,* warns mothers that there are indeed critical periods in the development of a child when he can best learn certain skills and concepts. He quotes Dr. Burton L. White, Director of the Pre-School Project at Harvard University, as saying, "By the age of 3, children should have acquired the ability to understand most of the language they will use in ordinary conversation. . . ."

6. Yvonne Brackbill[10] suggests that children will demonstrate a pacification effect if they are continuously stimulated. While she was not referring directly to constant stimulation of a screaming, overbearing, emotionally abusive mother, it seems clear that the withdrawal of some of these children is related to her findings.

7. Similar studies by Tronick et al.[11] from Boston's Children's Hospital indicate that face-to-face interaction between mother and infant may cause some significant behaviors in a child. If, for example, a child is stimulated with facial gestures on the part of the mother, he becomes extremely excited.

8. Infantile rumination has been reported by some to be a distant effect of certain maternal child interaction problems at key points of the child's development. Reports by Fullerton and others support this view.[12,13,14]

9. The delay in talking is reported by Filippi and Rousey[15] to be related to significant interpersonal disturbances at critical areas of child development.

10. Certain hyperactive children (apparently not all) may demonstrate significant interpersonal problems that have occurred in their family during critical areas of the development of the child in question. Whether the hyperactivity is actual or perceived on the part of the parents is something that is discussed by Kenny et al.[16] On the other hand, 58 percent of the children were not felt to be hyperactive by the staff who observed them.

11. Condon and Sander[17] report that as early as the first day of life the human neonate moves in precise and sustained segments of movement that are synchronous with the articulated structure of adult speech. This indicates that the neonate has a role to play in the interaction with his mother and is an active participant rather than a passive listener. If this is true, then withholding this type of interaction from the child at certain key times in his development may well indeed decrease the ability of the child to actively participate with those about him.

12. Ashley Montagu[18] states, "The failure to satisfy tacticle needs in the human infant shows how damaging such deprivations can be, and how important such early satisfactions are."

I presented the above thoughts to Dr. John McKinney, a developmental psychologist, and to Dr. Ruth Kempe, a child psychiatrist, with these comments: "I don't know much about developmental psychology or psychiatry, but it seems to me that what I'm seeing in these young parents who abuse and neglect their children is the result of some very bad and misguided early child development. These parents haven't learned the basic skills, so how in the world can they transmit them to their children?"

After many conversations, the first step seemed to be to write down of the basic aspects of developmental psychology, plus the observations and findings in child psychiatry, that might apply to this "world of abnormal rearing."[a] The following two sections are a beginning. Hopefully others will be stimulated to apply these concepts to our day-to-day work, developing new diagnostic and therapeutic approaches from them.

---

[a]The concept of the "World of Abnormal Rearing (WAR) was first presented to the Ambulatory Pediatric Association in a presidential address, San Francisco, 1973. This never-ending cycle was first published in *Pediatric BASICS,* vols. 10 and 11, by Gerber Company in 1974. Later the WAR was revised and published in "Child Abuse and Neglect: Diagnostic Process and Treatment Programs" by the Office of Child Development, publication #OHD 75–69 (Ray E. Helfer).

## SECTION TWO

### Related Aspects in Developmental Psychology
### John McKinney

Before beginning this discussion some of the psychologist's terms should be reviewed. *Development* refers to both maturation and learning. Developmental psychologists have been interested in both these processes and in their interaction. The first of these, *maturation,* refers to the biological growth of the child and specifies the limits within which his or her behavior can change at any given time. Its course is generally thought to be primarily the product of genetic predisposition. *Learning,* on the other hand, specifies those changes that occur via the child's environment within the limits imposed by maturational status. Maturation, then, is thought to be less influenced by environmental stimulation, while learning actually requires it.

For the most part, we learn how to behave. This is true whether we are children or adults. The same principles apply to learning how to walk, or talk as apply when we learn how to drive a car or to solve problems in calculus. These learning principles apply to the acquisition of adaptive behaviors such as taking care of our health, as well as such maladaptive behaviors as smoking cigarettes or drinking too much. The behavior may be prosocial, like sharing, or antisocial, like hitting a child. In both cases the behavior is learned, and in both cases the same principles of acquisition apply.

Child abuse can be thought of as a disease[19] or as a behavioral disorder. As a disease it requires a healing agent—a "physician"—and the proper treatment. As a behavioral disorder its acquisition can be understood by an examination of the principles of learning. Its elimination can then hopefully be effected by an application of those principles to a new, more adaptive, more prosocial set of behavioral responses.[b]

The purpose of this section, then, is to examine child abuse not only as a disease but also as a learned behavior, behavior that can also be unlearned and in place of which new behaviors can be learned. How a person learns to be abusive to a child, and what the child learns who is being abused, must both be explored. Each of these approaches—i.e. abuse as disease and as learning disorder—share one distinct advantage: they make the whole issue of guilt irrelevant in the treatment or relearning. Only when the behavior is considered "sinful" or "immoral" does crippling guilt get in the way of making treatment or education more difficult. The position of the learning theorist is that a person need feel no more guilt over not learning appropriate child rearing techniques than he feels over not learning to speak Turkish, or to do calculus.

---

[b]The more that is learned about child abuse, the greater tendency there is to move away from the after-the-fact disease/treatment model to the more preventive learning model.

Perhaps the first principle of learning to mention is the one that most clearly distinguishes the learning approach from the pure disease approach. This principle states that the learner is an active organism. The person who is sick requires treatment—i.e., to be cared for. The person who is learning becomes an agent (active) rather than a patient (passive). The learner must be able to change behavior requiring an active participation in the process.

## Modes of Learning

**Learning by Association.** There are three major modes of learning that have commanded the psychologist's attention. Each of these is relevant to the issue of child abuse and neglect. The first is learning by association. This is the classic conditioning paradigm of Pavlov.[20] It applies not only to dogs learning to salivate at the sound of a bell, but also to a child's learning to be afraid[21,22,23] or to love.[24] When an emotion-arousing stimulus is paired with a neutral stimulus, the neutral stimulus can elicit the same emotional response from the child as the emotional stimulus—i.e., the learning was accomplished by association.

Watson and Raynor[21] demonstrated in 1920 that this emotional conditioning followed the well known principles of learning, including stimulus generalization. For example, a child taught to fear a rabbit by association with a startle-eliciting noise will also fear other furry objects. It is not surprising, then, that a child taught to fear his father's voice (by association with a blow on the head) will fear other men's voices, other men, or even other people in general. Learned fear can serve as a motivation in the learning of other behaviors—for example, avoidance and escape. This may well be related to the tendency for abused children to avoid interpersonal signals such as eye contact.

**Learning Through Outcome.** A second way in which learning occurs is through the effect that behavior has in changing one's environment. This is the well known principle of reinforcement. The experimental research in this operant conditioning has demonstrated that some patterns of reinforcement (or after effect) are far more effective in changing behavior than others. In general, a partial or intermittant reinforcement schedule has been found to be more effective than one in which the reinforcement always follows the behavior. Variable schedules—those in which the reinforcement comes as irregular intervals or following after an unpredictable number of behaviors—are more effective than fixed schedules. If parents were consistent in abusing their children, the likelihood of the children's learning avoidance behaviors would be less than if they were inconsistent. Whatever behaviors these abused children learn in the avoidance of this aversive stimulation, they learn effectively by the erratic manner in which the stimulation is delivered.[c]

[c]The reader should take note that one of the most consistent findings of the "high risk" parents who responded to the predictive questionnaire was their degree of inconsistency.

In the same way, much of the positive socialization of children occurs because of the rewards that are given intermittently for good behavior. In other words, the "happenstance" learning that goes on in the home is, from the point of view of the learning theorist, extremely effective. In some respects this is very comforting, since very few of us are able to be 100 percent consistent in our rewarding of appropriate behavior. It is good to know that as long as our general reinforcement schedule is a positive one, we don't have to worry about "dropping the ball" now and then. In fact, it probably insures even greater social learning in our children.

Reinforcement can effect behavioral change in two major ways: positive stimulation can enhance the likelihood of the behavior's occurring subsequently and aversive stimulation can decrease that probability. Both of these undoubtedly operate in abusive parent-child interactions. In a neglectful setting, where little environmental change is contingent on behavior, a child may paradoxically find that being hit is better than being left completely alone. He may learn to repeat whatever brought about a stimulus change. More commonly, however, children learn to avoid those behaviors that lead to aversive reinforcement. Avoidance conditioning, and the use of punishment, especially if extreme, entails a number of hazards.

The side effects of stern punishment have been powerfully documented by Adah Maurer.[25] Not the least of these is the sense of shame and self-disdain especially in the young child who does not distinguish between himself and his behavior. Under those conditions the effects of punishment can be seen to generalize, so that the child learns not only that his behavior is reprehensible, but that, by cruel logic, so is he. The child taught not to talk back to his mother by being burned may learn also not to talk—perhaps not to look at her—in effect, not to respond to normal stimulation. Whatever emotions the child was experiencing when hit, she may easily learn not to express. Indeed, one of the characteristics of abusive parents, many of whom were themselves abused children, is this blunted affect, as well as an inability to separate feelings from behavior.[26]

Parental lack of impulse control suggests either an inability to label emotions before they are acted upon (i.e., no adequate mediational devices) or a preoperational logic that treats behavior and emotion as the same thing. This lack of differentiation is common in normal babies and in neurotic adults, but seems to be extreme in abusive parents. It is as though any expression of anger were tantamount to violent behavior or any expression of joy were identical to an outburst of satisfaction that may suddenly be taken away, leaving one more bereft than ever. The only available emotional expressions seem to be overreactions, or underreaction. Learning not to respond seems to be a major component of the abusive parent who was also an abused child. Selma Fraiberg[27] writes of a mother who, incredibly, when her child was crying, acted as though she didn't hear her baby's cries. One is forced to ask, "Has she learned not to respond to normal stimuli?" The history Fraiberg details of the mother's own upbringing confirms the suspicion.

**Learning by Observation.** The third major way that learning takes place is via the imitation of powerful others who model behavior.[28] The likelihood of imitating a model is enhanced when the model is powerful and is seen as a controller of important resources. Thus adults, especially parents, with whom children identify closely, can be effective models for teaching a wide range of behaviors, including aggresion. The early theory that frustration was the necessary and sufficient condition, leading to aggression[29] was later modified to include this notion of social learning. Aggresion is a more likely response from those who have observed it in others, whether in reality, or on film.[30]

As mentioned above, it has been well documented that abusive parents have themselves often been abused children.[26,31,32] Some interpret this fact to mean that emotional deprivation in early life makes one incapable of expressing normal affection as an adult. Support for this position comes also from Harlow's animal research,[33] which has demonstrated that female monkeys reared in social isolation, devoid of mothering, became inadequate mothers themselves. Of interest is the difficulty these monkeys had in conceiving and giving birth to infants. "Most of the monkey motherless mothers ignored their infants . . . but other motherless mothers abused their babies by crushing the infant's face to the floor, chewing off the infant's feet and fingers, and, in one case, by putting the infant's head in her mouth and crushing it like an eggshell."[33]

Many abusive parents see the abused child as a transference object and regard him or her as a hopeful substitute for their own parents. Indeed, many abusive parents complain that their children have been unable to satisfy their emotional needs, as though they had hoped to gain a parent by having a child. Even in normal, healthy families parents have expectations for their children and are influenced by their children's behavior and their conformity or nonconformity to parental expectations. It was once thought that, while parents influenced their children's development, children had little effect on their parents' behavior. There is now, however, ample evidence in the literature of normal child development that the socialization of parents is indeed affected by congenital factors in the child.[34,35] It is no longer possible to consider child socialization a one-way street with no input from the child's behavior and temperament affecting the parents' responses. Behaviors of the child, such as extreme activity or passivity, affect the parents behavior such that some children may be more "predisposed to abuse" than others in terms of the signals they emit. The relevant parameters need examination.

### Attributes of Child Abusive Parents

The question that remains is, "What have abusive parents learned in their own childhood that predisposes them to be abusive?" From the foregoing one can predict that abusive parents may have acquired some or all of the following patterns: uncontrolled aggression, avoidance of social interaction, fear of authority, feelings of guilt, low self-esteem, and ineffective communication patterns. In reviewing the literature on this topic, Melnick and Hurley[32] cite studies that attribute each of these personality traits to child-abusing mothers. In addition, they find her described variously as "chronically aggressive . . ., highly frustrated by the restrictions of the maternal role . . ., locked in a power struggle with the child . . ., responding violently to a host of social stresses . . ., unstable, emotionally immature . . ., dependent and narcissistic. . . ."

Their own research, however, is far more controlled than much of that which they cite and their conclusions are more cautious. They tested ten abusive mothers for the presence of eighteen personality traits, by comparing them on these dimensions to a control group of mothers, matched for age, social class, and education. They found that their abusive mothers, rather than being "chronically hostile" or "overwhelmed by maternal responsibilities," had a low self-esteem, a low need for nurturance, low family satisfaction, and scores revealing frustrated dependency needs. Melnick and Hurley interpreted the abusive mothers' inability to empathize with their children as evidence of their own emotional deprivation. Their inability to nurture is undoubtedly related to their own unfulfilled succorance needs.

Since their own emotional development has been arrested, it isn't surprising to find that abusive parents have little concept of what constitutes normal emotional needs in their children. A number of studies have documented that abusive parents do not know the basic stages of development and the behaviors expected at each.[26] Typically, abusive parents expect too much from their children and often treat them like adults.[36] It is as if their own needs to be nurtured intrude even into their relations with their children.

Earlier in this chapter, reference was made to our first conversations on this topic. The brief discussion about what "children must learn" during their formative years raised several questions in section one. These were precisely the things that an abused child could not learn and later as an abusive parent, could not teach. The research literature supports these speculations. One therapeutic answer would seem to be, as many have already urged, reparenting, or retraining. Having some idea of how early learning has gone wrong, perhaps we are in a better position to design programs of reeducation.

## SECTION THREE

### Related Aspects in Child Psychiatry
### Ruth Kempe

By far the most disturbing and consistent finding in observation of young children who have been abused and neglected is the delay, or arrest, of their development. The extent and consistency of these deviations vary from one child to the next, as do the rates of the different developmental parameters. developmental parameters.

### The Abused Infant

What characteristics do we see in abused children in relationship to their development? In young infants under the age of six months, one frequently notices difficulties in the feeding situation. Some children have great difficulty in being satisfied, others become disinterested in feeding and respond in an apathetic manner. The mother and child do not seem to have made a good adjustment to one another in a major area of interaction. Many infants who are abused seem unusually irritable, with a high-pitched, particularly irritating cry. Here it is difficult to know how much the innate characteristics of the infant contributed to the problems within the parent-child relationship. Some young, isolated parents who have had no personal experience of good care and have high expectations of performance from their baby *and* themselves as parents, may do reasonably well if they have a very easy infant for which to care. They can enjoy success and begin to develop a fairly good relationship. But, if that infant is difficult, they have no inner resources on which to draw and are incapable of getting help from others.

During the first six months of age, one can begin to notice, with some abused children, the beginnings of a delay in motor and social development. They are somewhat slow to turn over, to reach out for toys, and later to sit and crawl. Of interest is a finding of poor muscle tone, which seems to be characteristic of the apathetic infant. An additional important finding is the comparative delay in social response such as smiling and vocalization to the human.

Between six and twelve months the lack of social response or variations in its quality become more striking in the abused child. Here one begins to see children who do not seem to notice separation from their parents, who do not seem to have the usual kind of stranger anxiety, and who instead seem to respond with indiscriminate pleasure to any new relationship. This lack of discrimination continues throughout the next few years and is one of the more striking characteristics of many abused children. In contrast (and the extremes often seem to be the rule in behavior with abused children), there are a few young abused children who remain very much attached to their parents, who will persist in their attempts to receive attention from their parents with very little reward. They continue to "work for it," even without encouragement.

Disturbance in object relations is accompanied by other developmental delays. Frequently there is a generalized apathy or passivity, a lack of activity in relationship to people and objects alike. When offered toys for play, they may engage in an activity, but as soon as the toy is removed or the activity changed by an adult, the child passively accepts the loss of the toy or the change of activity without any protest and, indeed, without apparent notice. For example, if the toy is dropped, the child may make no effort to retrieve it. This apathy also extends to the way in which these children use toys, frequently making little effort to explore their potential, manipulating them in a rather primitive and crude way suggesting not only lack of experience with the toy itself, and a lack of stimulation or education in its use, but also a lack of interest.

In their paper "Deprivation in Institutionalized Infants,"[37] Sally Provence and Samuel Ritvo have described disturbances in the development of relationship to inanimate objects that describe very well some of the reactions of our abused and deprived children to toys. To quote from the paper, "the infant's reaction to toys and his use of toys depends in very important ways upon the relationship of people. . . . [T]he infant's capacity to develop a belief (a mental concept) in the consistency and constancy of the inanimate object, i.e., a world of things, is dependent upon the consistency and constancy of the human object."

The state of "frozen watchfulness" can be seen in comparatively young children of nine or ten months who have been abused. The child sits or lies quite passively and immobile, but is alert, watching intently what goes on about him. This behavior is contrasted in the hospital where normally reared children, after a brief period of scanning their environment, will reach out to their parents or other adults for help and will become more active and responsive. Sometimes the abused child will remain an onlooker for days before he becomes to any extent integrated into the activity of the ward.

When seen for evaluation, children between one and two and one-half years of age are somewhat difficult to test because they vary their performance from day to day. At first, the abused toddler may be unable to perform a given motor task. Persistent and patient repetition of the task will show that he can perform some, even though his response is unreliable and haphazard. There is some evidence that the child's capacity to respond to a test situation may improve within a few days in a "safe" and supportive environment. This raises the questions of rapid learning factors and motivation to stimulate attempts at new activities. A single, rapid test of any abused child's capacities may give one a very false impression of the child's underlying potential.

Preliminary findings of the developmental ability of small children known to be abused reveals a general delay of adaptive and motor activity, such as in the use of toys and the capacity to play. In addition, there is consistently seen a considerable delay in speech. Equally as striking is the lack of social development. These children do not relate well and fail to show a tendency to use eye contact. They passively accept the relationship, are acquiescent and somewhat indiscriminate in their acceptance of a contact with a strange adult. They often show little evidence of anxiety, even at time of separation. In a few days as relationships within a new, supportive environment are made, the child may play out, or express fear of abandonment.

One abused boy of two and one-half years, during a play interview in the hospital, suddenly spent ten minutes throwing the mother doll on the floor and repeating in a tone of desolation, "Dead! Dead!" In reconstructing possible reasons for this, he was felt to be reliving episodes in which his mother had made suicidal gestures in his presence.

Particularly striking is the frequent passivity these children show both in accepting whatever requests the examiner makes and their lack of active resistance to those requests they seem to find unpleasant. They tend to remain stationary. Some abused children between the ages of fifteen to eighteen months have poor motor coordination and very poor muscle tone, in the absence of any neurological disorders. This appears to be associated with the lack of activity rather than a neurological defect. Some present with spasticity.

At the age of twenty-three months, Terry, the fourth child in a family of five neglected and abused children, was seen for a play interview. She sat, never moving from the two spots she was placed during the hour. She never smiled, although her depressed, impassive expression lightened slightly when the interviewer tried unsuccessfully to play peek-a-boo with her. The two words she spoke were "Momma" and "Bye" after being reunited with her sisters. She used her hands awkwardly and with little interchange. Feeding a baby doll with a bottle when invited to do so, she then tried to combine the bottle with other toys inappropriately and without apparent purpose. Her use of all toys was equally haphazard and perseverative and totally without pleasure. Her inability to relate to the interviewer as a person was almost complete; she rarely looked at her or used her in any interchange except for two instances of imitations. Now, at age three and one-half, Terry has been adopted and is described by her psychologist as having "developed beautifully."

### The Abused Preschool Child

A group of thirteen preschool abused children between two and one-half and four and one-half years of age were assessed. Most parameters of development were delayed. The response to psychological testing was highly variable within different test items. This seemed to be related to the child's preoccupation with the examiner and the examiner's approval or disapproval, rather than to the task at hand. Only one child was able to obtain a score of 100 on psychological testing with the Stanford-Binet or McCarthy tests. Four of these thirteen children had clear neurological symptoms and might well be considered to have retardation on this basis. The remainder demonstrated a variability in response with clear evidence that they were able to answer questions with ease which, during the anxiety provoking test situation were not answered.

A general evaluation of their ability to perform many similar tasks made it probable that at least half these children had normal intellectual potential. Their responses to the tests seemed to be more an evidence of their coping style in anxiety-provoking situations than a lack of knowledge or their capacity to perform the task. Variations in response to testing included some children who immediately gave up when an item became at all difficult and said, "I don't know." Others attempted to charm or tease the examiner and divert her from the question. Occasionally children became negativistic and simply refused to answer. Only one child became distressed and overtly anxious in an appropriate way at not knowing an answer. He was the child who obtained the highest score.

This same group of thirteen children also demonstrated, on psychiatric evaluation in a permissive play situation, severe difficulties in other areas of development as well. Not one child related to the adult with comfort and confidence, in contrast to normal children. In relating, they seemed to be anxious, fearful and expecting of punishment, disapproval, or criticism. These expectations were not changed by reassurance. Some of the children were overly compliant and totally preoccupied with pleasing the adult. Others were passively aggressive and negativistic. None appeared able to express feelings readily and seldom revealed any capacity for pleasure, enjoyment, or playfulness. Pain or unhappiness were never expressed, even when a few questions concerning family or separation were asked. At such times the chief evidence of the underlying discomfort was revealed in an abrupt change of subject or activity. They seemed to have difficulty in recognizing, as well as verbally expressing, any of their feelings.

In addition to poor performance in testing, the preschool children revealed comparative lack of interest and ability to play, to make use of toys and to organize their behavior into any kind of planned or structured activity. Movement from one toy to another was haphazard, impulsive, without using the adult as an adjunct in the play. Fantasy was not used to elaborate the play. Many expected criticism or punishment, and seemed to have a very poor image of themselves, saying that they couldn't do an activity which they had not yet even tried. Failure was anticipated; when encouraged by the interviewer, success was a surprise and followed by a hesitancy to try again.

Speech was delayed, often with poor enunciation and vocabulary. These children found it hard to express their feelings and avoided talking of their family or their life outside the playroom. Describing what they were doing or what they would like to do was difficult. Communication as part of their ongoing activity was limited. Most of the conversation was concerned with defining their limits by questioning what they were allowed to do, what toys could be used, or how much candy could be consumed.

A few of the children were considerably more active, aggressive, and negativistic. Just as the other children were restricted within a passive mode of coping, these children were restricted to a negativistic, defensive and somewhat aggressive mode of coping. Their use of "no" seemed inappropriate, even for furthering their own pleasure. Their aggressive verbalizations was used for many other feelings as well. Perhaps the anger of these children was the only feeling they were accustomed to expressing. It substituted for more appropriate expressions of anxiety or unhappiness.

### Early School-Aged Child

Another group of seventeen older abused children, age four to seven, were evaluated prior to being seen for play therapy as a study of efficacy of the treatment modality. These children, many of whom were in school, were found as a group to be mostly of normal intelligence with IQs ranging from 76 to 117 on testing with the WISC. They revealed many of the findings that were seen in the younger age group, namely, difficulties in relating to another person, considerable difficulty in establishing trust, lack of capacity to enjoy play, an inability to show pleasure, poor self-image, and a preoccupation with many fears.

Although findings varied somewhat from one age group to another, difficulty in relating to others was a constant problem. Other parameters that remained part of the picture throughout were delays in maturation of speech and verbal expression of feelings. The use of spontaneous language to promote their relationships was rarely seen. As a group they remained passive, if not in motor activity, at least in attempting to master their environment by actively organizing their own behavior.

One of the most consistent findings was delay in development without sufficient neurological explanation for this delay. Subsequent improvement when environmental stimulation and unsatisfactory relationships were provided was consistently noted. Very striking in the children was their lack of exploratory activities, their passivity, and the way in which they failed to reach out to control the objects and people in their environment. They remained circumscribed in the scope of their activities. One might postulate that passivity is not accidental but has become an available coping style.

### Observations of Parents

Making the assumption that these developmentally arrested children are reacting to an unfavorable, abusive, and neglectful environment, an appropriate question is how the relationship with the parents can produce such delays. Studies of abusive parents have indicated clearly that one of the several major areas of difficulties is their unrealistic and inappropriately high expectations of performance from the child. These expectations often are due to the belief that the child is capable of meeting the parents' emotional needs. This entails a disregard of the child's emotional needs.

Such a reversal of roles is clearly seen in both parents and children alike. The inappropriateness of parental expectations might *seem* to derive from a lack of knowledge of child development. While the lack of knowledge is certainly present, teaching child development is not an adequate solution. The distortion in perception of the child's needs seem to derive from the developmental issues of the parent. Having been expected, when they were children, to meet their parents' needs rather than their own needs, they have still to find a way of fulfilling their own needs. If, during the course of their lifetime, this has not yet happened, they then may reproduce this situation with their own children, reversing the roles and expecting from their children the acceptance, love and care they had not received as young children themselves. Only during treatment, when they have matured enough that the child's needs do not seem to be in competition with their own, do they seem motivated to make use of developmental knowledge and parenting skills in dealing with their own children.

Valuable information has been obtained regarding a mother's spontaneous reactions to her newborn. Delivery is apparently a time of crisis when defenses are less stable than usual. A mother's spontaneous reactions to her newborn child can be most revealing. Work by Brazelton and his group[38] has emphasized the importance of the individual capabilities each newborn infant shows in all his reactions. They demonstrated the patterning of these capabilities into a sequence of behaviors that ordinarily brings an appropriate response from his mother.

Such a response, however, depends upon the mother's ability to perceive her child's needs accurately and her motivation to attempt to meet those needs. For the mother raised in an abusive atmosphere, this seldom happens. A minimum of physical care, with little empathic understanding of emotional or social needs, represents her total parenting ability. When such a mother has a placid or difficult to arouse baby, she may not make the effort to interest him in waking and in making adequate efforts to suck. If, on the other hand, her baby is very active and difficult to manage and is frequently hungry, the mother may well fell overwhelmed and easily discouraged.

Abusive and neglectful parents misperceive age-appropriate behavior as willful disobedience. Crying is often misinterpreted as critical and accusatory: one abusive parent said of her young infant, "I felt that when she cried, it showed she didn't love me, so I hit her." Such a major distortion, not only of what is to be considered normal behavior for an infant but also the misinterpretation of its significance, demonstrates some of the pathological "sets" with which the abusive parents approaches parenthood. The mother is truly confused as to the relation between the child's needs and her own. Too often there is no capacity to perceive what normal infantile needs are because the mother is still preoccupied with her own needs. Because of her own experience of being parented in this way, she assumes the child is the only appropriate means by which she can have her needs met.

Those behaviors of the child which do not fit with the parent's wishes are ignored or misinterpreted. These behaviors at first are most apt to be crying demands for attention and holding. As the child grows older they are the normal. exploratory behavior that leads to messy eating of solid foods; resistance to a passive, supine position in diapering; and reaching for any object within grasp.

Very early, some abused children learn these behaviors are punished, and gradually they learn to inhibit them. In a quotation from an unpublished paper by Kay Tennes, she describes

> . . . a family in which the boy named Keith was 7 months olu and beginning to have activity which was increasingly irritating to his mother. Activity during diapering she found most unbearable and she said, "I had to whack him again and again to make him hold still." Keith was observed during diapering, lying completely immobile, intently watching his mother's hands with a serious expression on his face. Three months later, mother complained that Keith had learned his lesson only too well. During diapering and dressing, he now became quite limp, failing to hold up his hands to have his shirt put on. Mother said she would "have to show him he could only go so far before he got the flat of her hand again." This baby boy's infantile ego faces a difficult if not impossible task. First, he must learn to inhibit movement to avoid punishment. Not much later, he must learn special circumstances under which movement must be started in order to avoid punishment.[39]

### Reading (Decoding) Responses
### Between Mother and Baby

How does such inhibition of "normal" behavior take place? the most usual method would be to develop inappropriate response on the part of the mother to the infant's affective declaration of need (crying, smiling, reaching out). Gerald Steckler[40] has described the increasingly efficient way in which most parents read the infant's signals of distress and make appropriate responses with feeding, changing, and holding. When the baby's needs are met, the infant responds, indicating success of parental maneuvers; instead of crying, the baby now smiles, babbles, or goes to sleep. This positive, affective response then signals to the parent that the parent is doing the right thing and meeting the baby's needs.

Success sets the stage for repetition of a mutually satisfying experience. For the baby, this sequence (which Steckler calls a "sensory-affective system") depends on the willingness and the ability of the mother to cooperate. If successful, this system can lead to the capacity of the infant to learn how to influence what is happening to him. In this view of things, the mother is not only the provider of stimulation, but a key link in the "information feedback loop" that provides the baby with his only means of altering the outer world. This continues until that age when he can accomplish direct motor-effectance on the environment.

In another relevant study, Tromick and associates[41] have shown how quickly an infant responds with what appears to be confusion and stress to a lack of social response on the part of an ordinarily responsive mother.[d] The difference

---

[d]The description and interpretation of these tapes is made following a public viewing of of them and may not represent the opinions of Dr. Tromick or his associates—Ed.

between two episodes recorded on divided screen, audiovisual tapes is very impressive. In the first sequence, the mother and baby engage in mutually stimulating pleasurable social exchange. In the second sequence, the infant greets the mother as usual, and when she remains totally impassive, makes several repeated attempts with diminishing vigor to elicit a response from her. Gradually, after a brief period of a minute or less, the infant subsides with a look of real distress. This distress was immediately followed by a "frozen" state of unresponsiveness.

The impassivity and unresponsiveness of their mothers was remarkably similar to the apathetic and unresponsive reactions to their babies of some mothers filmed at the time of delivery and of some mothers observed with their abused or failure-to-thrive infants at a later time. Our assumption is that the lack of response, or the inappropriate response, of a mother to her young infant breaks the "mother-baby decoding" cycle, and thereby obviates the baby's opportunity to alter what happens to him. Without appropriate response, there is no reinforcement for his next effort at mastery of his environment. Learning cause and effect as it relates to the significance and usefulness of his own behavior is obviated. Provence et al.[37] state,

> In several areas of behavior there was a discrepancy between the maturation of the apparatus and its use in the infant's adaptation to his environment. In these areas the investigators found that the apparatus matured according to the biological timetable, but the emerging potentials were not put to use in the normal fashion . . . they did not come under the control of the infant's developing ego as readily as in family-reared infants.

Michael Lewis[42] comments on Provence's work, "It was not how much of the skill or structure that was important in differentiating the infants; rather it was the motivation to use the skills." Lewis goes on to state,

> The data, both our own and those of others, seemed consistent and strongly suggest that an important expectation is learned in early infancy—namely, the expectation that the infant's actions can have a payoff in its environment. Further, the date indicate that without this expectation, the organism's performance, as well as subsequent maturational development can be seriously affected. Moreover, we believe this expectation is learned through the early mother-infant interaction as a function of a contingency of infant and maternal response sequence.

In a study by Maier et al.,[43] experiments exposed animal subjects to a series of *unavoidable* shock experiences. Following a series of such shocks, the animal lost the ability in subsequently altered circumstances, to avoid the shocks as other animals were able to do. The conclusion was that "the animals are given expectations about the outcome of their acts." Lewis comments on these studies: "It is clear that this learned motivational principle of helplessness is extremely important in determining the course of subsequent behavior, such as cognitive development or learning."[42] While transfering data from animal experiments to the situation of the abused infant who receives punishment in response to his efforts at getting attention from his mother or father may not be appropriate, perhaps those shocks and punishment are equally painful and equally unpredictable. Punishment provides a very powerful and highly negative deterrent to the infant's efforts to influence his environment by physical activity or affective signals such as crying.

There are at least two ways in which negative or inappropriate parental actions might affect the infant's activities. First, by failing to reward with success his primitive attempts at communication of his wishes, and second through painful punishment or a total lack of response, by leaving him with a feeling of helplessness and futility. There may be a lack of another very important positive ingredient in this developmental process, namely, the stimulation and encouragement of his activities by the parent. The neglecting or abusive mother or father is preoccupied with his or her own needs and tend to have little energy or interest available to recognize the infant's needs.

### Summary

These three sections have emphasized that children, during their first several years of life, experience certain critical periods in their development. When these periods are arrested or frozen—or fail to develop at all—the results are lasting. These arrested states are seen, in childhood and later in adulthood, in a variety of ways. Their most devastating effect is the inability to adequately relate to oneself or to others. The loss of interpersonal skills has a snowballing effect on almost every other aspect of one's adult life. Were these insults to the individual not enough, the lasting effect is that this lost skill prevents any semblance of reasonable parenting skills from developing. The next generation is affected, and the cycle continues.

 Chapter Four

# Family Pathology as Seen in England

Christopher Ounsted and Margaret A. Lynch

## TWO BIOGRAPHIES

### David

On the 17th May, 1973 David N was beaten to death by his father. His father was found guilty of wilful murder and sent to prison for life. After the trial a tribunal was set up to enquire into the events leading up to the child's death. There were at least seven biographical moments in the brief life of the child at which preventive intervention was openly called for, but not given. (See Addendum at end of this chapter.)

The father came from a family of violent people. He was reared by blows and shouts. At the age of seventeen he had a personality crisis. He broke with his family and became a social failure and took to drink and petty crimes. He was jobless. In his nineteenth year he made two suicide attempts, going to a psychiatric hospital after each attempt but rejecting treatment. It was at this stage that his biography became entangled with the mother's. She was also reared harshly and was deeply bonded in hate to her own mother with whom she had a hostile dependent relationship. She had started running away from home between fourteen and fifteen years of age. She was committed to an Approved School, where, on testing, it was found that her intelligence was low. On discharge from the enforced care of the institution she became jobless and homeless. She met her husband. The mating between the two was clearly assortive; the bonding predictably aggressive. Within three months of their coming together the mother had charged the father with inflicting "Grievous Bodily Harm" on her and, throughout the time we shall be considering, he had hanging over his head this charge, which he knew might send him to prison.

The baby was conceived before marriage. The gestation was grossly disturbed.

*75*

The parents showed no "nesting behavior"; they made no preparation for the baby; they bought neither pregnancy clothes nor baby clothes. They had nowhere to live. Periodically the mother returned to her mother and was infantilized by her. The baby was born at full term on January 29, 1973 and weighed only five pounds. He was thus a small-for-date baby and at risk for physical and mental handicap. He was not followed up medically. On the 18th of February, less than two weeks after discharge from the maternity hospital, the mother took the baby to a policeman on the street corner. The child was bleeding from the nose and mouth, with the diagnostic injuries of child abuse. She told the policeman that her spouse had inflicted these wounds. She was advised to attend the hospital accident service and she did. The injuries were treated. There was no followup, and notes of this episode did not come to light until the tribunal was heard.

This first "warning" was not read. Nine days later another "open warning" was given. The mother brought the child to hospital very sick. He was in shock and the temperature subnormal. The diagnosis of chest infection was made. A chest x-ray was taken and passed as normal. This x-ray showed six fractured ribs and one fractured clavicle. The baby was then kept in hospital under the care of a general physician for thirteen days. (At no time was a paediatric or psychiatric opinion sought.) The baby was discharged to the parents, who at this time were homeless, spending the nights "shacked up" with a friend. Seven days later, on the 17th of March, the baby was back in the hospital, the family doctor actually raising the question of child abuse. Chest x-ray was repeated and once again passed as normal. Seven obvious healing fractures were present. For the next six days the baby was kept on an acute children's ward with erratic visiting by the parents. During this time, the mother's maternal incapacity became apparent. The nurses tried to train her in mothercraft but were unsuccessful.

The warnings continued. The mother, at the time of the readmission, showed a nurse the baby, again bleeding from the nose and mouth. At the end of March the father visited the ward, and when he left he showed the nurse in charge that the child's foot was covered with blood. He asked, "Did I do it?" The nursing staff kept a watch on the father at subsequent visits. Seven days later, however, gross bruising of the belly was found after the father had just left the ward. A transient house physician (intern) once again raised the question of child abuse. The physician in charge later said that the injuries were unlike anything he had ever seen. A color photograph was taken and placed in the medical notes. No further opinion was sought. Three days later the child was found grossly bruised around the chest and shoulder after the father had left the ward. Again the lesions were photographed but no action was taken.

Thirty-six days now passed while the child was kept on the ward because of the poor social conditions of the parents. On the 15th of May the mother showed the social worker that she had a flat to live in. On 16th of May the mother came to the ward and asked for her baby. The baby was given to her that evening. On the morning of the next day the mother gave the last "open warning," just as she had given the first. She took the baby at eleven o'clock in the morning, bleeding from the nose and mouth, to the policeman on the corner. Again she was advised that the injuries should receive medical attention.

At 5:30 p.m. the same day the father came home and beat the baby to death. At necropsy there were sixteen separate injuries. A full skeletal survey made after death showed three further diagnostic injuries in the limbs in addition to the seven fractures which had been missed in the x-rays made during the baby's period in the hospital.

There are, in this brief biography, at least seven points in the series of steps leading up to the murder, when "open warnings" were given by one or other of the parents that the child was gravely at risk. At these biographical moments intervention might well have been prophylactic, and certainly investigation would have been diagnostic.

### Simon

The critical path of our next biography illustrates how one child within a sibship may be abused while others thrive and develop naturally.[1] It also shows how, in a totally "unpromising" family, the abused child can be rehabilitated and the whole family can become a happy and integrated one with no further abuse occurring.

On the 5th of June, 1973 the police telephoned the Park Hospital for Children. They had removed a child from his family on a legal order. They were asked to bring the child directly to the hospital. Simon had been born on the 1st of May, 1970 and was three years and one month when brought to our hospital. His right leg was in a cast. The records show that he had attended an emergency room and a spiral fracture of the right tibia had been treated one month before. He weighed only 27 lbs. 4 oz. (below the third percentile). His limbs and buttocks were wasted, and his belly swollen and full of gas. His skin was dry and scaling and his hair was thin. The left leg showed an extensive ulcerated burn.

Simon showed the behavioral signs of "frozen watchfulness." His face was alert, but wholly expressionless. He was silent, responding neither to friendly nor painful simulation. He stayed in hospital for a month. The "frozen watchfulness" lasted about seven days and then, quite suddenly, he began to change into a lively, happy, alert and active child. His concentration became good. He was demanding and liked his own way, but when reassured he would play contentedly for long periods, provided that an adult was near.

During this time intensive psychotherapy was undertaken with the whole family, including the maternal grandmother. The background of Simon's parents was grim indeed. The father, himself an abused child, was wholly rejected by his own family and from the age of two and a half had spent his childhood in a community home. He was a total educational failure and, although not unintelligent, had never learned to read or write. He had developed an intense distrust of authority. The mother came from a sibship of five. Her father died when she was only three. She had always been dominated by her mother. This had been all the more necessary because of her subnormality.

The parents met and a premarital pregnancy quickly followed. They were, however, happy together and a normal baby was born. They did not marry and lived with the maternal grandmother. The patient, Simon, was the result of the second pregnancy. This too was premarital, but provoked both a marriage and a removal to a very isolated house of their own. The pregnancy was a stormy one, being complicated by mother's hospitalization with an antepartum hemorrhage. Delivery was at 32 weeks and the birth weight 4 lbs. 10 oz. Because of prematurity and illness the child stayed in hospital for his first four months of life. On discharge he was cared for by the maternal grandmother until he was one year of age.

In retrospect it was clear that there had been no healthy bonding between the parents and this child. His father said, "He never seemed to be part of the family." The father began to develop paranoid feelings that this child was not really his. Two further pregnancies followed in quick succession and resulted in two normal, healthy babies, who thrived and developed well. In the meantime Simon, who had returned to his parents, failed to thrive. His slow development contrasted unfavorably with that of his siblings, and he had multiple minor infections.

The family had no near neighbors and they became more and more isolated. Neither of the parents could manage a telephone. The demands of the four children meant that leaving the house was becoming increasingly difficult. The mother was overwhelmed by her domestic and family duties. The father found his mounting frustration focusing on Simon. The burnt leg had occurred when the father was trying to wash him and had put the leg on a hot tap for about ten minutes. The fracture of the other leg had occurred when the father had twisted it forcibly when trying to replace a shoe, kicked off on a country walk. Following this episode Simon's father had burst into tears and taken him at once to the hospital. A month later the child presented at our hospital in the condition described.

The family made a remarkable response to intensive psychotherapy. Simon's physical condition became excellent. His frozen watchfulness disappeared and his behavior was indistinguishable from that of a normal child. A juvenile court assembled to decide whether the child should be removed from his family or not. Agreement was reached between the lawyers of both sides, together with the physician, that the medical evidence that child abuse had occurred could not be disputed. The entire case was then taken through without any cross examination of the witnesses, the physician being asked to address the court. The outcome was that all the children were allowed to go home with their parents. This, then is an example of the therapeutic court, which we shall discuss later.

The next few months were made extraordinarily difficult since father had been charged with inflicting "Grievous Bodily Harm" but was not brought before the court for many months. The family moved from crisis to crisis and, in each of these, the therapeutic team was deeply involved. A total of more than 40 home visits had to be made. When the trial was finally heard, the physician was again able to speak in defense of the father. A sentence of twelve months imprisonment was given. While the father was in jail he was visited regularly by members of the therapeutic team. He found the prison setting familiar to him because of his institutional upbringing and became a good prisoner, earning a remission of his sentence.

In followup the father has sustained a healthy parental attitude. All four children are now emotionally and developmentally normal. The mother has been able to accept continuing help and is running her family well, in spite of her mental handicap. This then was a family who looked completely hopeless but, having formed stable bonds to our hospital, has managed to develop well, and there has been no further child abuse.

## CONCEPTS OF PSYCHOPATHOLOGY AND PSYCHOTHERAPY

In order to guide our understanding of the processes that lead to child abuse, and those methods of psychotherapeutic intervention that prevent it, we have drawn up eighteen concepts in psychopathology and matched these with eighteen concepts in psychotherapy. The list is given in Table 4–1. We have deliberately put our concepts in simple catch phrases, since many of those who have to use them have had no formal psychiatric training.

**Table 4-1.** Eighteen Concepts in Psychopathology and Psychotherapy

| | *Pathology* | *Therapy* |
|---|---|---|
| 1. | The Hostile Pedigree | A New Beginning |
| 2. | Basic Mistrust | Trust Us |
| 3. | Fantasy Governs | Truth Releases |
| 4. | Blind Alleys | The Safe Place |
| 5. | Assortive Mating | New Bonding |
| 6. | Childlike Parents | A Chance to Grow |
| 7. | The Hospital's Baby | The Family's Hospital |
| 8. | The Ritual | Astonishment |
| 9. | The Releasing Drugs | A Clean Brain |
| 10. | The Little Stranger | Getting to Know |
| 11. | A Sick Family | Health Restored |
| 12. | Crying in the Trap | Smiling a Welcome |
| 13. | The Open Warnings | Trials of Freedom |
| 14. | Gaze Aversion | Facing the Facts |
| 15. | The Cataclysms | Crises Resolved |
| 16. | Collusion | Acceptance |
| 17. | Isolation | Liberating Bonds |
| 18. | Closed System | The Open System |

The concepts listed below use the same numbering system listed in Table 4–1 giving the pathological issue first, followed by the therapeutic concept.

1. **The Hostile Pedigree.** Many abusive parents were themselves battered. For generations communication in these families has been by violence. Often they are bonded in hate to their own parents. The women in particular have angry yet dependent relationships with their own mothers. In many there is a hostile attitude towards all authoritative figures, an attitude which itself evokes anger in others. The bond between the parents is itself often hostile but nonetheless extremely close.

**Therapy—A New Beginning.** A new system of individuals is introduced. They help the family break away from the effect of the hostile pedigree which has so weighed down their biographies. They are given a chance to shed their anger, an opportunity to end the "family curse."

2. **Basic Mistrust.** "Loved ones cannot be trusted." In childhood, abusive parents have constantly been let down by those close to them; this continues into adult life. In Eriksonian terms[2] they have been unable to pass the first developmental hurdle establishing a balance between trust and mistrust. An extreme manifestation of the child's mistrust emerges as the syndrome of "frozen watchfulness."[3]

**Therapy—Trust Us.** To learn to trust is a new experience for these families. This means that everyone dealing with them must be seen to be dependable, honest, and predictable. The treatment team must replace the good parents these families have never had.

3. **Fantasy Governs.** These people escape from the truth into a world of fantasy. They have unrealistic ideas and expectations about all aspects of their lives: their relationships with each other, their job prospects, the kind of car they can afford, the kind of house they expect. At no point do fantasy and reality meet. Most important of all are the expectations they have of their children and their behavior. The fantasy child, as Pollock and Steele have pointed out[4] often bears no relation to any conceivable normal infant. Fantasy also takes over when abuse has occurred. The explanations offered are not clever attempts to conceal a crime but rather fantastic suggestions, whose very unlikelihood often leads those who hear them to accept them as true.

**Therapy—Truth Releases.** An essential goal in treatment is to obtain the parents' reconciliation to the truth. This is a gradual process, for it is not easy for them to yield the fantasies which have always been a necessary escape from the harsh realities of their world. Once a trusting relationship with a therapist has been established, the parents begin to find themselves able to face the truth and to admit to the assault, with relief.

4. **Blind Alleys.** The parents can often see no way out. All hope of a happy future has gone. They are overwhelmed by the number of difficulties to which

they can find no solutions: there may be large debts, a deadend job, unsatisfactory housing. They cannot foresee success in either marriage or parenthood.

**Therapy—The Safe Place.** Before these families can begin to change they need a refuge from the pressures surrounding them; a chance to escape from the blind alley. When we take the family into our hospital we offer them a safe place where they and their children are protected from aggression.

5. **Assortive Mating.** This phenomenon occurs between the parents of abused children. It is not surprising that people with such biographies meet and are accepted by only those of similar backgrounds. Such common assortive mating does not prevent a mismatch for intellectual ability, however. In our series we have encountered a young woman with an intellectual capacity in the top 2 percent of the population but whose emotional immaturity was such that she started truanting in her teens and later married a youth who was truanting from a local school for subnormal pupils.

**Therapy—New Bonding.** We aim to form a bond between the family and hospital which is both nonneurotic and real. The relationship between therapist and patient is often spoken of in terms of the Freudian transference, but this is not the bond that we form with these families. It is rather the bond a child forms with his parents, an enduring one, and the basis on which true trust can develop. New healthy bonds can then form between the parents, their children, their friends and extended family.

6. **Childlike Parents.** Often the parents, especially the mother, are, both in actual age and in emotional age, too young for parenthood. In a recent series 40 percent of the mothers were under the age of twenty when they had their first child. In our area less than 9 percent of all maternities occur in mothers under twenty years of age. The childishness of these parents makes them easier to treat; they are actively seeking mature adults to whom they can bond. In the past when they have sought such persons they have failed to find them. Identity diffusion in Erik Erikson's sense is extremely common.

**Therapy—A Chance to Grow.** When the parents are admitted to the hospital they are, in practice, allowed to regress to the status of babies, although great care is taken to respect their dignity as people. They are now in a place where they are cared for totally and without any expectations of payment or return. They are housed, fed, and cared for by day and by night. The routine initially is wholly undemanding. Often the exhausted mother takes gratefully to her bed and is nursed for several days. The abused child and the other children in the family are cared for. Much help must be given by deed rather than words, for basic trust is established in the preverbal years of development. In this setting the metamorphosis towards mature adulthood is often amazingly fast.

7. **The Hospital's Baby.** By comparison with their brothers and sisters, children who are abused are more frequently prematurely born or are ill in the neonatal period and therefore require admission to a special care baby unit. The

parents thus can make little, if any, physical or other contact with the baby. Peering through the window they see their child in the center of the necessary machinery; an inhuman mechanism controlling a naked object elicits no pride or joy. Fear is the inevitable response. Parents will often report later, "He never seemed to belong to me." When later hospitalizations occur, the parents feel acutely that the baby has been taken over by the hospital and that they are being excluded.

**Therapy—The Family's Hospital.** Each member of the family is given equal attention; no one individual is singled out for special concern. This may be very different from previous experiences when all the attention had been focused on the ill child. We offer the family a hospital where *all* the members are welcome and accepted. Each family has their own front door key and key to the family room, and they are allowed to come and go as they please. This often means they have more freedom than they have ever had before. All parts of the hospital are open to them and a member of the therapeutic team is available at all times. This means that the team must coordinate its efforts in an apparently effortless way. This is only possible when the members are mutually supportive and have a common sense of commitment.

8. **The Rituals.** These families under stress set up ritual patterns of behavior. Their interactions are formalized, each response being a step in the process leading to inevitable disaster. When dealing with health professionals, a ritualistic way of talking is easily learned, set questions are asked and expected set answers given. A doctor presented with an "open warning" commonly accepts the fantastic explanation offered for the diagnostic injury because he is part of a ritual that simply involves treating the immediate wound and not looking beyond that.

**Therapy—Astonishment.** Our aim is to break into the ritualized cycle, eliciting astonishment from the parents. We feel this astonishment to be a necessary precursor of any effective psychotherapy. The majority of families experience amazement when they find that, for the first time in their lives, everything is given to them for nothing. They are not condemned for their behavior nor criticized. They are instead treated as people. The astonishment often induces panic, as would any totally new experience. The parents often threaten to leave, but calm, kind intervention by the staff overcomes their fears of being rejected yet again.

9. **The Releasing Drugs.** In a recent series of families presenting with threatened or actual child abuse, 90 percent of the mothers were taking drugs of the benzodiazepine group or the tricyclic antidepressant group. These drugs are extremely dangerous in families under stress. There is excellent evidence[5] that the so-called tranquillizers will, like alcohol, in a stressful situation remove inhibition and release hostility and aggression. The mothers themselves, on recovery, will often describe the way in which their moods changed dangerously when on these potent drugs.

**Therapy—A Clean Brain.** Weaning the parents from psychotropic drugs is the primary task. Help is also given where alcohol has become a problem. Since we are hoping to induce a radical change in the behavior of both the parents, it is essential to have their brains functioning at optimum capacity and unimpeded by chemical barriers.

10. **The Little Stranger.** The child may indeed be a stranger to his parents. He may have spent a long time in a special care baby unit or in a pediatric ward. In his absence fantasies of his behavior have been built up in the parents. When he arrives home the rigidity of the parents' behavior means that they cannot adapt to the reality of the actual child. In other cases a child fails to live up to the parents expectations and ideas, often in direct contrast to a sibling.[6] As the gap between fantasy and reality widens, the child becomes more alienated.

**Therapy—Getting to Know.** We offer the parents a chance to get to know their child, perhaps for the first time. Help is given with mothercraft and mothering; time is spent helping both parents to play with their children and to understand and cope with their behavior, while at the same time learning realistic ideas of development. We have learned from experience that these families cannot be taught in a conventional sense. When a trusting relationship is established they will learn by example and begin to ask questions for themselves. They can then get to know their child and enjoy and accept him as he really is.

11. **A Sick Family.** When we compared the biographies of battered children with those of their unharmed brothers and sisters[1] we found that the biographies of the abused children were notably full of physical ill health. One must also be alert to the possibility of undiagnosed illness. The rest of the family needs a full medical checkup. Often much sickness is revealed: we have seen cerebral tumors, pulmonary tuberculosis, renal disease, multiple sclerosis, dystrophia myotonica, and leprosy, among others. Minor health problems, such as dental caries, gynecological troubles, are common in the mothers. Brothers and sisters may also have minor but irritating health problems, such as wheezing and eczema. Psychiatric ill health, both acute and chronic, has featured in these families for generations. Serious mental illness, psychopathy, and inadequate personalities are all found.

**Therapy—Health Restored.** The restoration of health is a most urgent and practical point for all members of the family. Careful medical histories are taken and, where indicated, investigation and treatment are initiated. Routine dental treatment is arranged and a gynecologist from the local family planning clinic makes a weekly visit to our unit. In a large number of cases we have found mothers much more able to cope with their problems when physical fitness is restored. Settling the pattern of feeding and sleeping is usually necessary for both the abused child and his siblings. This, together with treatment for irritating minor ailments that these children so frequently suffer, further alleviates the stress in the family.

12. **Crying in the Trap.** The whole family is trapped in a situation from which there is no escape—and the inconsolable, persistent crying of the child is the last straw. The infant cry is the most compelling of all signals. A response is called for from virtually any adult who hears it. These parents cannot leave, but they cannot calm the child either. Something has to happen. The outcome is the cataclysmic loss of control and assault.

**Therapy—Smiling a Welcome.** In the routine of the hospital the child in whom crying was a major feature loses this as a standard reaction, and the child who showed frozen watchfulness quickly loses this behavioral pattern. On admission many of the children are bonded in fear and hate to the parents who have treated them so badly. But in the secure, predictable atmosphere of the hospital a bond of love and affection can form. The child's smile of welcome confirms to the parents that this has been achieved at last.

13. **The Open Warnings.** The case studies we have presented show clearly how open warnings are given and how they are, sadly, so often ignored. In the majority of cases, parents have taken their child to a doctor, an emergency room, or a policeman, and displayed minor, but often diagnostic injuries. These are too often ignored or brushed aside and only in retrospect is their true message read.

**Therapy—Trials of Freedom.** When the family has learned to trust, open warnings are no longer necessary. They know that they can talk openly with the staff and that, if the stress becomes too great, help is available. It then becomes possible to encourage them to take over more responsibility and care of their children. We arrange for the family to go home for several days before their final discharge so that both parents can be together with all the children, including, if possible, the abused child. The family knows that they may return without any warning if things go wrong.

14. **Gaze Aversion.** Human behavior is such that we see what we want to and positively avert our gaze from that which we cannot bear. That is how it was on the road from Jerusalem to Jericho: it needed a Samaritan to take notice of the Jew who had fallen among thieves. The battered baby syndrome was not described in medical literature until 1962, although it has been with us since family life began. It needed the compassionate eyes of Henry Kempe and Henry Silver to discern that many—perhaps most—injured babies were victims of adult attack. Many of the families in which child abuse occurs seek aid because of their uncontrollable aggressive urges. But they are often told, "Oh, you would not do a thing like that!" Unfortunately they not only would, they do. So would we all; that is why gaze aversion happens and why reassurance is so dangerous.

**Therapy—Facing the Facts.** Acknowledging that a cataclysmic outburst of rage in response to infantile signals is inherent in all of us is the first essential step in establishing empathy with these parents. Only then can true healthy bonding arise between family and therapist. A child ten months old was admitted with the classical injuries of child abuse. He had had seven hospital admissions and it was not until his admission to our service that he was found to be congenitally blind. The parents had maintained a totally defensive attitude until they were given this diagnosis. Then their defenses fell. "He cried and cried and never looked at me," said the mother. The father said, "It was my fault. I knew what was happening really. I should have stopped it." The mother then asked the physician, "Could he have done it?" and he answered sincerely, "Yes." This honest answer led to an open relationship.

15. **Cataclysms.** By definition a cataclysm has occurred when a child is abused. The final provocation is often minor—crying or food refusal. Initially we may not know what the final trigger was because the parent committing the assault may have a true amnesia for the attack. This lasts for a variable length of time, but usually the memory returns. The paroxysm of violence is similar to the other paroxysmal behaviors, such as uncontrollable vomiting, laughing, orgasm, labor, and epileptic seizure.[7] Once it has begun it cannot be halted. When it is over the rage is satiated and immediate help for the injured child is usually sought. Occasionally, however, the denial may extend so far as a refusal to recognize that the injury has in fact occurred.

**Therapy—Crises Resolved.** The inevitable crises that occur during treatment are resolved, making them the antitheses of the cataclysms that brought the family to notice. There are legal crises involving civil and criminal court hearings. There are crises about housing. There are crises about marital relationships. There are crises between the parents and the grandparents. There are crises between the parents and the therapeutic team, when the parents initially try to manipulate the staff. At each point the team must maintain equanimity and be united in their psychotherapeutic aims, while at the same time supporting wholeheartedly the family as a unit. This is particularly well seen when going through court. The example given at the beginning of the chapter show how the drama of the court can itself be cathartic. Such court hearings often have a quality of confession, absolution, and penance.

16. **Collusion.** The partner of the abusive parent nearly always knows what has happened but colludes in the fantasy story proposed. Professionals also often collude with the confabulatory stories, since they too unconsciously wish to deny the possibility of such behaviors and hence repress the obvious.

**Therapy—Acceptance.** It is essential that acceptance of the whole sequence of events leading to the abuse should occur. It must be accepted that the past cannot be changed and the chain of "what would have happened if?" must be broken. Ritualized discourse intended to change the past must be avoided. It is better to concentrate on providing achievable goals for the family.

# CRITICAL PATH FOR BABY N

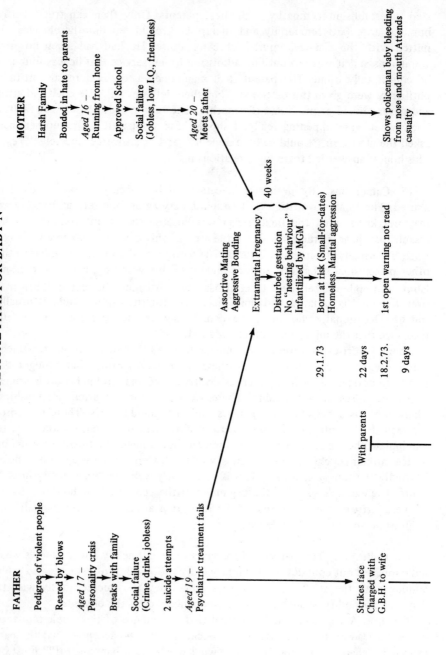

**MOTHER**

Harsh Family

Bonded in hate to parents

*Aged 16 –*
Running from home

Approved School

Social failure
(Jobless, low I.Q., friendless)

*Aged 20 –*
Meets father

Shows policeman baby bleeding
from nose and mouth Attends
casualty

40 weeks

Assortive Mating
Aggressive Bonding

Extramarital Pregnancy

Disturbed gestation
No "nesting behaviour"
Infantilized by MGM

Born at risk (Small-for-dates)
Homeless. Marital aggression

1st open warning not read

29.1.73

22 days

18.2.73.

9 days

With parents

**FATHER**

Pedigree of violent people

Reared by blows

*Aged 17 –*
Personality crisis

Breaks with family

Social failure
(Crime, drink, jobless)

2 suicide attempts

*Aged 19 –*
Psychiatric treatment fails

Strikes face
Charged with
G.B.H. to wife

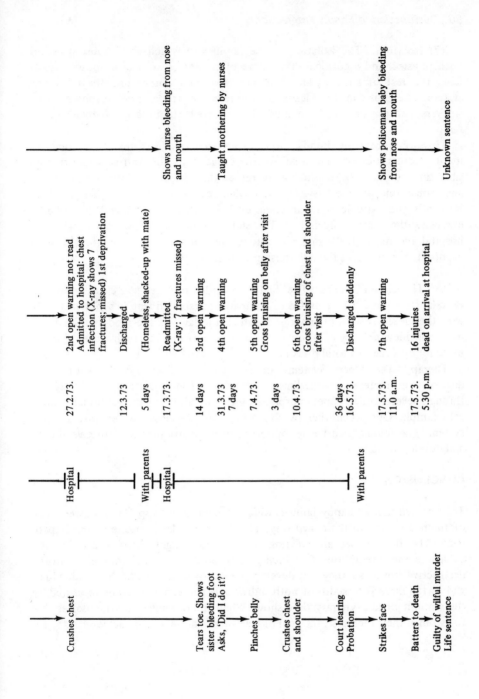

17. **Isolation.** The isolation of the families in which child abuse occurs is both physical and emotional. They have often elected to live in houses cut off from the rest of society. Many do not have, and cannot use, the telephone system. Their basic mistrust leads them to reject overtures from neighbors, social workers, and physicians. Once abuse has occurred, the isolation is then intensified.

**Therapy—Liberating Bonds.** It is an apparent paradox that firm bonds to mature adults are preconditional for the capacity to choose freely and responsibly and to face the world openly rather than withdraw into isolation. Yet analogous concepts are basic to the physiology of stability and change: Claud Bernard's "La fixité de milieu interieur est la condition essentielle de la vie libre" expresses the matter precisely.[8] The stable bond for the parents is with the hospital and its staff. We make no attempt to end the family's relationship with us, nor do we interpret the relationship verbally to them.

18. **The Closed System.** The final state can be regarded as a closed system in Bertalanffy's sense.[9] It is useful to compare the isolated trap in a violent family with the closed system of physics, in which the laws of thermodynamics determine the inevitable progression to maximum entropy. All such closed systems inevitably proceed to total disaster.

**Therapy—The Open System.** In contrast, an open system is one that develops an increasing orderliness over time. The evolution of the zygote through several orderly metamorphoses into the adult is a conventional biological example. Our psychotherapy aims to convert the closed system into an open system. The family then has an opportunity for continuing constructive growth and development.

## CONCLUSION

Tolstoy said that all happy families were alike, while unhappy families were each of them unhappy in their own way. This is the precise opposite of our experience. The families we are treating have become highly stereotyped in their behaviors and interactions. Our final goal is to release them from their neurotic, destructive bonds so they can develop their own identities, both as individuals and as families. The health of both individuals and families can be measured by the amount of idiosyncrasy they show. When these families are themselves able to astonish their therapist, the goal of treatment has been truly achieved.

**Part II**

# Evaluating the Family

# ✳ Introduction

The comprehensive assessment of all members of a family caught up in the problem of abuse or neglect is the most important first step. This requires the coordinated efforts of a variety of skilled professionals. What must be accomplished is summarized in the following.

| TASK | BY WHOM |
|------|---------|
| 1. Complete medical history | Pediatrician/Family Physician |
| 2. Complete physical examination | |
| 3. Laboratory studies | |
| 4. X-ray examination | |
| 5. Family psychodynamics/the child's environment | Some combination of: social worker, psychologist, psychiatrist, nurse, pediatrician |
| 6. Is the child a special child? | |
| 7. Ability to handle crises | |
| 8. Is the home safe? | All of above |
| 9. Long term treatment plans | |

Once completed, the recommendations for long term treatment and learning can be implemented.

In Chapter Five the child protection team in Denver discusses their problem oriented approach to the assessment of the family during the time of crisis. Drs. Ruth and Henry Kempe team up in Chapter Six to review a variety of methods helpful in identifying pathology within the family. Their suggestions and ideas will be useful to the social worker, pediatrician, psychologist, psychiatrist, nurse, and others confronted with the need to evaluate any given family. This material supplements the information presented in our previous two books.

Chapters Seven and Eight present comprehensive reviews of sexual exploitation within the family. The problem of sexual abuse and its adverse effects on the child have been ignored too long. This presentation of the psychodynamics involved with incest should be beneficial to all who encounter this difficult problem.

C. Henry Kempe
Ray E. Helfer

✳ Chapter Five

# The Child Protection Team:
# A Problem Oriented Approach

Barton D. Schmitt, Candace A. Grosz,
and Claudia A. Carroll

Multidisciplinary teams have become a critical element in the evaluation and management of the complex problems of child abuse and neglect. The main purpose of this chapter is to describe the inner workings of a diagnostic child protection team during the assessment and dispositional phase. The unique feature of our team is that it is problem oriented. This means we utilize a problem oriented form of record keeping, case discussion, and follow up. In addition, our team has found that the data base must be standardized in order to avoid missing data. We have also standardized the collection responsibilities for different parts of the data base. This type of role definition and clarification prevents duplication of effort, plus unnecessary frustrations and crises. The role of the physician, the social worker, and the coordinator are discussed in this chapter. Ground rules for team conferences and the use of the problem oriented record are also provided.

## THE PHYSICIAN'S EVALUATION

The physician's main role in child abuse and neglect is to be an accurate diagnostician. His other roles are to report confirmed cases to the local child protective service, to hospitalize the child in need of diagnosis and protection, and to fully arrange for the evaluation of the abused child's personal, medical, and psychological needs. (see Table 5–1).

The physician who initially sees the child, be he or she a pediatrician, family practitioner, or surgeon, may be uncomfortable in carrying out the tasks listed below. In which case, the physician should seek consultation as he would were this a case of heart failure, kidney problem or the like. Every community or region must develop appropriately trained consultants in child abuse and neglect.

**Table 5-1.** Medical Evaluation Checklist

| | |
|---|---|
| 1. | History of injury |
| 2. | Physical examination of patient |
| 3. | Trauma X ray survey |
| 4. | Bleeding disorder screen |
| 5. | Forensic vaginal examination |
| 6. | Hospitalization of selected patients |
| 7. | Nutritional rehabilitation program |
| 8. | Color photographs |
| 9. | Physical examination of siblings |
| 10. | Official medical report in writing |
| 11. | Behavioral assessment |
| 12. | Developmental assessment |
| 13. | Attend dispositional conference |
| 14. | Keep parents involved and informed |

### History of Injury

A complete history should be obtained as to how the injury allegedly happened, including the informant, date, time, place, sequence of events, people present, time lag before medical attention sought, and so forth. If possible, the parents should be interviewed separately and exact details obtained. No other professional should have to repeat this detailed, probing interview. The physician must talk with the parents directly so that his history is not looked upon as hearsay evidence if the case comes to court. In some cases, obtaining the history from the parent on the phone may suffice if they cannot come in. The physician commonly forgets to interview the child himself, which is often helpful if he is over age 3 or 4. This should be done in a private setting without the parents present. In sexual abuse cases the history is usually the most critical datum of all.

### Physical Examination of Patient

All bruises should be recorded as to size, shape, position, color, and age. If they resemble strap marks, grab marks, or a blunt instrument, this should be recorded. The oral cavity, eardrums, and genitals should be closely examined for signs of occult trauma. Eardrums may be perforated in cases of direct slap over the external ear. All bones should be palpated for tenderness and the joints tested for full range of motion. Special attention should be paid to the retina for hemorrhages that may point to serious head injury. The height and weight percentiles should be plotted. If the child appears malnourished, this must be carefully followed. In sexual abuse cases, the mouth, anus, and external genitals should receive careful inspection for signs of trauma.

### Trauma x-ray Survey

Every suspected case under five years of age should receive a radiologic bone survey consisting of long bones, hand, foot, skull, rib, and pelvis x-rays. Over age

5, x-rays need be obtained only if there is any bone tenderness or limited range of motion on physical exam. If films of a tender site are initially negative, they should be repeated in two weeks to pick up calcification of any subperiosteal bleeding or nondisplaced epiphyseal fractures that may have been present. When the films are positive, there is often no overt fracture. The most classic finding is a chip fracture or corner fracture.

The most diagnostic x-ray of all is one that includes multiple bone injuries at different stages of healing. Such an x-ray implies repeated assault. X-ray findings usually last for four to six months after an injury, and rarely are seen twelve months following the last insult. Babies with nutritional deprivation need trauma x-rays because approximately 10 percent of them have associated skeletal injuries indicating trauma has occurred. Sexual abuse cases rarely require x-ray surveys. (See references 1 and 2 for further details on the radiological aspects of child abuse.)

### Bleeding Disorder Screen

If there are bruises and the parents deny inflicting them, or the child allegedly has easy bruising, a bleeding disorder screen should be obtained. This bleeding panel would include a platelet count, bleeding time, tourniquet test, partial thromboplastin time, prothrombin time, and occasionally thrombin time. A normal bleeding panel strengthens the physician's court testimony that the bruising could not have occurred spontaneously or with minor injury. Observations that the child does not bruise easily in a controlled environment, i.e., hospital or foster home, are most helpful.

### Forensic Vaginal Examination

Suspected sexual abuse cases usually need to be referred to a gynecologist, who has the expertise to perform a forensic vaginal exam that can stand up in court. Evidence (e.g., hair specimens, fingernail scrapings, acid phosphatase, sperm tests, etc.) is collected, transported, and analyzed, utilizing a patient identification system that fulfills legal requirements. All rape cases (postpubertal and prepubertal) should be referred to gynecology for this procedure. Incest cases should be referred only if intercourse has taken place in the last 48 hours (evidence for sperm rarely persists beyond this time period). Often these cases can be confirmed only by the history. Molestation cases not involving intercourse may not need a gynecology referral. Vaginal discharge can easily be examined for sperm. The first pelvic exam in a girl should be preceded by careful explanation and preparation from the clinic nurse. Cases at risk of pregnancy should be handled according to the families' and patients' wishes. Those at risk of venereal disease must be treated according to current recommendations of the American Academy of Pediatrics.

### Hospitalization of Selected Patients

When a Protective Service worker or police officer brings in a child, they usually want a physician to document the medical evidence for physical abuse. This may or may not require hospitalization depending on the ability of the protective services worker to provide temporary shelter for the child. By contrast, when a parent or guardian brings a child with suspected nonaccidental trauma to the Emergency Room or clinic without any prior agency involvement, the child should be hospitalized so that an adequate diagnosis is made and treatment begun in a protective environment until protective services can become involved and an assessment of the safety of the home can be completed. The extent of injuries is not relevant to this requirement for hospitalization. A child with a minor inflicted injury could return home and receive a second injury on that same day that proves to be fatal.

The parents must be told the truth—i.e., that the cause of the injuries is uncertain and that studies and further evaluation must be done. The possibility of nonaccidental trauma is optimally not discussed in this setting unless brought up by the parent. On the rare occasion when a parent refuses hospitalization, a police or court hold can be obtained. Failure-to-thrive cases suspected to be secondary to nutritional or emotional deprivation must be hospitalized for diagnostic assessment and treatment. These patients are extremely difficult to follow as outpatients, there is a 10 percent risk of concomitant physical abuse and in some cases death from starvation has occurred because of inadequate followup. In sexual abuse cases, the first priority is to prevent continued sexual exploitation of the child. This may require immediately placing the child in a hospital or foster home.

### Nutritional and Emotional Rehabilitation Program

A nutritional rehabilitation program is the starting point for reaching a definitive diagnosis in failure-to-thrive cases. The infant should be placed on unlimited feedings of a regular diet for age. The type of formula should be identical to the one used at home. Rapid weight gain on a special formula free of cow's milk protein or lactose would prove little in terms of previous underfeeding. Supplemental vitamins should be provided, the daily caloric intake should approach 150 cal./kg./day (ideal weight). This diagnostic trial of feeding should be carried out for a minimum of ten to fourteen days.

The underweight infant who gains rapidly in the hospital is a victim of underfeeding and/or emotional deprivation at home. A rapid weight gain can be defined as greater than 1.5 oz. per day sustained over ten to fourteen days. Sometimes the hospital weight gain is less than this, but if it is two or three times greater than a similar period at home, it is diagnostic. Average weight gains for normal children vary according to age: 0.9 oz. per day in the first three months, 0.8 oz. per day from three to six months, 0.6 oz. per day from six to nine months, and 0.4 oz. per day from nine to twelve months. Additional confirmation comes from the observation that these underfed babies are ravenous, demanding feeders in the hospital.

### Color Photographs

Color photographs are required by law in some states. In most juvenile court cases they are not essential to the primary physician's testimony. In cases where an expert witness who has not actually examined the child is to testify, they are mandatory. In cases where criminal court action is anticipated, they will usually be required and taken by the police photographer. In nutritional deprivation, "before" and "after" photographs will be helpful. In sexual abuse cases that involve physical harm, the police will usually arrange for photographs.

### Physical Examination of Siblings

There is approximately a 20 percent risk that a sibling of a physically abused child has also been abused at that same point; and there is almost a 100 percent chance that the siblings of an abused child will be emotionally and developmentally impaired. Therefore, all siblings should be brought in for total body surface examinations within twelve hours of uncovering an index case and a more complete assessment at a later date. If the parents say they can't bring them in because of transportation problems, the protective service agency can assist them. If the parents refuse to have their other children seen, a court order can be obtained and the police sent out. In sexual abuse cases, female siblings should be interviewed, since seeing more than one child to be victimized is not uncommon.

### Official Medical Report in Writing

This report is required by law in all states and should be phoned and written by the examining physician. Since it is an official document, it is best if typed. The accuracy and completeness of this report is extremely important. This report should not be simply a copy of the admission workup or discharge summary, because the evidence for the diagnosis of child abuse is often lost in those highly technical documents. This report should include the following.

1. History—the alleged cause of the injury (with date, time, place, etc.).
2. Physical exam—description of the injury, using nontechnical terms whenever possible (e.g., "cheek" instead of "zygoma," "bruise" instead of "ecchymosis").
3. Lab tests—x-rays, blood work, etc.
4. Conclusion—statements on why this represents nonaccidental trauma, the severity of the incident in terms of long term handicaps, plus the risk of repeated abuse.

### Behavioral Assessment

The abused child is likely to have associated behavior problems. Some may be primary behaviors that make the child difficult to live with and hence prone to abuse such as negativism and hyper activity. Other behaviors may be secondary to abusive treatment such as fearfulness and depression. Often the abused child's individual need for therapy will be overlooked unless these symptoms are uncovered.

### Developmental Assessment

Child abuse and neglect leads to serious developmental delays. These problems can be recognized by routine use of a complete developmental history, Denver Developmental Screening Test (DDST), or other developmental exam in this age group, and a careful observation of this child. A school report may be helpful in the comprehensive assessment of the abused school-age child. (See Chapter Three for further details on the developmental defects in child abuse and neglect.)

### Dispositional Conference

The pediatrician or family practitioner who carries out the above functions must attend the conference of the child protection team members. (This is discussed later in the chapter.)

### Informing Parents

The physician is in a unique position to gain a good rapport with the parents. Extreme pains must be taken to keep them always informed as to progress, plans, and anticipated events. Always tell them the truth; all parents respond better to the truth, even though they may not agree, than to some vague, partially true bit of information. After the diagnosis of abuse is made, the parents must be told the results. For example: "Peter has received several injuries at different times. While I am uncertain exactly how they occurred or who was at fault, I am certain that they occurred. I am more interested in helping you make certain this doesn't occur again than I am in finding out the exact circumstance for each of his injuries." Three days after a mother and father were told of the findings and interpretation, the mother broke down, cried, and said, "I'm scared to take Peter home."

## THE SOCIAL WORKER'S EVALUATION

The initial phase of intervention with a family requires that a variety of tasks be addressed by the social worker, and further, that these tasks be performed expeditiously. The role of the social worker during the diagnostic phase may be seen as being comprised of the following four areas, all of which are closely related: (1) evaluation of the safety of the home, (2) intervention with and support of the parents, (3) initiation of legal action, and (4) initiation of ongoing treatment services to the family (see Table 5-2). Some of these tasks may be counterproductive, some best accomplished in the home, and some in the hospital setting. For these reasons there usually need to be two social workers—the medical social worker in the hospital, and the community-based social worker (protective services worker).

**Table 5–2.** Social Worker's Checklist

---

**Evaluation of the Safety of the Home**
   Assess each parent, perception of child and prognosis for reabuse.
   Refer selected families for psychiatric consultation (see Chapter Six).
   Present evaluation and tentative treatment recommendations at dispositional conference.

**Intervention with and Support of the Parents**
   Convey attitude of understanding to the parents.
   Interpret information on behalf of the parents to others having contact with them.
   Be predictable with the parents by helping them anticipate all agency or hospital actions
      in advance.
   Help the parents understand what is happening around the child's hospitalization.
   Encourage parental involvement with child's hospital care.
   Help the parents with concrete needs.

**Initiation of Legal Action**
   Request police and/or court action when indicated.
   Share assessment of family with those who are identified to help the family.

**Initiation of Ongoing Treatment Services to the Family**
   Remain actively involved with family until on-going treatment worker becomes available.
   Allow and/or encourage parents to direct anger toward initial social worker so they may
      have positive relationship with second social worker.
   Keep in touch with your own feelings and those of the staff.

---

### Evaluation of the Safety of the Home

This question requires careful evaluation of each parent, an assessment of the total family functioning, the perception of the child by each parent, and the prognosis for future abuse to occur. A home visit will usually be necessary to gather some of this information. Compilation of all these data is required to begin to determine what patterns are characteristic to this family. Only then can realistic planning for discharge of the child from the hospital and followup services to the family be initiated.

The social worker has specific responsibility at the dispositional conference to present a succinct yet sufficiently detailed report around (1) personal history of each parent, (2) significant information about the child and his role in the family, (3) principal features of the family, (4) diagnostic impressions, (5) safety of the home, and (6) tentative treatment plans or recommendations. These treatment recommendations may be modified as needed by the team at the meeting. The protective services worker and medical social worker must be in attendance at the dispositional conference.

### Intervention With and Support of the Parents

Keeping in mind that abusive parents characteristically have extremely poor self-images, no one to turn to in times of stress, and a limited capacity to use help, it is the job of the social worker to convey to them that someone is interested in them and can help them in this overwhelming situation. Treatment with the abusive parent begins with the initial contact, whether it be with a physician, nurse, or social worker. The attitude conveyed by those who come in contact with the parents does much to set the stage for engaging the parents in long term treatment and ongoing planning.

At times the social worker needs to interpret information, on behalf of the parents, to a variety of individuals (e.g., to the house staff of the hospital) explaining how a parent lost control with the child, what the parent's behaviors mean, and so forth. In this way all professionals having contact with the parents will have a better understanding and appreciation for them as hurting, "abused children grown up." Insuring good communication with the hospital staff and involving them with the planning of the child protection team regarding the family are essential to the management of a child abuse situation.

Most parents during this initial period of time have many questions, along with associated anger mixed with depression, regarding what is happening to them and their child. Being completely honest with the parents is the most productive way of handling both their questions and their feelings. For example, it is necessary to tell the parents of the referral to the department of social services, the filing of a child abuse report as required by law, and discussing with them what legal steps may or may not be initiated.[a] Maintaining a firm yet sensitive attitude conveys the message that we are interested in them, see them as people who can be helped, and will stand by them until their situation improves.

One of the universal goals in all child abuse cases is helping the parents learn to trust others. This begins during the initial assessment. The best way to gain trust is by being predictable with parents and helping them anticipate all agency or hospital actions by preparing them in advance. Examples of this predictability would include sharing with the parents—before any court hearing—the team's report and recommendations, discussing with the parents the recommendations of the dispositional conference, letting them know when the social service department is notified and the role of this individual, and letting them know if the police will be contacting them.

Another aspect of the social worker's role is helping the parents understand what is happening around the child's hospitalization and physical condition. Something as simple as changing the child's hospital room can be extremely upsetting to the parents if they haven't been told of this change. They may interpret this move as an attempt to "keep the child from them." The social worker should encourage the parents to visit as frequently as possible, facilitate

---

[a]Protective service workers must feel comfortable in telling parents who they are or for whom they work. Parents must be told early that, "I am a protective service worker. I am here to be helpful in every possible way." Any attempts to hedge on this issue will inevitably create distrust.—Ed.

their involvement with the child and his care during the hospitalization, and make arrangements for the parent(s) to room in with the child when feasible. The social worker can also be of assistance to the parents in helping them work out such concrete problems as transportation, child care, financial problems, hospital bills, and so on. Many of these parents move from crisis to crisis, and help in these areas often needs to be provided so that the parents can become less overwhelmed.

### Initiation of Legal Action

Among the legal considerations during the acute phase of involvement are: (1) whether a police hold is necessary to keep the child in the hospital temporarily for his protection, (2) reporting of nonaccidental trauma cases to the local social services department, and (3) whether juvenile court action is indicated immediately. While the hospital social worker may request certain legal action for the immediate protection of the child, the community protective service worker must see that the subsequent legal steps are carried out properly, both in timing and detail.

### Initiation of Ongoing Treatment Services to
### the Family

If the social worker can be a positive, moving force during the crisis stage, it is more likely that the parents will accept services and intervention during the next phase, that of the long term treatment with the family. In most situations the families will be in need of a variety of intensive services from several different agencies. The social worker involved in the initial phase must stay actively involved with the parents until the ongoing treatment worker can be introduced into the situation. During this period the parents need someone on whom they can rely for continuous support and understanding.

In those situations where there is such intensified anger expressed by the parents that in no way are they going to perceive the social worker as a positive link to help, she or he can still serve an important function by allowing, and even encouraging, the parents to direct their anger, possibly seeing the social worker as "the bad guy who started all this," and thus freeing the protective services worker to be the "good guy." This concept can be instrumental in leaving the parents a positive relationship with the second social worker inasmuch as they have been able to express their anger at the first worker.

The four tasks comprising the role of the social worker have been discussed in terms of the hospital-based assessment. However, these tasks are not unique to the hospital setting; with minor modification they are also identified to the responsibilities when the assessment is carried out on an outpatient basis. Throughout the whole process the social worker must keep in touch with his or her own feelings and help others involved with the family to do likewise. Saying to the harassed physician or nurse, "You sure seem upset over this case" may be just the right bit of therapy needed at the time. Basic trust among the team members is critical. Feeling comfortable to share the intense feelings that are inevitable is not only helpful but mandatory if the team is to survive and function effectively.

## COORDINATOR'S ROLE

Three major goals outline the coordinator's responsibilities in the assessment phase. First, she aids in gathering information for the team's diagnosis and evaluation process and insures that a complete data base is collected for each family. Second, she plans the dispositional conference so that it will be an effective and worthwhile meeting. Third, she provides consultation and support to others in the community who are requesting aid in case assessment for abusive and neglectful families (see Table 5-3).

**Table 5-3.** Coordinator Checklist

---

**Diagnosis and Evaluation**
   Gather information from medical staff, social services, Central Registry, police, other agencies.
   Report suspected child abuse to designated agency by phone.
   Schedule consultation and special testing.
   Provide liaison with hospital staff and community.
   Keep all Child Protection Team records up to date.

**Preparation for Dispositional Conference**
   Contact participants for each family to be discussed.
   Prepare problem oriented team report.
   Bring pertinent material.
   Share team's decisions and evaluation information.
   Schedule team's recommendations.

**Consultation to Others in Community**
   Arrange immediate medical evaluation if child has injuries.
   Arrange immediate social work home visit for potential cases and self-referrals.

---

### Diagnosis and Evaluation Duties

**Gather Information.** The coordinator supplements information from the pediatrician and social worker, who have interviewed the family directly, by contacting other related agencies. This includes previous medical resources such as clinics, hospitals, private physicians, or visiting nurses. Primary questions include: has the child received treatment for any injuries; what is the history of each injury, the date, and the treatment received; was there any suspicion about the circumstances of this injury? A record of well child care, illnesses, or other medical conditions is also obtained. Telephone contacts should also be made with the Central Registry for Child Abuse, the county department of social services where the family lives or has previously lived, the police, or other agencies who have been recently involved. Inquiry should include nature of the involvement, assessment of the family's functioning, concerns for neglect or abuse, and what services the agency can provide the family.

**Report Suspected Abuse or Neglect.** When it is determined that the injury is nonaccidental, a call is placed immediately to the county department of social services or other agency designated to receive these reports. To decrease the anxiety about reporting cases and improve the cooperation and service between agencies, a contact person at each agency should be developed. The coordinator also needs to be certain that the physician completes, and signs, an official, typed medical report.

**Schedule Consultations.** The coordinator may need to schedule appointments for family members with psychiatry, psychology, specialty physicians, or for laboratory work and x-rays. Some cases will also require photographs for court documentation or medical photographers for teaching purposes. The coordinator needs to be able to expedite these procedures by knowing when consent is required according to state law and how all the necessary consultations can be completed without conflicts. The parents must receive careful explanation regarding consultations, and clear communication as to times and locations of appointments.

**Provide Liaison with Hospital Staff and Community Workers.** If the child is hospitalized, it is important to keep the physicians, nurses, and ward clerks informed of any changes in status, for example, a police hold that is obtained, the projected date for discharge, whether the child will be going home or to foster placement, specific recommendations for the family, and current cooperation and emotional status of the parents. These should be recorded in written form in chart notes, not relying on verbal exchanges with one or two people. When the child does not require hospitalization, the coordinator attempts to expedite an outpatient assessment. When foster home plans are made final, the coordinator facilitates this by making arrangements between county workers and the hospital staff regarding the discharge time and orders. She also keeps hospital staff informed of times and places of any court hearings for which they may be needed.

**Keep Child Protection Team Records Up To Date.** The major focus is to implement a system that can be efficient and facilitate the followup process. A card file for quick reference, a statistical sheet, and an individual family file are helpful. The family file includes a face sheet, a master checklist to show the dates certain actions were completed by the physician, social worker, and coordinator; as well as problem oriented team report (see below), social history, psychiatric evaluations, ongoing brief notes regarding current status, and follow-up sheets. A separate card file, divided by months, helps to order the followup system and show which cases need review each month.

### Preparation for Dispositional Conference

**Contact Participants for Each Family to Be Discussed.** All persons who are currently involved, as well as those who will be receiving referrals to be working with the family, should be contacted to attend the dispositional conference. If someone cannot attend this meeting, the coordinator should still contact the person getting information about his involvement with the family, sharing with him tentative recommendations, and outlining his questions for discussion. Sometimes a conference telephone call can be used when a particular person cannot attend.

**Prepare Problem Oriented Team Report.** Prior to the meeting, the coordinator prepares the typewritten problem oriented team report and completes this report by soliciting diagnostic impressions and tentative recommendations from each of the persons who has made a direct evaluation (see below).

**Bring Pertinent Materials.** The coordinator needs to anticipate and have available all the materials the team will need to adequately discuss a case. These include case records, hospital charts, photographs, x-rays, and information about previous medical care or services provided to the family.

**Share Team's Decisions and Evaluation Information.** Following the dispositional conference, the coordinator revises the problem oriented team report and mails this, along with evaluation reports from the physician, social worker, and others, to persons supplying ongoing service, who include county social service workers, visiting nurses, physicians, or mental health workers. If juvenile court is involved, a copy to the county attorney for the department of social services, the Guardian ad Litem, and parents' attorney should be made available. While confidentiality must be respected, those working directly with the families must be informed if help is to be given and the child protected. State laws generally concur with this view. While consideration is needed for the privacy of the family, the focus is to provide protection for the child and integrated treatment services for the family by sharing team diagnosis and recommendations.

**Schedule Team Recommendations.** Frequently, followup appointments for health care or for additional evaluations for psychiatric or developmental problems are needed. The coordinator helps to schedule these and implement other treatment services. Calls are made within two to three weeks from the dispositional conference to determine that services are being provided and that diagnostic information has been received. Subsequent followup calls are made on high risk or serious cases according to particular case needs. Usually these calls are scheduled two to three weeks prior to the next court hearing, to provide feedback information for team members, supportive consultation to ongoing workers, or to determine the need to reconference prior to the court hearing.

**Transferring Coordinating Tasks.** Transfer of coordinator from the acute crisis period to long term therapy is necessary. This may be her counterpart for long term care or a primary therapist identified for the family. The protective services worker does not have the time to do this for each case.

### Consultation to Others in the Community
Frequent calls are received from private doctors, visiting nurses, school personnel, or social workers requesting guidance in case management.

**Suspected Cases.** If a child has received injuries, the coordinator can arrange for the child to be brought immediately to the hospital clinic for medical evaluation and possible reporting. This would require that another person—e.g., nurse, social worker, teacher—accompany the child and his parents, to insure that the child is brought in.

**Potential Cases.** When it is not known if the child has received injuries, or when the concern is the presence of a potential for child abuse and neglect identifying information and a summary of current status is obtained from the concerned person. The coordinator can then call the appropriate community resource and make an appropriate referral. This course of action is recommended to show support for the individual making the referral and to eliminate as much red tape as possible. In this way they are encouraged to refer other cases and the concern is assessed quickly. The plan must be explained to the concerned caller. In some cases, all the appropriate services may already be in effect and the coordinator may need merely to listen, sharing the worry about the situation, and offering encouragement and understanding.

**Self-Referrals.** Parents may call at a time of personal crisis to ask for services. The goals in managing these cases are to offer support and arrange for someone to contact the family directly and assess the situation. Usually this requires patience and frequently an extended phone call with the parent to offer reassurance and develop enough rapport and trust so that the parent will share his name, address, and telephone number. The coordinator then calls the appropriate agency to arrange an immediate home visit by a social worker. The parent must know that a social worker will be requested to see them immediately.

## GROUND RULES FOR EFFECTIVE
## TEAM CONFERENCES

The most critical component of team functioning is the multidisciplinary team conference. The professionals who have actually evaluated the family, such as the hospital social worker, the protective service worker, the pediatrician, and the public health nurse are present, as well as the consultants who make up the permanent diagnostic consultation team attend (these may include a regular pediatrician, psychiatrist, psychologist, lawyer, etc.). At this meeting the individual professionals pool their knowledge and understanding of a given family, and attempt to assimilate and analyze all their data. Finally, an accurate picture of the family's strengths and weaknesses comes into focus: at this point a reasonable treatment plan can be designed.

The multidisciplinary team conference also requires ground rules if it is to be productive and efficient. One question that frequently arises is whether or not the parent(s) should attend the conference when their case is being discussed. When they do, many of the professionals feel uncomfortable. And yet the parents do have a right to be heard. This question needs to be assessed for each family and a group decision made as to how to proceed. The following 25 ground rules help to bring about a meaningful conference.

1. *Hold Regular Conferences.* Teams should meet on a scheduled basis so that the time becomes built into the members' schedules. Most teams meet weekly. It is much easier occasionally to cancel a meeting if it is not needed than to schedule each conference separately.

2. *Discuss All Cases.* The exposure of all disciplines to the full spectrum of child abuse cases and normal accidents is important. The more cases discussed, the more accurate and efficient the team becomes. Cases of repeated abuse or death must be fully discussed, much as one would insist upon at a medical inquest.

3. *Have All Team Members Present.* This is important for two reasons: each member has input into the final decisions, and the late veto from an absent member is prevented. Especially important is the presence of the juvenile court attorney so that he fully understands the reasons for seeking court action. However, the team must be able to move ahead with recommendations even if some members are absent.

4. *Have Presenters Come Fully Prepared.* Before the meeting all participants should have collected a complete data base in their area. Each should have thoroughly analyzed their data and made as many decisions as possible. Ideally, each participant should already have met with his supervisor. Identifying the existing problems and making tentative recommendations allows for a more in-depth team discussion.

5. *Have Agency Representatives Come With Decision Making Power.* The

person who attends the meeting must have the power to agree or disagree with team decisions without checking with his or her supervisor.

6. *Appoint Team Leader to Enforce the Rules or Guidelines.* Every team needs a leader or moderator who is in charge of case management discussion, pacing the meeting and keeping to the time schedule. The leader should also foster an informal, democratic atmosphere with free give-and-take discussion.

7. *Conference Time Limit—Two-Hour Maximum.* By two hours everyone is exhausted. The meeting must have an agenda and a timetable so that it stays on schedule. The team leader should adjourn the conference early whenever possible.

8. *Case Time Limit—30 Minutes Maximum.* Staying within the time deadline for individual cases so that all members are still present when the final decisions on that case are made is important. Complicated cases will take 20 to 30 minutes to review. These time limits will usually be difficult to adhere to without implementation of the problem oriented record.

9. *Formal Presentation Time Limit—Three Minutes Maximum.* Most of the case time should be reserved for open discussion. All formal presentations, both medical and social, should be precise and prepared in advance. They should concentrate on pertinent findings, current problems, tentative recommendations, and available treatment resources. Usually the medical presentation can be limited to two minutes, describing the medical findings and how they allegedly occurred. The social work and psychiatric presentations may require four minutes, but should stay with a capsule view of the personalities. These individuals should be told of the time limit in advance of the conference. This distillation of essential data is usually more important for social workers and psychiatrists, who frequently have volumes of materials and anecdotes that could be presented on each family.

10. *Start on Time and Stay on Schedule.* The meeting that starts late is unlikely to ever catch up. If a time schedule is adhered to, direct service workers can attend the portion of the meeting that discusses their particular family without being kept waiting unduly.

11. *Present the Evaluation in a Logical Sequence.* A basic sequence for presenting each case should be developed. Our usual sequence is medical diagnostic information, information from the reporting source (e.g., public health nurse, police, teacher), the social worker information, the psychiatric information, and then other agencies involved with this family. This sequence can be modified when it is not appropriate for a specific case.

12. *Utilize the Problem Oriented Record (POR) Format.* This subject is fully discussed in the next section; it involves identifying and numbering the total problems in each family under discussion by the team. Ideally, this is done prior to the team meeting. Visitors who bring cases to the team for consultation must prepare their cases in this style.

13. *Address All Comments to a Specific Problem Number.* The participants should be encouraged to preface their comments and questions with a specific problem number (e.g., "My comments relate to treatment for #3, the mother"). This helps to keep the meeting focused.

14. *Postpone Program Discussion Until Staff Meeting.* Team functioning problems may come up during this meeting, but full discussion of them should be tabled until case discussion is complete and a staff meeting can be held.

15. *Record the Team's Recommendations During the Meeting.* This is preferably done on a chalk board or somewhere visible to all the participants. The person who records these data should be someone who is not presenting on that specific family, since it may be difficult to do both. Often this person will be the team leader. In addition, a secretary or some other willing person should be simultaneously recording the chalk board recommendations onto paper before their are erased, for later typing up.

16. *Focus on Critical Decisions.* The team should spend the maximal amount of time on serious deliberations about four major decisions. First, is the home safe for the child or is foster care required? Second, what are the optimal treatment recommendations for this family? The team should be certain that each identified problem has a plan. Third, who will be responsible for each treatment recommendation? Fourth, is the data base complete or have some problems been overlooked? The main purpose of the meeting is to coordinate therapy; decisiveness and setting priorities are two of the hallmarks of an effective team.

17. *Consultants Must Give Practical Recommendations.* The advisory members or consultants must offer attainable advice rather than idealistic advice.

18. *One Consultant Cannot Overrule a Primary Member's Diagnosis.*[b] The consultant can try to persuade the primary team members about a specific point such as an injury was not accidental, but they should not have veto power on this matter. A case should not go to court when the team of experts cannot make up its mind about the diagnosis, because one cannot expect the court to resolve a diagnostic question. The diagnostic process is not trying to determine who abused the child, but rather whether abuse did in fact occur. Obviously, a case can go to court without knowing exactly who abused the child.

19. *One Team Member Can Demand a Court Hearing in a Confirmed Case Regarding a Treatment Question.*[b] If a team member feels a child should be removed from his home for his safety, he(she) should be allowed to

---

[b]Keep in mind that the community protective service worker is a primary member of the child protection team. The law gives her/him the mandate to carry the ball and be responsible during this acute intervention phase. Occasionally mistakes will be made; our aim is to lessen their number. These team conferences will help give this worker the guidance and support for this difficult decision.—Ed.

overrule all the other team members in this regard, at least to the point of giving the child his day in court. This is the kind of treatment decision that judges are prepared to make. A Guardian ad Litem should be appointed and a hearing date set.

20. *Give a Five-Minute Warning Before Closing Case Discussion.* This provides the team members a last opportunity to raise important questions.
21. *Summarize the Team's Recommendations at End of Case.* This should be done by the same person who leads and directs the overall meeting.
22. *Gain Team's Approval of Recommendations.* Although the team is rarely unanimous in its decisions, one should expect the majority of the team members to form a consensus about recommendations.
23. *If the Team Does Not Approve the Recommendations, the Recommendations Should Be Modified at this Point,* until they are acceptable to the majority of people. The discussion of a case should never close until a consensus has been expressed. Occasionally the team leader must force this decision solely by a show of hands regarding two alternative situations.
24. *Set a Date for Case Review by the Team.* Often this followup report will take only two or three minutes.
25. *Have the Team's Final Recommendations Typed and Distributed to All Involved Professionals and Agencies.* The child protective service's attorney should receive a copy of the team's deliberations so that he might better prepare his case for court and possibly submit these documents into the court record.

## THE PROBLEM ORIENTED RECORD

The problem oriented record (POR) is a new form of record keeping. It was introduced by Dr. Lawrence Weed in the late 1960s. Those who use it feel that it leads to more logical thinking, writeups, presentations, and meetings. This section will discuss three years of experience utilizing the problem oriented record in child abuse and neglect cases at Colorado General Hospital. Until now, medicine has applied the POR to the analysis of a single patient; however, in child abuse and neglect, the problem oriented record must analyze an entire family.

The critical step in problem orienting a child abuse and neglect case is problem formulation. There is always one point where the professionals involved in a case will have considerable data available to them; this is usually a few days after the report is received. At this time the family's problems should be listed, clarified, and each given a permanent number. A plan must be written for each recorded problem. Thereafter, all progress notes and followup conferences on this family must be cross-indexed using the same numbers. An index sheet (a master problem list) is placed on the front of the record as a guide to its contents. In this way, the family's chart becomes organized. The POR does not ask any professional to change their evaluation. Instead, it requires that data be reorganized.

### The Master Problem List

Child abuse and neglect is a symptom of family problems. Hence, the entire family needs evaluation if rational decisions are to be made. The master problem list contains standard nomenclature for family diagnosis in child abuse and neglect. The same system is used for every case seen. Specific details for individual family problems are listed under these major problem headings. There are a maximum of twelve problem areas.

1. The specific Child Abuse/Neglect category (e.g., physical abuse, failure to thrive, sexual abuse, medical care neglect, intentional drugging or poisoning, emotional abuse, abandonment, lack of supervision, severe physical neglect, high risk child, true accident, etc.).
2. Patient's physical problems.
3. Patient's emotional problems or status (e.g., deprivation behavior, depression, discipline problem, developmental lags).
4. Siblings' emotional and physical problems or status.
5. Parents' physical problems.
6. Mother's emotional problems or status.
7. Father's emotional problems or status.
8. Emotional problems or status of other important people in the home (e.g., baby sitter, aunt, grandmother).
9. Marital problems or mate relationship.
10. Personal crises (e.g., death, desertion, divorce, recent move).
11. Environmental crises (e.g., inadequate home, heat, water, food, job, medical insurance, child support payments).
12. Safety of the home (i.e., composite data from above that relate to decision for or against foster care placement).

These twelve categories were arrived at by revising the list many times until any type of family dysfunctioning or problem could be fitted into it. Obviously, the majority of cases will not have all twelve problems operational. Problem 1 will be present in all cases, because it is a description of the specific kind of child abuse or neglect that has taken place. Problem 12 is an important category that should be present in all cases; namely, a listing of the data that pertains to the safety or danger of the home in terms of the likelihood of a life threatening recurrence of abuse.

### The Master Treatment List

The master treatment list contains the treatment options for the specific problems listed in the master problem list. There are a broad range of possible recommendations for each of the problems. In any given case, only a few of the possible treatment recommendations will be chosen. Treatment is individualized and tailormade for every family. Legal decisions are always listed under 12—Safety of the Home. The two types of intervention seen in every case are followup of the family by one assigned social worker and the identification of a primary physician or nurse. Table 5–4 gives some of the treatment options on the master treatment list.

**Table 5–4.** Treatment Options on the Master Treatment List*

1  **Child Abuse or Neglect Category—Recommendations**
Formal (written) Report to Protective Services
Routine medical follow-up by private MD, house staff MD, neighborhood clinic, etc.
Increased medical visits, if not in foster home, etc.

2  **Patient's Physical Problems—Recommendations**
Pediatric specialty clinic for evaluation and/or treatment
Obtain release of information for evaluation done elsewhere
Dental services
Etc.

3  **Patient's Emotional Problems—Recommendations**
Child rearing or discipline counselling by CPS worker, pediatrician, PHN, young mothers
group sessions, parent education classes, etc.
Infant stimulation program, day care, nursery school (especially for developmental lags)
Referral for individual psychotherapy (e.g., play therapy)
Therapeutic play schools or regular school involvement
Foster grandmother in the hospital
Child companion, Big Brother or Big Sister program
Speech therapy, physical therapy, etc.
Petition to court
Etc.

4  **Siblings' Emotional and Physical Problems—Recommendations (same as 3)**

5  **Parents' Physical Problems—Recommendations**
Medical specialty clinic for evaluation and/or treatment
Dental services
Etc.

6  **Mother's Emotional Problems—Recommendations**
Public Health Nurse services (PHN)
Parent aide/lay therapist counselling
Group contact (e.g., Parents Anonymous, drug abuse group, Alcoholics Anonymous, or
other self-help groups)
Individual psychotherapy (clinic vs. inpatient unit) (psychologist vs. psychiatrist vs. SW)
Family counselling
Crisis outlets: 24-hour hot lines, crisis nursery, install a phone, provide workers' home
phone numbers, emergency home visits
Job training/have the mother return to work
Homemaker services/babysitters
Family planning
Reality therapy: forbidden to babysit by staff physician or police warning
Suicidal precautions
Etc.

7  **Father's or Mate's Emotional Problems—Recommendations** (same as 6)

8  **Other's Emotional Problems—Recommendations** (same as 6)

9  **Marital or Mate Relationship Problem—Recommendations** (same as 6 plus)
Marital counselling/sexual counselling
File for divorce

**Table 5-4.**  (Continued)

---

**10 Personal crises—recommendations**
Crisis intervention, crisis hotlines, crisis nursery, emergency babysitting services
Crisis anticipation and prevention

**11 Environmental Crises—Recommendations**
Environmental crisis therapy; i.e., financial assistance, emergency funds, food stamps, food, shelter, transportation, etc. (Note: These items should have first priority in order to restore some equilibrium to the home )

**12 Safety of the Home—Recommendations** (all above plus)
Close supervision accepted, child in the home (e.g., close followup via school, day care, PHN, or MD using total body surface exams twice weekly)
Court-ordered supervision, child in the home
Court-ordered supervision, child in foster care
Older children advised to call CPS for help if reabuse occurs
Voluntary foster home
Encourage voluntary relinquishment for adoption
Initiate termination of parental rights petition

At the bottom of the Master Treatment List the following is in capital letters:

THE COORDINATOR FOR THIS LONG TERM TREATMENT PROGRAM FOR THIS

FAMILY IS ___(give name)___ . THIS CASE IS TO BE REVIEWED ON ___(give date)___ .

---

### Example of a Problem Oriented Child Abuse and Neglect Report

Table 5–5 is a copy of a problem oriented summary of a multidisciplinary team diagnostic conference. This family has nine problems that have been delineated. Each is assigned a permanent number. The data that demonstrated the existence of each problem are listed. Under the emotional problems of a given person, an attempt is made to also list that person's strengths and assets. These might include special work skills, character strengths, family ties, close friendships, and so forth. Do not think of a problem as only deficits or bad. Families may have many positive attributes that make a given problem area much less significant.

Each of these nine problems has a recommendation written for it with an identical number. This fulfills one of the prerequisites of the problem oriented record; namely, that every problem must have a treatment plan. There is also a section called Additional Data, which includes important interview findings that don't fit into the above format. A final statement is recorded as to when the child protection team wants to review the case. All future progress notes made on this family in the child protection team's chart will begin with the appropriate problem number.

**Table 5–5.** A Child Abuse and Neglect Report

| | |
|---|---|
| **Dispositional Conference, 1/6/75** | Barton Schmitt (MD, Child Protection Team) |
| DOB: 7/12/73 | Marilyn McDonald (MD, Colo. Gen. Hosp.) |
| CGH# | Barbara Knapp (Nutritionist) |
| County: Adams | Elaine Clemmens (SW, Family Learning Ctr.) |
| 17-month-old boy | Debbie Palmer (Adams Co.) |
| Name: _____ | Pat Beezley (SW, Child Protection Team) |

## Problems and Recommendations

1 **Physical Abuse**
   33 bruises (1 strap mark, some grab marks); trauma X-rays negative
   Mother admits father caused several of the bruises

   **Recommendations**
   Written report to CPS
   Medical followup—CGH Peds Clinic (Dr. Gerrard)

2 **Question of Failure to Thrive**
   Height and weight 3rd percentile (father also short)
   Poor appetite/no gain in first 4 days
   Gained 600 gm. in 3 days but only with behavior modification

   **Recommendations**
   No validation of underfeeding; final diagnosis—short stature

3 **Patient's Emotional Problems**
   Developmentally slow
   Withdrawn; failure to respond appropriately to others
   Rare smile or interaction

   **Recommendations**
   Infant Stimulation Program

4 **Siblings' Emotional and Physical Problems**
   Two girls (ages 3 and 4) take care of mother and fearful of father
   Strength: not afraid of adults in general

   **Recommendations**
   Day care arranged

5 **Father's Physical Problems**
   Severe headaches, blurred vision, occasional unconsciousness, untreated since 1969,
      probably psychogenic

   **Recommendations**
   Thorough neurologic and physical workup at CGH Neurology Clinic

6 **Mother's Emotional Problems**
   Does not protect 3 children from father
   High expectations of children
   Pervasive denial and avoidance of conflict
   Beaten by father; domineering mother
   High risk score of 52
   Strength: has longstanding, close friend who is supportive

   **Recommendations**
   Treatment at Family Learning Center or Adams MHC
   Case worker counselling and followup; give 3 phone numbers for crisis or suggestion of
      suicide in husband

**Table 5-5.** (Continued)

---

7   **Father's Emotional Problems**
Currently "under a strain" at work: acutely depressed for more than 9 months
Possible thought disorder
History of deprivation; father died when his son was 6 years old
High risk score of 85

**Recommendations**
Full psych evaluation and urgent intensive psychotherapy at adult psychiatry clinic
Consider hold and treat order for psych hospitalization

8   **Environmental Problems/Crises**
Mother returned to work recently
Father must babysit evening hours

**Recommendations**
Father must not babysit; mother work days or other sitting arrangement

9   **Safety of the Home**
Severe bruises, different ages
Young age of child
Father is dangerous person currently
Mother not protective of children

**Recommendations**
Temporary foster care, court enforced
Review in one week
Case Coordinator ____(name given)_____

---

### Implementation of the Problem Oriented Record
### Format at Multidisciplinary Team Conferences

The first step in implementation is to have all team participants agree upon a standard nomenclature for problems in these cases. The previously listed twelve problems have gone through several revisions and are a good starting point. Ideally, a tentative listing of problems and recommendations should be prepared prior to the team meeting. This requires that each professional who evaluates any member of the family submit his tentative problem list and recommendations to the team coordinator. This would include the pediatrician, social worker, psychiatrist, and others. The premise behind this approach is that, if a person can perform a standard evaluation, he can also condense his findings into conclusions with a brief listing of the hard data that substantiate these conclusions. The coordinator then combines these problem lists prior to the meeting into a tentative team report. Each case discussion starts with time allotted for the team members to read the case summary to themselves. This permits the meeting time to focus on major decision making. After full discussion, the recommendations are usually modified and then retyped.

Another method of implementing this system is to have one team member who is familiar with the problem oriented format record the main points of the dispositional conference on a chalkboard during the meeting. After all the involved professionals have presented their evaluations, the team leader can focus peoples' attention on the data as he has recorded it. The team should then be encouraged to modify the data until agreement is reached. A team member who is not presenting can record the final version of the problem oriented notes as they appear on the chalkboard. These can then be typed after the meeting and distributed to all persons providing direct services to the family.

The problem oriented approach can be useful in the management of child abuse and neglect cases. The two prerequisites are a standard nomenclature for family problems and a willingness of professionals to organize and condense their data to fit this format. Once implemented, multidisciplinary team dispositional conferences should become both more relevant and efficient.

## ✳ Chapter Six

# Assessing Family Pathology

**Ruth Kempe and C. Henry Kempe**

The fundamental dysfunction in family interactions has been present long before the episode of abuse that brings the child to the attention of the community. The pathology involves all members of the family—father, mother, and their children. As family data are gathered, the preceding generations (at least the grandparents) also show difficulties, particularly in parenting skills. The pattern is often so clear-cut and so obviously present before the abusive incidents that the assessment of difficulty in parenting can be made in a predictive way (see Chapter Twenty). Unfortunately, in many situations parents are not seen until the difficulties have exploded into at least one episode of abuse. At this time of crisis for the entire family an assessment of the pathology must be made before any decisions can be taken as to the safety of the home and the child, as well as the potential of the family for treatment.

A generally accepted principle in psychiatry is that evaluation and treatment are most effective when offered as close to the time of crisis as possible. Parents ordinarily find the acknowledgment, even to themselves, of inflicted injury very difficult. If there is to be questioning by the police for any kind of criminal or legal procedures, there is pressure for the family to develop a story of the injury that seems to meet the needs of the situation. This interferes with an assessment of their true feelings. Parents become so concerned with keeping their story straight and defending it that their response to others may be minimal.

The social worker or physician who sees the family should not be concerned primarily with fixing blame, but rather with the possibility that abuse, having occurred once, could occur again. The degree of potential to abuse or neglect a child must be documented. The initial crisis offers an opportunity to gather necessary information and help the family when they are most in need. Defenses are ordinarily less intact, parents are more ready to express their true feelings, and there has been less time for them to become concerned with ways in which they might please the hospital staff and reassure community, legal, or protective workers that a true accident really did occur.

A comprehensive family assessment should be made as soon after the injury to the child as possible: within the first 24 to 48 hours if feasible. In spite of this rapid schedule, the time available to the parents should be as leisurely as possible in order that the worker not feel rushed and compelled to ask rapid-fire questions. On the contrary, the interviewer must encourage the parent to express feelings freely, listening for the subtle nuances that indicate areas of potential difficulty. This ordinarily means that a time period of approximately one or one and one-half hours should be available for each parent, both together and separately, in order to cover completely the material needed and to allow time for each parent to discuss those things that are of concern and for which advice, support, or information is needed.

Which personnel are most appropriate to do an evaluation of family pathology? If one uses a team approach, which is strongly advocated, there are many members of the team who will have something to contribute to this evaluation. The primary responsibility for assessing family pathology—i.e., determining the potential for abuse as seen in the psychosocial background of the family—will ordinarily be taken by the social worker, by a psychologist or psychiatrist if available, or some other suitable professional who has been trained in interviewing techniques and evaluation of psychological illness. Specially trained personnel may not be available and the evaluation must be done by the nurse, physician, or social worker who has the opportunity to see the family.

## WHEN IS PSYCHIATRIC
## ASSESSMENT MANDATORY?

There are occasions when psychiatric or psychological evaluation is absolutely necessary. This is true when the injury has been severe and the possibility of termination of parental rights or long separation is likely to be recommended. Court action involving as serious a decision as termination of parental rights often requires professionals designated as "expert witnesses." There are some courts which permit a specialist social worker to be so designated, but other courts insist that the social worker's evaluation be backed up by another professional, in which case psychiatric or psychological evaluations must be done. Professionals who originally see the family in an emergency room, hospital clinic, private office, school, or community facility can make a preliminary judgment concerning this question, and also arrange for total psychiatric evaluation at the earliest time when it would be most helpful to the family.

Ideally a competent psychiatrist and/or clinical psychologist should be available and involved in the assessment of *every* case of serious abuse or neglect. While nice, this clearly is not feasible in many, if not most, communities. When, then, *must* a psychiatric assessment be made? An experienced clinician (social worker, nurse, physician) may get a "feeling" when all is not right, but this is not sufficient. The following are some of the more clear-cut indications for psychiatric assessment.

1. When the family dynamics don't fit or match many or any of the standard classic histories found in 80 percent-plus cases of abuse and neglect. That is, an obvious case of serious abuse and neglect where the parents are not found to have a poor rearing experience, isolation, poor self-image, unrealistic expectations of children, and so forth.
2. When premeditated abuse has occurred—e.g., a father who planned the setting of the house on fire to burn his children.
3. When torture has taken place, such as tying a child to a chair and burning him with a cigarette.
4. When one part of the body is constantly picked on—e.g., the left arm is repeatedly broken or the penis is repeatedly twisted.
5. When there is distortion of reality and what the parent says just doesn't make sense—e.g., "My baby is a whore". . . . "*I* caused my parents' divorce when I was 20 because I was conceived out of wedlock."
6. Inappropriate responses to questions indicating a loss of affect—e.g., "How do you feel today?" "I don't have feelings."
7. Severe depression.
8. Religious or culturally-based fanaticism.
9. Ongoing drug/alcohol addiction.
10. Bizzare ideas that seem to make little or no sense.

The special contribution by the psychiatrist or psychologist, in addition to the assessment of the quality of parenting, is to determine the presence or absence of serious psychiatric illness through the medium of a mental status examination and a general psychiatric evaluation. This is important in order to establish the immediate safety of the home, the treatability of the parents, and the type of treatment that will be most appropriate for the family.

Approximately 10 to 15 percent of parents seen have psychiatric diagnoses that make their potential for treatment very poor. These diagnoses include parents who are psychotic, particularly those who appear as paranoid schizophrenic or schizophrenic patients with a delusional system that involves the child as part of the delusional system. Some psychotic parents are so disabled by their illness, at least at the time when they are first seen, that they are not able to function in any caretaking capacity. This may be true of *severely* depressed parents, who do not have the energy or the capacity for the involvement required to care for a small child. A few schizophrenic patients appear able to function well as parents; but this may change as the child develops and his behavior no longer fits into the parent's pathological ideation. Such a situation needs careful monitoring if the child is to remain with the parent.

In addition to psychoses and severe neurotic depressions, there are a group of parents who present as very severe character disorders or sociopathic personality disorders. There are parents who have often been in severe trouble with the law, who tend to explode in violent behavior. Prognosis for improvement in these patients is comparatively poor. Other diagnoses with poor prognosis for treatment include severe alcoholism and severe drug addiction. Alcoholic and drug addicted parents are minimally capable of caring for children since their intoxication makes them unsafe unless they are in a controlled, safe environment. Treatment may be very long and difficult, and significant improvement must occur before these parents are able to care for a child on their own. Many in this group will never be able to parent adequately, for the urgency of the child's own developmental timetable will preclude such a delay.

A final group which has responded very poorly to treatment is a comparatively small group of parents who are "fanatic"—those parents who have a highly fixed set of ideas that are ordinarily considered eccentric and that probably represent obsessional ideas in psychiatric terms. They are frequently related to a fundamentalist religion or an unusual philosophy of life. They may sometimes be extremely moralistic, very successful and very well respected people—"pillars of society"—making the diagnosis very difficult. When their ideas include unusual exploitation of children, and establish deviant standards of behavior plus unusual and cruel punishments, this becomes a very dangerous environment for children. Their rigidity is a well established ideational system, and they are very resistant to treatment.

## ASSESSING THE MORE TYPICAL
## ABUSIVE PARENTS

Having ruled out a group of parents with a poor treatment prognosis, approximately 85 percent of abusive parents will remain whose personality diagnoses cover the spectrum seen in the general population. A comparatively high percentage of these parents have severe difficulties in coping with life. Their symptoms vary: depression, immaturity, impulsive behavior, inadequate personality, and passive-aggressive personality are all common descriptors. What they all do share are specific difficulties in parenting, and these seem to occur frequently in a constellation of findings as follows.

1. Historically they were abused or deprived as children.
2. However successful or effective they appear, their emotional relationships are inadequate. Isolation, distrust, and minimal support systems are the rule.
3. They cope poorly with many crises, most often when they are made to feel rejected or inadequate.
4. They show role reversal, expecting their children to meet *their* needs and make *them* feel better. They see physical punishment as an appropriate reaction to failure of the child to respond as they wish in meeting those needs.

5. Their self-image is defective; they are convinced they really aren't "any damn good."

When the family is first seen, many falsely assume that seeing the mother is sufficient. A mother alone may, on initial contact, seem to present herself and the family as within "normal" limits; yet when the father is seen, the difficulties may become apparent, the relationship between the parents presenting with more obvious pathology. Both parents must be seen. In families where only one parent is present and a boyfriend or girlfriend functions as a part time parent or caretaker, he or she should also be evaluated. There are many situations in which it has been found that the mother, having lost her husband, will form a relationship with another man or succession of men who minimally care and provide for her with the support she desperately needs. In the process this new man may be abusive to her children, and often to her. Because she depends on him and feels herself unable to function alone, she tolerates the abuse of her children and herself in order to maintain the relationship and her own support. She may even feel she deserves the abuse. Another example of the importance of the relationships between the parents and its effect upon the question of abuse occurs when a father is competitive with his children for the attention and love of his wife. He may feel deprived when she seems more concerned with the child's welfare. Under such circumstances, the father may become quite angry at this deprivation of his own needs and vent his rage upon the child rather than upon his wife.

Not only must the parents be fully assessed, but each child in the family should also be fully evaluated. Almost without exception the children will be found to have psychological symptoms and developmental deficits stemming from the physical abuse and attendant neglect of their needs. Even when the injury does not cause serious physical damage, the child is in emotional jeopardy. All siblings in the family must be assessed, for they have suffered either psychological or physical abuse by their very presence in this environment. They may have escaped the notice of the community but are still in urgent need of professional help.

When the parents are seen initially, they should be made to feel that the time is not set aside for questioning them so much as to determine how someone can be helpful to them. Whether the parents are first seen together or separately will depend to a considerable extent on their own wishes. Certainly when they are seen together, one can develop a clearer picture of their relationship. One learns who may be dominant in the relationship and the extent to which they can both agree not only upon the story of the present injury, but upon their perception of their family. The parents must also be seen separately. Frequently one finds that differences of opinion and discrepancies in personal and mental history become apparent. A better understanding of each parent as an individual as well as the relationship between them is gained when they are no longer being defensive with one another.

The material to be covered in the evaluation of the parents includes the story of the incident and the crisis that occurred leading up to injury, as well as the situation in which the parents now find themselves. The needs of the parents to discuss their worries, their anxieties, their possible anger at the events that have already taken place must be recognized. The hospitalization of the child, the question of abuse, the physician's refusal to accept the accidental nature of the injuries, the intervention of many new people, are all most upsetting. The parents' discomfort and unhappiness concerning these events can be recognized without being dishonest with them or offering false assurances. Frequently a discussion of their feelings may be the first time in which they find someone concerned for them as individuals. Someone who is able to be empathic with the discomfort and fear they feel, but is also able to help them discuss the realities of their situation, is a rarity in their lives.

Accusation and critical questions in a disbelieving way are devastating to these parents. Descrepancies in the parents' stories are compared when different interviews obtain inconsistencies. Accusation and skepticism only confirm for the parents their expectation that they will be once more criticized and punished and that no one can understand or help them. In talking with someone who can understand their feelings, if not approve their behavior, they have made an initial step toward being able to accept themselves. One can often be mislead by the apparent anger and self-defense of parents, who will loudly proclaim they have done nothing wrong or that the child deserved the punishment he received. Many months later, after considerable treatment, that they may admit to their feelings of guilt and even to the fact that the punishment and injury actually was inflicted by them.

The social worker or physician may have difficulty in being able to empathize with the parents since he has seen the injury suffered by the child. Recognizing and handling one's own feelings about the family is mandatory. Parents who are abusive are not easy to like until the world from which they came is understood. Since these parents have never learned to give feedback or cues that enhance interpersonal communication, those who work with them must be very astute to pick up the innuendos of acceptance that, finally, appear. For example, keeping an appointment (albeit two days late), returning a phone call, asking a question, lifting a head to look at you, eventually even a smile—unless these subtleties are picked up, the task of assessing these families can be most discouraging.

Family discord and stress before the episode of abuse are likely. Such crises may at times be major, and involve the loss of a job, the threat of breakdown of the marriage, or illness of the child. At other times they may be comparatively minor and only seem the final straw in a generally unhappy life situation for either parent. At these times the comparatively minor external stress is bound to have special significance for the parents and to represent some kind of psychological loss. For example, criticism by a mother or mother-in-law or disappointment from a potential friend may lead to feelings of anger and misery which cannot be expressed, finding their final outlet in overreaction to a minor provocation by the child.

In discussing the family's present situation, the importance of social-economic factors will become readily apparent. Frequently there are financial difficulties, which can contribute to the stress of relationships within the family. The parents may have difficulty making friends, and one finds that they are socially isolated with no people to whom they can turn in time of trouble, no people whom they truly trust. This often includes their immediate family, whom they have generally found do not provide help and assistance in time of need. As children they had to pay for such requests for help by being criticized, made to feel inadequate and guilty, ultimately loosing their own self-respect. Under these circumstances, isolation is often preferable, until they become desperate.

Sometimes difficulty with the law—particularly in situations in which the spouse is a sociopathic personality and frequently in trouble—may add to the family stress. Physical health is often poor for the parents or for their children, causing additional worry and actual difficulty in the performance of parental function. A history of "nervous breakdowns," or psychiatric help and treatment, often hospitalization, may indicate the longstanding and serious nature of the emotional difficulty. All these potential areas of stress may be seen as contributing to the difficulties in the marriage and to the parents' relationship with their children.

The marriage or relationship between the two mates is of great importance both historically and at the present time. Helpful information includes knowing when in their lives and why the parents were married. Often they married very young in order to get away from an uncomfortable home situation; marriage may have been impulsive and without adequate knowledge of the strengths and weaknesses of each partner. The early history of each parent is thus of great importance, including memories of their childhood and happenings in the early history of their relationship with their own parents. Frequently such episodes will be unhappy, traumatic, and often involve severe physical punishment and/or continual criticisms. The parents often see their own parents as having always been dissatisfied with them, always ready to criticize or punish, and frequently as violent or brutal. In talking of their *present* relationship with their own parents one may find that, while they begin with a bland statement of how good their parents are, one soon finds that with further details there is a strong element of disappointment; that their parents rarely provide any support.

Information concerning a parent's siblings is also helpful. The parent himself (herself) may have escaped severe physical punishment by making a major effort at pleasing his parents. A coalition between the child and parents against an abused sibling may have been established. Information concerning these siblings' current life adjustment is thus very useful. Frequently siblings have had difficulties with their own children and may perhaps have been abusive or lost their children because of neglect or nonaccidental injury. Knowledge of possible separations, divorce, illness, or death, resulting in children being deprived of one or the other parent, may indicate long periods of time in which the children's needs were not adequately met. Emotional and perhaps physical deprivation often occurs during these periods. Such parental loss may contribute to serious problems in adult life.

School adjustment, intellectual capacity, reactions to school authority and teachers, as well as relationships with other adults, all indicate a capacity to form relationships and develop support outside the home. Inappropriate relationships with peers and minimal capacity for friendships is also relevant and may indicate isolation or a tendency toward violence and fighting developed at an early age. How far the parents went in school and the reasons for their leaving are indications not only of their capacity to perform intellectually but also of the degree of stability and personal expectation. Inadequate stability may have resulted in leaving home at an early age, either to take a job or to marry. Job history indicates, again, the reactions to authority, capacity to sustain self-discipline, to get along with others and develop new skills. Frequent job changes may demonstrate either difficulty in interpersonal relationships of a major degree, a high degree of impulsivity, or inadequate skills. Another particularly useful area in questioning is how the parent sees himself. If a parent has a very poor self-image—sees himself as stupid, bad, or unable to make friends because no one likes him—that parent is extremely vulnerable to crises and stress.

### How the Parents See Their Child

With this background the potentially abusive and/or neglectful parent decides that a baby becomes the only possible hope finally to meet his or her own needs through the love expected from the child. The generational cycle has gone full circle and again one has a parent with unrealistic expectations and hopes for his child, a parent poorly prepared for the very role he or she desperately desires. Lack of emotional preparation, few supports systems, poor personal relationships, inadequate social skills to deal with the difficulties of mature adult life, all result in one ill-prepared parent.

The next step is to evaluate how the parents see their child and their own role as a parent. When a parent is asked to describe the child in detail, a worker may find that the description focuses on how well the child meets the parent's needs. The child is perceived as a "good child" if he is capable of meeting these expectations and as a "bad child" if he does not. In asking for the parents' ideas of appropriate behavior for a child of a given age, one discovers that their perception has little relationship to normal child development. An abusive parent states, with approval, that a four-year-old little girl is good because she has helped to toilet train her two-year-old brother, clean up the living room every morning, and is always watching out for her two younger siblings, playing with them and showing concern for their safety. Of course she is also expected to take major responsibility for her own care.

In such a description one finds that the child is attempting to meet the parents' needs by helping with parenting and housekeeping functions. There is little or no recognition on the part of the parent that the child, herself, needs support and the opportunity to develop on her own timetable without the interference produced by such role-reversing burdens. However, if the child becomes difficult or disobedient, unwilling or unable to meet parental expectations, then she is perceived as deliberately bad, disobedient, or stupid, and may be punished for disobedience or unwillingness to perform impossible tasks.

When one has all the information described above—(1) psychiatric diagnosis, (2) current life situation, (3) potential for abuse, (4) capacity to be a parent, and (5) motivation for treatment and change—then one can make an appropriate treatment plan. This may require hospitalization for those parents who are acutely psychotic or depressed, or a referral for long term therapy as an outpatient, which offers a more supportive and less insight oriented treatment.

## EVALUATING THE ABUSED CHILD
## AND SIBLING

Evaluation of the abused child and his siblings should come second only to the evaluation of the parents' capacity to keep them at home. Almost without exception we have found that when these children are adequately evaluated by the professional staff, they show evidence of severe emotional pathology, resulting from the psychological abuse, neglect, and deprivation which always accompanies physical abuse. While the long term importance of these factors has not been fully established, our impression is that physical abuse is a symptom of poor parenting and as such does not necessarily play the major role in the developmental effects upon the child. Psychological deprivation may be far more damaging to personality development. This is why the abused child's sibling may be in as much jeopardy as is the victim. In the young developing child the primary pathway for the expression of damaging influences seems to be interference with and delay in the developmental process, (see Chapter Three).

In diagnosing the effects of abuse upon the children, the physical status of each child in the family is first considered. When physical injuries have occurred there may be possibilities of physical abnormalities, brain damage, or crippling. As examples, poor growth from failure to thrive, and localized smallness of a limb from an epiphyseal injury in a long bone can occur. The neurological examination is of prime importance because many children suffer neurological injury in addition to other physical trauma. Approximately one-third of 58 children followed by Martin et al.[1] had neurological deficits. While some of these neurological deficits may have preceded the injury, the greater likelihood was that they were the result of physical injury or failure to thrive at an early age.

In addition to the physical and neurological examination, the abused child and his siblings should have a developmental assessment or a psychological testing. Very useful are nurse's, social worker's or homemaker's observations of interactional behavior with his parents and with other individuals. For the young infant, observations during appropriate hospital or clinic situations, such as feeding, diapering, and playing, will give considerable information concerning the interaction between the parents and the child. Are the parental expectations of the child realistic and is the child acting his age? These are the key questions. A comparative lack of interaction—for example, holding the child far away from the body on the edge of the lap, handling him roughly when feeding or diapering, and not talking to the child—are indications of the lack of a close, warm relationship between parent and child. A parent may often express disapproval of a child's responses, making threats of punishment if he is messy in eating or does not remain quiet during diapering. Even though such threats may be made in a joking way, they indicate the way in which the parent thinks of the infant.

Developmental data should be obtained in a more systematic fashion by the use of any one of standard tests, such as the Denver Developmental Screening Test, the Bayley or the Yale Developmental Scale. These may indicate delays in development and a comparative lack of social response. Such delays begin to occur quite early, sometimes observable in the third or fourth months. In the older infant and toddler while developmental examination and observation are also appropriate, one might wish to use a modified psychiatric play interview in order to provide a child with more opportunity for spontaneous reaction. Play interviews provide a standard set of toys chosen to provide a scope of differing interests, plus an expression of common affects and impulses. They encourage the supportive, nondirective, but encouraging participation of the professional, trained to respond appropriately to a child of such an age. Even with children under two, one can derive a wealth of information as to their capacity to deal with a relationship with a stranger, to use an adult for help, to seek enjoyment and communication with his world.

The observer can also document the child's gross and fine motor skills, language and capacity to utilize the toys in an appropriate and satisfying way. Speech evaluation becomes important during the second year of life. When a delay in speech—which is one of the most striking findings in abused children—becomes apparent, abuse has been present for some time. (For further discussion on speech delay, see Chapter Three).

Inhibition of affect is also noted in some children who seems not to feel pain, pleasure, or anger in an appropriate way. During a play interview, the minimal capacity of the abused child to respond to an interpersonal relationship, his anxiety, expectation of criticism, disapproval, or punishment may be readily seen.

Unusual compliance and efforts to please the adult are also noted. Many abused children will see themselves as bad and stupid, having a poor self-image at a very early age. Approximately three-quarters of the children seen will be unduly compliant and the remainder are negativistic and aggressive. Very active and aggressive children may be seen as a possible example of neurological involvement leading to hyperactivity. On occasion an organic basis for the hyperactivity may be present. In most situations, however, the hyperactivity observed is an expression of the child's intense, overriding anxiety. Whether hyperactive or aggressive, a supportive, warm, yet highly structured environment is most helpful to the hyperactive child, whether or not medication is used.

The school-aged child also benefits from evaluation including physical and neurological examinations, psychological testing, and psychiatric evaluations. These children are less apt to have speech difficulties still present, but their ability to communicate, especially feelings, is impaired. Symptoms are now being noted in a child with a personality of increasing complexity in whom many types of coping styles are developing; for example, compliance may begin to give way to aggression. For his own protection the child has a tendency to collude with the parents in denying the abuse, even though the child is most aware of its occurrence and results. This leads to confusion on his part, since he is also beginning to realize he is not always at fault. However, the school-aged child is still very apt to accept blame for his punishment, to accept his parents' evaluation of him as bad, stupid, or disobedient and therefore deserving of his unhappy situation.

The aggressive, hyperactive child finds that his symptoms cause considerable difficulty in attempting to adjust to any school situation. Many of these children become academic and social failures almost immediately upon entering school. An additional complicating factor in older children is that their educational and behavioral difficulties are often seen as intrinsic, and the possibility of abuse as a major causative factor may not be entertained by the school. This is true particularly when no such medical diagnosis has been made prior to the child's entering the school system.

## IMPORTANCE OF EVALUATION

Evaluation of the abused child and his or her siblings is of enormous importance because at the present time a variety of treatment modalities are being developed that can begin to offset and reverse the detrimental effects of inadequate parenting. For the young infant and toddler one can provide alternative rearing experiences in a safe and supportive environment without breaking ties with the parents if the situation warrants continuation of the child at home. Until we have learned how to help parents improve their parenting skills much more rapidly than at present, this is by far the most desirable plan.

Disruption of the relationship between parent and child further increases difficulties in interaction which are already so threatened by the parents' intrapsychic problems. In addition to these alternative rearing experiences a program of stimulation through play, with the participation of the parent if at all possible, using professional personnel as a teaching and parent modeling resource is most beneficial. If the parent is not available or not sufficiently motivated, preschool and school personnel may be used to offer this very important treatment modality to the very young abused child.

When the child must be placed in a foster home for safety requirements, the foster parents must provide a stimulating and supportive developmental environment. Foster parents should be seen and trained as lay therapists so the treatment can continue within this setting. The individual evaluation of the child will serve to identify those areas in which special help is most urgently needed in order to reverse developmental delay. This is accomplished by encouraging the development of speech, emotional expression and the building of more appropriate and satisfactory relationships.

This diagnostic assessment can be used not only in specialized therapeutic preschool but also in preschool or day care settings with available advisory personnel able to interpret findings and consultation with the staff. For some children who are more severely disturbed, often the hyperactive and aggressive child, individual psychotherapy in a playroom setting may be an additional necessity to supplement the day care, preschool, or head start program. The need to include individual psychotherapy and possibly other treatment modalities such as speech therapy, physiotherapy for neurological and physical defects, will depend upon the completeness of the individual child's diagnosis and the community's responsiveness to the needs of these troubled children.

※ **Chapter Seven**

# Sexual Exploitation

Marshall D. Schechter and
Leo Roberge

## INTRODUCTION

A month before Christmas, the patient appeared decidely ambivalent about vacationing with her parents. She was 26 years old, single, a research assistant with a Master of Science degree from a major university. She had been in psychoanalysis for two months at that time. Her concerns about the vacation at home were voiced with evident anxiety which increased as she indicated her desire to see, but fear of being physically in contact with her father. With great hesitation she told of her father's sexual involvements with her since she was 11 years of age. No matter how many times she verbally objected, no matter how long she was away from home, no matter how many sexual affairs she had, no matter how many times she asked her mother to intercede (the requests were rejected each time), within a few hours of her return home her father was insisting on sexual contact. This pattern continued throughout college and thereafter. Her father, a banker and former mayor of his city, had a PhD in business administration.

The reason this woman came into treatment was because of compulsive promiscuity and difficulty in attaining any long lasting or satisfying inter-personal relationships with male or female friends. There were no signs of psychotic defenses. Diagnostically she fell into a category of a characterological disorder. As she described her initial involvements with her father, it retro-spectively appeared to her that of the three children (she had a younger brother and sister) she had always been her father's favorite. When she was eleven, under the guise of helping with her bath, her father washed her genitals to the point of orgasm. Manual manipulation continued for some time before she was asked to touch his genitals manually, then orally, with penetration vaginally not occuring until she was 14 years of age. Dating was permitted when she was 16, but her father insisted on interrogating each boy at the first meeting and required her back home by 11:30 no matter what the occasion.

For the first few years, the patient talked to her mother because she felt guilty about the sexual contact with her father. On each occasion her mother told her not to bother her with this information and that if she was uncomfortable in the relationship with her father that she should handle it herself. As she recalled it, her mother on the last few times they spoke of this became quite angry, telling her to leave her alone and never to speak of these things with her again.

## HISTORY OF SEXUAL EXPLOITATION

Moses was born of the union of his nephew and his aunt (Num. 26:59; Ex. 6:20). Abraham was married to his paternal sister (Gen. 20:12) and Jacob married two sisters (Gen. 29:21 ff). It was suggested by the writer of the book of Jubilees that the sons of Adam married their sisters (Jub. 4) indicating that one reason for incest was to populate the earth or, in subsequent times, to insure good stock (cf. Gen. 24:3–4ff; 28:1ff). This also was described in the story of Lot and his daughters (Gen. 19:31–35).

As evidenced in Leviticus, the book of Laws, prohibitions against such relationships with one's "near of kin" were severe and exact (Lev. 18:6, 18: 7–18, 20:14). The exact description of consanguinity defined also which punishments should be inflicted from death by burning or some divine punishment while in Talmudic law, punishments ranged from death by stoning or burning to flogging. Incest was included as one of three offenses along with murder and idolatry which could not be committed even to save the individual from certain death (Sanh. 74a), or in order to save another person's life (Tosef Shab 15:17) or for any medical reasons (Shab 14:4). A female's enjoyment during incestuous relationships was connoted as constituting an overt act for which her punishment was to be flogging (Tos. Bk 32a).

In the case of incest in the Corinthian Church, Paul stated: "Let him who has done this be removed from among you. . . . . You are to deliver this man to Satan for the destruction of the flesh" (I Cor. 5:2, 5). Isaac Levy[1] gives a modern day and sympathetic view of historical documents in the following: "Leviticus XVIII contains a comprehensive list of the unions between the sexes which are repellant to the finer feelings of man. In this connection it may be said that while there are some whose sensitiveness is revolted by such detailed descriptions of the various forms of incest referred to in Lev. XVIII, and are even appalled that this passage should form the selected reading from *Torah* on Yom Kippur afternoon, its inclusion in the *Torah* is indicative of the "true to life" approach which scripture adopts towards such intensely human situations.

In Babylonia, the Hammurabi code (circa 2000 B.C.E.) was established defining legally, among other things, incestuous alliances with mother, step-mother, daughter and daughter-in-law. Various cultures in the past related social misfortunes to incestuous relationships as the Galelareese of Halmahera explain torrential rains, the Celts of ancient Ireland regarding crop failures and the people of Thebes concerning the sterility of both women and cattle as well as other disasters because of the actions of Oedipus. The mythological stories of Cronus and Rhea, Zeus and Hera, and Osiris and Isis indicate that gods, like more modern day kings, married their sisters, possibly to ensure their title to the throne.[2]

### Definition

The sexual exploitation of children refers to the involvement of dependent, developmentally immature children and adolescents in sexual activities that they do not fully comprehend, are unable to give informed consent to, and that violate the social taboos of family roles. This article will particularly focus on incest rather than child molestation in general because of its more insidious, collusive, secretive, and chronically pervasive course within a family.

The word incest derives from the Latin *incestum,* which means unchaste and low. Anthropological studies have noted that incest most closely approximates a universal taboo.[3] Whether Freud's concept of a primal horde, in *Moses* and *Monotheism,* concerns about genetic inbreeding or the Bible's ferocious proscriptions in *Leviticus* shaped this particular behavior, people today still view incest as the riskiest of family secrets.[4] Approaches to study and intervention in this disorder invariably arouse "gallows humor," collusive denial, or severe retribution. Nevertheless, the topic frequently intrudes into literature, (e.g., O'Neill, Proust, Freud, Shakespeare) movies (e.g., *Chinatown*), and other art forms as if seeking a covert resolution. Data collection and scientific study have been markedly impaired by what has been euphemistically referred to as a "family affair."

### Incidence

Incidence reports on incest are particularly unreliable. Families involved fear dissolution if discovered. Physicians express marked discomfort at such major social improprieties or have a lowered index of suspicion as to its existence. Courts insist on the strict rules of evidence which make family members adversaries with marked biases in their testimony and low conviction rates. In contrast to sexual molestation in general, the family as a whole supports actively or passively their own "incestuous equilibrium." Usually case finding occurs adventitiously with family quarrels, pregnancy, psychoses, or some criminal charge. How often incest passes undetected at present remains in the area of conjecture. Weinberg estimated at the turn of the century an incidence rate of one to two cases per million population.[5] More recently, the Children's Division of the American Humane Society reported 5,000 cases annually for the United States.[6]

When compared to reported child sexual abuse in general, incest comprises 10 percent of the total.[7] In a prison population of sexual offenders, only 2.5 to 4 percent involve incest.[8] Eaton and Vastbinder reported 28 cases of incest yearly from a population of 33,361 emergency room visits in Columbus, Ohio.[7] In an unselected psychiatric population, the historical evidence of incest occurred in 4 percent of the cases.[9] Most of these authors generally view these figures on incest to be but the tip of the iceberg. With the added strains placed on the family unit, the ready availability of birth control and abortion to deal with embarrassing pregnancies without question, and the loosening of sexual prohibitions, there are probably even greater numbers involved.

### Socioeconomic Status

Most studies of incest implicate lower socioeconomic groups, where factors such as crowding and lack of intergenerational privacy are felt to be involved.[9,10,11] Sarles notes, however, that data biases for this group occurs because of the greater dependence on anonymous public institutions for their care.[12] The stereotype of poor mountain people living in remote areas and inbreeding often dominates our thinking on incest. Such factors as limited social access, geographic barriers, and the need to maintain ethnic identities do promote incestuous behaviors. However, European royalty successfully promoted intrafamilial incest in order to maintain wealth and power.

The private practitioner who has known a family for some time and on whom his reputation and remuneration rely, can more readily be manipulated into complicity with this family secret. In conversations with such private practitioners, many report significant examples of middle and upper class involvement in incest (cf. Case Reports below). Sociocultural factors may contribute to incest, but obviously it is not a critical factor in this multidimensional aberration.

### Intelligence

Intellectual subnormality is often implicated in incest. Williams and Hall reported that of 68 persons convicted of incest, 24 percent were of low or subnormal intelligence.[13] In a complementary study of the sexually abused children, 30 percent of these 8 to 14-year-old girls were considered retarded.[14] Takagi has tried to explain this in terms of the discrepancies in the retarded between physical and cognitive-social development, a greater familial dependency because of their emotional and physical needs, and the narrower range of interests in their lives.[15]

Where retardation is a factor in the child, the incestuous relationship tends to be more prolonged. However, the majority of incest cases seem to involve average to above average intelligence in the participants. The great concern of parents that their retarded child may be unduly sexually compromised may be a projection of their own feelings in addition to the more generally accepted reality concerns. Intelligence in itself probably only plays a minor role in the problem of incest.

### Age

Data as to age of the incest partners generates interesting developmental hypotheses. Three-quarters of all incest involves father-daughter relationships. The father is usually middle-aged (30–50 years old) with the average onset age in the mid 30s[9,13,16] In men, these years are characterized by reassessment of their goals and a more realistic appraisal of their future potential. For many this is a sobering and often depressing period of unfulfilled expectations. Realization of diminishing potency in their lives, and the sometimes accompanying rejection by their spouses, provides a psychological backdrop for regressive sexual behavior.

The daughters of these middle-aged fathers are usually entering adolescence, with all its profound physiological and social changes. The increased sexual drive frequently produces an acceptance of the incestuous relationship if not at times seductive partner whose tenuous oedipal resolution make her especially vulnerable. She oftentimes is the eldest daughter. The girls involved in incest ranged in age from 5 to 16 with an average age of 8½ at the time of onset in Lukianowicz's series.[9] Other males involved are often brothers, other family members, baby sitters—all of whom the child knows well and with whom she has many affectionate ties.

### Sex

The sex of the child and the perpetuator have very definite patterns. The active aggressor almost invariably is a male and the passive recipient is usually female, although homosexual acts are also reported with males. Stoenner published a ratio of ten girl victims to each boy.[6] Seventy-eight percent of all reported incest involves father-daughter; eighteen percent sibling; 1 percent mother-son; and the remainder, multiple relationships within the family.[5] It has been observed, however, that mothers sleeping with their school-age sons, referring to them as "lovers," or actually sexually stimulating them has greater cultural acceptance than similar acts between father and daughter. These covert acts beyond the toddler age might represent the grey area of incestuous sex. Only the most disturbed of these relationships seemingly warrant societal condemnation. Weinberg noted that in his series, such mothers were severely disturbed, and oftentimes the son as well.[5] (It is a curious fact that mother-daughter relationships are never mentioned in the context of incest.)

### Nature of the Incestuous Act

Violence rarely accompanies the incestuous act. Seduction, passive compliance, or sexual curiosity and exploration promote such relationships.[7,16] At times it can be seen as a vengeful or competitive challenge to the other spouse by the adolescent.[17] The onset of incestuous sexual relationships frequently follows frustration in the marital sexual activity by illness, death, absence, or refusal and disgust by the spouse.[16] Occasionally, the rejecting wife offers the daughter as a compensation to her husband for her own promiscuity. Usually the contacts are frequent, even daily, with other members of the family actively avoiding or passively complying with the situation. These relationships often occur over many years' duration, usually terminating with the daughter leaving home for marriage or a career. The next oldest daughter may then take on her sister's role. Occasionally such relationships are thrust into community awareness because of extraneous factors such as an unrelated family quarrel.[12]

Guilt seldom plays a significant role in the majority of cases especially if the relationship is mutually satisfying.[18] Defenses such as denial, rationalization, and projection ward off threatening affects. One mother, when asked about her feelings concerning her recently revealed husband-daughter incest, replied, "He gave up smoking and needed something to help him through." Sarles reports the surprise on the part of the parent that the community should be so concerned: "I was only trying to show her the right way before some rough kid hurt her," a father replied to accusations of sexual abuse of his daughter.[12] The daughters might rationalize their feelings by stating that they never enjoyed it. Most of the guilt and shame arise from disclosure or the growing awareness of the adolescents of acceptable social roles.

### Personality Factors

The personalities of incestuous fathers have not been examined in rigorous scientific fashion to rule out sample bias. Particular categories and trends, however, have emerged through the literature. Weinberg has categorized them as follows: (1) An introversive personality with extreme intrafamiliar orientation and with minimal extrafamilial social contact; (2) a psychopathic personality characterized by indiscriminate sexuality, inability to form tender attachments with spouse and children, and who views them as objects; (3) a pedophilic personality who is psychosexually and socially immature and who seduces both his and other children.[5]

Sebhard could distinguish no characteristic personality differences between a population of incestuous fathers and other sexual offenders. Weiner examined a group of five middle class incestuous fathers and discovered no psychosis in any, above average intelligence, and difficulties with adult male identification.[17] Paranoid traits and unconscious homosexual strivings have also been reported by Cavallin.[19] The designations of inadequate personalities, aggressive psychopaths, and alcoholics recur frequently in the literature describing incestuous fathers.[5,9,17]

Lukianowicz also draws attention to the father's family background.[9] Many have originated from broken homes, have little formal schooling, and early (e.g., 15 years old) departures from home.[16] Often he has a history of being sexually demanding and has a poorly integrated social conscience. Frequently the father has a poor work history and is unemployed during the time of the incestuous activity. In summary, these incestuous fathers do not exhibit severe psychopathology or marked cognitive deficits but rather have a poorly integrated social perception that can affect many other areas of their lives in addition to their inappropriate sexual incursions.

The wives in these father-daughter incest families may either exhibit immaturity and passive dependency or can actively encourage the incest relationship as a means of compensating for their own promiscuity. The incest frequently is precipitated by the wife by sexually frustrating her spouse[13] or recoiling in disgust at his behaviors and excesses (i.e., alcoholism, infidelity, pedophilia). Many of these wives exhibit pathologic dependency on their spouses which outweighs any sense of outrage at their husbands' behavior. These mothers seek to preserve their families at all cost. This dependency often derives from a similar relationship to their own mothers. Never having achieved any sense of an autonomous adult female sexuality, they in turn foster premature pseudomaturity in their daughters, thus completing the three-generational psychodynamics of incest.[9,12,20]

The daughters are in turn caught up in this triadic family "love affair." Struggling as they may be with their own emerging sexuality and oedipal feelings and fantasies, these young girls are particularly vulnerable to family pressures. They may be even influenced by siblings as well to reduce the marital tension and preserve their family from disintegration and possible abandonment. Their own mothers have been inadequate models for sexual identification or protection. How difficult it is to share such a secret with the outside world with its not uncommon idiosyncratic responses.

Daughters who have had these developmentally inappropriate responsibilities thrust upon them, and no one with whom to safely share their dilemma, often develop resentment towards their parents and early separation from them. Hypochondriacal or neurasthenic symptoms may develop in response to such multiple stresses or occasionally a full blown hysterical conversion.[12] More chronic responses include characterological defenses against sexual feelings, developing symptoms of promiscuity and/or frigidity. Any guilt felt in these relationships by the daughter seems to derive mainly from society's responses. Weiner noted that their denial may take the form of never allowing themselves to enjoy the sexual experience. The later development of frigidity and hysterical personalities might well derive from this defense.[17]

Incest occurring before the daughter's adolescence appears to have less pernicious effects on the later sexual identification of the daughter. The harsher conscience of the adolescent and the active involvement in identity formation and peer group standards probably contributes to the heightened psychological trauma of incest during adolescence. Ramussen reports that of a series of 54 women involved previously with incest, 46 appeared to be unaffected by their experience and were functioning normally in the community.[21] Those girls showing most psychopathology (i.e., promiscuity, prostitution, petty theft, and disorderly behavior) also came from the most disturbed homes with predominantly psychopathic fathers.[9]

## CASE REPORTS

### Patient No. 1

Presenting complaints of depersonalization and difficulties in concentration, a professional musician indicated that these symptoms had been present off and on for most of his life. His description of his early life included parental separation and then divorce when he was four years of age, with subsequent severe financial difficulties for his mother. The two lived in a small, one-bedroom flat (he was an only child). He felt that his mother isolated herself from all contacts, devoting herself entirely to meeting his needs. Being extraordinarily precocious playing the clarinet, he was given scholarships to study with the most superior teachers leading to a complete scholarship to a major conservatory where he graduated with honors. When he was around 10 years of age his mother suggested he sleep in her bed during a cold winter spell. Although initially quite comfortable with this arrangement, the patient began noting the feelings of depersonalization after awakening many times with his mother touching his genitals. The sleeping arrangement continued, and as the patient entered puberty his excitement markedly increased as he would awaken in the middle of the night. He would touch his mother's breasts and genitals, surreptitiously he thought, leading to his ejaculation but ostensibly without his mother awakening. According to the patient, intercourse never did occur.

Although he continued to perform very well in his profession leading to positions with major orchestras, he was isolated socially, only telephoning his mother nightly. He was very constricted in all aspects of living, being only able to attend to and concentrate on his music which he practiced obsessively. It was when he was playing for an orchestra not in his home city, that he met the violin playing daughter of the conductor. She was an excellent musician who included the patient in many activities—social and musical. She was the aggressor sexually which the patient found exciting and satisfying. Despite objections from his mother, the patient married and moved permanently to an orchestra geographically quite distant from his mother.

He and his wife decided against having children at all, but when it was discovered his wife was pregnant, the patient first noted a marked decrease in his concentrating ability resulting in a number of errors during performances. At first this was excused, but, when it continued, he was referred for psychiatric evaluation. His wife noted an increase in irritability, isolation, sleeplessness and an increase in ritualistic behaviors. His thinking was deristic and irrational. The fantasies which were evident during wake and sleep periods were primarily sexualized with fears of being engulfed by an overpowering, witchlike mother. Diagnostically it appeared that he was suffering from a schizophrenic process having its origins in the incestuous relationships initiated by his very withdrawn and disturbed mother.

### Patient No. 2

After an unsuccessful attempt at beginning psychotherapy for obesity, this 15-year-old girl was finally brought back for treatment when she was three months pregnant. Besides the obesity, promiscuity was then revealed as another primary sympton. Her parents divorced when she was 3 years old; but her mother had maintained a relationship with the father even after his remarriage to "keep up friendly relations."

Her father made no attempt to see her or to do anything to show her the tangible signs of affection or interest. However, the patient persisted in the fantasy that he cared for her intensely but didn't dare show it because her mother would be offended. When she started dating, he did ask about her sexual involvement with boys. He insisted she let him initiate her before she allowed anyone else to have intercourse with her. This she did when she was 14 and the sexual relations with him continued. In addition, she engaged in casual pickups of older men until the second referral. There was a real question if the child was her father's.

During the initiation and continuation of sexual relations with her father, her mother feigned a lack of interest and knowledge of what was happening between father and daughter, although they secreted themselves in his den for an hour at a time. Her explanation to the therapist was that her former husband, a PhD in mathematics, was coaching his daughter in algebra! Following an uncomplicated delivery, the patient had resolved many of her underlying depressive responses and decided to adhere to a stringent diet. Her mother then began baking and bringing home desserts for the first time in seven years. Her father never came for interviews but from the history developed by his former wife and daughter, one might assume he diagnostically fell into the category of a sociopathic character structure.

### Patient No. 3

Everyone at the clinic agreed that the patient was one of the most attractive teenagers they had ever seen. Her blonde hair, fair skin and startlingly blue eyes were compliments to a magnificently adult figure. She was accompanied to her appointment by her parents and two younger siblings. As the brother and sister waited, the parents in her presence described to the psychiatric social worker that they had just discovered that she had been involved sexually with the mother's brother for over a three year period. Their concern was for their daughter who stared vacuously around the room throughout the recital or played with a tattered doll the parents brought with them. The uncle lived a few blocks from this family and was 25 years old. He had been used as a sitter for this family for ten years and was a frequent visitor to the home after school and on weekends. A graduate of high school, he was employed as a shipping clerk and was characterized by this family as shy and somewhat socially isolated.

The parents had been aware of developmental problems with their daughter within the first few years of her life. There were delays in walking and talking, which were related to mental retardation of unknown origin. Because of her blondeness and blue eyes she was repeatedly considered a possible case of phenylketonuria but this diagnosis was never substantiated. Her parents, both college educated, felt she had done quite well in an ungraded special education class where she was learning many self-help skills. Her intelligence quotient on repeated examinations was around 50.

The sexual involvements came to light when her mother overheard her trying to induce her 10-year-old brother to play the same game she played with her uncle. At first, her description seemed to be an innocent game of chase leading to capture and then some wrestling which the mother had witnessed many times before. However when the girl pulled her brother on top of her and told him to touch her "privates" like the uncle did, their mother interrupted the "game" and began to ask the patient more about what had transpired. Her description clearly indicated that petting was involved and very possibly intercourse. This latter activity was denied by the uncle, although it was evident that some genital contact did occur.

The parents were desirous of a complete psychiatric evaluation to help them determine how much inner self-control in the sexual area they could expect in the future and whether they should consider either the use of birth control methods or even sterilization if these controls might prove inadequate. They were very much aware of the "Lolita" quality of their daughter's appearance and were fearful of the possible effect on their child if men forced their attentions on her. Psychologically there did not seem to be any adverse effects of the prior involvements with her uncle to whom she was greatly attached, and guilt was not evident in regard to their activities. The visits from her uncle or to family gatherings where he would usually be present were stopped by the uncle who became increasingly embarrassed the first few times after he was confronted with the parents' knowledge of his actions and as the patient would suggest to him that she wanted him again to play "their game."

### Patient No. 4

The patient, who was 13 at the time of referral, had been shifted into her third foster home in two weeks. Her mother had died when the patient was five. She and her brother, two years her senior, traveled with their father who was in military service and then had a job as a truck driver. Periodically their paternal grandmother cared for them and at other times a succession of different women who lived with their father. He was frequently drunk, and when in this state was physically abusive to everyone in the family. It was after a particularly severe beating of his common law wife when she decided to report this to the police that his daughter (the index patient) told her that her father had been forcing her to have both oral and genital contact with him for at least a year. The police then incarcerated the father.

When he was released on bail, the department of social services removed the girl from her home and placed her in a foster home. She was relocated in a few days because the foster parents expressed negative feelings toward the child indicating that she was either making up stories about her father, or, if there was any truth to the sexual involvements, it might really have been because of the patient's seductiveness. The second placement was terminated in a few days because of an emergency in the foster family. Social Services wanted to have a psychiatric evaluation in order to secure the current placement. It looked like the patient would be out of the parents' home for at least a year while the criminal charges against the father were being prosecuted.

Psychiatrically this adolescent was quite bright and in general had age appropriate and healthy psychological structures. However, even though her academic performance was good, indicating a competence in her concentrating abilities, she evidenced periods of confusion, episodes of anxiety and difficulty sleeping. She was fearful of her father's wrath when they would be back together again. But she was also afraid of her own power which she felt potentially could destroy the family entirely if she ever "reported" any inappropriate behavior from her father in the future. She had seen that her current stepmother had retracted her complaint against her father so that her father, stepmother and brother were all together while she was shifted from home to home having to live with strangers. When asked about ultimate plans about marriage for herself, she indicated that she expected to remain unmarried and was seriously considering becoming a nun.

### Patient No. 5
Questionably resolved was the case of a previously convicted pedophilic discovered involved with one of his own children who left the state when his wife threatened to bring criminal charges against him.

### Patient No. 6
There were three girls in the family, 10, 8, and 4 years of age. Their father, who was a manual laborer, had been out of work for a long period of time. Their mother had an evening job as a waitress besides her regular daytime secretarial position to increase the income for the family. The father was left to handle the household chores and care for the children. He was terribly unhappy and angry in this role and took every occasion to declare his masculinity including periodically brutalizing his wife and children. The eldest daughter was found crying at school one day quite uncontrollably. When her teacher and a very sympathetic, competent school nurse questioned her in the nurse's office, she described continual sexual involvement by her father with her and her sisters. For at least a year, she had had intercourse with him and he practiced sodomy and had the younger girls perform fellatio on him.

It was the youngest of the three children who concerned the social workers the most. She seemed possibly retarded and was without affect except when she was around a man. At these times she would become coy, smile at the man, and then rub her genitals against the man's knee and reach out to touch his genitals. Mental status examination revealed a child who was insecurely attached emotionally to her parents. Her attempts to make contact were conditioned by her previous experiences that offering sexual overtures was the bridge to affection. This suggested ultimately a sadomasochistic substructure to her character. She was not retarded but rather was preoccupied with prematurely stimulated sexual impulses.

The father was convicted on the criminal charges and jailed for a minimum of seven years. When the youngest was asked what she would wish for if she had three wishes, the patient stated: "1. To have my Daddy back. 2. To have a new doll. 3. To be a grown-up lady."

### Patient No. 7
A 14-year-old Indian youth was brought to the emergency room following what appeared like a grand mal seizure. Thorough neurological examination demonstrated no organic cause for the seizures. History revealed that this boy had just heard in church that incestuous activities with sisters as well as with mothers was forbidden. As he walked through an open field on the way back from church, he thought he heard a sound behind him. He looked back over his left shoulder, feeling an overwhelming sense of oppression. Believing that severe infractions morally would be punished by a "ghost," he was certain that this spector was upon him and he fell into the seizure state. Since he had had sexual relations with his 16-year-old sister for two years, he felt he needed considerable expiation for his guilts. The result was a conversion reaction, which yielded to individual psychotherapy and concomitant counselling with his family.

### Patient No. 8
A 7-year-old girl began treatment for a hysterical paralysis of her lower limbs. She revealed that her 15-year-old brother had on numerous occasions stimulated her genitally and most recently lay on top of her while they were both nude. When he was questioned by their parents as to the validity of his sister's story, he with relatively slight reluctance admitted the truth of it. Both he and his sister were adopted, coming from different biological parents, and the boy indicated no guilt regarding his behavior as he felt no incest taboo could possibly be operative.

### INTERVENTIONS

It is our experience that the majority of complaints come through the police department primarily initiated by school personnel and/or physicians. Since sexual exploitation occurs most frequently during the latency or adolescent period and since the experiences are involved over a considerable period of time (in contrast to the single episode often of sexual molestation), the real crisis revolves about the handling of any unusual or acute emotional reaction within the child. Because the need of society for retribution when incest taboos are broken is so great, the crisis is most frequently in the "eye of the beholder." People tend to react with a totality that starts with an interrogation of the child, seeking the most minute sexual details, and then placement of the child in a foster home and/or incarceration of the offending adult. Almost always a criminal charge is lodged against the adult or there is an active attempt within the family to completely deny the allegations.

Quite frequently demands are made that a physical examination be done of the child. At this time of heightened emotionality in the child, such an intervention can create even more shame and fear. The question needs to be addressed as to whether the information thus obtained really is of any value in determining whether sexual exploitation has occurred. Our experience suggests that when a child below age 10 gives a very explicit, detailed story about the sexual involvement, this is prima facia evidence that it has indeed occurred. Given a kindly, interested, and sympathetic listener with little probing, this type of experience can be elicited. In its sharpness and clarity of description, actual sexual involvement can be distinguished from fantasy.

In the adolsecent, the validity of the information given can best be authenticated and accepted when accompanied by an affect indicating distress. A high index of suspicion must be entertained when the details of the sexual involvement are described in a flat, affectless manner. In this latter situation, the confused and ambivalent feelings could be the result of a psychotic-like reaction. If physical examination is required of any minor it must be done with the utmost tact and gentleness, especially with the younger child, since anogenital injury, infection, or inflammation may be present, as well as evoking increased anxiety about this unfamiliar procedure.

The familial history often will be the most revelatory. As in most cases of child abuse, a positive history of disruption in intrafamilial, interpersonal, and social relationships can be obtained. A background of problems, including sexual, between the parents can be causative in the development of sexual usage of a child. The quite constant presence of an adult male who is left alone with young children is suggestive of a potential source of sexual exploitation. Whenever anxiety states, phobias, conversion symptoms, psychophysiological disorders, suicidal attempts, and even psychoses occur in children and adolescents, sexual exploitation should be considered etiologically in the dynamics of the differential diagnosis.

Legally, sexual exploitation is considered part of child abuse in most communities. However, it is clear that validated cases of incestuous sexual behavior invariably lead to criminal charges against the offending adult. In a recent report, a father of sixteen children who had pleaded quilty to sexual relationships with two of his teenage daughters was given probation, the judge stating that incest was a family affair and did not endanger the public (*Playboy,* Dec. 1975, p. 60). There is much question if the separation of the adult from the seduced child/adolescent really stops the activity, or whether this method of handling incest increases the tendency to hide this "family affair."

Laws were established very early on in the development of civilized societies against this type of activity. The fact that laws were so explicit and the punishment so detailed is highly indicative that these activities occured with sufficient frequency to develop a legal code for dealing with them. Our current laws reflect these influences and suggest that incest represents one of the last taboos within our social structure. Because of these societal attitudes, most of these cases are subject to the legal adversary procedures. This inhibits or totally prevents an explication of the motivation and circumstances of the seduction on the part of the adult as well as an opportunity to fully investigate the psychological responses of the child.

There is often tremendous shame and fear connected with incestuous activities, usually in the child and frequently in the offending adult as well. Those instances, as noted in one of the case reports where the adult seemed to have a psychopathic character structure, suggest that some adults may not have any overwhelming guilt over their activities. Guilt plays such a tremendous role not only at the time of initiation of incest but also becoming a potent motivating force in the development and continuation of psychopathological responses in the child.

It has been our experience that the adolescent female and most of the latency age girls who are so used do not develop major psychotic breaks. This is not the case with males who are involved in mother-son or father-son relationships. In the male child, there is greater likelihood that psychotic defenses will be utilized, whereas in the female minor, psychophysiological reactions, sociopathic behaviors, characterological disturbances, anxiety states, and some depressive neurosis are much more likely.

There is often a need for a long term therapeutic involvement with these children and their parents. These psychotherapeutic endeavors might include individual, group, family or marital therapy, or any combination thereof. The initial attempt beyond making meaningful contact is most often the alleviation of guilt which is often compounded by the societal response to hearing of these forbidden activities. Along with the guilt, anxiety and depression are frequent accompaniments, in addition to the very real threat of disruption of the total family and of long term incarceration of the offending male.

Group treatment—the minor with peers and the parents with similarly involved adults—offers an opportunity to see themselves in situations that have affected others as well. These people often have envisioned their plight as unique and without parallel, making the shame that much greater. Within the group context, these "wicked" and "impure" actions can be exposed more readily, allowing active growth potentials within the individual to progress to more integrative and adaptive levels. With the minor in any of the psychotherapeutic modalities utilized, the emphasis should be the establishment of age appropriate activities and friendships with permission given to move away from home psychologically (and even geographically) without guilt.

In similar fashion the parents are helped to reestablish adult relationships with each other and find satisfaction in actions and social ties outside the home. During family sessions the therapist might, as an example, sit next to and support in many fashions the offending father, who perhaps has very low self-esteem and is introversive generally. The intent in any of the therapies is to reestablish interpersonal relationships, with appropriate generational boundaries.

## DISCUSSION

Sexual exploitation has been described as a complex, multidimensional social problem. Factors such as age, sex, intelligence, and socioeconomic status have been shown to be contributory. Three-generational familial dysfunction, however, is particularly central to violations of this ancient taboo. Poorly socialized individuals with particularly characterological defenses of denial, rationalization and projection perpetuate future generations of sexual exploiters and victims.

The sexual exploitation syndrome in many ways compares with the society's reaction to the battered child syndrome of thirty years ago: it is rarely recognized for what it is, and is usually dealt with in some inappropriate fashion. The emphasis at present is on the two extremes: benign neglect, or severe retribution. The families involved exhibit the characteristic collusive "stone-walling" that permits social institutions to respond with a certain psychological blindness. When society has its rigid proscriptions violated and its defenses exposed, the courts have too often responded by dissolving the families and creating an atmosphere of guilt and hatred for the individual involved.

Unlike physical abuse, sexual abuse has little concrete evidence to identify it. There are no characteristic physical scars or radiologic tests. The victims are usually adolescent and frequently willing. The damage is usually psychological and evolves over an extended period of time. Some studies even suggest that psychological harm is not done in many cases. Fantasies particularly abound in any area of sexuality but especially incest. Our only therapeutic lever is a greater acceptance of the historical data and its often courageous history taker. The use of data needs to be helpful and not a punitive concern by community agencies. This will more likely encourage other family members to talk through their feelings and difficulties in an accepting environment. Societal support of the vulnerable individual best safeguard generational boundaries and role limitations. The combination of open social concern and helping programs are the same attitudes that made child abuse a treatable clinical entity.

Child protective coordinating committees play a vital function in providing the necessary community input to protect and support these dysfunctional families. Courts most profitably need to encourage reporting and then allow these families to work through their difficulties under proper supervision. Because incest is not a sudden act of passion but rather a long standing, deliberate pattern of behavior, it requires equally long term therapeutic planning. Flexible use of family, marital, peer group, and individual therapy is the cornerstone of successful interventions with man's most universal taboo.

✳ Chapter Eight

# Humanistic Treatment [a]
# of Father-Daughter Incest

Henry Giarretto

The incest taboo is found in all known cultures, ancient, primitive, or civilized. It is generally agreed among social scientists that the essential purpose of the taboo is to optimize the survival and expansion of social systems.[1] Incest rules remain the most sternly enforced regulations for sexual relations and marriage throughout the world. But as social systems differ so do incest rules. To this day, laws defining and penalizing incestuous relationships vary markedly among nations and in the United States. In England, the law regards incest only as a misdemeanor. The penalties for incest in the U.S. range from a $500 fine and/or 12 months in Virginia, to a prison term of 1 to 50 years in California.[2] In most but not all states, first cousin marriage is illegal. Rhode Island permits first cousin marriage only between Jews.[3] For the purposes of this chapter, incest is defined as sexual activity between parent and child or between siblings of a nuclear family. The focus will be on father-daughter incest, as treated by the Child Sexual Abuse Treatment Program (CSATP).

Dread of incest is buried deeply in the unconscious of man and evokes emotions that are volatile and unpredictable, among them, repugnance, uneasy fascination, fear, guilt, and anger. This confused state finds expression in obscene comments or nervous disinterest when the subject is brought up in conversation, or quickly erupts into hostile behavior when an incestuous situation is discovered. Professional helpers themselves are not free of the incest dread. Many react either evasively when a case is referred or irresponsibly by failing to comply with child abuse reporting statutes. Nor can criminal justice personnel claim immunity from the panic induced by incest since their effect on sexually abusive families usually adds up to either rejection of the child's plea for help, if the evidence is not court-proof, or severe punishment of the entire family if the offender confesses. Finally, social scientists must also be afflicted

[a] A condensed version of this chapter appeared in *Children Today*, July–August, 1976.

with the dread of incest. How else can we account for the paucity of studies on incest which, with few exceptions, are superficial in conception and scope?

Typically, the repertory of law enforcement officials in the handling of father-daughter sexual abuse is ineffective and unpredictable. In one instance, the police officer or the district attorney may simply drop the case because of insufficient evidence even though there is strong suspicion that the victim's accusations are based on fact. The emphasis on a provable law violation has the effect of the community's turning its back on both the child and the family, thus leaving them in a worse condition than before. The child feels abandoned and must now face her hostile father, mother, and siblings alone. Often the father, though he may not repeat the crime, uses subtle retributive measures such as restrictions, extra chores, ostracization, etc.

In another instance, the criminal justice system, seeking sound, indisputable evidence, descends on the child and family with terrifying force. From the clinically detailed police reports, it appears that the only interest in the child is for the testimony she can give towards conviction of her father. The entire family is entangled in the web of retribution. The child is picked up and brought to a children's shelter, often without the mother's knowledge. The father is jailed and the mother must place her family on welfare. In sum, the family is dismembered, rendered destitute, and must painfully try to find its own way to unification.

Neglect of the sexually exploited child by the American community is vividly dramatized by Vincent de Francis in a 1971 report presenting the results of a three-year study in New York. He stresses that, "the victim of incest is especially vulnerable. The child is overwhelmed by fear, guilt, and shame. Substantial damage to the point of psychosis may ensue." As a rallying cry for action he adds: "I firmly believe that no community, rural or urban, can say such cases are unknown to it. Suffice it to say the problem of sexual abuse is a real one! It is a problem of immense proportions! It is pervasive!"[4]

## INCIDENCE AND EFFECTS OF INCEST

De Francis's alarm may not seem justified in view of the small number of detected incest offenders recorded annually by western nations. Over the period 1907–1938, Weinberg[5] determined that detected incest occurred in about one to two cases per million people in the United States; in Europe, the number of detected incest offenders ranged from one to nine cases per million. These rates seem to hold up to 1960.[6] All writers agree, however, that the low figures are the tip of the iceberg; that the laws discourage detection, and that data gathering methods render comparative studies extremely difficult if not impossible.

In the United States some improvement in detection and treatment of child abuse is developing as a result of rising public agitation. One tangible outcome of this pressure was the passage in 1974 of the Child Abuse Prevention and Treatment Act, which led to the establishment of a National Center on Child Abuse and Neglect in the Children's Bureau. Douglas J. Besharov, director of the Center, clearly spells out the position of the new federal resource on the overall problem of child abuse and neglect:

> The reality of child abuse is so awful that a harsh, condemnatory response is understandable. But such reactions must be tempered if any progress is to be made. If we permit feelings of rage towards abusers of children to blind us to the needs of the parents as well as of the children, these suffering and unfortunate families will be repelled and not helped. Only with the application of objective and enlightened policies can treatment, research, prevention and education be successfully performed.[7]

Other hopeful signs are the expansion and bolstering of child abuse reporting laws by many states, the increased attention being given by the media and the growing number of hotlines, several offering 24-hour service exclusively to calls on child abuse. Though major interest has been on child battering and neglect, some attention is slowly turning to sexual molestation. In a recent issue of *Children Today,* devoted entirely to child abuse, Sgroi[8] submitted an article in which she deduces that the above-mentioned developments had much to do with a sharp increase in reported incidents of child sexual abuse in Connecticut. The number of such incidents reached 76 in fiscal year 1973, and rose markedly to 172 cases in fiscal year 1974, apparently as a result of strengthened child abuse reporting statutes, the opening of a hotline, and a persistent public education effort.

The CSATP serves Santa Clara County, which has a population of 1,159,500 (December 1973). In 1971, its first year of operation, 36 cases were referred. The annual referral rate increased slowly over the following two years, but during fiscal year 1974 the rate accelerated sharply to 180 cases. This burgeoning rate can only be attributed to added coverage by the media and to growing confidence in the CSATP approach. Even the rate of 180 cases of recorded incest in a population of 1.1 million inhabitants does not provide an accurate estimate of the actual prevalence of incest in Santa Clara County. Although this is a large increase from the two incest cases per million estimated for this country by the writers cited above, the true incidence of incest has yet to be established. All available figures are at best educated guesses.

More telling than guesses on the number of actual cases is the social price paid for the neglect of incest, which is beginning to surface through recent studies revealing the effects of incestuous experiences on child victims. James[9] interviewed 200 prostitutes in Seattle and found that 22 percent of the women had been incestuously assaulted as children. For several years, Baisden[10] has studied Rosaphrenia: "An individual who cannot accept her own sexuality regardless of how she practices sex." He discovered that an inordinately high percentage of women so afflicted were raped as children. (Here, rape is defined as sexual exploitation of girls by much older males.) Concentrating on a group of 160 women, whom he tested for Rosaphrenia, he found that 90 percent had been raped during childhood, 22.5 percent by fathers or stepfathers.[11] The Odyssey Institute in New York interviewed 118 female drug abusers to ascertain their sexual history. It was found that 44 percent of the women had experienced incest as children. The 52 incest victims confided that the 93 different incestuous offenders, a total of 60, were in the parental generation, and of this group 21 percent were fathers or stepfathers.[12] It is notable that in each of these three studies of troubled women, a background of father-daughter incest emerged in over 20 percent of the subjects.

## FATHER-DAUGHTER INCEST

Father-daughter incest is potentially the most damaging to the child and family. Certainly it is the form most frequently prosecuted by the courts. A typical father-daughter incestuous relationship imposes severe stresses on the structure of the family. The father, mother and daughter roles become blurred and this engenders conflict and confusion among family members. The most bewildered is the daughter, who is at an age when her budding sexuality requires a clear and reassuring guidance. The familiar father has suddenly put on the strange mask of lover. She never knows which role he will play at any given time. Her mother, too, becomes unpredictable. At one moment she is the usual caring parent, at another she sends subtle, suspicious messages that can only come from a rival. The girl's relationships with her siblings are also adversely affected as they become aware that she has a special hold on their father.

Of course, each family has its own unique cast of personalities and the dramatic twists and turns which they enact are of infinite variety. But the following composite case history is fairly typical of the families we have been treating, and how the authorities reacted before CSATP.

### Leslie

Leslie is ten years old when her father begins his sexual advances. She has always been close to her father. When he tentatively begins to fondle her, she finds the experiences strange but pleasurable. Slowly the sex play becomes more sophisticated as it progresses to mutual oral copulation and, at puberty, to intercourse. Their meetings, which at first were excitingly secretive, now become furtive and anxiety-ridden. Leslie is about to enter the difficult teenage years when the mounting tension within her becomes unbearable. Her father is now interfering unduly with her peer relations. She senses that his fatherly concern over boys who are paying her attention is tainted by jealousy. She no longer can tolerate body contact with him and tries to resist, but he refuses to stop. Ashamed to confess the affair to her mother, she turns desperately to an adult friend, who immediately calls the police.

Though the policeman tries to be kind, Leslie is frightened by the power and authority he represents. His probing questions are excruciatingly embarrassing. But an odd feeling of relief intermingled with exhilaration comes over her as she realizes that her secret has now been exposed and her father's power over her broken. Her anxiety returns when she is brought to a children's shelter. Despite friendly attempts by attendants to make her stay pleasant, Leslie feels alone and threatened. This is the first time she has been forcefully separated from the family. She is overwhelmed by mixed emotions of fear, guilt, and anger, and is convinced she will never be able to rejoin her family or face her friends and relatives. Since there is suspicion of inadequate protection by her mother, a foster home is found for her. But she will not adjust to the new family, as this confirms her fears that she has been banished from her own family. Though often told that she was the victim of the incestuous relationship, Leslie believes she is the one who is being punished. She enters a period of self-abusive behavior manifested variously through hostility, truancy, drug abuse, and promiscuity.

### Jim

Jim, Leslie's father, a successful accountant, is in his mid-thirties when he becomes aware of deep boredom and disenchantment with his life. He feels stalemated in his job and his prospects for advancement are poor. There is growing estrangement between himself and his wife. She no longer seems proud of him; in fact, most of her remarks concerning his ability as a provider, father, or husband are critical and harrassing. Their sexual encounters have no spark and serve only to relieve nervous tension. He fantasizes romantic liaisons with girls at work; but he has neither the skill nor courage to exploit his opportunities.

Jim finds himself giving increasing attention to Leslie. Of all his children, she has always been his favorite. She is always there for him, accompanies him on errands, snuggles close beside him as they spend hours together watching TV. (His wife has no interest in this pastime; at night she is either taking classes or studying with her classmates.) As Leslie cuddles beside him he becomes keenly aware of her warmth and softness. At times she wiggles on his lap sensuously somehow knowing that this gives him pleasure. He begins to caress her and "relives the delicious excitement of forbidden sex play during childhood," as one client expressed it. But this phase is soon engulfed by guilt feelings as the relationship gets out of hand and he finds himself making love to her as if she was a grown woman. Between episodes he chokes with self-disgust and vows to stop. But as driven by unknown forces he continues to press his sexual attention on her. He now senses that she is trying to avoid him and no longer receptive to his advances. Though he doesn't use physical force he relies on his authority as parent to get her to comply. He becomes increasingly suspicious of her outside activities and the seemingly continual stream of boys who keep coming to the house. With a sinking feeling he notices that she is beginning to respond to one of the boys. He cannot control the feeling of jealousy the boy evokes or his craven attempts to force his daughter to stop seeing him.

Jim's trance is suddenly shattered one evening as he returns home from work. A policeman emerges from the car parked in front of his home and advises him that he is under arrest. Numb with shame and fear he is transported to the police station for questioning. Though informed of his constitutional rights, he finds himself making a fully detailed confession. Jim is eventually convicted on a felony charge and given a jail sentence of one to five years. His savings are wiped out by the lawyer's fee of several thousand dollars. He finds imprisonment extremely painful: from a respected position in society he has fallen to the lowest social stratum. His fellow inmates call him a "baby-raper." No one is more despicable. He is segregated and often subjected to indignities and violence. His self-loathing is more intense than that of his inmates. He gradually finds some relief in the fervent resolution that, given the chance, he will more than make it up to his child, wife, and family. A well-behaved inmate, he is released from jail in nine months. But he has lost his job and after weeks of job-hunting, settles for a lower position. Jim faces an uncertain future with his wife and family.

### Liz

The explosive reaction of the criminal justice system leaves Jim's wife, Liz, in shock and terror. She is certain that her family has been destroyed. There are subtle hints that she may have condoned the incestuous affair in the questioning by police and even others she once regarded as friends. She has failed both as wife and mother. Her feelings toward her daughter alternate between jealousy and motherly concern. Her emotional state vis-a-vis Jim is also ambivalent. At first Liz is blinded with disgust and hate at the cruel blow he had dealt her and vows to divorce him. Her friends and relatives insist this is her only recourse. But the rest of the children begin to miss him immediately and she realizes that, on the whole, he has been a good father. Liz is also sharply reminded that he has been a dependable provider as she faces the shameful task of applying for welfare. Nagging questions, however, continue to plague her. If she takes him back what assurance does she have that he will not repeat the sexual offenses with their other daughters? Will her relatives and friends assume that she has deserted her daughter if she allows him to return home? Will the authorities ever permit her daughter and husband to live in the same home again? Is there any hope for their marraige?

It is evident that typical community intervention in incest cases, rather than being constructive, has the effect of a knockout blow to a family already weakened by serious internal stresses. The average family treated by the Child Sexual Abuse Treatment Program is not at all like the incestuous family described in the literature. Weinberg, for example, reported that 67 percent of the families he studied were in the low socioeconomic bracket and that 64 percent of the incestuous fathers tested were below normal intelligence. He also noted that there was a disproportionate number of blacks in his sample.[13]

The 300 families who have been referred to the Child Sexual Abuse Treatment Program constitute a fair cross-section of Santa Clara County. The families are representative of the racial composition of the county, which is 76.8 percent white, 17.5 percent Mexican-American, 3.0 percent Oriental, 1.7 percent black, 1.0 percent other. The makeup of the work force leans towards the professional, semi-professional and skilled blue collar. Average income is $13,413 per household. The median educational level is 12.5 years.

## THE CHILD SEXUAL ABUSE
## TREATMENT PROGRAM (CSATP)

In 1971, cases similar to the representative one described above aroused the concern of Eunice Peterson, a supervisor of the Juvenile Probation Department. She conferred with Dr. Robert Spitzer, consulting psychiatrist to that department. Dr. Spitzer felt that family therapy would be a good first step towards constructive case management of sexually abusive families. I was invited to undertake a pilot effort limited to ten hours of counseling per week for a ten-week period. Initial criteria were:

1. The clients would be counseled on-site at the Juvenile Probation Department.
2. The therapeutic approach would follow a "growth" model predicated on Humanistic Psychology.
3. Conjoint Family Therapy as developed by Virginia Satir[14] would be emphasized.

It was soon apparent that the new approach held high promise of meeting a critical problem of the community. The initial effort expanded slowly due to meager funds. But the pressure of client needs was so strong that perpetuation of the new community resource was assured. As the program got underway, I quickly discovered that conjoint family therapy alone was inadequate and, moreover, could not be usefully applied during early stages of the family's crisis. The fundamental aim of family therapy—to facilitate a harmonious familial system— was not discarded. Incestuous families are badly fragmented as a result of the original dysfunctional family dynamics, which are further exacerbated upon disclosure to civil authorities. The child, mother, and father must be treated separately before family therapy becomes productive. Consequently, the treatment procedure was applied in this order: (1) individual counseling, particularly for the child, mother and father; (2) mother-daughter counseling; (3) marital counseling, which becomes a key treatment if the family wishes to be reunited; (4) father-daughter counseling; (5) family counseling; and (6) group counseling. The treatments are not listed in order of importance, nor followed invariably in each case, but all are required for family reconstitution.

Another important finding during early phases of the program was that traditional counselor-client therapy though important, was not sufficient. The reconstructive approach would be enhanced if the family was assisted in locating community resources for pressing needs such as housing, financial, legal, jobs, and so on. This required close collaboration between the counselor and the juvenile probation officer assigned to the case. In 1972 another development adding to program productivity was the formation of the self-help group now known as Parents United. The insight that led to this step came when a mother of one of the first families treated was asked to make a telephone call to a mother caught in the early throes of the crisis. The ensuing conversation went on for over three hours and had a markedly calming effect on the new client. A week later, three of the more advanced mother clients met together for the first time, and after a few meetings, to which several other women were invited, Parents United was formally designated and launched. The members meet weekly, and after a brief conference to discuss progress in growth and effectivity, the members form various groups: a couples group; an intense couples group size-limited to five pairs; a men's group; a women's group; and a mixed group. A separate organization, self-named Daughters United and composed of teenaged girls, meets earlier in the evening.

### Objectives of the CSATP

1. Provide immediate counseling and practical assistance to sexually abused children and their families, in particular to victims of father-daughter incest.
2. Hasten the process of reconstitution of the family and of the marriage, if possible, since children prosper best in normally functioning families headed by natural parents.
3. Marshall and coordinate all official services responsible for the sexually abused child and family, as well as private resources to ensure comprehensive case management.
4. Employ a treatment model that fosters self-managed growth of individuals capable of positive contributions to society, rather than a medical model based on the vagaries of mental disease.
5. Facilitate expansion and autonomy of the self-help groups, initiated by the program known as Parents United and Daughters United; provide guidance to the membership, such as training in co-counseling, self-management, and intrafamily communication; and in locating community resources—i.e., medical, legal, financial, educational.
6. Inform the public at large and professional agencies about the existence and supportive approach of the program, especially to encourage sexually abusive families to seek the services of the program voluntarily.
7. Develop informational and training material to enable emulation or adaptation of the CSATP model by other communities.

### Treatment Model
The therapeutic approach of the CSATP is based on the theory and methods of humanistic psychology, in particular the relatively new incorporation by the field of the discipline known as psychosynthesis, founded by Roberto

Assagioli.[15]   Other writers of importance to the CSATP are Carl Rogers, Abraham H. Maslow, Virginia Satir, Frederick Perls, Haridas Chaudhuri, and Eric Berne.

Assagioli agrees that many similarities exist between psychosynthesis and existentialist/humanistic views. Principal similarities are: (1) the method of starting from within, experiencing self-identity; (2) the concept of personal growth; (3) the importance of the meaning a person makes of his life; (4) the key notion of responsibility and ability to decide among alternatives; (5) the emphasis on present and future rather than regrets or yearnings for the past; and (6) the recognition of the uniqueness of each individual. In addition, Assagioli stresses: (1) the will as an essential function of self; (2) the experience of self-awareness independent of immediate I-consciousness of the various parts of ourselves; (3) a positive, optimistic view of the human condition; and (4) systematic use of didactic and experiential techniques that follow an individuated plan for psychosynthesis, the harmonious blending of mind, body, and spirit around the unifying essence—the self.[16]

Central notions in the treatment model are: the building of social responsibility; the realization that each of us is an important element of society; the belief that we must actively participate in the development of social attitudes and laws or be helplessly controlled by them. Chaudhuri gives firm emphasis to this imperative: "Since psyche and society are essentially inseparable, one has to take into account the demands of society. . . . One may criticize society or try to remold it. But one cannot ignore society or discard it."[17]

### Major Premises

1.  The family is viewed as an organic system; family members assume behavior patterns to maintain system balance (family homeostasis).
2.  A distorted family homeostasis is evidenced by psychological/physiological symptoms in family members.
3.  Incestuous behavior is one of the many symptoms possible in troubled families.
4.  The marital relationship is a key factor in family organic balance and development.
5.  Incestuous behavior is not likely to occur when parents enjoy mutually beneficial relations.
6.  A high self-concept in each of the mates is a prerequisite for a healthy marital relationship.
7.  High self-concepts in the parents help to engender high self-concepts in the children.
8.  Individuals with higher self-concepts are not apt to engage others in hostile-aggressive behavior. In particular, they do not undermine the self-concept of their mates or children through incestuous behavior.
9.  Individuals with low self-concepts are usually angry, disillusioned, and feel

they have little to lose. They are thus primed for behavior that is destructive to others and to themselves.

10. When such individuals are punished in the depersonalized manner of institutions, the low self-concept/high destructive energy syndrome is reinforced. Even when punishment serves to frustrate one type of hostile conduct, the destructive energy is diverted to another outlet or turned inward.

Productive case management of the molested child and her family calls for procedures that alleviate the emotional stresses of the experience and of punitive action by the community; enhance the processes of self-awareness and self-management; promote family unity and growth, and a sense of responsibility to society. The purpose is not to extinguish or modify dysfunctional behavior by external devices. Rather, we try to help each client develop the habit of self-awareness (the foundation for self-esteem) and the ability to direct one's own behavior and life style.

### Method

It is necessary to generate a warm, optimistic atmosphere before productive therapeutic transactions can ensue with families that have broken the incest taboo. They must be given hope and reassured that their situation is not as singular or as disabling as they have been led to believe. Feelings of despair, shame, and guilt must be listened to with compassion, as natural expressions of inner states. Awareness and acceptance of current feelings, without evaluation, allows the clients to assimilate them and to move on with their lives.

I know that I must continually work at developing this attitude within myself. When I met my first family, it was easy to maintain an attitude of acceptance with the child and her mother. But in preparing myself for the session with the father, I read the lurid details of his sexual activities with his daughter, which included mutual oral copulation and sodomy at the age of ten. The compassionate, therapeutic attitude which I can now write about so freely (perhaps pompously) completely dissipated.

I was forced to go into deep exploration of my unconscious for its own incestuous impulses and found that my early religious upbringing had done its repressive work thoroughly. After confronting the revulsion and anger that I was projecting on my client, I was able to assume a reasonable therapeutic mien. When I actually met with my client, my problem was much less difficult than I had anticipated. The raw feelings of despair and confusion had needed to be attended to, and my own hangups had become less intrusive. I cannot overemphasize the importance of self-work on the part of the therapist. This is the central theme of workshops I conduct for individuals who want to help incestuous families.

### Self-Assessment and Confrontation

Once a working relationship has been established and the highly charged emotional climate subsides, the clients begin to take an inventory of personal and family characteristics. Initially, during this exploration, I underscore the positive traits. What does the girl, for example, like about herself? What does she appreciate in other family members and the family as a whole? Before she can be motivated to work actively for personal and family growth, she must be convinced that she and the family are worth the effort. From this positive stance, the clients can then proceed to identify weaknesses and maladaptive habits that need to be improved or eliminated. These might include uncontrolled use of drugs, food, alcohol and cigarettes; hostile-aggressive behavior that interferes with progress in family, school, and work-relations; sexual promiscuity; inconsistent study and work habits; and, typically, the inability to communicate effectively, especially with important persons in their lives.

As the clients gain confidence in their search for self-knowledge, they begin to probe the painful areas connected with the incest. In what may be termed a confrontation-assimilation process, I encourage the child, father, and mother, as well as other family members, to face and express the feelings associated with the incestuous experience. It is indicated that buried feelings (fear, guilt, shame, anger), if not confronted, will return as ghosts to harass them. The feelings cannot be denied; they will have their effect somehow. If confronted now, they will lose their power to hurt them in the future. With some clients, the pain-provoking memories can be dealt with fairly early in the therapy; with others I find it prudent to proceed more slowly.

Although, I listen with compassion and understanding to the father's feelings, I will in no way condone the incestuous conduct or go along with pleas for mercy, such as that he is cursed and forced into incest by evil forces, or that he suffers from an exotic mental disease. He eventually is induced to admit the bald fact that he was totally responsible for the incestuous advances to his daughter. No matter the extenuating circumstances, including possible provocative behavior by his daughter, his actions betrayed his child and wife and their reliance on him as father and husband. Personal responsibility for the incestuous behavior is often objectively acknowledged by the men during group therapy and in sessions with their wives and daughters.

As a general rule, the mother will admit eventually that she was party to the incestuous situation and must have contributed to the underlying causes. Certainly, something must have been awry in her relationships with her husband and daughter. In order to relieve the daughter of feelings of self-blame and guilt for endangering the family, she is firmly told by her mother and, as soon as possible, by her father, that she was the victim of poor parenting. This step is also important for regaining her trust in her father and mother as parents. In time, however, she will confide that she was not entirely a helpless victim and is gently encouraged to explore this self-revelation.

Up to this point, the therapeutic approach is similar to that used by many humanist psychologists, particularly those of the Gestalt school.[18] The major objective of these first steps is to bring to awareness certain conscious and unconscious components of the individual personalities, as well as those that comprise the "personality" of the family. An important feature of the treatment is deliberate coaching in the techniques of self-awareness so that each individual can develop independently the skill of observing his own growth process and that of the family.

### Self-Identification

The last two phases of the treatment program draw on the writings of Dr. Assagioli and others in psychosynthesis. A key notion during the later phases is that the self is a unique entity which is more than the changing functions of mind, body, and spirit. A strong sense of self-identity must be internalized by an individual before he can experience self-esteem. Developing this line of thought, the counselor points out that the self in each family member should be a relatively stable center, which is more than the roles each plays as daughter, student, mother, wife, father, husband, or worker; more than the transient feelings of hostility, guilt, shame, etc.; more than the changing body states of pain and disease. Further, it is indicated that the marriage and the family also have integrating centers that are also more than the daily drama enacted by the principals.

### Self-Management

Once the idea of the self is entrenched and distinguished from the changing elements of personality, the concept of self-management is introduced. The assumption is that everyone can learn to control the way he behaves and ultimately the course his life will take. Each person in the family can behave purposefully to realize his potential and move deliberately toward self-actualization. The marriage and the family, conceptulized as separate organisms, can also be given purposeful direction. A major milestone is reached when the client acknowledges that all his past and current experiences are available to him for personal growth. He will assimilate all experiences, disown none.

A particular psychological school or discipline is not rigidly adhered to in attempting to satisfy the aims of the therapeutic model. Though the model roughly falls under the umbrella of humanistic psychology, other theories and methods, such as the psychoanalytic or the behavioral, are not denigrated or dismissed a priori. To avoid a mechanical, step-by-step approach, the last three phases of the therapeutic program are not developed in strict sequence. After initial efforts to bring about a good working relationship, I use an iterative strategy in guiding the client through the concepts and processes of self-assessment, self-identification and self-management. They are developed more in parallel than in serial fashion.

A variety of techniques are employed in implementing the therapeutic model. None is used for its own sake; instead, I try to tune into the client and the situation and try to apply a fitting technique. In most instances, experiential techniques are called upon that elicit affective responses, however, cognitive and spiritual needs are not neglected. When indicated, I will briefly discuss the strategy and progress of the therapy and answer questions from the client.

Certain clients who begin to internalize and practice the techniques at home report profound spiritual experiences. These clients are given special exercises that help them to expand and integrate the spiritual awakening.

Principal sources of the techniques comes from psychosynthesis, Gestalt therapy, conjoint therapy, psychodrama, Transactional Analysis, and personal journal keeping. To maintain continuity, exercises that can be done at home or at work between meetings are given to the client. Many of these techniques were described in detail in an earlier publication.[19]

## Preliminary Results and Milestones

1. No recidivism reported in the more than 250 families receiving a minimum of ten hours of treatment and formally terminated.
2. Compared to preprogram outcomes the integrated, compassionate approach indicates that:
   (a) The children are returned to their families sooner; 90 percent within the first month, 95 percent eventually.
   (b) The self-abusive behavior of the children, usually amplified after exposure of the incestuous situation, has been reduced both in intensity and duration.
   (c) More marriages have been saved (about 90 percent) many confiding that their relationships are even better than they were before the crisis.
   (d) The offender's rehabilitation is accelerated since the counseling program is started soon after his arrest and continues during and after incarceration. Previous to CSATP, individual and marriage counseling, if any, occurred after release from jail.
   (e) In father-daughter incest, the difficult problem of reestablishing a normal relationship is more often resolved and in less time.
3. Parents United has grown from three mother members to about 60 members, of which half are father-offenders. Daughters United, comprised of teenaged victims of incest, has also grown substantially. Both groups are becoming increasingly self-sufficient; several of the older members act as group co-leaders.
4. In addition, to self-help benefits, the Parents United formula is proving to members that they can become a strong voice in the community; a significant realization to those members who used to regard themselves as the pawns of civil authorities.
5. Offenders, who formerly would have received long jail or prison sentences, are now given suspended sentences or shorter terms due to increasing recognition of the CSATP by the judiciary as an effective alternative to incarceration.
6. The difficult goal of mobilizing typically disjointed and often competitive services into cooperative efforts is gradually being reached.
7. Due to the public education work the referral rate has increased to about

180 families annually; about 60 percent of the referrals come from agencies other than the police or Juvenile Probation Departments, or directly from people heretofore fearful of reporting the problem.

8.  The CSATP is receiving nationwide coverage by the media. Staff members and, more importantly, members of Parents United have appeared on several TV and radio programs, and the CSATP has been the subject of numerous newspaper and magazine articles.

9.  Hundreds of informational packets have been sent to requestors throughout the country to abet the aim of having the CSATP serve as a model for other communities.

10. Several presentations and training seminars are conducted each year for professional groups by the writer and staff members. The presentations now include mothers, daughters, and fathers of the families treated for incest who are willing to answer questions from the audience—a significant breakthrough.

11. The CSATP is involving many volunteers and graduate students, who make valuable contributions while being trained.

12. The CSATP is unique also in that it constitutes the only substantive attempt extant to apply the principles and methods of humanistic psychology to a serious psychosocial problem. Currently the program is obtaining financial support direct from the California legislature.

## DISCUSSION

Current attitudes and laws regarding incest are myth-ridden and ineffective. Society is not attending responsibly to a problem vital to its own survival. The impact of civic authorities on incestuous families, particularly those in which the father is the offender, commonly adds up to either rejection of the victim's plea for help or disruptive punishment of the entire family.

I do not suggest that criminal laws in support of the incest taboo should be abolished and offenders should be dealt with exclusively by mental health workers. Reliance on the weekly therapeutic hour alone has not proved successful in the histories of several CSATP families. Typically, the mother had become aware that her husband was sexually exploiting their daughter and threatened to breakup the marriage if he did not obtain psychiatric treatment. The offender complied but stopped going to the therapist after a few sessions. A month or two later he resumed the sexual abuse of his daughter. In two instances the fathers continued their offenses even while undergoing treatment. The motivating drive and/or therapy alone were not sufficient and the troubled family was left with its problem. In five other cases in which punishment alone was employed, the deterrent effect hoped for proved equally inadequate. After serving long sentences, the five men came to the attention of the CSATP for repeating the offense with other daughters or step-daughters.

The CSATP works closely with the criminal justice systems of Santa Clara County and other local counties. The promising results would not have occurred without the cooperation of the police, probation officers, and the courts. The police and probation departments are major referral sources. A distraught victim, mother, or friend will usually turn to the police for immediate help since they are available 24 hours a day. It is now a common practice for officers who investigate the cases to refer offenders and their families to the CSATP.

For the offender the implication is that involvement in the CSATP is likely to be strongly considered by the judge and prosecuting attorney during court proceedings. His own lawyer will also urge him to join the CSATP. Though all offenders hope that their penalties will be softened by participation in the CSATP, many find it equally compelling to do so for the aid the program gives to their families. Usually each man soon realizes that the program will help him understand and control his deviant impulses and to reestablish sound relationships with his wife, the daughter he victimized, and the other children.

In all cases the authority of the criminal justice system, and the court process, seems necessary in order to satisfy what may be termed an expiatory factor in the treatment of the offender and his family. It appears that the offender needs to know unequivocally that the community will not condone his incestuous behavior and that he must face the consequences. The victim and her mother also admit to deriving comfort from the knowledge of the community's clear stand on incest. All family members, however, will do their best to frustrate the system if they anticipate that the punishment will be so severe that the family will be destroyed—that they, in turn, will become "victims" of the criminal justice system, including the child-victim herself.

No matter what the reasons may be for admission of an incestuous family into the CSATP, it is our responsibility to help the family reconstitute itself as quickly as possible, hopefully around the original nuclear pair. Even if the offender comes to the CSATP only for the purpose of saving himself, it is up to us to show him that he can reap more substantial benefits both for himself and his family from honest participation in the CSATP. Of course, the CSATP is not equally effective with all clients. About 10 percent of referrals will elude our efforts. They will not come in for the initial interview or will drop out soon after treatment has begun. Four couples were dismissed from the program because the father and/or his wife would not admit culpability and placed the blame entirely on the child-victim and her seductive behavior. In these instances extraordinary effort was required in the treatment of the deserted child. After many attempts, three of the girls successfully adjusted to foster homes. They are now married and apparently doing well.

The CSATP is a growing community resource. Some of its objectives have only partially been achieved; others will be added, or dropped, or modified. But there is at least the beginning of a response to Vincent de Francis's clarion call to the American community to protect the sexually molested child.[20] Moreover, the CSATP complies with Besharov's request for enlightened intervention that considers the requirements of the entire family, the parents as well as the children.[21]

By working integrally with the criminal justice system, the CSATP shows promise of developing into a model for other American communities. Each community must be given the opportunity to treat incestuous families in a manner that is neither permissive or cruelly punitive. A national position should be taken on the incest taboo and laws enacted that are effective and consistent; the community must publicize these statutes and the penalties for violating them.

To prevent incest the public must be educated to become aware of predisposing conditions and to take appropriate action. Finally, comprehensive procedures similar to the CSATP must be established in each community to treat sexually abused children and their families in order to enhance their chances for reconstitution and to prevent future violations.

# Part III

## Family Oriented Therapy

✳ **Introduction**

Once the family assessment has been completed and the long term plans developed, the next step is implementation. This requires a personal involvement which in many situations may continue for years, not weeks or months. This is a commitment which many communities have been unwilling to make. Somehow, we all are able to say to the overburdened protective service worker, "This is your problem." Not so! This is our problem. Protective service cannot be expected to be involved with all these families for years; theirs is mainly a job of acute crisis intervention. The long term care givers for these families are found everywhere in the community. They must be organized into a coordinated group with the main task being the delivery of comprehensive care/services to abuse and neglectful families.

In Chapter Nine Dr. Steele begins Part III with a review of his concept of the interdisciplinary approach. Without this, families cannot be treated adequately. The next three chapters present a variety of methods to helping these parents and their children. Beezley, Martin, and Alexander summarize treatment programs from parent aides to Parents Anonymous in Chapter Ten. The innovative and exciting residential program at Oxford, England is reviewed in Chapter Eleven by Drs. Lynch and Ounsted. Their residential family oriented program is called "A Place of Safety." And this Part concludes with some very practical suggestions from Australia by Margaret Jeffery that may benefit parents and therapists alike.

The problem of child abuse and neglect is worldwide. This section presents ideas from the United States, England, and Australia. Although the programs vary in their approach to treatment, one theme is consistent over modalities: learning; learning what was missed in early childhood. Trying to experience early child development as an older child or an adult is difficult, but it is not impossible.

Ray E. Helfer
C. Henry Kempe

*161*

## ✳ Chapter Nine

# Experience with an Interdisciplinary Concept*

**Brandt F. Steele**

Our basic assumption is that child abuse and neglect is a very complex phenomenon manifested by a distorted, destructive, maladaptive pattern of child rearing. Our aim is to alter and improve such parental patterns through accurate diagnosis and pertinent treatment. Removal of the child to a place of safety is sometimes necessary but this in itself does not significantly alter the parental patterns that must be changed.

Maltreatment of infants and children is seen as the final overt act of caretakers whose entire lives have been in some degree of significant difficulty. This is true whether the abuse and neglect occur in mild isolated instances or whether there is more severe or continual maltreatment. The documentation of the causes of this rather unusual form of human behavior characterized by neglect or attack of their own offspring by parents has not been easy. Many things have been suggested to account for the condition, including neurophysiological abnormalities, psychiatric disorders, poverty, social disadvantages, ethnic tradition, religious conviction, environmental stresses, or simple lack of knowledge of parenting skills. All these factors may be found in different cases of abuse, but there are so many exceptions to each one that it is impossible to consider any factor in this list as the necessary and sufficient cause of abuse of children. In our own experience, the single most common denominator is the history that, almost without exception, abusive parents had been exposed to emotional and developmental neglect, with or without significant physical abuse, in their own earliest years.

Considerable statistical data has been accumulated concerning abusive

*Special recognition is given to the Grant Foundation for the support of some of Dr. Steele's work in this field.

parents. We know a lot about the age, sex, and marital status of the abusers, their educational achievement, their IQs, socioeconomic status, psychiatric diagnosis, employment record, and so forth. We also have information about the age, sex, ordinal position, and legitimacy of the abused infants, as well as about their birth history and whether or not they were premature or are afflicted with congenital abnormalities. We even have data about the time of day and season of the year in which abuse occurs. All these data have relevance but they do not answer why, in the particular family, a particular child was abused; or why some children in the family are physically well cared for, while another is constantly maltreated or tortured. To understand these specific problems of abuse and neglect, we must investigate the family as an unique phenomenon and not try to deal with it as some form of a standard entity to be put into a certain pigeonhole.

Abuse and neglect must be understood as problems of interaction between members of a family. A "family" in this sense is the situation in which there is a man, woman, and children. Most commonly this is mother, father, and children, but it may be mother, boyfriend, and children, or father, stepmother, children, or various other combinations of these factors. Abuse occurring in a *truly* single parent family is rare—but possibly so is a truly single parent family. On the other hand, it is not unusual for a mother to be involved in abuse while the man of the household is away on military duty, at a job in a distant city, or even away out of an angry separation. Fathers, too, also abuse when left alone with their children, but these are not truly single parent families. In all instances it is difficult to understand the abusive behavior without detailed information concerning the interaction between the two parental figures as well as some understanding of each of them as individuals.

In order to make a valid prognosis and to develop an appropriate treatment program, a broad knowledge of the family must be developed. Some families are in a constant state of disarray due to adverse socioeconomic conditions or serious psychopathology; with them, abuse and neglect seem to be constant, daily occurrences. The prognosis in such situations, of course, is much less optimistic than in those families in which abuse is a periodic, intermittent occurrence. In these families the parental response to individual instances of misbehavior of the child in addition to the presence of external stresses, often precipitates trouble. For instance, a mother may not abuse her child each time he soils the bed but only on those occasions when the bed soiling has been preceded by argument and emotional estrangement with the father or a disastrous argument with the mother-in-law over the telephone.

To understand these complex patterns one must uncover and consider a great number of variables involved in this tangled web of human behavior. How is an understanding of this phenomenon in a family attained? More pertinently, can such knowledge be obtained by one person alone? On occasions considerable usable data about family interactions may be obtained by a single interviewer.

On the other hand, I cannot recall a single case in which it was not only useful but actually necessary to have information developed by several different people becoming involved in the case.

A multidisciplinary approach is mandatory if we expect to make an adequate diagnosis of the problem for which we must prescribe a course of treatment In all but the most blatant cases of abuse, a pediatrician's opinion as to the origin and extent of the injuries is required. Only he (she), with the help of his other medical consultants, can decide whether injuries fit the picture of nonaccidental trauma. The pediatrician is also the only one who can validly determine whether a case of failure to thrive is due to parental neglect or to some medical condition. Psychiatric interviewing is also a necessary part of the evaluation in many families. A mental status examination is necessary in determining the caretaker's basic intellectual capacities, which in turn has some bearing on the kind of treatment to be prescribed and the chances of the parents responding to it. Psychopathology of serious degree can seriously compromise any form of rehabilitative treatment and must be discovered at an early stage. More important than any specific psychiatric diagnosis that can be made is the determination of what, if any, relationship exists between the psychopathology and the parent's abusive or neglecting behavior. Parents can have many psychiatric problems that have no direct influence on their caretaking abilities.

If the abused child is in the hospital, the observations by nurses of the child's behavior and notation of those things to which the child responds most negatively and positively, as well as direct observation of the interaction between parents and child, are all of crucial value. Similar observations can be made by visiting nurses who have had the chance to observe families in the home environment, bringing in an entirely different kind of information. Observations made by nurses and other personnel in the outpatient clinic or emergency room, as well as by interns and residents during the first interactions with parents in these settings, are also helpful.

Social workers, both those in the hospital and those who visit families in their homes, bring to the diagnostic process information obtained from a different viewpoint and by different techniques. Such information casts new light on the problem by corroborating or elaborating other data. All these observers may at times cast doubt on previous information and bring about a reevaluation of the situation with broader, fuller understanding. Like the public health nurse, the social worker often has the chance to see the family in its own home, with direct observation of parents' behavior with each other and with their children. These data are entirely different from that obtained only by observation and interviewing in the sterile environment of hospital, clinic, and welfare office.

The value of getting information derived from several disciplines in order to provide as broad a base as possible for diagnosing family problems is only part of the issue. It is equally important both that these observers are of different disciplines and that they are essentially different people. They are often of different sex and of different personalities. They approach the family—and are received and dealt with by the family—in very different ways. Concepts are derived from this experience as to how the parents react to people of the same or opposite sex and to people who represent different degrees of authoritarianism and intrusion or assistance to them. This multidisciplinary approach not only provides different types of technical data but very valuable interpersonal human behavioral data. We often do not make enough use of this latter information, either in understanding the problems of the family or in outlining treatment plans. The reactions the parent has to different people of different sexes is very revealing and can be used to help in understanding the stereotyped difficulties that have haunted the patient since early life and that are still interfering with present adjustments.

Those involved in abusive, neglecting behavior have a tendency to tell different stories. Such varied information is similar to pieces of a jigsaw puzzle which, put together, make an understandable picture. On the other hand, they may be bits of information which contradict each other. Such contradictions should not be dismissed as mere lying or attempts to cover up, but rather be regarded as valuable clues to the conflicts and problems the parent must cover up in his own defense and protection.

As the data obtained in a multidisciplinary approach to diagnosis are pooled and combined, the multiplicity and pervasiveness of the parent's conflicts become clarified. This combined picture gives a better clue to prognosis than single observations made by a psychiatrist, social worker, nurse, or pediatrician. Prognosis is determined not only by the degree of pathology and interpersonal difficulty present, but is also based on the degree to which there are positive elements in the patient's life. One interview may obtain data relating to some relatively good experiences or relationships with a warm, supportive person in the parent's early life. The degree to which such a person was available and was used by the parent during his development is the most valuable clue we have toward optimism in our prognosis. And yet, only one of the several persons seeing this parent may obtain this vital bit of information.

The multidisciplinary approach provides our greatest opportunity for the beginnings of treatment. If several persons are involved with the abusive parents early on, there is a better chance that the parent will find one of the group with whom he can feel a safer relationship. It does not matter basically whether this is pediatrician, nurse, psychiatrist, social worker, or medical student on the ward. The important issue is that the first stepping stone from which other treatment can take off and progress is provided in continuation with the same therapist or with some else close to the situation. Providing the parents with someone to be close to and someone else against whom they can vent their anger, is of equal importance.

Treatment that is multidisciplinary is automatically multipersonal. There are advantages in this, not the least of which is the value and comfort to the therapists themselves in having someone with whom they can share information and responsibility. In general terms we think of the treatment of abusive parents as providing the facilitating environment that opens up new channels of growth, development, and maturation that were blocked and distorted in their early lives. In this sense one can see that the provision of more than one therapist, particularly ones of different sex, is like reestablishing in a useful form the growth of a child with two parents. Only rarely will one find families in which there is not a need for help from social workers or nurses to act as a primary therapist in working with the family. No one person can be all things to all abusive parents, no matter how much we wish to be or how hard we might try.

This facilitating environment must provide two things in variable balance according to the needs of the individual parents. One is the chance to have new kinds of relationships with other adults, thus enabling the parent to develop trust, confidence, and pleasure in life, plus new concepts and techniques of child care. The other is a form of therapy that enables the parent to look at himself and his own psychic functioning, to understand and thereby change those unconscious automatic patterns of dealing with the world which have been plaguing him or her since early life. Both opportunities must be provided for the parent.

It seems unlikely that individual attention to psychic states and their improvement can adequately affect the total behavior of the parent unless there are inputs and help from other disciplines. Parents cannot accomplish social changes without some attention to specific intrapsychic conflict. It therefore is essential that many modes of therapy must be made available. An individual prescription for how much of each mode would be most useful can be made. And there should always be available the possibility of using any combination of modalities, including social case work, individual psychotherapy, group therapy, lay therapy, marital counseling, education in parenting techniques, and so on.

Although the ability of abusive parents to develop a sense of trust in other adults may of necessity have to begin with one person, parents must inevitably learn during treatment that they can have trust and confidence in relation to many people. This can only be reached through the experience of having several people, usually of different disciplines, involved in the therapeutic process. Through this method the socializing ability of parents, which had been so sadly defective, can finally be accomplished. Through this channel there can also develop lifelines to obtain help and manage crises as well as relationships that can bring pleasure and satisfaction to the parents in an adult world. Only after this has occurred can the parents become capable to care for their children in new and better ways.

The problems of abuse cannot be solved by treatment of the parents alone. The children, too, are in dire need of help. Such help may be that of direct medical intervention, particularly early in life; later it must involve the expertise of psychologists, child psychiatrists, teachers, social workers, and other child care experts—all of whom must work together toward bringing the child back into a better stream of emotional, physical, and intellectual development. Expert diagnosis is required so that special attention may be given to those areas that have suffered the greatest damage due to inadequate parenting. Treatment of child alone or parents alone does not work. Concomitant treatment of the two not only helps them individually but enables a feedback interaction between parent and child that enhances the development of both.

While many of the positive values and advantages of a multidisciplinary approach to treatment have been considered, one must also keep in mind that there are problem areas too. The various persons involved must have respect and confidence in each other. This is not always easily or quickly come by. There must be adequate sharing of data and communication between workers, and for busy people this is not always possible. If communication among therapists is delayed or temporarily impossible, there must be ability of workers to carry on independently and to cope comfortably with any misunderstandings that may occur. Some workers are temperamentally disinclined to work with others and can only be comfortable if they are working as "loners." Others may be so dependent upon constant communication and support from others that they cannot work independently. The presence of either one of these extremes makes multidisciplinary approaches difficult or even impossible.

Abusive parents have a great tendency—often much more so than other patients—to play off one therapist against the other. Difficulties are thus created if therapists fall into a trap of becoming antagonistic with each other, rather than using this pattern as a clue to conflict that needs treatment. Another difficulty that can often arise is that of each therapist having some tendency to "dump" the patient's problems into the laps of the other members of the multidisciplinary team. Working with these parents is always an exhausting, trying experience, and it is all too easy to slip into a pattern, when we are overworked ourselves, to "let George do it."

Although having open lines of communication among therapists is an essential part of the multidisciplinary approach, we must keep such communication in proper perspective. "Sharing" and "communicating" can subtly drift into being ends in themselves, and therapists can unwittingly feel they have accomplished their work by talking to each other, while the patient has been neglected. There is always the great need for those involved in therapy to have others with whom they can share worries and responsibilities, and from whom they can get help. Yet this very valuable source of assistance must not be misused. Care should be taken not to become too specialized, or to keep individual work purely and simply in the line of expertise, thereby avoiding the multiple interactions that occur in the total behavioral problems of the parents and children. Despite all the problems that can occur in a multidisciplinary approach, it offers the best chance for the rehabilitation of families in which abuse and neglect occur.

## Chapter Ten

# Comprehensive Family
# Oriented Therapy

Patricia Beezley, Harold Martin
and Helen Alexander

All members of the family of an abused child have need of psychological help. The parents have a right to help for themselves, apart from the interventions aimed at improving their relationships with their children. The abused child has a right for treatment for himself regardless of his parents' prognosis. And siblings of the abused child have psychological needs that are relevant and important in their own right.

Integration of the various separate treatments for the different members of the family is a difficult but necessary task. The professionals involved will need to meet together periodically to clarify their roles, to share information openly, and to share jointly in decision making. The timing of the introduction of various treatment modalities into the overall family treatment plan is critical. After the abused child and his siblings are assured of physical safety, primary efforts must be directed toward helping the parents feel better about themselves, apart from their parenting role. If too much is expected from them too quickly in terms of attending parent education classes and improving the quality of their child care, they will not be successful; their bad feelings about themselves and their anger towards their children will be reinforced.

Treatment for the abused child and his siblings can begin fairly quickly, but not until the parents feel reassured that someone will continue to be available to help them. When the children's therapy begins, it will be necessary to increase the contacts with the parents for a brief period. The parents will need frequent, scheduled contacts with the child's therapist to work through problems of competitiveness, jealousy, and reluctance to see the child grow more healthy.

In this chapter we focus on the treatment needs of abusive parents, abused children and their siblings, and on various efforts to meet these needs. All successful work by the Child Protection Team (see Chapter Five) is dependent on the availability and appropriate utilization of comprehensive and coordinated services to the whole family, rather than being limited to provide only crisis intervention.

## THERAPY FOR THE PARENTS

The main goal in working with abusive parents is to help them relinquish their abusive, neglectful pattern of child rearing and to replace it with a method of caring that is more rewarding to both the parent and the child. This necessitates focusing the treatment initially on the parents and increasing their own growth and development. Therapy for the parent includes helping him to build up his sense of self-esteem; helping him to develop better basic trust and confidence; helping him to learn how to make contacts with other people in the family, neighborhood, and community; helping him to establish responsive lifelines; and helping him to develop the ability to enjoy life and have rewarding, pleasurable experiences with adults and with his own children.

To accomplish these goals, treatment for abusive parents usually needs to be a two-part process. The first step is a *restitution*—that is, a nurturing or "reparenting" process. During this phase a more positive model of parenting than what the parent had as a child is offered. The therapist provides support of and interest in the parents for their own needs, regardless of the child's situation. There needs to be a considerable degree of tolerance for dependency, which had never adequately been met in the parents' own early lives. This process of nurturing on an "as needed" basis is frequently enough to stop the parent from using the child to meet his or her own needs and to stop the physical abuse. However, to make such gains more permanent and to alter the long term emotional relationships, a *resolution* of conflict, with some emotional insight and understanding, is usually necessary. Many parents can profit from some insight therapy and an in-depth reworking of historic conflicts. We must keep in mind that cognitive, intellectual understanding without experiential relearning results in a parent who can explain his or her dynamics but who has changed nothing. For other parents insight therapy is contraindicated, but they still need help in rearranging their lives to lessen the stress-reproducing situations that get them into difficulty.

The treatment needs of abusive parents differ somewhat from the treatment needs of other psychiatric patients. They differ in the following respects.

1. **Involving More Than One Person in the Treatment process Is Essential.** More than one person must be involved so that there is some multidisciplinary support in decision making. These families are extremely difficult to work with and many of the decisions made in treatment are critical to the lives and well-being of the children. It is crucial at times that there be a second opinion about the family's progress. To make these decisions alone and to have to then handle the potential failures alone, can be devastating to any therapist.

Abusive parents have very early developmental conflicts that include the splitting of objects. They frequently see issues as either black or white and treatment persons as either good or bad. It takes approximately six to twelve months in treatment to begin to help the parent incorporate both the positive and the negative aspects into the same person. In the meantime, we must help that parent stay in treatment; therefore, an alternate figure can play a supportive, giving role while the other person is the "bad guy."

Since treatment with abusive parents requires both restitution or nurturing, and a resolution of conflict, treatment can be very intense and time demanding. Although the primary therapist will need to provide some nurturing and reparenting as well as some help in the insight process, it is much more practical to have the primary nurturing come from another person. In this respect, lay therapists, public health nurses, homemakers, and church people can be extremely useful.

2. **Treatment of Abusive Families Requires Much More Outreach and Availability of Services Than Is Normally Provided in Traditional Psychotherapy.** Abusive parents are the types of patients who, if put on a waiting list, are never seen in mental health clinics. They require involvement during their time of crisis and constructive help for them to decrease the anxiety about the treatments that are being offered. It is extremely difficult to establish an alliance with an abusive parent despite the verbal outpourings, which are frequently defensive in nature. These parents expect to be criticized and told what to do, and therefore frequently avoid therapy at all costs. To help them with this process, home visits are necessary. This may mean going to a family's home more than once without an answer at the door but with someone behind a closed curtain. Although therapy has to be started in the home, it can frequently be transferred to the office once a parent is more comfortable. This outreach also means more phone calls to see how a family is doing and to show interest in them.

> Dorothy was afraid that she might injure her seven-month-old son. Another child had died four years ago under highly suspicious circumstances. Although Dorothy wanted help, she never was able to follow through on her appointments at the mental health clinic. A lay therapist began making home visits. After several months of nurturing, the lay therapist offered to accompany Dorothy to the clinic for therapy appointments. Dorothy is now able to go alone to therapy, but spends considerable time talking on the phone to her lay therapist prior to and immediately following each appointment.

Outreach also means being available by phone on a 24-hour basis. It means putting no pressure on parents about their being late or missing appointments. The psychoanalytic mode of discussing with the patient why he showed up on the wrong day and at the wrong time would only prevent this type of parent from ever coming back again. This outreach also means that the secretary's role is absolutely critical. If the parent is able to get to the office, the secretary can make or break the entire situation. The offering of refreshments or low key small talk helps the parent come back again, even when he does not as yet have a good relationship with his therapist.

> Diane, a young mother of four children, was at the end of her rope when she attempted to call her therapist. Kathy, the secretary, knew immediately what was happening. She encouraged the mother to bring the children to the crisis nursery, and meanwhile located the therapist. When Diane arrived, Kathy was there with a comforting hug and a cup of coffee. Although the therapist wasn't available for over an hour, Diane did not mind waiting. While she sat in Kathy's office, she read, chatted with passers-by, and began to feel very good about the fact that *this* time she had avoided a full-blown crisis.

This outreach also means lowering expectations in regard to a patient's being able to state what his problem is, why he is there, and what he wants to work on. Too frequently abusive parents are labeled as "unmotivated" and "resistant," and are abandoned. This may not be the case if we only will see it as our task to help them with their initial anxiety and get them started in the treatment process. Availability of services also means that the therapist must be ready to respond to crises and to help plan for ways to divert future crises. It also means providing backup during the vacations of those involved so that there is always someone ready to help the parents.

3. **Treatment for Abusive Parents Must Go On For A Longer Period of Time Than Is Currently Being Done In Most Mental Health Clinics and Child Welfare Departments**. Crisis intervention alone or even short term treatment cannot adequately meet the needs of abusive parents. The intense treatment with these parents frequently needs to continue for eighteen months to two years, with the absolute minimum being one year. During that time appointments can be decreased but the parent must be helped to feel that the door is always kept open for him to return.

Frequently, the contacts with the parents will go on for many years, with them calling back when they are in crisis, especially around a major change in their lives such as a new job or move or loss of someone important in their lives. These contacts are often on a very short term basis, sometimes no more than a phone call. At this point, the parents are using their lifelines, which is a significant indication of progress. But they often have lifelines other than the therapist at this point, and therefore, the contact usually is not intensive or as long term as it had been during the initial crisis situation.

4. **One Component of Therapy With Abusive Parents Needs to be "Doing-With Experiences" to Enhance the Parent's Self-Esteem, to Help Him Experience Pleasure, and to Improve Basic Child Care**. Although much of the therapy will

continue to be further discussion based on a psychiatric model, the parents will benefit greatly from opportunities that they can directly share with the therapist. Lay therapists frequently spend time with the parents, taking them to lunch, going shopping, beginning a new project or hobby with them. A therapist may spend some time with the parents and children, teaching some basic parenting skills and child development theories in a nonthreatening way (see Chapter 12). As the parents develop a better sense of self, the child will also be seen in more positive terms as an extension of the parents' own good self. When a parent begins to experience pleasure, it is easier for him to allow and appreciate the child's pleasurable experiences.

The specific treatment needs of abusive parents and the goals of the two-part treatment process can be met through various treatment modalities and are best met through some coordinated combination of them. The following sections will describe some of the many treatments that are available for abusive parents, with the emphasis being on their advantages and limitations.[a]

## AVAILABLE TREATMENTS

### Casework Services

Casework services are highly divergent, depending as they do on the level of expertise of the caseworker, the priorities of the child welfare department, and the size and nature of case loads. A caseworker with a Master's degree in social work and special training and experience with abusive and neglectful families is more qualified to investigate and treat these dysfunctional families than a worker with a bachelor's degree straight out of college.[1] While some child welfare departments legitimize protective service workers to provide long term, supportive, and/or insight oriented psychotherapy, other departments limit their caseworkers to investigation and short term crisis care. Heavy case loads are common and frequently prevent workers from providing the quantity or quality of services that are necessary. Also, the social worker is frequently in a very difficult position regarding her role with the family. She is required to investigate the family situation, make recommendations to the court, and frequently testify on material that leads to the judge's decision that the children should be placed in foster care. With distrustful and suspicious parents, it is difficult to begin a therapeutic relationship following these initial steps.

Despite these variations in the quality of casework services and the common drawbacks, casework has unique advantages. It provides an opportunity, with legally mandated authority, to coordinate services with other agencies so that treatment for individual family members is procured and continued. It is also the only modality that combines an opportunity to view the family as a whole with an ability to procure concrete services that the family is needing, such as medical

---

[a]The reader may find it helpful to review the manual published by the Office of Child Development (Washington, D.C.: U.S. Government Printing Office No. OHD 75-69) entitled "The Diagnostic Process and Treatment Programs" written by Ray E. Helfer. This gives an overview to the material covered in detail in this chapter.—Ed.

care, housing, food, and school placements. Casework provides for direct access to the child, assuring that the child's point of view is constantly represented. Observations of the child's growth and development and his physical safety can be made on a firsthand basis.

Because casework services are frequently provided through home visits, parent-child interactions can be observed and altered through direct suggestions by the caseworker. Although the caseworker's dual role of investigation and support have built-in conflicts, they also have some unique advantages. Abusive parents tend to split the people around them into either "good" or "bad" objects. If the caseworker is comfortable and will continue to strive to have a relationship with the parents, some parents will learn the important developmental task of combining negative and positive aspects into the same person.

### Individual Psychotherapy

Individual psychotherapy is usually provided by psychiatrists, clinical psychologists, or psychiatric social workers in an office by appointment. Therapy can be very diversified depending on the particular patient, the therapist's experience and style, and the many treatment techniques that can be used. The one commonality is that the psychotherapist is usually in tune to unconscious material, even though he may choose not to use that material directly.

The motivations for parents to go into psychotherapy vary. Many parents feel differently about going to see a therapist and going to see the protective service caseworker. To begin therapy usually implies some acknowledgement of personal psychological problems rather than simply more general problems with life. However, some parents begin therapy motivated by a wish to have their child returned from foster care rather than any desire to make personal changes.

One of the distinct advantages of most forms of psychotherapy is that it focuses on more than just here-and-now reality problems. There is some exploration of the parents' behavior and feelings with a goal of intellectual and emotional insight. However, as previously mentioned, the parents must also reexperience the nurturing and good parenting they missed as children. Without the latter, they may intellectually understand their abusive behavior but be unable to positively change their interactions with their child. Therefore, it is advantageous to provide psychotherapy in conjunction with some less traditional modalities of treatment such as lay therapy and Parents Anonymous to insure that the parents receive adequate support and nurturing.

One of the limitations of psychotherapy is that it frequently is not available and, even where it is available, it may not be obtained. Most abusive parents are too distrustful and too erratic in their behavior to come to an office on time for a 50-minute hour. Unless the psychotherapist is willing to make extensive phone calls or home visits in an attempt to elicit the trust of the parents, therapy may be futile. One of the most serious limitations of individual psychotherapy is that the focus is primarily on intrapsychic conflicts in the parents, not on parent-child interaction. This is primarily due to the therapist's orientation and his lack of training in dealing directly with parent-child relationships. The therapist may also have little access to information about these relationships or about the child in general. Changes in the parents' behavior toward the child may be too slow to protect the child's psychic and physical development. Therefore, unless someone else is directly involved with the child, his needs, including his need for physical safety, may not be met.

### Marital Treatment

Marital treatment is primarily provided by clinical psychologists and psychiatric social workers in an office setting. The husband and wife are seen together, preferably by cotherapists, with the focus being on marital problems. This modality is especially useful when the parents are aware that anger from their marriage is getting displaced onto their child. With improved communication and increased gratification of needs within the marraige, the child is less at risk. Marital treatment is contraindicated when the parents are so dependent and hungry for attention that they need a one-to-one relationship with a therapist. Such parents in marital treatment often end up competing for the therapists' attention and get little work done.

Such treatment is also not indicated if one parent is psychotic but the other has much more ego strength. In such cases it is more useful to work individually with the healthier parent so that he might unilaterally work out some long range plans for himself and the child. One of the limitations of this type of treatment is that marriage counselors can vary greatly in quality and training and there are very few state licensing regulations that govern them.

### Lay Therapy (Parent Aides)

Lay therapists, also called parent aides, are paraprofessionals who are parents themselves and have highly satisfactory family relationships. The primary role of the lay therapist is to provide long term nurturing to the parent. Most of the work is done through visiting in the home several times a week and providing transportation and social experiences for the mother or father. From the beginning it is clear that the lay therapist is there for the parent and not primarily for the child, although the child will benefit in the long run. The lay therapist cannot be responsible for protecting the child. If, however, a situation of jeopardy for the child arises, the lay therapist will alert others involved with the family. The intensive involvement of a lay therapist with the parent is around eighteen months to two years' duration. This is followed by a gradual lessening of contact but the relationship never formally terminates. The expectation is that the lay therapist will continue to be available when needed for as long as the family remains in the area. Even after families move, continued contact occurs through phone calls, letters, and birthday cards.

The advantages in a lay therapy program are numerous. Lay therapists can provide a tremendous amount of service at very low cost. It saves valuable social work and psychiatric time for other types of treatment. This modality is extremely useful with most abusive and neglectful families, for it provides a supportive relationship that the parent has never before experienced. Frequently, lay therapists are much less threatening to these families than a more traditional mental health professional would be. With the help of a lay therapist, many families have been seen to improve in their ability to cope with and enjoy life, as well as to improve in their relationships with their children.

Lay therapists have also been safe persons for the parents to use in times of crises and have often linked parents to community resources and more traditional psychotherapeutic modalities. Voluntary foster care and crisis nursery placements for a number of families in times of stress were accomplished because of the lay therapists' involvement with the families. Also, several voluntary permanent relinquishments were possible because of the lay therapists' ability to help parents consider this option and not feel condemned for their decision.

Lay therapists are contraindicated when the parent is psychotic, sociopathic, extremely violent, an addict, or so disturbed in some other way that a paraprofessional would likely become overwhelmed. Some of the other limitations of lay therapy include the difficulty in recognizing significant problems in the parents, especially problems that are uncomfortable for the lay therapist personally; difficulties in recognizing medical or psychological problems with the children; overidentification with parents and seeing other therapists with a negative view; overidentification with either the husband or the wife in a marital conflict; and difficulties with keeping the parents too dependent because the lay therapist is receiving a great deal of gratification from that dependency. These limitations should not, however, cause serious jeopardy to any lay therapy program. With supportive consultation from a social worker or psychiatrist, the lay therapists can usually move forward in their work with the family. It is a danger to attempt to train lay therapists to become professional psychotherapists, because it is their spontaneity and total lack of clinical jargon that makes them so successful.

The selection of the lay therapists is the key to the whole program. The criteria are "soft" in that they are based on personal qualifications, including parenting experience, rather than on education or work history. Initially, all potential lay therapists are interviewed in depth regarding their own early life experiences, their present family situation, and their feelings regarding abusive families. It is important to learn whether they felt truly loved and accepted by their parents or other significant persons in their early lives, whether they feel successful in their roles as parents now, and whether they have adequate support systems in their present lives to allow them to give freely and not feel overdrawn emotionally. Potential lay therapists should have the ability to empathize with the abusive parents' plight and have come to some understanding of their own aggressive feelings toward their children.

This does not mean, however, that lay therapists cannot have experienced any personal difficulties. Rather, they should have found some useful ways of coping with life's daily problems. The motivations of potential lay therapists vary, and when given enough time, many lay therapists screen themselves out of this program. Requiring lay therapists to be parents themselves is a very valid requirement, in that they have then experienced both the joys and pains of parenting and have a better understanding of the difficulties that abusive or potentially abusive parents face. Experience indicates that lay therapists who have children of school age are the most effective. The abusive parents generally view these persons as peers or friends and can accept nurturing from them.

Training begins with the initial interview, in which the program and the kind of commitment expected are explained. From that point on, potential lay therapists are brought to group meetings where they hear discussions about child abuse and specific families. They also learn how lay therapists and other staff have worked with these families and what the expectations for lay therapists are. Some individual conferences are held with each new therapist and reading materials and audiovisual tapes are provided. The period of time involved from the first interview until a lay therapist is assigned a family is about three months, or longer if appropriate for the particular lay therapist. On the few occasions that a lay therapist has been assigned within a shorter period of time, there have been difficulties. The lay therapist needs adequate time to become integrated into the team and to feel that he or she has the necessary background and support to attempt this type of work.

After a lay therapist picks up a family, he or she continues to come to group meetings and gradually may carry as many as three to four families, working up to twenty hours a week. Weekly consultation is available from both a social worker and a psychiatrist. All families assigned to a lay therapist must be evaluated by a professional, preferably the social worker, who will provide the ongoing consultation. The social worker provides the primary support for the lay therapist and is available by phone on a daily basis, as needed. Frequently, the social worker knows all the families who will be followed by the lay therapists so she can provide a backup when lay therapists go on vacation or are ill.

Lay therapists are employed on a part time basis up to one-half time or twenty hours weekly. This was established as the maximum amount of time a person could reasonably give of themselves in such emotionally draining relationships. Although there are many advantages in paying the lay therapists, some successful programs have been established on a volunteer basis. Remuneration, even though it may be quite small, helps the lay therapists to feel that they are a part of the multidisciplinary team, helps validate the consultant's role in making suggestions that are to be followed through on by the lay therapists, and helps the lay therapists at least break even financially for the transportation and food they will be providing for the families they are helping.

### Group Psychotherapy

Group psychotherapy for abusive parents is usually provided by clinical psychologists and psychiatric social workers, although professionals from many other disciplines may be involved. The purposes of groups vary, depending on the type of people involved and what they are choosing to focus on; a group may be primarily dealing with individual problems, marital problems, or with child management issues.

The advantages of groups are numerous. They provide an opportunity to reach more people with fewer professional staff; they provide a means of decreasing the isolation of parents and facilitating mutual support systems; and they also increase confrontation of denial and problems among group members. This usually takes place earlier and more intensely than it would in one-to-one treatment. Parents can also feel through a group experience that they can be helpful to others. Groups provide beginning socialization and pleasurable activities for the parents; the amount of this varies with groups, but many of these parents continue their contact following a group meeting. Many groups also provide accurate child rearing and child development information when the group members are ready for it. Group psychotherapy is especially indicated for those parents who are not extremely threatened by exposing their feelings to others.

Despite all these advantages, groups are not indicated for all abusive parents. They are contraindicated when a parent is in a severe crisis situation, for abusive parents usually need one-to-one support during this time. Also, parents who are extremely disturbed may be disruptive in groups and may experience further rejection. Some parents are extremely threatened by exposing their feelings to others and prefer a one-to-one therapeutic experience. For some parents, it is safer to approach Parents Anonymous than a more traditional group.

The issues of time, place, transportation, babysitting, group size, therapists, and pregroup preparation are very important issues, which need to be carefully thought out before a group is begun. Any group of abusive parents will need a safe place to meet where they can be sure that no one outside the group can hear them. A consistent meeting room and a consistent day and hour of the week are crucial. Many of the parents may initially have transportation difficulties, and some concrete help should be provided for them. Also, babysitting is frequently a problem and child care may need to be provided so that parents can attend the group.

A cotherapy model is important in all groups, regardless of population, but it is especially important with abusive parents, who tend to split "good" and "bad" figures. With two therapists, the group can feel comfortable in verbally attacking one, and yet have another therapist who is able to be of support and comfort to them. If one therapist leaves on a vacation, the group can continue, since there is another therapist. Whenever possible, the cotherapists should be a male and a female. Such a model facilitates the expression of feelings regarding parental figures.

The size of the group is a critical issue that is often difficult to control. The ideal size of an interactional therapy group is approximately seven, with an acceptable range of from five to ten members. With less than five, a group may cease to function as a group and the treatment may become individual therapy within the group. With more than ten members, the individuals may not get ample opportunity to express their feelings nor to receive the attention they so desperately need. Although a closed group with total stability of membership has many advantages, it usually is neither practical nor feasible. Many abusive parents will drop out of the group after the first few meetings or their attendance will be sporadic. Therefore, most groups will need to be open-ended, accepting new members when it becomes necessary in order to maintain a size of approximately seven.

Preparation of abusive parents for group treatment is an important issue that is frequently overlooked. Pregroup, individual sessions with both therapists can provide an opportunity to build rapport with the parents, to lessen the parents' fears and misconceptions about group therapy, and to explain how the expression of feelings in a safe group can be therapeutic. Such preparation frequently helps parents get through periods of discouragement when they may want to flee treatment.

Finally, it will be necessary for the therapist to make outreach efforts to the parents during difficult periods. Phone calls and occasional home visits or individual sessions should be part of the treatment plan. In our experience, group treatment with parents is most beneficial when the parents are also receiving some type of individual therapy. To prevent the emotional burnout of the group therapists, it is useful to have the individual treatment provided by other professionals, such as caseworkers and mental health clinicians.

### Parents Anonymous

Because so many abusive parents seek help and anonymity at the same time, self-help parents groups such as Parents Anonymous as well as child abuse "hot lines" are now rapidly spreading across the United States. Parents Anonymous was founded by Jolly K., an abusive mother who felt the protective service system unresponsive to her needs time after time. In its first year or two (1969–1970) fathers were not prominently sought, but the mothers' groups still accomplished a great deal by providing anonymity, emergency lifelines to other group members whose telephone numbers were shared, and by facing the problem with others rather than alone. From this start the groups include families involved in past or potential physical abuse, physical neglect, emotional abuse, emotional neglect and verbal assault, and sexual abuse. Nonjudgmental and unconditional mutual acceptance within the group has led to remarkable results in families, who may become able to accept professional help with the encouragement of the group.

A number of protective service departments have formed a sympathetic liaison with Parents Anonymous chapters and refer families as an additional modality of treatment. In recent years Parents Anonymous has included the concept of a sponsor—generally a social worker or psychologist, sometimes a nurse or a physician—who is used as a resource but is not the identified leader of the group. The sponsor, who should not be working in the area's protective service department to preserve member anonymity, has as one function the further individual contact some members may require after a particularly disturbing session.

### Crisis Nurseries

Most abusive parents have very few lifelines; when they are under stress or in a crisis situation, they frequently have nothing to do but to stay at home, cooped up with their children. The close proximity to the child and the lack of alternatives for the parent frequently result in injury to the child. Crisis nurseries can help provide needed services at these stressful times. The primary purpose of a crisis nursery is the prevention of injuries to children. However, many other goals can be achieved through such a facility. Parents can be helped to feel comfortable about getting away from their children; using the crisis nursery is often a prelude to their finding acceptable babysitters and day care facilities in the community. Some parents may not have injured their child as yet but desperately need to get away.

Occasionally the nursery can be a stepping stone to a voluntary foster placement. It can provide short term care so that the parent has time to sort things out and consider alternatives. The nursery can also be used as a holding facility between the time of hospitalization and foster placement, although this is of lower priority. A nursery can also legitimately be used for child care while parents are having their therapy appointments. The children frequently look forward to these structured visits. The nursery can also be a positive benefit to the children by providing age appropriate stimulation. In no way should the nursery be considered simply as babysitting. Older children can be helped to express their feelings and conflicts. They also can receive the support and stimulation they may not be getting at home. Seeing the children in the nursery can often provide access to getting developmental assessments and perhaps treatment for a particular child.

The nursery can often provide a means of engaging the family into other treatment modalities. When a family visits the nursery and begins to develop some trust, they also learn of other programs available and frequently ask to become involved. Crisis nurseries can be located in foster homes, day care and preschool settings, and in independent facilities. The crisis nursery at The National Center in Denver is licensed as an extended care facility of Colorado General Hospital. If crisis nurseries are provided through foster homes, the primary issues then must be how to supply adequately trained staff to help the foster parents and how to provide adequate physical space for separate rooms for playing and sleeping. Most crisis nurseries give priority to newborns and children up to the age of 5 years. Older children can be accepted on an individual basis, but frequently there are other services within the community that may be more satisfactory than a nursery.

A crisis nursery must be staffed twenty-four hours a day, seven days a week, fifty-two weeks a year. Although foster parents and paraprofessionals can provide much of the care for these children, it is essential that multidisciplinary professional staff be involved in the project. Many abused children are emotionally disturbed, have developmental lags, or have medical problems. Some are extremely difficult to manage; they frequently require good diagnostic assessment and treatment planning. Unless an early childhood special education teacher, a nurse or doctor, a social worker, and other child development specialists are involved in the project, it will be merely a holding facility, though even that may save lives.

There are few limitations and barriers to a crisis nursery, although the maximal duration of stay is 72 hours. Although there are always a few parents who are extremely manipulative, who continuously test limits, and who will leave their children at a nursery and never pick them up on time, this is the exception. Most abusive parents are hesitant about using babysitters and a nursery. It requires a great deal of time to help them feel comfortable in even leaving their children. The nursery is contraindicated for children with severe emotional and medical problems, which cannot be handled by paraprofessional staff. For example, a psychotic child with self-destructive behavior needs a residential treatment facility, not a crisis nursery. In general, if a child can be managed in a foster home, day care, or preschool setting, he can be taken care of by crisis nursery staff. Abusive parents also have particular treatment needs and there are several known effective treatment modalities, which are best utilized in some combination. For example, a parent may be in group therapy, have a lay therapist, and also utilize the crisis nursery on a regular basis. Whenever one provides treatment to these parents, the effects on other family members must always be kept in mind.

## THERAPY FOR THE CHILD

There has not been sufficient experience with various treatment modalities with children to consider each of them separately or to detail the advantages and limitations of each. We do know what the treatment needs of these children are. This section is therefore oriented around the needs the children have, with some comments on our experience on trying to meet those needs.

All abused children have a variety of needs for which various types of therapeutic intervention are indicated. Before exploring those needs and interventions, emphasis should be given to consider the relative paucity of investigations into the therapeutic needs of abused children. It is ironic that the specific problems of abused children have obtained so little recognition to this point. Impetus for professional interest in work in the area of child abuse surely included a sincere interest and concern for abused children. And yet, the developmental and psychological wounds of abused children so often go unnoticed and untreated. While there seem to be a number of reasons for this paradox, perhaps the most important basis for ignoring the treatment needs of abused children came from a somewhat distorted way of thinking of child abuse.

The early work in child abuse usually took a medical model, or occasionally a social-legal model. Under the medical model the physical trauma the child suffered was viewed as the problem or "disease" from which the child was suffering. The physical trauma was the reason the child was recognized and the reason a variety of medical and social interventions were undertaken. Gradually, however, we have shifted to seeing child abuse as a syndrome—that is, a grouping of various problems that make up a recognizable entity. This is another way of stating that child abuse is not a situation where there is a simple cause (the physical trauma) of a simple problem (the medical consequences). When this latter, simplistic thinking governs behavior, we need look no further than at ways to erradicate the cause of this physical phenomena: we need only to prevent nonaccidental injury to the child or prevent its recurrence.

But child abuse is not a simplistic problem that can be appreciated as a simple illness. It is a family problem. The nonaccidental injury to the child is but the indicator of a dysfunctioning family that brings the child and the entire family to our attention. We now know that when we encounter a family where a child has been abused, we shall in all likelihood find a whole host of indicators of family dysfunction: marital problems, emotional disturbance in parents, developmental and psychological problems in the child and his siblings. We cannot deal with this family dysfunction by only preventing the occurrence of one of the symptoms, that is (the abuse of a child). We need instead to treat the underlying causes of this syndrome; we must tend to and offer treatment for *all* the consequences of this situation, not just the medical consequences of the physical trauma.

The social-legal approach to problems has been another unsatisfactory way to deal with child abuse. In the social-legal setting, the reaction to child abuse is similar to the reaction to the commission of any crime. Child abuse is a crime, and society usually deals with the commission of a crime by apprehending the perpetrator. We may punish him, remove him from society, or make various attempts at rehabilitation so that he or she is unlikely to repeat this particular crime. We have taken all those approaches to abusive parents with various rates of success. When a crime is committed we try to prevent such crimes from being committed by others. Security measures may be instituted to protect potential victims. The parallels with child abuse should be obvious. Another parallel needs emphasis: the relative lack of interest in the victim of a crime. While child abuse is an indication of family dysfunction, and while we may view the abusive parent as more psychologically troubled than as perpetrators of a crime, nonetheless, insofar as child abuse is a legal phenomenon, there surely is a victim.

When child abuse is seen primarily as a criminal phenomenon, the approach under which society operates offers little help to the victim while focusing attention on the perpetrator, whether it take the form of punishment, banishment, or rehabilitation. However, courts, police, and welfare agencies have recently made steps toward seeing child abuse as a sociological problem of family dysfunction. The rather recent establishment of a guardian ad litem for the abused child is but one indicator of the concern of protecting the best interests of the child in legal proceedings. The move from handling child abuse in criminal court to managing the legal maneuvers in juvenile court is another such indicator of wholesome shifts in society's understanding of the child abuse syndrome.

In brief, we might see child abuse as a phenomenon wherein all members in the family are victims, including the parents, the identified abused child, and the siblings of the child. It is notable that little attention has been given to the siblings of the abused child. Our experience has resulted in two common situations of concern. First is the frequent experience where a specific child has been identified as having been physically abused, but there is a second child in the family, obstensibly uninjured, who is of greater concern to the parent than the identified abused child. This commonly involves the abuse of an infant while an older child is described as the real problem child. Whether physical assault has occurred in the past with the older child is often impossible to know with certainty. However, the parents' dynamics with the older abused child may be much more typical of the parent-child relationship seen in child abuse than is the case with the identified patient. There is also the frequent occurrence of several children being abused in the same family. At the time when only one child is identified as abused, it can easily happen that the other children in the family are not recognized as abused or potentially abused until at some later time.

A second situation of concern is the role of siblings in abusive behavior towards the identified patient. The siblings may be part of a family conspiracy towards a scapegoated child. Even when the siblings have not been party to abusive behavior, we have considerable concern for the siblings who have witnessed violent physical attacks on one of their siblings. Many children in abusive homes have witnessed the attack on a sibling which has resulted in the child's death. But whether fatal or not, the impact of witnessing or being aware of abusive behavior towards a sibling must be a momentous, psychological trauma. Some siblings react with guilt, assuming some part in the attack on their sibling or feeling that they are, in some manner, responsible for the physical assault. The sibling may feel that he could, and should, have prevented the physical abuse. Certainly the child who grows up in a home where there are physical attacks on one of his parents or a sibling must have vivid fear and anxiety, wondering whether, and when, the violent assaults might be directed towards him.

Terry, age seven, was being seen in play therapy because of symptoms of bed-wetting, excessive daydreaming in school, a generalized fear of adults, and a preoccupation with being good. Two years prior she had witnessed the fatal beating of her two-year-old brother. In her pictures and play she expressed her fear of dying should she ever elicit the rage of adults as her brother had done.

Both diagnosis and treatment must be directed towards the entire family—not only the parent and the abused child but also the siblings of the child. When a child has been identified as abused, the relationship of the parents to the other child must be explored. Even when there appears to be no danger of physical abuse to the siblings, the effects of the abusive incidents and the whole abusive environment on the siblings should be of concern to the child protection team. The siblings are part of a dysfunctional family and they are apt to pay a large price in terms of their own growth and development; their treatment needs should also be part of the treatment planning.

The effects of the environment on the abused child and the concomitant consideration of treatment needs is such a vast subject that another volume related to this is to be published soon.[1] However, the key points of the treatment needs and the attempts to meet those needs can be dealt with in summary fashion here. Three treatment needs of these children shall be discussed. There are: (1) the medical treatment of the child; (2) the treatment of developmental and psychological problems and (3) the establishment of an adequate home environment.

### Medical Treatment

The first priority in medical management is the treatment of the nonaccidental injuries the child has sustained, such as, bruises, burns, fractures, and lacerations. Such treatment is usually available to abused children. A second area of medical treatment involves the identification and treatment of long term handicapping sequelae to the nonaccidental injury such as brain damage, sensory loss, or other chronic handicaps. Such long term treatment is often not available from the same medical personnel who undertake the immediate medical treatment of the child. This then requires the consultation and referral to a variety of specialists who can, and will, offer long term care for the consequences of the physical trauma.

A third less obvious area of medical treatment involves attention to the medical problems of the child which are not related to the physical trauma per se, but are related to the inadequate parenting the child has received. Several studies of abused children have noted that from 30 to 40 percent of abused children are undernourished at the time abuse was diagnosed.[2,3,4] Anemia is a common finding in such children. It is our experience that abused children have had a higher incidence of ear infections and other respiratory diseases in their past than do other children. These children have had a great number of infections and medical problems prior to the abuse and they usually have had poor medical care.[5] Normal preventive medical care has often not been available, for many of these children are found to need immunizations. These children need to be under the regular care of a child's physician so that all their chronic medical needs can be met. This medical care should be established with a single doctor, a clinic or health station where recurring change of medical personnel must not take place. So often the medical personnel changes every time the child is moved from one home to another. The importance of sustained, long term medical care from the same medical resource needs to be emphasized.

### Treatment of Developmental and Psychological Problems

Almost all abused children will have significant developmental and psychological problems in addition to their somatic injuries. Elmer[3] found that 88 percent of the children in their study had significant developmental problems. A number of other authors have documented these problems in more detail.[1,2,5,6] The professionals who deal with child abuse must continually recognize such developmental and psychological problems. In every instance of child abuse, it is recommended that the child protection team routinely and regularly address the following questions.

1. What is the developmental status of the child? Does he have problems in the areas of learning, motor coordination, speech and language, and perceptual-motor function? If so, what help can be provided?
2. What is the personality of this child? How has he adapted to the abusive environment? How has he reacted to the abuse and all that has happened subsequently? What is the nature of his peer relationships, his adult-child relationships, his self-concept, his general state of happiness? What can be done to help the child with the psychological problems he has?
3. What will be the effect on the child of the various treatment plans being made? If the child is to be hospitalized, separated from his parents, placed in a foster home, what will the effects of these moves be on him? All aspects of management should be considered in terms of their relationship to the welfare of the child. For example, when the team is deciding on changes of visiting rights for parents of the abused child who is in foster care, the best interests of the child should be paramount. Visiting rights for parents are often used as some sort of reward for their "progress." And yet, even when parents do not "deserve" to see their children, it may well be in the best interest of the child to have regular contact with the parents. This position requires an awareness that much of what is done in a case of child abuse actually provides increased guilt and trauma for the child. We must then ask what we can do or provide so as to minimize the deleterious effects of our various treatment plans.

If these three questions are adequately asked—and answered—for each abused child, then there is little chance that the child will not receive the needed help. To answer such questions will often require the use of professional consultants such as child development experts, child psychologists, child psychiatrists, and speech and language pathologists, who frequently are not available to child protection teams. Most of the professionals working with child protection teams have more expertise in social systems, adult psychopathology, law, and medicine than they have in child development and child psychology.

The implications of child protection teams addressing the above questions of need are many. It might be that the composition of teams will have to change; that consultants to help the teams answer these questions will need to be found and utilized; that the child protection teams will quickly discover that services for children in their communities are very limited and some effort will need to be expended to increase range and availability of these services.

Some examples of the types of services these children require include physical therapy, occupational therapy, and speech and language therapy, in order to offer treatment for their various motor, perceptual, and communication lags. Another form of therapy that should be available to all abused children under five years of age is a preschool or day care setting. In the experience of staff at The National Center for the Prevention and Treatment of Child Abuse and Neglect in Denver, a group setting such as a therapeutic preschool can offer the most helpful type of treatment for these children. In such a setting there are a variety of goals that can be met that are rarely possible in another treatment setting. They include:

1. *Respite for child and parent.* The separation of child and parent for several hours a week removes some stress from the parents. It also allows the child a respite from an abusive or unloving environment.
2. *Developmental stimulation.* The stimulation of learning in a school or day care setting may be the only manner in which healthy motivation for learning, growth, and development will take place.
3. *Remediation of developmental lags and deficits.* A preschool is an ideal place for children to get specific help with delays and deficits they may have in speech and language, motor coordination, perception, and learning skills. There is a high incidence of such developmental lags in abused children. The use of preschool staff with consultation from appropriate professionals in other fields is an optimal use of manpower for providing treatment for these developmental deficits.
4. *Socialization.* The abused child has very poor models of interpersonal interaction. The preschool setting provides the opportunity for the child to learn how to relate to his peers and with the adult preschool staff. He can learn not only how to get along with others but also how to obtain pleasure and gratification in relating with other children and adults.
5. *Help with personality traits.* A psychologically sensitive preschool staff can identify and modify those personality traits that handicap the child and make him unhappy. They can help the child identify, acknowledge, and appropriately express his feelings; encourage the development of a sense of self and

improve the child's self-esteem and self-confidence; and loosen the inhibitions the child has around "messing," having fun, and expressing his normal aggressions.

We have primarily been speaking to the needs of the younger child where day care or preschool are available and appropriate for the developmental needs of the child. The important role of elementary school must also be mentioned, for in an elementary school these same therapeutic goals can be met. In addition to the classroom teacher, other persons may need to be available to the child. We have frequently found that when the public schools have been approached, they have taken over this broader role with an abused child. A school nurse, social worker, teacher, or counselor may be willing to spend some extra time with a child on a regular weekly basis to help the child deal with his reactions and adaptations to the abusive environment. This may be much more comfortable, and in the long run more helpful, than a more traditional psychotherapeutic setting. If nothing else, the message that an adult outside the family can enjoy the child, can tolerate his feelings, and is selflessly interested in the child's happiness can make a tremendous impact on the abused child.

The most important psychological need of abused children is to have someone to help them through the especially stressful events in their lives. The literature has addressed this in terms of children dealing with the stresses of hospitalization, death of a parent, divorce or separation of parents, or diagnosis of a chronic or particularly difficult disease with potential for fatality. But what of the abused child? He has to deal with having been physically and emotionally battered by an adult—usually a parent—on whom he is dependent for love and emotional sustenance. He has to deal with hospitalization and with separation from parents, with being moved to a strange family in a foster home, sometimes repeatedly. He is frequently the participant in legal and emotional storms where he is the center of attention. His emotional, physical, and developmental needs have been ignored, or at best have been met erratically and in a distorted manner. Deprivation, neglect, violence, and distorted parenting have been the rule.

The help he needs may come in various forms and from a number of different types of adults. The medical setting can provide a physician, nurse, or social worker. In a number of instances, child welfare workers have had the interest and ability to provide psychological help and support to the child. Foster parents occasionally are helpful to the child with such psychological issues. The staff of the preschool or day care setting can attend to the psychological problems of the abused child. We are impressed with the psychological problems of these children, even the children who are not thought to be problems by their parents, teachers, or child welfare workers. Some abused children will need and benefit from traditional types of psychotherapy. (The issues and results of such treatment are discussed elsewhere.[1])

The problem is that such help is usually fortuitous, depending on chance that such a suitable person is available to the needy child. But the provision of psychological help to the child should not be happenstance. There must be some child advocate who makes sure that the psychological problems of the child are specifically considered and that therapeutic help will *always* be provided. That advocate may be a member of the child protection team or the guardian ad litem, or any adult who has contact with the abused child.

### Establishment of an Adequate Environment

An adequate home environment provides a child with a family where there are parents who love and care about the child. The abused child has not had adequate parenting nor has he lived in a family where his psychological, physical and developmental needs have been met. The rapid establishment of an adequate home environment is the most important and critical need of abused children.

This need has a number of implications for our present system of foster care. If we start from the premise that adequate parenting is required for a child to properly grow and develop, then a number of corollaries follow. For one, this implies that foster parents, when needed, will be chosen on the basis of their adequacy as parents. It means that the agencies who are ultimately responsible for the dependent child will provide counseling and support for foster parents who have these troubled children in their homes. It means that a number of changes in policy will be directed at helping the foster parents take the role of psychological parents.[7]

Much of the basis for therapy for the abusive parents of the child should be directed towards just this goal—that is, to help them become adequate parents. Case work, group therapy, psychotherapy, and lay therapy for abusive parents have been incomplete if they have not dealt with the role of the adult as a parent. This issue will be taken up in the section on therapy directed towards improving family relationships. It is no easy task to describe or define in any detail what constitutes good parenting. We are more often able to identify inadequate parenting. We have some confidence that good enough parenting will be provided when we can see the following:

1. The parents can find joy for themselves. This includes increased mutual sexual satisfaction.
2. The parents see the child as an individual. This is a shift from seeing the child primarily as a need-satisfying object for the parents. It further involves a respect for the individuality of the child rather than viewing him as an extension of the parents.
3. The parents enjoy the child. When the parents are able to take pleasure from the child and enjoy his presence and behavior, then we have some assurance that adequate attachment and bonding are present.
4. The expectations of the child are age-appropriate. This marks a shift from the highly unrealistic expectations of most abusive parents.

5. The parents have the ability to tolerate the child's negative behavior. This involves allowing the child to have anger and express it in some manner; and it means the parents can appreciate the child even though the child may misbehave or give them negative feedback. This requires a sense of self and self-confidence as parents, so that absence of positive reinforcement does not threaten the ego integrity of the parents.

6. The parents can allow the child to receive emotional rewards from people outside the family. This has wide implications: it means that the family is not so isolated that need gratification must come from within the nuclear family; and it implies that the parents have loosened their unhealthy interdependency on the child. It further means that the parents will be able to allow the child to receive the recommended treatment and therapies. An altruistic love for the child which can endure the pain and struggle of allowing the child to grow up is seen.

7. The parents are comfortable about expressing positive affects to the child. Verbal and physical demonstrations of caring come easily to the parent.

These are the types of guidelines we use in determining whether parents are capable of providing a growth promoting family life for the child. They might be applied to parents when deciding when the child might return to the biologic home. They might also be applied to foster parents or to any proposed parent surrogate for the child. In a sense, this third goal of therapy for the child—the provision of an adequate family life—is the real crux of all treatment for the child; for when the child is in such a home, the parents will see to it that his medical needs are met. Such parents will also want the developmental and psychological needs of the child to be met. While it is undoubtedly true that "love is not enough," it is equally true that love and an adequate home environment are the foundations upon which other growth of the child can be built.

## THERAPY FOR FAMILY INTERACTIONS

The first two parts of this chapter have emphasized the treatment needs and treatment methods for abusive parents and their children. Every therapeutic effort we make for any member of an abused child's family may be seen as therapeutic for the whole; but without planning for and looking at the family as a unit, we may fall short of our goal of improving family interactions. The interpsychic issues for each individual are important, but also important is how these issues are affected by the relationship among all the family members.

A consistent and coherent look at the total family must be a part of the therapeutic efforts for both parents and children. Within the context of what is already established protective service practice, increased efforts can be made to assess the effects of treatment plans on the family and to assess the potential for the family's adequate functioning. This section will discuss separation and parent-child visits, home visits, parent education and modeling behavior, and family therapy in the context of family interaction.

### Separation and Parent-Child Visits

Hospitalization of an abused child and possible subsequent foster care placement have effects on the other family members and on their relationships with the child. One obvious result is a loosening of the familial ties; very tight pathological bonds often need this kind of disruption to allow a new realignment on healthier terms. Separation can be used to maximize this potential for altering unhealthy bonds without necessarily severing the whole familial relationship.

One valuable tool in trying to alter the relationship is to assess as early as possible what the relationship actually is. Where are the difficulties? Where are the strengths? What aspects can we build on and what needs to be changed? Few parents have a totally negative relationship with their child; however, in the period preceeding the abuse incident, the negative aspects may have taken precedence, leaving little energy or availability on either the parents' or child's part for sharing their healthier interactions.

The marital relationship must be given equal attention to understand how the respective partners counter and balance each other in respect to the child. Are the precipitating factors more in relation to how the child is used between the parents, or is the child an added stress the marriage cannot presently tolerate? Without a dynamic picture of how the total family operates we will be unable to know clearly how separation is affecting each member individually and the family collectively. Siblings need careful consideration at this point also. Will the absence of the abused child cause a shift for a sibling, thus placing him in jeopardy or added stress?

Separation then may have different meanings and uses, depending on the family structure. Certainly, in a broad sense, neglect or failure to thrive is an indicator of too little attachment of parent to child and separation may only reinforce the most difficult aspect of the relationship. Every effort must be made to keep parents and child in contact and to bridge the already existing distance in the relationship if reunion is planned. In abuse, pathologic bonding is more typical, but even in this situation a total rupture between parents and child will leave an added wound to heal.

There are ways to enhance the more positive aspects of the relationship while offering the relief to the parents as well as safety and care for the child. Visits between parents and the child become crucial in enhancing the more positive aspects of the parent-child relationship. However, such visits are often used by many of us as a necessary evil, not unlike one divorced parent's view of his estranged spouse's visits to their children. Difficult and painful though they are, visits are important therapeutic opportunities that are frequently overlooked. Planning visits based on the needs of the child and the parents as opposed to the needs of the agency or foster parents, or the availability of transportation could be a beginning in capitalizing on these important experiences.

Early in the separation the child needs reassuring contact with his parents to know that they have not deserted him. Short, frequent visits may be more useful to both parents and child than long, infrequent contacts. The usual "adjustment period," in which no visits are allowed, is unnecessarily cruel to the young child, to whom two weeks may be felt as "forever." Although visits may cause disturbing behavior in the children which is particularly upsetting to the foster parents, this behavior is a sign of true attachment to the biological parents and a realistic indicator of the pain the separation is causing. Avoiding visits when this behavior occurs, or because the adults caring for the child or his parents may find it too difficult to tolerate the child's distress is unwise. This should be seen as proper expression of attachment and pain. Visits are often used as a reward or punishment in attempts to control the parents. "If you do not come regularly for your appointments, you will not be able to visit your child." Although this is a tempting handle to use, it negates the very valuable use of visits to increase attachment and to alter the parent-child relationship.

For the parents, a contact should be provided with the child that is as positive as can possibly be planned for. The old hassles of eating, bedtime, or whatever has been particularly stressful for the parents should be avoided. Instead, the parents should have the opportunity to see the child in a less antagonistic and demanding way, at times when enjoyment can be maximized, and in a quiet and supportive setting. This may take time and patient help, as the parents' views of the child have become deeply fixed. However, there are excellent opportunities for modeling good parenting behavior. A sensitive and skillful worker should be used to facilitate the visits if they are to reap the benefits they hold therapeutically. Too often, lay people and the least experienced social workers are used for merely transportation purposes for the visits.

The worker must plan carefully to insure as useful a visit as possible. Snacks for the whole family to share, extra diapers, clean changes of clothes for the children, a comfortable setting, and words of encouragement from the worker will all help facilitate positive interaction. Reassuring explanations of the child's normal reactions to separation should be made, as parents most likely will interpret the child's behavior in terms of their own perception. They may feel that the child is being stubborn or hateful rather than seeing the child's behavior as meeting his own needs. Slowly, the parents may be able to identify with some of those feelings such as fear, hurt, or unhappiness that are similar to their own. If these guidelines are used and expanded, visits between parent and child will become a useful therapeutic tool.

### Home Visits by the Therapist

Home visits, when the child remains in the home or when he is returned to the home, offer a very valuable source of information that can be used to determine the effectiveness of other treatment attempts. Through the observations and monitoring in the home situation, changes and difficulties within the family can be objectively evaluated. Although outreach into the home is offered for a variety of reasons, one benefit can be the feedback about the family relationships. Whether a lay therapist, visiting nurse, case worker, or psychiatrist visits in the home, valuable information can be gleaned, especially if the home visitor is alert to specific areas where information is needed.

In general, the signs of good parenting listed in an earlier section of this chapter are the areas of concern. Specific examples for less experienced home visitors may help them identify what the signs actually are. Does mother say positive things about Johnny? Or does she make derogatory comments in his presence? Are there age-appropriate playthings for the children? Is there adequate supervision for safety? Does the child have freedom in play and movement? Can he express anger openly? Do the parents have friends? Do the children have friends? What is the parental interaction around the child? Do the parents vie for the child's attention? The kind of information the home visits provide can help individual therapists and child protection teams determine whether relationships are changing and whether therapy is becoming effective.

Home visits provide another opportunity for modeling behavior as parents see other ways of relating to their children. The nurturing, supportive relationship that often accompanies the home visiting is a parenting model directly experienced by the parents. The parents learn to love as they are loved. Demonstration in the home may be a rich opportunity, too little valued.

### Parent Education and Modeling Behavior

Parent education classes such as Parents' Effectiveness Training[b] require a very high degree of motivation which often is not present. The need for basic information cannot be ignored, as most abusive parents have serious deficits in their knowledge and understanding about child care and child development. Timing becomes a critical issue in attempting to provide information. Because of the parents' high degree of sensitivity about their parental deficits, they need time to develop trust and have some of their own emotional needs begun to be met before they have energy and interest available to learn about their child. Learning may need to be very elementary for some parents and might be offered through small parents' groups, to take the stigma off a single parent's or couples' implied lack of knowledge. Educational endeavors should not be expected to be a primary effort of changing the parent-child relationship; at best this will be a supplement to other interventions.

Modeling of appropriate child care methods and adequate parenting may be a more appropriate method of changing parent-child interactions. There are a

---

[b]P.E.T. is helpful for many parents. We have found, however, that considerable modification is necessary in the delivery if it is to be useful for many abusive parents. The developmental deficits are so great for some parents that the standard P.E.T. is like algebra II when arithmetic is needed.—Ed.

variety of places where modeling may be possible. Already mentioned are those possibilities existing in parent-child visits during periods of separation, and the home visits made when the child is living in the home. Letting parents have opportunities to observe others dealing with other children can also be valuable. The child's preschool teacher, day care worker, foster parent, and therapist can demonstrate alternative ways of dealing with the parents' child and with children in general. The parents' readiness to use these experiences will be critical, however. Also, such experiences should never imply criticism of the parents. In the Circle House Residential Treatment program at The National Center in Denver we have become aware how much parents do watch and learn as they see the child care staff handle their children. No lectures or attempts to teach could be as useful as the firsthand observations by the parents and their attempts to then try for themselves.

> When Burt and Irene moved into the family residential program five weeks ago, they had extremely high expectations of their five-month-old daughter, Susy. Because part of the treatment plan includes their observing one hour each day in the child care unit, they have seen what other infants and children are able to do at different ages. They are particularly eager to watch the child care workers manage demanding and aggressive children. Recently they told their therapist, "Susy isn't retarded after all, and if we stay calm when she is fussy, it doesn't last that long. Susy just doesn't seem to be the kind of kid we thought she was."

**Family Therapy**

Family therapy has not been used extensively in treating abusive and neglectful families. However, it may be a valuable method of directly dealing with family relationships. There are, however, some considerations in implementing this. The parents' level of frustration and anger with the child may be so high as to require some venting. Early expressions of anger may not be adequately countered with any positive reassurances to the child. Placing a child in a position of having to hear these feelings expressed over and over again may place unnecessary pain and stress on his already fragile sense of self-worth.

The child's anger may also require some expression and be unbearable for the parents to tolerate without alienating them further. The child may need an opportunity to have some control over this before dealing directly with his parents in this difficult and sensitive area. Severe marital discord may be a major issue needing resolution before the total family can begin to deal adequately with their relationships. The degree of emotional deprivation and needs in both parents and children suggest individualized care before therapists can be shared by the family. Individual attention may need to continue in order to help family members tolerate and continue in family therapy.

Family therapy has some very distinct possible advantages. Most obviously, it is the one therapeutic mode whose purpose it is to attend to the interrelatedness of the individual family members. There is, as in groups of any sort, less opportunity to distort reality and influence the therapist's opinion. Diagnostically, a great deal can be gleaned from family interviews even if this is not the ongoing treatment of choice. Family therapy is based on the family as a functioning unit with no single member as the identified patient. This very premise is correct in its lack of corroboration with perceptions of the "bad" child or failing parents; instead, the premise of each member's part in the total family problem is offered as a working base.

### Coordination of Therapeutic Efforts with an Emphasis on Family Interaction

The need for coordination was stressed in the opening comments of this chapter. Coordination of therapeutic efforts is another means of monitoring and affecting what goes on between parent and child. Planning and sharing among those involved can quickly help us identify how each family member affects the others. Regular reviews of the therapeutic progress or failures are essential: Are particular behaviors of the child causing unbearable stress to these particular parents? Can the child's therapist or play school teacher help him modify these behaviors to facilitate his parents' acceptance and pleasure with him? Can certain parental behaviors be altered to allow for the child's necessary growth? Do the parents need helpful handles to deal with specific child behavior? As we work individually in different ways and settings with family members our concerted efforts should bring forth a more harmonious, comfortable, and healthy family relationship.

### SUMMARY

Family oriented treatment for abusive families should be the goal of all protective service efforts. Too often the treatment needs of only certain family members are considered. Children as well as parents need treatment in their own right. However, even when treatments are used in combination for all members, the effects on the total family are frequently not considered. To truly improve parent-child interaction, the family must always be considered as a unit.

✳ Chapter Eleven

# Residential Therapy—
# A Place of Safety

Margaret A. Lynch
Christopher Ounsted

## INTRODUCTION

The inpatient unit described here is at the Park Hospital for Children
in Oxford, England. This is a National Health Service hospital dealing with disorders of brain function and development. The main
hospital has 30 beds. In 1964 a house accommodating three families was added
to the existing facilities in order to provide a setting for the treatment of whole
families. Initially it was thought that the main need was for psychotherapy for
the hyperpedophiliac parents and siblings of irreversibly handicapped children,[1]
but the last few years have seen a dramatic increase in the number of referrals to
our services for treatment of both actual and threatened abuse. In 1971–73
these cases represented about half the admissions to the unit; in 1974 the rate
had risen to 70 percent and in the first six months of 1975 to 80 percent. At the
present admission/discharge rate this means that in one year the facility can
expect to treat as inpatients at least 30 abusive families, with some 60 children.

## THE UNIT

The unit[2] is a modern bungalow set a few yards from the main hospital building,
and shares with it pleasant, parklike grounds. There are three comfortable
bed-sitting rooms. The families share the main sitting room, dining area, kitchen,
bathroom, and laundry facilities. Meals are available from the hospital kitchen or
mothers may choose to cook for themselves and their husbands. The mothers are
responsible for cleaning their own rooms and communal areas. Each mother has
her own front door key and is free to come and go at will. A telephone is
available within the unit, both for calls outside and as a link with the hospital.

*195*

The hospital where the children are treated has a wide diversity of rooms and territories in it. The design throughout is domestic and friendly. The staff wear no uniforms. There is an active school and a large, well equipped occupational/ play therapy department. The play rooms are equipped for children of all ages. There is a separate day nursery staffed by experienced nurses. The night nursery is in a different area from the day space and family unit.

The architecture and setting of the inpatient facilities are themselves essential aspects of the treatment. The buildings have been planned so that the families may have individual privacy and still have easy access to the hospital facilities and staff. For example, at night, the nursing and medical staff provide on-call cover for the unit. The parents can thus feel secure without feeling "spied upon."

## STAFFING

Medical staff with pediatric and psychiatric training run the unit on a day-to-day basis. At least one male and one female are involved. A social worker, a senior occupational/play therapist, and a psychologist have a special interest in the families. A key member of the team is an experienced nurse, who spends most of the day with the mothers and children in the unit. The mothers also mix daily with other members of the nursing staff, some of whom have been at the Park for many years and provide a stable background of well tried ideas and common sense. Backing up this treatment team is the Director, a psychiatrist, who does not interfere with day-to-day therapy, but who knows every family and is always available for advice and emotional support.

The team works closely together and its members share information and feelings frequently, both informally and at weekly staff meetings. The families are aware of these meetings. The hospital staff are usually joined by a community social worker, who is already or will be involved with the family on discharge. The family's health visitor (home visiting nurse) and family doctor are also invited to attend meetings.

The Unit staff also work in other inpatient and outpatient services of the Park Hospital, which as a whole has a relatively high staff-patient ratio. One great advantage of being part of a wider organization is that staff involved in the emotionally stressful and exhausting sphere of child abuse can, when necessary, find relief by working in another area of the hospital. It also makes immediately available to the families, staff with different areas of expertise, yet who are working together as an integrated team with a common sense of commitment.

Too often the diversity of facilities that these families need are provided by services that are both geographically and ideologically widely separated. Our aim is to contain the whole range of pediatric, psychiatric, social, and legal problems within the scope of one confident and mutually supportive team. This gives it the authority needed to provide comprehensive help to the families and to deal with their closely interrelated emotional, practical, and medical problems.[3]

## REFERRAL AND ADMISSION

To demonstrate the general characteristics of the families referred and admitted to our service, data collected about 50 families admitted between January 1973 and June 1975 is shown in Tables 11–1 to 11–9.

The families referred do not come predominantly from any one socio-economic group. Table 11–1 shows the social class according to the Registrar General's classification of the father's occupation for the 50 families. A significant number of these families, however, did not come within this classification, either because the mother was unsupported, or the father was unemployed or in jail. Four of the families were in the armed services. The families came from a wide variety of sources and from a wide area that includes both urban and rural districts (Tables 11–2 and 11–3).

The 50 families admitted brought in a total of 87 children. The aim was to admit all the children currently living in the family. Many of the parents had other children who had been left with a previous partner, adopted or taken into

**Table 11-1.** Social Class and/or Profession

| | *Social Class*<br>*(Registrar General's classification)* | | |
|---|---|---|---|
| I | 3 | Services | 4[a] |
| II | 4 | Unemployed | 3 |
| III | 12 | In jail | 3 |
| IV | 8 | Unsupported mothers | 9 |
| V | 4 | | |

[a]2 American, 2 British

*Code*
I, II Professional and managerial positions.
III White collar and skilled craftsman.
IV Semiskilled workers.
V Unskilled workers.

**Table 11-2.** Referral Source

| *Distance from the Hospital* | |
|---|---|
| Local | 15 |
| Within 25 mile radius | 24 |
| 25–50 mile radius | 10 |
| Over 50 mile radius | 1 |
| Total | 50 |

Local = Families within the City of Oxford and suburban villages and housing estates.

**Table 11-3.** Habitat

| *Habitat* | | |
|---|---|---|
| Urban  (Over 25,000 pop) | 28* | ( 56%) |
| Country town/village | 11* | ( 22%) |
| Rural | 9 | ( 18%) |
| Forces Accommodation | 2 | ( 4%) |
| *both include 1 caravan | | |
| Total | 50 | (100%) |

Rural = Farm cottages, isolated houses and villages under 1,500 population.

Care. Some teenage children remained in school and lived with relatives or friends, and in a few families there were children who had grown up and left home; one mother was already herself a grandmother. (Table 11–4).

The children ranged in age from ten days to twelve years, with a majority being under three years (Table 11–5). The mother's age at the time of admission and at the time her first child was born is shown in Table 11–6. This illustrates the early age at which mothers in families with a high potential for abuse embark upon maternity. The fathers tended to be a little older, but ranged in age from sixteen to fifty years.

A high proportion of referrals came from pediatricians, usually when a child had been admitted injured to the ward. Other referrals came from family doctors, psychiatrists, and social workers (Table 11–7). While some of the second group may have at some time been severely injured, the majority had only minor injuries or were in a severe "at-risk" situation. In some instances neglect or emotional deprivation was the predominant feature. An increasing number of parents who are recurrently abusing their child, yet inflicting minor or no trauma, are presenting themselves to their doctors and being referred to us.

**Table 11-4.** Number of children in each family admitted

| Number of children in family. | 1 | 2 | 3 | 4 |
|---|---|---|---|---|
| Number of families<br>t=50 | 26 | 13 | 9 | 2 |
| Number of children<br>t=87 | 26 | 26 | 27 | 8 |

**Table 11-5.** Age of Children on Admission

| | under 1 month | 1 month - 6 months | 6 months - 1 year | 1 year - 3 years | 3 years - 5 years | 5 years - 8 years | 8 years & over | Total |
|---|---|---|---|---|---|---|---|---|
| All children admitted to Unit | 1 | 18 | 11 | 26 | 10 | 17 | 4 | 87 |
| Children abused, neglected or at risk | 1 | 17 | 10 | 20 | 7 | 7 | 1 | 63 |

Table 11-6.  Mother's Age

|  | < 20 | 20-24 | 25-29 | 30-34 | 35 plus and over | Total |
|---|---|---|---|---|---|---|
| On admission | 6 | 24 | 14 | 5 | 1 | 50 |
| At birth of first child | 25 | 19 | 6 | – | – | 50 |

Table 11-7.  Referred By:

|  |  | Percent |
|---|---|---|
| Pediatricians | 17) | |
| Bed to bed transfer | ) | |
|  | ) | |
|  | ) | |
|  | ) | 40 |
| Pediatrician | 3) | |
| OP referral | ) | |
| Family doctors | 12 | 24 |
| Social workers | 6 | 12 |
| Adult Psychiatrists | 5) | |
|  | ) | 12 |
|  | ) | |
| Child Psychiatrists | 1) | |
| School Medical Officer | 2 | |
| Maternity Hospital | 1 | |
| Neurologist | 1 | |
| Neurosurgeon | 1 | |
| Police | 1 | |
| Total | 50 | |

When the cases admitted to the unit in 1971 and 1972 for a previous paper[2] were reviewed many "at-risk" children were initially referred to our service with other diagnoses: behavior disorders, seizure disorders, developmental delay; the previous abuse or "at risk" features of the case only became clear after the families were admitted. This now occurs much less frequently, and an increased awareness of the problem and willingness by parents to seek help more openly is now more common. Table 11-8 shows the reason for referral to the Park and a diagnosis, after assessment, for each child in the fifty families admitted to the Park between 1973 and 1975.

**Table 11-8.**  Diagnoses of the 87 Children Admitted  (January 1973 to June 1975)

| Reason for Referral | Diagnosis after Assessment | | | | | | |
|---|---|---|---|---|---|---|---|
| | *Actual Abuse* | *Probable Abuse* | *At Risk* | *Neglect* | *Other* | *'Normal' Sibling* | *Total* |
| Actual Abuse | 23 (21 families) | | | | | | 23 |
| Probable Abuse | 1 | | | | 2 | | 3 |
| At Risk | 5 | | 18 | 1 | | | 24 |
| Neglect | | | | 1 | | | 1 |
| Other | 1 | 2 | 4 | | | | 7 |
| 'Normal' Sibling | | | 7 | | 1 | 21 | 29 |
| Total | 30 | 2 | 29 | 2 | 3 | 21 | 87 |

Actual Abuse — Injuries known not to be accidental. This also includes attempted suffocation, strangulation, drowning, and poisoning.

Probable Abuse — Injury in a child at risk, but not proved to be a result of abuse.

At Risk — Where a child is in danger of abuse, recognised by others or the family itself. Also included outbursts of aggression not resulting in detectable injury.

Neglect — Deprivation of adequate physical and/or emotional care.

Other — Includes seizure disorders, behavior disorder, developmental delay, etc.

Where children had more than one diagnosis, only that related to abuse and neglect is shown in this table.

Not all families referred to us are admitted to our unit. Where the mother is grossly psychotic, or the abuse is of a truly sadistic nature, the family unit seems to be untreatable. Therefore, the individual members of these families are offered treatment and the abused proband often needs to be placed apart from his parents. Some referrals are managed as outpatients or by admitting the child alone. All too frequently we would like to offer immediate admission to a family but have no space.

A few admissions consist of families where a child has been removed and the workers involved felt that the parents had made sufficient progress for a reunion to be tried. It has seemed appropriate that this should initially occur in the supportive atmosphere of the Park, with a view to the child's returning home. Another recently introduced use of the unit is the admission of mother and baby straight from the maternity hospital, where previous family biographies and an accumulation of other adverse factors places a child at severe risk of bonding failure and abuse.[3,4] The majority of families admitted stay with us for at least three weeks, only a few staying more than nine (Table 11-9).

Most of the abused children admitted to our service have not been separated from their parents except for the acute hospitalization. The aim is to rehabilitate these families so that the child may return home safely without further separation.

**Table 11-9.** Length of Stay

| Under 7 days | 1-3 weeks | 3-6 weeks | 6-9 weeks | over 9 weeks | Total |
|---|---|---|---|---|---|
| 9 | 8 | 24 | 6 | 3 | 50 |

## ASSESSMENT OF THE FAMILIES

Every family needs a full medical, psychiatric, and social assessment. We go back into the pedigree and usually find that hostility and violence have ruled for generations. A full picture of the family's relationships has to be built up. This is a continuing process, which is greatly facilitated when the family is seen in a residential setting. It is important that every member of the family get a full medical assessment. Frequently we find that an abused child is the product of a difficult pregnancy, labor and delivery, or has been ill and separated from his mother as a neonate or young child.[3] Frequently he may still have continuing medical problems.

One must also be alerted to the possibility of undiagnosed illness in the proband.[5] Examples of this seen at the Park include blindness,[4] chromosome abnormalities, developmental retardation due to cerebellar ataxia, and hemophilia. Every child, proband and sibling, also gets a full developmental and psychological assessment.

The parents have a careful medical history taken and, where indicated, investigation and treatment are initiated. Most of the mothers have minor health problems; excessive tiredness, iron deficiency anemia, and headaches typically described as migraine. Many have minor gynaecological problems and are in need of contraceptive advice. A gynaecologist from the local family planning clinic makes a weekly visit to our unit. A few mothers have been found to have pregnancies on admission, some unwanted. Routine dental treatment is arranged. Severe medical maternal diagnoses have included chronic renal disease, thyrotoxicosis, tuberculosis, multiple sclerosis, bronchiectasis and leprosy. One mother died of a cerebral tumour some months after discharge.

Both parents need a thorough and sophisticated psychiatric assessment; this too needs to be a progressive process. Serious mental illness, psychopathy, and grossly immature personalities are found. Pathological jealousy, especially in the father, is relatively common. If these parents have been previously seen by a psychiatrist they are often labelled as personality disorder—untreatable. Until recently up to 90 percent of our mothers and many fathers had been or were on tranquilizers and/or antidepressants, usually benzodiazepines and tricyclics. These had been prescribed unwittingly for complaints of anxiety and depression by these parents. These drugs, by removing inhibition, may have precipitated a battering episode.[6,7] One of the first steps is to stop all such drugs. We also offer treatment when alcohol has become a problem. The majority of mothers are cigarette addicts.

A substantial number of our parents have severe marital and sexual difficulties, which exacerbate their feeling of frustration. In these cases marital therapy is offered. An assessment is simultaneously made of the family's social situation, as they may very well be in need of help with financial matters, housing, employment, and so forth. All too often every aspect of a family's life seems to be in a hopeless muddle. A common response to this "blind alley" situation is for the family to deny reality and escape into fantasy.

## THERAPEUTIC PROGRAM

The treatment program is adapted to meet the needs of each individual family. During the first few days the care of the child is taken over almost exclusively by the nursing staff. The parents are given a chance to escape from the angry hostile trap, where their only communication has been by shouts and blows. All the family members have felt frightened, unloved and unworthy; these feelings have to be reversed. All members of the family are offered care and attention from a variety of mature adults. Without their having to ask, the mothers are provided with food, warmth, privacy, and tranquillity—an undemanding routine. They are allowed to regress; and many mothers do indeed take to their beds.

One reaction is of astonishment, first discerned and described by our colleague Derek Steinberg. This is an important reaction, a positive predictor of the success of the psychotherapy. The situation of being cared for is something quite new for these parents. Often, together with this astonishment, comes panic, resulting in a phenomenon we have come to call "second-day packing." The mothers want to leave the unit and run away. Many of these mothers are indeed "runners," having been runaways in their teens and self-dischargers from hospital wards. On this occasion they are met with calm, kind intervention by the staff, the situation is resolved, and the mother begins to settle down to a regular routine, often for the first time in her life.

The involvement of the father has to be varied to fit in with his work schedule; but his willing participation in the treatment program is one of the conditions of the admission. He is encouraged to spend time off and/or weekends in the unit. He attends psychotherapy sessions, some play therapy sessions, and is helped to cope with feeding, bathing, and diaper changing. The more we have encouraged and expected fathers to be involved with their children the more they have responded. On the whole they are both willing and interested.

The parents also receive group, individual, and marital psychotherapy during their admission. A group is held in the mothers' unit every day with the psychiatrist and nurse. Each family has a doctor and social worker, each of whom sees them for several hours each week. Every child, proband and sibling, has a session with an occupational therapist every day, the parents being encouraged to attend too. The therapist makes developmental and behavioral observations of the children and on the interactions with their parents, as well as helping the parents to learn to play with their children and understand and cope with their behavior. The older children attend the Hospital School.

Much of the treatment that families receive is informal psychotherapy, role modelling, and practical help that all the staff, especially the nursing staff, give throughout the days the parents spend with them. Gradually the children settle into a happy routine, lose any frozen watchfulness, and are able to smile a welcome to their parents, who themselves are already beginning to feel more confident in their roles as parents. Their expectations of the children become more realistic. The children are able to enjoy being children and the parents, parents. Gradually the mother is able to take over more and more of the child's care until he will be spending most of the day and night with her, and the family will be ready to try a weekend at home.

As the family releases its fantasies they are able to face reality and frequently a catharsis occurs. This is often in the second week of treatment, when the parents with great relief admit to the assaults and abreact the emotions they have denied. During their stay the families become firmly bonded to the Park Hospital. We have termed this the "liberating bond." It is an open relationship, a new experience for these families, who have only known closed, destructive relationships. From this stable bond they are able to go on to make new bonds with their child, spouse, and other people in their lives. In Erikson's terms they have established basic trust.[8]

The time any family takes to move through the different phases of therapy naturally varies. In most instances we are able to predict the outcome within the first week to ten days. In cases where it becomes obvious that no healthy bond will form between parent and child, it is a matter or urgency to find a suitable placement for the child and to help the parents to come to terms with their feelings.

## LEGAL PROCEEDINGS

When the diagnosis of abuse is first made, the parents are usually defensive and may threaten to remove their child from treatment. This is most likely to occur when the child is transferred to us after an acute admission to a pediatric ward. The resulting crisis must at times be resolved by law. This can be therapeutic. Both doctor and parents know the child has been injured and that he must be placed where such injuries cannot recur. In the United Kingdom this is done with a Place of Safety Order obtained from Social Services or the police. This Order names the hospital and gives twenty-eight days in which a plan of treatment can be put into action. When we offer to admit the family of a child to our unit, the parents usually accept. In the sample of 50 families previously considered, ten children from nine families were at some time on Place of Safety Orders.

Subsequent court hearings need not damage the bond established with these families. An appearance in a juvenile court can act as a useful catharsis. Parents can purge themselves of their guilt openly and feel that they have begun to act as responsible people. The subsequent feeling of relief is enormous. The court, usually with our support and the parents' agreement, places the child in the care of the local authority; but in treatable cases this does not mean automatic separation from the parents. It does mean that the parents have legal protection for themselves and their child. Court proceedings followed for five of the ten children in the sample on Place of Safety Orders and Care Orders were obtained. Seven other children from five families were also made subjects of Care Orders. Of the total twelve children, four were reunited with their parents on discharge from the Park.

There were only two cases in recent years where there have been criminal proceedings and we were still able to maintain our relationship with the families. In the one instance where the father was jailed, psychotherapy was continued by regular visits by us to him in prison, and the family are now reunited. In the other case the judge passed a suspended sentence, and that child too is back in the family.

## DISCHARGE AND FOLLOWUP

Before families are discharged from our inpatient service arrangements are made for them to spend weekends at home—a "trial of freedom." The amount of involvement with each family after discharge will vary and will depend among other things on travelling distances. The family may return regularly for one day a week; the mother and children may attend a therapeutic outpatient group; the family may attend the outpatient clinic; or a worker may visit them at home. The followup is always shared with workers in the community, with the Park Hospital always available in times of crisis. Practical details, such as installation of a telephone, placement of children in day care, recommendations about rehousing, will have been worked out before discharge. If a Family Aid is to be used, she will already have been introduced to the parents and children. We never end our involvement with a family or attempt to break the bond they have formed with the Park Hospital.

## OUTCOME

The true effectiveness of our therapy can only be judged after years of careful followup of the children and their families. Eighty percent of the families in our unit between 1973–1975 returned home with their children. For twelve children in ten families (20 percent) separation was found to be necessary during the admission or after a short trial at home. Several of these families, after prolonged therapy, are now having their children returned; for others the separation must be seen as permanent.

In the 40 families returning home with their children there has been one serious injury (a fractured femur) and one death (in a brain damaged child). There have been no cases of proved reabuse reported, but for many families followup can only be measured in months. At least two children have subsequently spent short periods of time in foster homes, and many families have needed support and help in times of crisis. Now, however, instead of denying a need for help, it is being asked for and accepted.

## CONCLUSION

An inpatient program that incorporates medical, psychiatric, social work, and legal expertise provides an accurate and comprehensive assessment of each family. In treatable cases medical treatment, practical help, and the initiation of ongoing psychotherapy makes it possible for these troubled families to be rehabilitated without prolonged separations.

## EDITORIAL NOTE

In Amsterdam there exists a Socio-Therapeutic Institute, The Triangle. This is a residential therapeutic program for dysfunctional families. This began four years ago and to date the staff has treated 150 families. The Triangle is a large unit which can handle 18 to 20 families at any one time. A staff of 40 work with each family member as individuals and as members of their total family unit.

Their program accepts referrals from any social service professional, including agency social workers, physicians, court workers and the like. Families may stay in residence at the Triangle for up to six months. The therapy provided emphasizes family living and is seen as only the beginning of a long term treatment program. The referring agency must agree to continue working with the family during their stay in the Triangle and thereafter.

Three individuals stand out as strenghts of the program: Rob van Rees, Nicco Oudendgk and M. van Spanje. They and the staff working with these families are making significant advances in our understanding of the problem of abuse and ways to best help those caught in its cycle.

# Practical Ways to Change Parent-Child Interaction in Families of Children at Risk

Margaret Jeffery

Workers frequently remark on the negative nature of the interaction in the families of battered children; on the violent ways of handling situations of stress; on the use of punishment by abusive parents; on the unreal expectations and strong demands by parents; and on the way children adapt to these pressures.

Diverse social work techniques may be offered to the abusive family. Workers may follow Kempe's valuable prescription to give to the very deprived parent the love which they have been denied.[1] These may help to slowly change the negative quality of the interaction and make the family safer and more adequate for the child. Frequently parents want and need to learn new ways of behaving to their child in order to change the negative quality of the interaction as soon as possible. Workers can learn to help parents to learn such new ways. Changes in feelings and attitudes may follow changes in the actual behavior of parents and children.

This chapter describes simple and practical ways to help abusive parents to learn new ways of behaving to the child—in a word, to become more competent parents by changing negative interactions, learning to handle situations of conflict, controlling the child's behavior without punishment, having more realistic expectations, deflecting the actual aggressive acts, and changing the response of the child.

An assumption is made that many families can change and that most abusive adults can be helped to achieve competence as parents[2] so that the child is safer at home. No general prescription can be made. A period of observation in the home and discussion with the family is necessary. Together the family and the worker decide and agree on a plan of action.[3] The technique is to closely observe what is difficult, followed by flexibly and creatively trying to think what to do, and finally to evaluate the effectiveness of the intervention demonstrating that successful changes can occur.[4] Our aim is to communicate not just ways that have been found to be helpful, but the process, the approach.

There are, in spite of the uniqueness of each family and its difficulties, two strands that frequently appear and that directly bear on intervention: social isolation, and ambivalence towards violence and the use of punishment. In child abuse these aspects of western society are reflected in an extreme way. Social isolation[5] means that caregivers know less about children, learn less about handling children from other models, and have fewer people to turn to at the inevitable times of stress in bringing up children—no shoulder to lean on, no safety valve, no relief. Violence is the way caregivers frequently handle the inevitable conflicts with their children. In our society, physical punishment as a method of controlling children has origins in evangelical and later hygienist thinking.[6] In other societies,[7] for instance with Indian children in Malaysia, control is obtained principally by withdrawal of social approval.[8] Newson[6] found that in one very large British sample 17 percent of parents of one-year-olds smacked them for property destruction. Striking and yelling at children, depriving them of food, love, or play—these are ways caregivers strive to control their children. Maxim Gorky[9] unforgettably describes his violent early life where everyone was "choked by a fog of mutual hostility."

## CHANGING NEGATIVE INTERACTIONS

Some approaches to changing excessively negative interactions within families will be described here.

1. **A Simple Reinforcement Technique to Increase Positive Response to the Child.** Describing a single case will show the process of this intervention. The child was a 6-year-old boy in an abusive family, where both parents—noisy, simple, likeable people—interacted highly but excessively negatively with him. Here is an example taken from a tape recording (with their permission).

Child:  (crying).
Mum:   "Aw, stop your crying."
Dad:   "Who's crying? He's got to cry, he's just a little sook."
Mum:   "Want me to put a nappy on you?"
Dad:   "A nappy . . . "
Mum:   "Little nappy. Want a nappy? Ha ha ha."
Child:  "Not funny."

Observations showed a circle of negative interaction. Parents are angry, he cries and whines, parents are angrier still, and it all ends in the child being hit, or sent to bed, or reduced to tears. Sometimes he says or does quiet, friendly things, but these are missed by the parents. Occasionally parents are quiet or warm and positive to him, but rarely. They talk of putting him in a "home." Nobody, parents or child, likes the way things are. Who really wants the desperate stream of anger and abuse?

Initial observations at home, at first unstructured and informal and later fairly strict behavioral observations, revealed these patterns in the family. Baseline observations (rating of defined positive and negative behaviors with 82 percent reliability) showed that the very frequent interactions had high levels of both positive and negative behaviors, but with negative exceeding positive by 3 to 1[10] (see Fig. 12–1). The family could (sometimes) respond positively, and needed to more often for the child's sake, and wanted to more often for all their sakes, but did not know how to break with old habits.

The social worker and psychologist decided to try to give the family some outside incentive to help them to increase their positive responses. A simple reinforcement plan was made whereby a reward would be given to the parents for increasing their positive, friendly behavior in the hour's observation time each day for two weeks, the reward consisting of tokens to be traded in for posters to be put on the wall. The reward was to be given immediately, with social approval, if positive, friendly behaviors exceeded in number negative and

**Figure 12–1.** Reinforcement to Increase Positive Verbal Responses to a 6-Year-Old-Boy

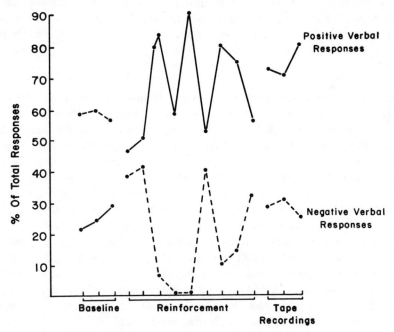

angry responses. The results of the reinforcement period can be seen in Figure 12–1, where positive responding is increasing and negative responding is decreasing greatly from the baseline measurements.

That was all very well for the time we were there observing, but what happened when we were away? Were things worse than ever? In other words, how could generalizing of the new interaction behaviors to the rest of the day come about? To attempt this, a tape recorder was used, with the family's agreement, to be turned on and off without anyone knowing. Again there was to be a reward if ratings showed there was, still, more positive than negative behavior. Figure 12–1 shows results of this stage, where positive responses have kept high and negative responses are still low. The tape recorder and the reward gave these parents an incentive to maintain positive interaction through the day.

Unfortunately, we were not able to systematically measure to see if improvement was maintained after the end of the taping period, although informal observations suggest that this has been the case. Times of stress in this family have led to a deterioration, but interaction has picked up again soon after. Learning to increase positive response did not end this family's difficulties, but it was the beginning of change. Social work supports (and help by a homemaker) have continued. There has been no reabuse, and no one talks of putting this boy in a "home" now.

The following four interventions also concern changing frequent negative interactions, but in situations where there are very limited positive behaviors to build on. These interventions, then, concern caregivers' learning new positive behaviors with the child. They may want terribly to get on better, but where to begin?

2. **Learning to Communicate (Listening, Responding, Talking) with Their Child.** Caregivers often do not attend to the child unless he is being very bad. All opportunities are missed for positive responding. The child *is* bad to them because that is all that they notice. Attending to, listening to, and responding to the child's communications are new behaviors to be learned, new for both caregiver and child. For his part, the child has learned that his strong negative behaviors do bring his mother to him, but his more subtle, quiet, positive ones pass by. Both children and caregivers have to learn to elicit positive responses and to emit positive responses.

A 5-year-old, in addition to being abused and emotionally deprived, had severely regressed speech, more like that of his 2-year-old twin sisters, perhaps in an attempt to get some of the positive response they got. Baseline observations found that there was excessively limited verbal communication between him and his mother. She talked to him about 2 percent of the time they were together, and that was mainly single-word, shouted commands: "Sit!" "Out!" "Come!" He talked to her about 6 percent of the time, quiet little soft things he said; but he soon gave up.

Figure 12–2 shows what happened before, during, and after a series of 15-minute "talking sessions," where we practiced talking all together, listening to the child and each other, expanding on what he said, playing with a tape recorder. The amount of time she and he talked to each other was marked on a graph, so that both could see what was happening. In other words, there was modeling, cuing, reinforced practice, and feedback. In addition there would be a shared reward if the mother could talk to her child for 30 percent of the 15-minute sessions together, and he to her for 50 percent of the time. Both therefore had to elicit and maintain communication in the other. A few weeks after the talking sessions were over, communication between the two, while lower than at the end of the practice and reinforcement period, was still much higher than in the first observations (mother now talking 21 percent of the time; the child, 30 percent; see Fig. 12–2).

**Figure 12–2.** Reinforcement to Increase the Time a Mother and a Son Talk to Each Other in 15-Minute Recorded Sessions

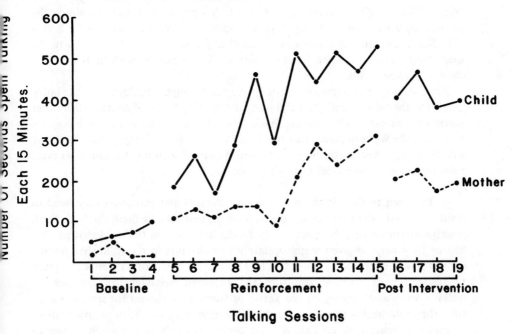

3. **Learning to Play.** It may be more appropriate to change other forms of communication, particularly with younger children. How can parents learn to have happy interactions? Play enables many kinds of positive responses to be practiced and learned—smiling, touching, talking, listening, eye contact—where there is an absence of positive interaction behavior. Playing comes relatively easily to children and is very important to abused children, but caregivers may

feel very remote from play. Are they scared of seeming stupid? Do they feel they will lose their authority?

Start with practice sessions. The worker can act as a model. It is easier to play if one sees someone else, especially someone from "the welfare," letting go, making funny noises, being "messy" and "stupid." Great sensitivity is necessary in using modeling, when one aims to help the caregiver to learn without making the caregiver feel inadequate and thus unable to model behavior of the worker. The worker can also help by giving social reinforcement—encouragement and approval—to the first tentative steps by the caregiver. Generally intrinsic reinforcements of satisfaction, pleasure in playing, or self-esteem are enough to maintain the behavior. After several sessions one mother said, "I quite surprised myself, I even like to play with them now."

It often helps caregivers to plan a special time every day—one hour, or even ten or fifteen minutes as a beginning—and to have a list of ideas and activities prepared according to the child. The need for help here is illustrated by the rigid father of an abused child who angrily criticized a box of "beautiful junk," by saying, "What's all this stuff in here? Linda has plenty of toys." To which the mother, who had been learning to play, responded, "What she's got is for 2 year olds. She needs stuff like this now." Another parent really looks forward to the special time after tea when he plays with his son, when he feels he is *with* the child, not *against* him.

Another way caregivers can learn to play is through a backyard or local play group for themselves and their children, also leading to social contact with other parents on an extremely informal basis. The play group movement is a positive growth in the Western Australian community, being self-helping and preventative and in some respects fulfilling extended family functions for some women, reducing suburban and nuclear family isolation.

4. **Learning to Give Positive Attention.**   Parents and caregivers may need to learn how and when to smile, touch, look at, and talk to their children. Such positive attention may be given rarely to the behaviors in the child that parents like or they may be given inappropriately to behaviors in the child that parents do not like, thereby increasing the child's negative behaviors. Parents can learn to suspend such positive attention to unwanted behavior, for instance by walking away and putting on the kettle or turning on the garden sprinkler each time the child begins to whine. At the same time, they can learn to give positive attention to what they do like. A third person can help to cue parents when to attend and when not to attend.

5. **Learning to Make the House Adapt to People.**   The lack of positive interaction may relate to actual household arrangements. In cramped flats or exceptionally clean and neat houses, it can be very hard for the child to do positive things that will bring approval (e.g., too many things not to touch, nowhere to play or to make a mess). It is hard to change your image of yourself

and your perfect house, but with encouragement and hope that it will make life happier for everyone, caregivers can follow suggestions to adapt their houses or part of their houses. Learning to increase positive interactions means that the parents may need to arrange households to make positive behaviors more likely and negative behaviors less likely.[11] This leads, of course, to the wider field of changing the community and social environment to allow for positive child behavior, which becomes in this respect a treatment procedure for child abuse.[12]

6. **Contracts or Agreements.** Contract or agreements between parents and children can be drawn up to avoid particular conflicts and situations which lead to negative interactions.[13] As an example, observations and discussions showed that one family had bitter battles about feeding the dog every night, leaving everyone bad tempered and letting fly by tea time. A contract was drawn up and agreed to by a father and his 7-year-old daughter (Table 12–1), who herself was not abused but whose 4-year-old brother was severely rejected and thought by the mother and by workers to be at risk of abuse. It was he who usually took the brunt of the tense, angry feelings at tea time. The approach here was to attempt to resolve the family conflicts surrounding this child. In the family's own words, "tea time became much 'sweeter.' " Table 12–2 lists other examples of contracts for a family over a three-month period.

7. **Learning New Handling Techniques.** Observations have revealed that there are frequently two basic family situations that lead to conflict and around which much of the negative interaction occurs. For example, when the child demands something and caregivers say, "No," or otherwise prohibit or deny the child. The child then demands more strongly and persistently, frequently ending in violent conflict and punishment. Parents are often not able to follow the frequently given advice to "ignore" without specific help. Distraction has been found to be a technique that caregivers can learn to use; it is one that is frequently used by caregivers anyway. Abusive parents have benefited by learning to use distraction more frequently and with more awareness. The conscious formulation of distraction as a technique arose from observations that chimpanzee mothers in their natural environment used distraction rather than prohibition or punishment with their infants: "Chimpanzee mothers, when their offspring persisted in trying to attain a desired objective, reacted on many occasions by tickling or grooming their children rather than by punishing them."[14]

If caregivers can learn to use distraction sometimes rather than saying "no" always, they will avoid conflicts and violence; they then become a guide and a model to the child rather than an authority (see Table 12–3). If, for instance, the child is about to climb out of the window, mother can practice not saying, "no," and instead quickly think of something else the child likes to do: empty out the toy box, make bubbles, have a drink, see what's inside here, turn on the tap, wave to Aunty. It may help caregivers to write down a list of what the child likes to do so that if they are at their wits' end, they can refer to the list *fast* for ideas for distraction.

The second conflict situation occurs when the caregivers tell the child what to do, to obey them, and the child says, "NO." In the words of parents, the child "wilfully defies" them, or "tests me out," or "won't do what she's told" or

**Table 12-1.** Agreement between Mr. L & M

1. If M feeds the dog by 5 p.m. each evening being reminded only once, Mr. L will swing her on the tire for 5 minutes.

2. If M does not feed the dog by 5 p.m., Mr. L will feed the dog and make no comment.

3. M will keep a record:——

| | *Feeding Dog* | *Swing* |
|---|---|---|
| Sun. | | |
| Mon. | | |
| Tues. | | |
| Wed. | | |
| Thurs. | | |
| Fri. | | |
| Sat. | | |
| Sun. | | |
| Mon. | | |
| Tues. | | |
| Wed. | | |
| Thurs. | | |
| Fri. | | |
| Sat. | | |
| Sun. | | |

4. If there are 7 ticks in a row, M can choose what tea will be that night.

7 Ticks In A Row

| *Yes* | *No* |
|---|---|
| - | - |
| Choosing Tea | - |

**Table 12-2.** Subjects of Contracts for L Family over 3-Month Period

1. If Y tidies her room on Saturday she can stay up to watch the movie on Saturday night television.

2. If M feeds dog by 5 p.m., Mr. L will swing her on tyre for 5 minutes.

3. If Mr. L says "hello dear," Mrs. L will not ask questions. If Mr. L does not say "hello dear" Mrs. L can talk and ask as many questions as she likes.

4. If M stays out of Y's room when her friend visits Y, then Y will play with M for 20 minutes afterwards.

5. If Mrs. L mends Mr. L's clothes he will buy new trousers and 4 new shirts.

6. If all the L's meet on Saturday evening, each person can have their turn planning a Sunday of family activities for fun.

**Table 12-3.** Ways of Avoiding Fights with E: Distraction

1. Have ready stuck to the fridge a list of "what E likes."

2. When you are nearly going to say "no" to E, quickly think of an alternative on the list or look at the list to find an alternative.

3. Then say, "let's do..." and not say "no."

"goes against me" or "gets at me." Parents can be helped to handle this situation more effectively than they do, and the technique has been called quietly telling without shouting. Reference to Figure 12–3 will show what is meant. Parents often doubt that the technique will work, but practice, with the worker present, often gives the parent confidence that it will work and is working.

Of course most parents—not just abusive parents—give far too many commands to their children anyway. For this reason it is often helpful to go through two steps before hand: first, for all caregivers to decide in what areas commands and instructions are necessary, with the aim of making a reduced list of rules and instructions for the child to keep; and second, to practice "double thinking" an instruction or command—that is, thinking twice about whether that particular command is really necessary right now. For instance is it necessary to tell the child to wash his hands if he is about to turn on the tap anyway? Luria's (1961) often quoted work on the role of speech in controlling the behavior of young children gave rise to the idea for this technique.[15] There is nothing new in this, of course: La Fontaine was saying the same thing in 1678! The La Fontaine fable, "The North Wind and the Sun," beautifully shows to some parents the process where their child builds up in resistance as they build up in more and more heated commands.[16] The greater the confidence of caregivers that they can control their child's behavior by using this technique, the easier it is to use; which is another way of saying that violent punishment is a reaction to feeling incompetent and inadequate.

A particular case enabled an evaluation of the effectiveness of these two handling techniques. A lonely mother of a 3-year-old girl fought with her daughter over these two situations, leading to constant slaps and crying when the worker was present. The mother was distressed but felt inadequate and incompetent to do anything else. Her daughter's behavior and her own forcefully reminded her of the fights between her own parents when she was a child, and her own fights with her husband before he left. She was given suggestions to distract rather than saying "No" (see Table 12–3) and to quietly and repeatedly tell her daughter what to do without shouting, in the form of a cartoon (see Fig. 12–3).

Baseline measures had been taken. There were other interventions before this (described below) but this is the situation after this mother and the worker practiced these two handling techniques: first in role playing, then in real situations with Edith. Here we measured three different sorts of behavior: verbal interaction, physical interaction, and the mother's compliance or refusal of the child's expressed wants. This intervention—handling instructions—lowered negative verbal interaction ratings, and raised compliance ratings. When practicing for the first time, this mother said with an unforgettable look, "It worked, didn't it?" A week later she wrote a note saying, "Since I have been keeping calm [quietly talking] and not saying "No," [using distraction] Edith is a bit better already."

Other handling suggestions may concern toilet training, going to bed, night disturbances, meals, bed-wetting, rocking, head banging, running away, and tantrums.[17, 18]

## AN INTERVENTION TO CHANGE ATTITUDES
## AND TO DEFLECT THE AGGRESSIVE RESPONSE

One intervention to change attitudes will be described. Parents so often have unreal expectations about their children, leading to constant trouble. For example, a mother of a 2-year-old sobbed, "She does not respect books, she tears them and draws on them." Sometimes quite ordinary behavior is seen as defiant, bad, abnormal, or a sign of failure. A constantly recurring theme in literature on child abuse is the parents' unreal expectations and lack of understanding of sequences of child development[1,2,19,20] what Richards[21] calls "a fragmentation of intergenerational transfer of knowledge about mother/child behavior."

A technique was devised to change attitudes through intervening *before* the

**Figure 12-3.** Quietly Telling Without Shouting

## not this.....

## but this.....

aggressive response to quite ordinary and typical behavior. First, a list of ordinary behavior is drawn up from published norms[22,23,24] to suit the particular child (see Table 12–4). For example, a pool of all possible items for a 4-year-old was collected, and particular items to suit the child extracted from the pool and made up into the list. Each time one of the behaviors occurred, the caregiver was to mark a stroke on the sheet (stuck on the refrigerator with pencil attached usually) *straight away* before doing or saying *anything else*. For instance, the child breaks mother's best bottle of perfume, and mother, *before* yelling and hitting, goes to the refrigerator, picks up the pencil angrily, and marks blackly against the item "breaks things" and says to herself, "Bloody 4-year-olds!" aggressively, or "Is that what kids of 4 do?" incredulously, or "Thats what 4-year-olds do" resignedly. The aim therefore is twofold: to intervene to redirect the aggressive response *on to the list* and to change the unreal expectation/critical attitude of the caregiver to quite ordinary behavior. Many lists have had jagged and dark and angry marks on them. Practice with the worker is necessary first. This technique aims to change attitudes and behavior at once.

Going back to the same 3-year-old child with her lonely mother as an example, this intervention lowered the negative response by half and dropped the number of refusals by the mother. This mother no longer expected so much of her child; what before had seemed like defiance, stupidity, or perversity in her child now came to look like proof of her being an ordinary 3-year-old. Experience with this mother, however, where self-recording was also used with a marked lack of success, suggested that changing expectations may need to go hand in hand with other interventions that give positive things to do: in this case, ways of handling as well, as described previously. It was after this attempt

**Table 12-4.** Changing Unreal Expectations—What to Expect from a Four-Year-Old

|  | Sun. | Mon. | Tue. | Wed. | Thurs. | Fri. | Sat. |
|---|---|---|---|---|---|---|---|
| Fits of rage. | ☐ | ☐ | ☐ | ☐ | ☐ | ☐ | ☐ |
| Hits. | ☐ | ☐ | ☐ | ☐ | ☐ | ☐ | ☐ |
| Throws stones. | ☐ | ☐ | ☐ | ☐ | ☐ | ☐ | ☐ |
| Breaks things. | ☐ | ☐ | ☐ | ☐ | ☐ | ☐ | ☐ |
| Runs away | ☐ | ☐ | ☐ | ☐ | ☐ | ☐ | ☐ |
| Loud silly laughter | ☐ | ☐ | ☐ | ☐ | ☐ | ☐ | ☐ |
| Kicks. | ☐ | ☐ | ☐ | ☐ | ☐ | ☐ | ☐ |
| Swearing. | ☐ | ☐ | ☐ | ☐ | ☐ | ☐ | ☐ |
| Does not do what he is told, and sometimes does the opposite of what he is told. | ☐ | ☐ | ☐ | ☐ | ☐ | ☐ | ☐ |
| Punishment does not have any effect. | ☐ | ☐ | ☐ | ☐ | ☐ | ☐ | ☐ |
| Makes up stories and lies. | ☐ | ☐ | ☐ | ☐ | ☐ | ☐ | ☐ |
| He can go up the street and back alone. | ☐ | ☐ | ☐ | ☐ | ☐ | ☐ | ☐ |
| He can visit neighbours. | ☐ | ☐ | ☐ | ☐ | ☐ | ☐ | ☐ |
| He runs ahead when walking up the street. | ☐ | ☐ | ☐ | ☐ | ☐ | ☐ | ☐ |
| Etc. | | | | | | | |

to change the mother's expectations that things first improved for this little girl and her mother.

## AN INTERVENTION TO CHANGE THE RESPONSE OF THE CHILD

So far interventions have been described which suggest that it is mainly the parent or caregiver who needs to learn. But this is a two-way process. Many authorities note the effect of the infant on the caregiver[25]: the child has to learn to elicit positive responses as much as the parent. Some work has concerned this, particularly infants who are unresponsive and unrewarding to their caregivers. Their lack of response seems to tell the mother she is not a good mother. Changing the child's response, if that is possible, helps him to become more rewarding to his caregivers and more able to benefit himself from his environment. The case of an individual child is presented where the ultimate aim was to accelerate development through perceptual and social stimulation by the present caregivers (see, for example, Richards[21] on the social structure of an institution affecting the ways caregivers relate to children).

An abused child was at home for six weeks with retarded parents, and since then had been hospitalized and institutionalized (he is now 8 months old). When he was 5½ months old his functioning was like that of a 3½-month-old baby. Was this developmental retardation due to institutionalization?[26] Was he retarded like his parents? Or was his retarded development because his earliest learning had been that people, the most interesting source of stimulation, were also disruptive and painful? He appeared to be a child who failed to evoke social stimulation. A chain of lowered stimulation lowered his response and elicitation of further stimulation towards him. Prechtl[27], Robertson[28], Blurton-Jones[29], Rutter[26], and all papers in Lewis & Rosenblum[25] demonstrate the effect of the infant on caregivers; sensitive (and microscopic) studies by Brazelton, Koslowski, and Main[30] indicate the mother's response can modify cycles of attention and withdrawal in the infant, and they comment that failures in mothering (failure to thrive, child abuse, autism) may relate back to such basic patterns of interaction.

A program of intensive stimulation was planned by the author and Lee Goddard. There have been many reports in the literature of the raising of particular developmental behaviors by plans of extra stimulation.[31-36] The program was intended to artificially improve "appropriate environmental experience".[30] Baseline measures were taken of the infant's behavior, and of the behavior of others in his field, and there was a further developmental measure just before the beginning of the program, where at the age of 6½ months his functioning was like that of a 4¼-month-old baby. The program began with all staff who were concerned with this baby discussing all his behaviors and being asked how each could be responded to. Then for each fifteen minutes of his waking time, staff were instructed to "talk, touch, and play" (TTP) with him. In 1975 Elardo et al.[37] found that at six months the opportunity for variety in daily stimulation was a factor that had one of the most significant relationships with cognitive development later at three years. The staff were to record each TTP. This lasted two weeks. Measures were again taken: baseline behavioral measures and another developmental assessment.

Results are shown in Figure 12–4, where the actual development of the infant is compared to expected development of infants of his age, before and after the intensive stimulation. This clearly demonstrates that after the stimulation program this baby's development accelerated. At the age of eight months he was functioning at the 8.2-month level. While merely *looking* at objects decreased, active reaching and touching objects with his hands increased after the stimulation period of two weeks. All responses to people—gazing, smiling, reaching, and touching—increased, which was the most encouraging change of all. Vocalizing increased, while at the same time crying and finger and thumb sucking (self-stimulating and comforting behaviors) decreased. There was little change in the motor behaviors of crawling position, crawling movement, and rolling over. Very significantly, the behaviors of caregivers towards him increased markedly (vocalizing to him, touching him, smiling to him, and holding him).

**Figure 12-4.** The Effect of a Stimulation Intervention on the Development of an Infant from 5½ Months to 8 Months

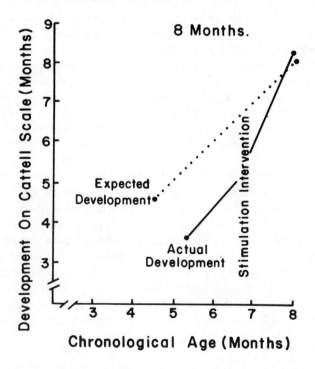

Two things can be learned from this: early patterns *can* change (this infant should now be able to be adopted and have an ordinary life); and much of the work can be done by intervening at the level of those in daily contact with the child, rather than a worker's being directly assigned to the child. Of course this infant was institutionalized, but it has been possible to carry out a similar sort of plan at home, where the parents actually give the increased stimulation for a short period to increase the rewarding responsiveness of their infant to themselves. This may be especially useful where an infant has been institutionalized or hospitalized and is returned home if he appears to have a lowered level of response. Further work has concerned a socially understimulated and unresponsive infant where a homemaker has carried out similar sessions to help a passive mother learn to elicit response from her child. The spreading of skills to nonprofessional workers has definitely benefited the now interested, responsive baby.

## CONCLUSIONS

When one small thing changes, other changes may be set in motion. Ways have been described to begin such changes. Of course, all such interventions and new learnings need to go hand-in-hand with other forms of treatment such as homemakers, social supports, 24-hour telephones, counseling, housing and financial changes. Systematic evaluation can be helpful in showing both worker and family that changes are happening. In general the aim is to help people do what they want to do but feel they cannot, so that they no longer feel so helpless or fatalistic in the face of their child, their family, and society.

## ACKNOWLEDGMENT

Acknowledgements and thanks to my fellow workers of the Child Life Protection Unit: Jean Hamory, June Roe, Kathie Forwood, Anne McKenzie, Irv Davidson, Norm Shakespeare, Helen Skehan, and Rhonda Monaco for help with the manuscript; to Matron Grant and Sister Ellis and all the Sisters and Nurses of Ngal-a, and to Matron Parker of Lady Lawley Cottage for their cooperative hard work; to Keith Maine, Director of the Department for Community Welfare, Western Australia, Ailsa Smith, Joy Schapper, and Bruce Dufty for their support and advice; to Professor Birnbrauer; to Patricia Lowe for her careful scrutiny; and especially to Lee Goddard for constant help and support, and to the parents and children for their willingness and trust in trying new ways.

**EDITORIAL NOTE**

There are over eight million people in the city of New York. Approximately two and one-half million are children. One percent of these children were reported in 1975 to the Bureau of Child Welfare as suspected cases of child abuse and/or neglect. That's *26,536* children! One out of five children in New York City live in families whose income falls below the poverty level; three out of five live in families headed by the female parent. While the number of reports of suspected abuse and neglect in the city is huge, essentially the same number of suspected abused or neglected children are seen any time there are eight and one-half million people living in a defined area. The incidence in Michigan (8½ million population) are virtually the same.

In the midst of the financially troubled city of New York there is an "island of safety" for a few of these 26,536 children and their parents. In 1972 Dr. Vincent Fontana at the New York Foundling Hospital Center for Parents and Child Development developed a child abuse treatment and prevention program to deal with child abuse in the urban setting. One of its key components is a residential program—an inpatient facility in Manhattan for the mother and her baby, plus a "half-way" boarding home in the Bronx where help can be provided to the young family before they return home. In addition, there is a multidisciplinary staff, paraprofessional surrogate parents, a hotline, and an outpatient facility.

The establishment of such a program has required considerable cooperative effort on the parts of several agencies within New York City. This is brought to your attention to demonstrate that a helpful program can be established in the megalopolis. One doesn't need to be in Oxford, Denver, Perth or Amsterdam to be witness to a center of excellence.

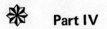 **Part IV**

# The Community

❋ **Introduction**

Hopefully, by this point, the reader is convinced that the assessment and treatment of any abusive and/or neglecting family cannot be successful without a multidisciplinary team effort. This, then, requires a community cooperative endeavor. Rarely will any community have an existing structure with the required trust and cooperation already in existence. This has to be built. Chapter 13 provides the builders with a blueprint that should be used and modified to meet particular needs within a given community. One thing is certain: without a cooperative, comprehensive program these families in trouble cannot receive the help they so desperately need. John Miller's contribution on "Child Abuse in the Military" gives the perspective of the problem in this setting. The final chapter in this section by Kawamura and Carroll offer helpful suggestions in the organizational and financial aspects of these community endeavors.

C. Henry Kempe
Ray E. Helfer

## Chapter Thirteen

# The Community-based Child Abuse and Neglect Program

Ray E. Helfer and Rebecca Schmidt

## BASIC COMPONENTS OF THE COMMUNITY PROGRAM

The three basic components of a community program are depicted as three interacting circles (Fig. 13–1). Circle A represents the acute care and diagnostic assessment component, Circle B the long term therapeutic component, and C, the education, training, and research component. Each of these components and coordination points are discussed in detail below.

Prior to developing the details of a community program, the definition of a community should be established. *A community is a defined area with specific geographical boundaries in which live approximately 400,000 to 500,000 people.* A community must not necessarily be confined to county lines. For example, a city of 200,000 people located within a given county should expand its program to a more regional concept that includes surrounding communities and counties to cover a realistic geographical area containing approximately 500,000 population. On the other hand, in large megatropolises such as Detroit, New York, or Los Angeles, it is necessary to have multiple communities with specific geographic boundaries in which live approximately a half-million people. As will be pointed out subsequently, certain components of the community programs can extend beyond the 500,000 limit and others cannot (component A being one that cannot).

We can no longer afford the archaic system of maintaining county governed child protection services and expect to make progress in the area of child abuse and neglect. It is an impossible task to develop a child abuse and neglect program in each of 3,300-plus communities within the United States. Regionalization must occur and these programs must be state run, not county run. On paper, many states appear to have supervision over county protective service programs, but in reality there is little if any control by the states.

Figure 13-1.   Community Program Basic Components

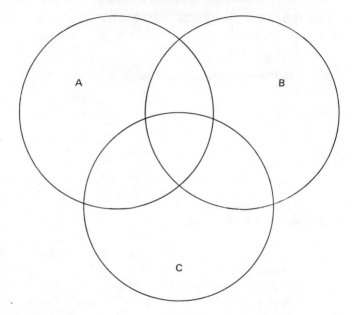

## COMPONENT A—THE ACUTE CHILD PROTECTION TEAM

### Putting Protective Services in Perspective
Successful functioning of a multidisciplinary, diagnostic, and acute care crisis oriented group of professionals requires broadening of the current concept of protective services from that of a unidisciplinary social agency to a comprehensive team of professionals who work together as a single unit. The example provided by the child protection group in Honolulu should be considered. The great majority of this group is made up of protective service workers and their supervisor; in addition there is a full time medical director, psychologist, part time lawyer, full time public health nurse, and a liaison with the police department. This child protection group is depicted in Figure 13–2.

It will be impossible to provide significant and meaningful acute care services to abused and neglected children and their families if we persist in the concept that protective services is a single disciplinary unit, i.e., social service. A social worker, even though he or she is an indispensable member of the child protection team, cannot be all things to all people. Where departments of social services place their protective service workers in a position of having to make medical, legal, psychiatric, and law enforcement decisions without appropriate

**Figure 13-2.** Component A—Child Protection Team

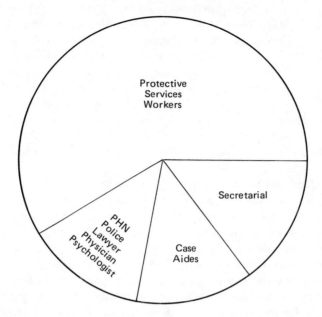

and sometimes without any backup, children and families can be lost, killed, or permanently injured. Child protection teams must be multidisciplinary in nature; they must work together as a unit, like a cardiac care team or a football team.

The members of this child protection team must be specialists in their respective fields. Not every social worker or physician, for example, has been trained to deal with this difficult problem. Each member of the group must be subsidized (receive a salary), since the fee-for-service system in the area of child abuse and neglect (much like many specialties) cannot be expected to support the individual members of the protection group. Each group should service a 400,000 to 500,000 population area. The minimum number of individuals on the team are as follows:

Protective service workers—15
Public health nurse—1
Pediatric specialist—½
Psychologist or psychiatrist—1
Lawyer—1
Law enforcement—¼
Case aides—3 to 4
Clerical support—sufficient for case load

### Function of Child Protection Group

The function of the child protection team is quite specific. It should do the following: (1) receive reports of suspected abuse and/or neglect; (2) make a diagnostic assessment; (3) perform crisis intervention whenever necessary; (4) develop an immediate plan to protect the child; and (5) develop recommendations for long term therapy. In addition, each member of the child protection team has a specific responsibility to be liaison with their respective professions within the community. For example, a doctor on the child protection team should be available for consultations to physicians who have difficult cases with which they need help. The same function would be true of the psychiatrists and/or psychologists, the lawyer, the law enforcement officer, and so on. These specialists do not provide *all* the services offered by their respective disciplines, rather they coordinate and oversee these services. In difficult cases the professionals on the team work directly with the protective service worker in providing the necessary services.

It should be clearly understood that the child protection group is an acute care crisis oriented team which should neither be responsible for long term therapy nor be the social service arm of the juvenile court. Long term care of families who are abusive and neglectful requires a different type of approach, by a person who may have a different personality and a service system that allows considerably freedom and flexibility. These are not necessarily the prerequisities of an acute crisis oriented protection team. Asking members of the crisis team to be responsible for care or coordination of therapy for six months to six years would be analogous to having the intensive care nurses and physicians on a cardiac care unit required to do long term therapy, home visits, and followup for months and years after each patient is discharged. This is not possible and should be resisted.

Being the social service arm of the juvenile court is equally as devastating, as these cases require coordination and follow-up long beyond the acute crisis oriented phase. When long term care and acute crisis care are intermingled, long term therapy and its coordination will suffer, as acute crises need immediate intervention.

### Community Affiliations

Every child protection team must have close affiliations within the community in which they function. There must be strong ties—some of which may be contractual in nature—with (1) one or two hospitals which have an active pediatric service; (2) juvenile court; (3) foster placement; (4) supportive and crisis services; (5) long term therapy programs; and a (6) community child abuse program.

If within a given community there is a large pediatric inpatient service in a given hospital, then two or three alternatives are available. This hospital *must,* under all circumstances, have an in-hospital child abuse and neglect consultation team. Delegated members of the community child protection team must be very closely affiliated with this team, and one or two of the child protection group members should serve as members of the hospital team. For example, any children's hospital in a given community must have a child abuse and neglect team. The physician on the community child protection team and the hospital team may be common to both. The child protection team within this community must also delegate one or two protective services workers to the hospital team as direct liaison between the child protection team within the community and the child abuse consultation team within the hospital. Similar arrangements will be possible in large communities where the juvenile court has a separate child protection part or unit, direct liaison with certain degree of commonality of members of both teams is mandatory. Figure 13–1 indicates that the child protection group (Component A) is directly linked to the community child abuse program. This is of critical importance, since neither can function autonomously.

### Administrative Structure

The administrative structure of Component A must be developed to enable the state department of social services (*not* the county) to run these multidisciplinary acute care service programs. There should be a division of child and family services, which in turn is divided into three major regions: one dealing with rural programs, another with metropolitan programs, and the third dealing solely with megatropolis programs. The problems and issues that arise in each of these three areas are very different and should be approached administratively in a different way. For example, the establishment and running of a child protection team in the Upper Peninsula of Michigan (some 300,000 people) would be administered differently from child protection teams in the city of Detroit.

There should also be *direct line* relationships to the state region which handles these three major areas, and the county department of social services should be bypassed. A program for physical abuse and neglect to small children should not be administered at the local level; rather the state department, with competent people in each of the several regions, must have direct authority over these programs. This stand will no doubt cause considerable consternation, but a program this complex cannot be developed in the 3,500 (approximate) counties in this country. State departments of social services do not usually include disciplines other than social workers except on a case consultation basis. This policy must be changed. The psychiatrist or psychologist, physician, lawyer, and nurse who are part of the child protection team should be considered as much a member of the group as are the protective service workers. Their function is not to deal solely at the case level but to get involved with programatic problems and issues as well. (This will be discussed further in subsequent sections of this chapter.)

Since many physicians and psychiatrists will not be comfortable working under the rules and aegis of Civil Service, a direct contract may have to be written with a given physician or group, medical school, law school, or department of mental health for the services of these individuals. Some developers of community programs will have had such negative experiences with their local department of social services that they may be tempted to go it alone, developing a program in child abuse and neglect bypassing the D.S.S. Every effort should be made to avoid the temptation of developing this A component—the child protection team—without including protective services. This department, after all, is generally mandated by law to carry out this function. The B group (long term care) should be developed outside D.S.S. but with their help and support.

### Community Image and Public Relations

Unlike the police and fire department within a given community, the departments of social services have not, over the years, had a community public relations arm. Since child abuse and neglect is the responsibility of everyone in the community, and since the services provided to families with this problem cut across all economic, racial, and religious boundaries, it behooves the child protection teams to develop community information and public relations services. This function can be carried out by the education and training component of the community program (to be discussed). This education and training unit should also serve as a resource to help the personnel in these child protection groups with their data gathering and the development of specific observational and research projects.

### Personnel Fatigue

One of the problems in any child protection team is the tremendous physical and emotional fatigue that overcomes the workers after spending one to two years (or less) in this front line operation. This is much truer of protective services workers than of other members of the group, since the latter are either part time or can divert their emotional stresses by performing other duties within their discipline. Protective service workers, however, "wash out" in this period of time unless very careful attention is paid to this problem.

One of the distinct advantages of having a group of this type is that decision making in sometime life-and-death situations can be shared by the group and the emotional stresses ofttimes diminish. This may not be sufficient, however. Rather than lose a good worker because of fatigue, he or she should have the problem recognized well in advance and an "R and R" program developed for that individual. It is strongly recommended that each 4–6 weeks all protective service workers have a block of time in which no new cases are assigned to them. This should be at least 2–3 weeks per quarter, hopefully longer. This would give workers time to catch up on old cases, do some community relations, give talks at a local school system, do a special project for a group, and so forth. Although on the surface this may appear to be a waste of time, whatever the cost, the decrease in turnover of workers will readily balance the apparent added expenses. It is not possible to function as an acute care worker in a child protection group without extended time built in for diversion.

## COMPONENT B—LONG TERM THERAPY

Three interacting circles were depicted to represent the three major components of a complete and comprehensive child abuse and neglect program for a given community. These are represented in Figure 13–1 where Component A represents the Acute Child Protection Team, Component B the long term therapy section and C the education and training unit. This section will discuss Component B, therapeutic development. Figure 13–3 depicts Component B with its *working* committee and subcommittee striving to define, redefine, develop, innovate, and move ahead in a coordinated fashion.

**Figure 13-3.** Component B—Long Term Therapy

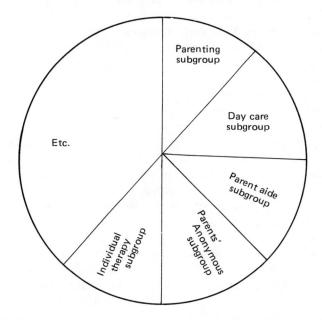

Who is responsible for getting this committee together, calling the first meetings, being the chair? In a subsequent section, the concept of the prime mover is discussed. Someone—anyone—has to pick up the ball and run with it.

As mentioned earlier, the acute care and diagnostic component (the child protection team) should not be responsible for the providing or the coordination of long term care. It is equally important, however, for the community child abuse and neglect program to identify a group of individuals who will be responsible for this vital component. If significant time and effort is not delegated to the development of therapeutic programs within any given community, the work of the child protection team will go for naught. These two components (A and B) must proceed concurrently; if component A has more referrals than component B can handle, the total program, as well as the abused and neglected children and their families, will suffer.

Most communities have existing services that are available to abusive and neglecting families. These services are often sporadic, short term, and independent of other community service programs. Families in trouble need *many* services, from family planning to budget management to psychotherapy. Separate service groups working in isolation trying to serve families who are scared and nontrusting just won't suffice; there is no way any one agency or service will meet all the needs of these desperate people.

Two things are of critical importance at the outset: first, to realize and admit that departments of social services (protective service units) are not in a position to provide long term therapy. Second, a coordinated community long term treatment program will not happen by sitting around and complaining that D.S.S. is not doing its job. Some group has to get moving.

### Committee to Develop Therapeutic Programs

Component B is made up of a group of individuals whose major function is as follows:

1. Establish goals in relation to community needs and resources.
2. "Beat the bushes" within the community to develop new treatment programs.
3. Help existing programs and services make necessary modifications to treat abusive parents and their children.
4. To explore new and innovative approaches for treatment.
5. To coordinate long term programs within the community.
6. To coordinate long term therapeutic endeavors for difficult cases (see section on coordination).

The makeup of this committee should be those individuals who are the supervisors, sponsors, and workers in long term treatment programs and services. For example, the supervisor of a parent aide program, a sponsor of a Parents Anonymous program, the supervisor in mental health who is responsible for a group therapy program, the supervisor of a program for special nursery school programs, the parent training teachers, Head Start workers, and so on. These individuals must meet regularly to discuss problems, community needs, and methods of developing new and modifying old therapeutic programs.

The functions of components A and B must be separated. Although component A participants must be aware of component B programs for referral purposes, they cannot be responsible for setting up these services. As was stated above, it is humanly impossible to do crisis work and long term work at the same time; in addition, the two tasks often require different skills and personalities.

### Who Is Responsible for Long Term Care?

There is no existing agency within our communities throughout the United

States that has the mandate to either provide or be responsible for long term therapy of abusive and neglectful families. Somehow this aspect of our therapeutic endeavors has been overlooked. If one examines carefully the role and responsibility of the protective services units around the country—almost all of which are administered through the state department of social services (with great county autonomy)—one finds a crisis oriented, acute care service which ends within a period of one to three months.[a] Since abusive and neglectful families require both crisis intervention *and* long term care (sometimes for years), and since the child protection team cannot and should not provide this long term care, who then will pick up this responsibility? Currently no one is; and our case failure rate is related to this deficit.

It is impossible for departments of social services to pick up this deficit in long term care responsibility because existing rules and regulations, both federal and state, prohibit their involvement with families on a long term basis unless that family is eligible (or almost eligible) for income maintenance (AFDC). Even for those on AFDC the departments of social services cannot provide the necessary long term involvement because of their current methods of followup and the case loads of their income maintenance case workers.

How this problem will "shake loose" over the next several years is uncertain. Some group or agency must be given this long term responsibility through legislation. If a case goes to juvenile court, as 20 to 30 percent of *physical* abuse cases do in some communities, the court *may* assume this task, but only for the child and often not for the family. Juvenile court cannot be given the task of long term therapy. If the department of social services in the state structure is to assume this responsibility this will require some major changes in both their rules and philosophy, since for years departments of social services have been serving poor people during crisis periods only. Their administrators have not and do not see their role as providers of long term therapy.

Who, then, should be responsible for the treatment required by these families? We obviously have misgivings about suggesting that departments of social services be delegated this task, but to date we have no better suggestion. One thing is certain: the job must get done, and it must be done by some type of bureaucrative agency, otherwise there will be no uniformity within any given state. Currently, every community must resolve this problem and "rediscover the wheel" for themselves. We believe that a therapeutic development committee should be formed, long term programs initiated, and some type of long term coordination organized (see subsequent section). In considering this problem, such a committee may find the following guidelines helpful.

1. There are essentially three phases of treatment.
   A. *The acute-crisis phase*—during which diagnostic assessment and crisis resolution take place and long term plans are formed. This usually takes one to four weeks and is accomplished by component A.

B. *The transition phase*—at this time the A and B components are trying to make a reasonably smooth transition from one service component to the other. Often both groups are involved periodically during this period. (This is schematically depicted below in Figure 13–4, at coordination point 2.)

**Figure 13–4.** Coordination

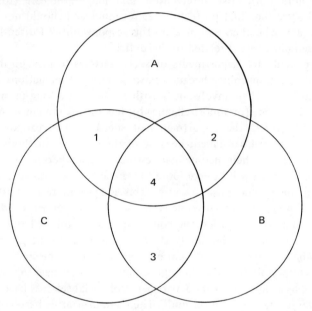

C. *The long term phase*—this is where the treatment plan gets locked in, programs for a given family are identified, and crises become fewer (but rarely ever go away). Currently no agency or group is responsible for making certain that the plans for treatment actually take place, and families fall through the cracks. This phase can continue for many months to years.

2. In some family situations the treatment plan need not go beyond the transitional phase, for some show significant improvement with "minimal" intervention.

3. Even though a given family has been picked up for treatment by two or three different therapy programs, one person must be responsible to make certain that the plans developed during the acute phase are working or modifications made if necessary.

4. While the development of long term programs outside the department of social services structure is necessary, the D.S.S. must still be involved with the planning. They must see this need, for eventually they may have to pick up this responsibility for at least the coordination of the long term treatment if

not the actual treatment itself, since they are the only existing bureaucratic agency even remotely structured to do the job.

### Therapeutic Programs

This chapter is not intended to be a review of all therapeutic programs currently underway in a variety of communities throughout the country. (The reader is referred to Chapter Ten for this discussion.) However, two very specific points must be made as the therapeutic development committee considers its tasks. First, none of the treatment programs is sufficient unto itself. For example, Parents Anonymous or parent aides should not be considered an end in themselves but only an adjunct to another form of therapy. The second point is that most of the therapeutic endeavors available in a given community, such as mental health services, Catholic social services, child and family services, must be modified in some way in order to make their services useful and appropriate for these families. One must not assume that an existing mental health program can automatically assume responsibilities for care of these families without significant modifications in their approach—and often in their basic philosophy.

### Affiliations

The therapeutic development component of a community child abuse and neglect program must be affiliated with any number of existing service agencies and program within that community. As indicated, the supervisors of these programs and their workers should make up the membership of the therapeutic development committee. In addition to developing these affiliations, this committee must be strongly allied with the total community child abuse and neglect program as indicated in the schematic of Figure 13–1. How these programs are tied together administratively and how they are coordinated is discussed subsequently.

Backup services from skilled social workers, psychologists, psychiatrists and pediatricians must be available for every therapeutic endeavor in this field. For example, parent aides must have a direct line to their supervisor, who is generally a social worker; and these supervisors, in turn, should have consultation readily available. The therapeutic development committee itself does not run these programs, nor is it administratively responsible for them. These programs should remain the responsibility of the agency and/or organization under which they are developed. One critically important area must not be forgotten. Parents who are abusive or neglectful are constantly finding themselves in crises which they, individually, cannot resolve. The skills of a crisis oriented supportive service team (component A) must be readily available to these families and their long term therapists.

### Prevention

As the development of treatment options and improved diagnostic services proceed, the need for earlier intervention will become apparent. Many professionals will begin to note early signs of danger prior to abusive behavior, such as parents who express fear and/or frustration over their parental responsibilities. An additional responsibility for this treatment development component then becomes the planning for inclusion of these parents in some type of preventive training and treatment program. This chapter is not intended to discuss in detail the concept of early recognition and prevention (see Part VI).

## COMPONENT C–EDUCATION, TRAINING, AND RESEARCH

The necessity for a diagnostic assessment and crisis intervention multidisciplinary child protection team (component A) as a separate entity from those who provide long term therapy (component B) has already been emphasized. These concepts were discussed above and schematically depicted as two of three interacting circles (Figure 13–1). Component C, the education, training, and research unit (Fig. 13–5) is, in the long run, probably the most important and influential segment of any of the community child abuse and neglect components. This training unit overlaps both A and B and can become a very powerful tool in unifying the community, helping to establish consistent philosophies, and developing mutual trust among those involved.

**Figure 13–5.** Component C–Education and Evaluation

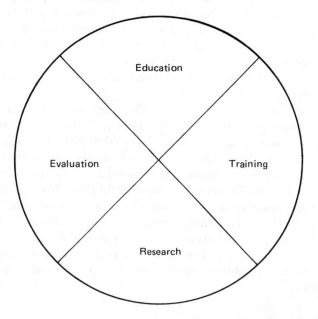

Traditionally, social workers, nurses, teachers, and others have participated in "in-service training" programs. While these educational endeavors may satisfy certain needs, nothing fosters "inbreeding" and traditionalism—and actually inhibits multidisciplinary service programs—more than "in-service" education. Failure to develop communitywide educational and training programs results from the false assumption that every discipline involved with this problem assumes that the professionals in the other disciplines have been trained to handle their role in this problem. Doctors assume social workers have the necessary skills and answers, and vice versa; social workers think police have been trained; and we all know that lawyers and judges have the insight and education to deal with these difficult issues.

The point is, of course, that none of us can look back at our formal education with any degree of satisfaction in how we were prepared to help abusive and neglecting families. Doctors aren't taught much about child development or family dynamics, laywers have little training in family and child law, social workers experience minimal training in protective services, some judges have no understanding of family interaction, and so on down the line. This, of course, is changing; but all too slowly. Realizing these deficits, a community child abuse and neglect program must develop an education, training, and research unit to make up for the many weaknesses we all had in our formal education.

### Functions of the Unit

The basic functions of this unit are as follows.

1. To develop, in conjunction with those who are to be trained, specific objectives to be achieved.
2. To organize these objectives into a variety of learning experiences appropriate for the specific content, skill, or attitude wished to be learned.[b]
3. To develop ongoing and periodic evaluations of the educational experience, the professionals in the program, and of the program itself.
4. To coordinate public informational programs, using mass media, at appropriate times through the year.
5. To initiate and stimulate research projects in the area of child abuse and neglect.

While these functions are broad and all encompassing—and may even be threatening to some—they can be done at the outset on a small scale, with minimal costs and few extra personnel. These points are discussed in more detail below.

### Makeup of the Unit

One person in the community should assume the overall responsibility for the coordination of this training and educational component. This individual need not—in fact probably should not—be an expert in the area of child abuse and neglect. His or her skills should be in the field of education and training. Ideally this person should work for an educational institution, such as a community college, local university, or public school system. This institution must be one that sees *community* educational endeavors as one of its primary responsibilities. This educational and training coordinator should have ready access to some skilled individuals—e.g., those knowledgeable in audiovisual equipment, group leaders, trainers, as well as content experts in the field of abuse and neglect. Almost every community can identify individuals with these backgrounds and skills if the "word is out and the search is on."

### Process of Development

What is being proposed is not a large $500,000 operation analogous to a large regional training center (such as one can find in Denver) with others being funded by the Office of Child Development. Every community needs to tap the resources of these centers as well as develop their own ongoing, multidisciplinary training programs. These educational programs should begin on a small scale; for example, a one-day training session for new parent aides or nurses. They can then expand into a more ambitious venture such as a three-day empathy training or interpersonal skills marathon for protective service workers. Some programs might be held monthly, others semiannually. As trust begins to develop within a given community, several disciplines can be trained together, picking areas of common needs for a small group which might consist of a lawyer, physician, hospital social worker, nurse, police woman, and mental health worker.

The number of training units required varies with the size of the community. As indicated above, there should be one child protection team for every 500,000 population. While each protection team needs a training unit, one such training unit may service more than one child protection team. For example, a city the size of Detroit would need five or six child protection teams, but only one or two training units.

Rarely will significant amounts of *new* money be necessary to develop these training units if the various agencies and services involved with child abuse and neglect within a community are willing to pool some of their resources and "in-service" training funds. This certainly will take a good deal of give and take, but it is feasible and can be one of the many tasks of the program coordinator (see below).

### Public Education

Community education is often achieved through the mass media. This needs to be directly related to the development of an awareness of the problems, services available as well as the need of improving therapeutic services. It is a mistake to *begin* by encouraging the public to report suspected cases; advertising has invariably shown a dramatic rise in the reporting rate. This rise can be beneficial *after* treatment gains have been made; if it occurs too soon, the increased case load can overwhelm agencies and services.

These public educational endeavors serve not only to inform but also to alter public opinion regarding the treatment potentials for abusive parents and to provide an avenue for concerned citizens to direct their interest and time to the abuse and neglect problem. They can volunteer, donate money, be advocates, etc. The media can also provide needed legitimacy and recognition of dedicated persons involved in program operation. All too often the media is utilized to promote out of town speakers and administrators rather than line workers. Local people must be given credit. Seeing your name or group written up in the local paper is a small reward for the long hours spent in the provision of services, but it is at least some compensation.

Care must be taken to develop a good working relationship with media people, for they can be either helpful or harmful. Dramatizing the brutal beating and death of a child on page 1 and reporting on the therapeutic endeavors of a community program on page 30 may not be all that beneficial. Media people are very willing to help but they need to know how and when to be helpful.

### Educating Those in Positions of Authority

Administrators, commissioners, legislators, judges, and senior law enforcement personnel, although needing education in the area of abuse and neglect, are all too often reluctant to become involved in formal training programs. But they must not be neglected and allowed to "escape" the educational arm.

These individuals can be reached through several avenues. First, they can become involved in discussions of difficult cases, particularly cases that demonstrate certain key problems or issues requiring resolution. Second, they should be asked to attend meetings to specifically discuss the problems, such as role of police vs. protective services, prosecution vs. treatment, and so on. Third, they can be approached for their opinion or approval—e.g., what should a doctor's statement for a court case of abuse include; can photographs be taken in the emergency room of the hospital? Fourth, attempts should be made to provide them with educational materials such as articles on the role of the hospital or judge in abuse cases. Fifth, invite them to participate in upcoming seminars locally or nationally on child abuse. Sixth, ask them to appear on local panels and television shows on child abuse and neglect: nothing educates faster than having to appear as an expert! Finally, hold a "take-a-judge-to-lunch month" campaign.

Not every administrator needs to become an expert in abuse and neglect. Rather, these key individuals need to know how they can help in local matters and how their particular agency or service can be helpful to the community program. Educational aims should be directed toward letting them know to whom they can turn for further information and help. Finally, don't forget that one way to educate someone is through the spouse or children.

### Education of the Front Line Professionals

Front line professionals are defined as those persons involved in case management and treatment. This group includes physicians, lawyers, social workers, psychologists, psychiatrists, police workers, teachers, public health nurses, and others. There are essentially two ways to reach this group. One is through a didactic approach and the second is experiential. The didactic includes reading materials, discussion groups, lectures, case studies, and the like. Experiential includes role playing, practice interviews, and getting them involved with actual cases.

It is probably most effective to provide both kinds of training. Initially, interest can be generated through didactic materials; if actual skills are required, experiential learning becomes mandatory. The opportunity to practice methods of interviewing, for example, provides a "safe" opportunity to practice new ideas. Unless skill learning is available, the client becomes the opportunity for practice, making learning and/or changing more threatening as well as providing slower growth in skill development.

Not all front line professionals play a role in the day-to-day involvement of treatment or diagnosis, but they still need to be aware of current practices. (These professionals include nurses and receptionists in the hospital, the beat policeman, welfare workers, teachers, etc.) Education for this group can best be accomplished if it is goal oriented. For example, a new hospital child abuse and neglect team, and the procedures for referring to the team, can be presented to the general hospital staff through a series of staff training sessions. These people do not need to know how to handle a case of abuse but rather how best to get a case or knowledge of a case to the proper person or agency. Note: if training is done before standard procedures and protocols are established, this can cause as much havoc as increased reporting when it occurs before programs are ready.

### Paraprofessional Training

The training of parent aides and other paraprofessionals such as crisis hot line workers needs to focus on the development of existing skills. The danger in training paraprofessionals is one of overkill. While this group begins their work with the feeling of inadequacy, it is important that they not try to compensate by becoming junior psychiatrists. Excessive use of professional jargon contributes to this feeling of inadequacy and fosters the junior therapist role.

One method of training is to make use of practice interviews, attitudes and values clarification exercises plus didactic material. This is helpful not only with lay workers but with professionals as well. Practice interviews focusing on feelings, with audio or visual taped replay of the interview, have been developed by Norman Kagen at Michigan State University.[c] This method of training, in combination with didactic information, is suited to aiding workers involved with abusive families.

### Research and Evaluation

Not every community program will be able to perform formal research studies but all programs should record and document what they are doing. This in itself will be useful to others for further funding opportunities and especially to assess what is being achieved. Writing down in advance what one hopes to do in subsequent months will help assure that you don't end up someplace else without even knowing it. When formal research is feasible, it should be encouraged. Very talented researchers are always looking for things to study, measure, and record. Local colleges and universities are bulging with Masters and PhD candidates with time and in need of a project. These efforts must be coordinated and controlled, but should be encouraged.

State social service departments are notorious for discouraging "outsiders" from having access to their inner workings, often under the guise of confidentiality. While a person's rights *must* be respected and safeguarded, there are ways of doing honest research and maintaining these rights simultaneously.

### Affiliations and Administrative Structure

The education, training, and research group can originate from staff positions of the community child abuse and neglect program or it can be provided by staff from community colleges, schools, or mental health centers. If provided by institutions not associated with the community program, close ties with that institution must be developed. Since training and education provide not only for skill development but also for legitimacy, publicity, and coordination, it is imperative that educational goals be related to the activities of components A and B. If education is approached as a vital resource it can be utilized to further the advances or initiate new ideas in the community operation. Occasionally participation in these courses can provide college credit for the participant.

## COORDINATION WITHIN EACH COMPONENT

Consideration has been given to the three major components of a community-based program for abused or neglected children and their families. At this point, the need for coordination must be given high priority. Any time several agencies or disciplines must work together to achieve a common goal, the single most important factor is that a coordinated effort be maintained. The basic coordination points in this community endeavor fall into three areas.

1. Within each of the three components—i.e., within circles A, B, and C.
2. Where each of the three circles overlap—i.e., points 1, 2, and 3 in Figure 13–4.
3. Where all the circles overlap—i.e., point 4 in Figure 13–4.

### Acute Care Coordination (Within Component A)

The complexities of case management during the acute crisis intervention phase following a report of child abuse or neglect are enormous. The handling of this difficult problem is the responsibility of the child protection team. Each case must have a specifically defined person responsible for the coordination of efforts, someone not necessarily responsible to carry out all that must be done, but rather responsible for the coordination of these efforts. With rare exception, this acute phase coordinator should be the protective service worker. This is his or her basic task: to weave this complex case in and out of the diagnostic assessment team, pull together the data and people involved, and hold a team conference at which time the case is assessed and a long term therapeutic plan developed.

The responsibility for the case remains that of the protective service worker until all data are gathered, crises apparently resolved, and a transfer to a long term coordinator can be made (see below). All this acute coordination occurs within component A, using outside services and helpers where indicated. The protective service worker is heavily dependent upon the other members of this child protection team during the time the case is in the acute phase period (generally a matter of days or a few weeks).

### Long Term Case Coordination (Within Component B)

This is the very point where almost every community in the country is hung up. Either it is not realized that our traditional protective service system provides only acute care and *not* long term (months and years) therapeutic services, or, if this is realized, many either don't wish to admit it or are unable to do anything about it. The result—families by the scores fall through the cracks (more likely gaping holes) and return only when abuse or neglect has recurred: back to the acute care service worker.

One of the primary functions of the therapeutic development committee, in addition to helping the community organize and implement long term treatment programs, is to see to it that a specific individual is responsible for long term case coordination. This coordinator is not responsible for the actual delivery of this care, but rather for its coordination. As the protective service worker is the coordinator of the acute care, this person or persons coordinates long term care. The coordination of long term therapy was discussed earlier under component B. This gap in services presents a serious problem for every therapeutic effort in every community. Who is to make certain these efforts are carried out by those responsible? As indicated, the following seem inevitable and must be facilitated.

1. For D.S.S. to assume the responsibility for coordination of long term therapy.
2. For D.S.S. to drop all financial eligibility for such coordination to occur (clearly the public health departments purify water for all, not just the poor).
3. For D.S.S. to develop a separate but related division, apart from the child protection team which has the responsibility for long term coordination.
4. For D.S.S. to work closely with the community service system, which must implement the long term treatment since D.S.S. cannot and should not be responsible for implementation, only coordination.

The administrative structure of the coordination required for components A and B is depicted in Figure 13–6.

The major function of a long term case coordinator(s) is as follows.

1. To maintain records on all cases referred for coordination.
2. To review records on the average of once every three months (more often early in the case) to determine if plans are being carried out. If not, the case coordinator must pull together the appropriate individuals to reassess previous plans, explore problems, and develop new plans.
3. To identify consultants within the community who are willing to meet with long term workers to discuss specific cases.
4. To organize and attend these regularly scheduled review and consultation meetings with component B workers to facilitate the coordination of the long term therapy problem.
5. To give feedback to the members of the child protection team (see below).
6. To meet regularly with the community program coordinator (see below), keeping him or her informed of service gaps and problems.

### Training, Education, and Research Coordinator
### (Within Component C)

This is probably best achieved by a small committee with a good leader. The function of this component is described above and the carrying out of the necessary coordination should be done by the committee. The individual must maintain close contact with the community program coordinator to assure ongoing communications are maintained. Where funds are available a specific person may well be delegated (hired) to coordinate these endeavors. A committe, however, can perform the task.

Figure 13–5 depicts interface points 1 and 3, which are where the actual training and education takes place—A workers and/or B workers participating in an educational happening. The committee clearly has responsibilities outside of the program as well (i.e., to the community).

### Interface Point 2

The transition of a case from acute to long term care is where many, if not most, problems exist. The transition may not be complete for several weeks or months. Even after the transition is made, crises will again recur and the services of some or all the A team members are required. B workers must not find it necessary to do A work; thus, a family in long term therapy has a child who gets a fracture; is this fracture accidental? This should be the function of the A team to help out and make this decision. Another example: a family in long term therapy has a house that burns down, the father is injured, and no money is coming in. B workers may take 20 hours to contact the right people to resolve these crises. An A worker could do it in one to two hours.

Close contact must be maintained at interface point 2. Workers must trust

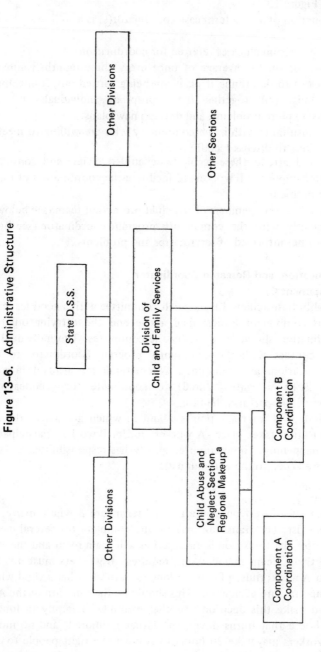

**Figure 13-6.** Administrative Structure

aRegional make up will have to vary according to population, i.e., the needs of rural, metropolis and megopolis are different.

each other and bail each other out. Movement from A to B must be carried out through close communication between the coordinators within each circle.

## PROGRAM COORDINATION

Emphasis must be given to the difference between case coordination (acute or long term) and program coordination. Communities that have only a traditional protective service unit within a department of social services are in desperate trouble because they have no program. Protective service is a service, not a program. The demands made upon the traditional protective service workers are impossible; these social workers must be physician, lawyer, psychiatrist, police officer, investigator, friend, therapist, and child protector all in one person. One has little doubt why the protective service workers around the country stay in their jobs for only one to one and a half years on the average.

Every community must have a child abuse and neglect program with the three components described above. Where the components intersect (see Figure 13–5, point 4) is the pivotal point where the program coordinator and her or his board evolve.

### Role of the Program Coordinator

This task must be delegated to a specific person, the program coordinator, who is salaried and whose role it is to do exactly as his or her title depicts—i.e., coordinate this total endeavor. The coordinator is in a position to gain access to people, programs, problems, and supporters. She or he must be a sales person with forceful tactfulness, personal stability, and organizational capabilities. This often is a lonely job with few short term rewards (and many failures), but with great long term satisfaction and benefit.

Of primary importance is that the coordinator write down specific objectives (ones that are small and manageable) which she hopes to see accomplished within the first six months, year, etc.[d] She should see herself as a facilitator and coordinator, *not* an expert in the field of child abuse and neglect. If she is seen as a child abuse and neglect expert by the community, she may lose her ability to coordinate and become a threat to some agencies or individuals. Each community will find it necessary to write their own job description for their program coordinator. The one used in some communities is given in Appendix B to this Chapter.

In order for the coordinator to function, a small group to whom she can report and receive support must exist. At first this group does not need to be an elaborate board; a small task force of dedicated citizens and professionals will suffice. The main requirement of this informal group is to (1) provide support and advice to the coordinator, (2) act as a sounding board for suggestions to problem resolution, and (3) provide legitimacy to the role and person in this position of program coordinator. Rarely should the task force dictate specific duties, for the role of coordination requires such flexibility that only general goals and guidelines must be considered rigid (see description of board of directors below).

### Impediments to Coordination

In order to implement each of the three components in a given community, several problems must be examined and resolved by the coordinator and task force. The problems outlined below can be expected to emerge at some point in the project development and, if anticipated, will not seem so overwhelming.

1. A *lack of trust* between agencies and professionals is often apparent. This has developed from competition for funding and professional specialization, use of unidisciplinary jargon, and status hierarchies. Ironically, abusive parents have a problem since they cannot trust, while professionals trying to help often have a similar problem.

2. In overcoming this problem the coordinator and task force play the role of *mediators,* the guardian ad litum for the community. If a certain judge is throwing doctors' statements out of court, the coordinator requests the judge to spell out his requirements for a doctor's statement, or sets a meeting up between the doctor and the judge. A lawyer on the task force who knows the judges can be especially useful in this example. By involvement in the diagnostic and treatment team meetings, the co-ordinator is able to facilitate communication between team members and between the team and other community agencies.

3. Resistance to working together is evidenced by arguments regarding *confidentiality.* In order to provide coordinated care from the diagnostic to the long term treatment phase, professionals must share case material and concerns. This resistance can be attacked through discussions of case disasters where coordination was in short supply. This confidentiality fear stems more often than not from a fear of professional exposure rather than client exposure. A "let's learn from our mistakes" attitude during team meetings helps alleviate this fear.

4. Another problem will occur in the area of treatment development. The present *lack of treatment resources* exists because agencies are set up to provide outpatient therapy to motivated clients, inpatient therapy often being used for an unmotivated client. Abusive parents are often found to be unmotivated (due to lack of developing this attitudinal frame in child-hood) but rarely need inpatient care, thereby being eliminated from both categories.

5. Therapists from treatment agencies are professionally trained to discourage *dependency of clients,* something that is most critical during the early phase of treatment. Therapists, fearful of admitting their own negative feelings toward abusive parents, use the "unmotivated client" and "dependency" arguments for terminating cases.

6. Treatment development facilitators must help agencies to see the *uniqueness and treatability* of abusive parents. Accepting the uniqueness and providing structural changes to facilitate the referral of parents is the agreement required with treatment agencies. Involvement in a coordinated treatment team enables the therapist to overcome his or her negative feelings toward clients.

7. *A further problem* exists for both diagnostic and treatment personnel in an uncoordinated community. Everyone's natural inclination is to punish or ignore the parents and protect the child. A real psychological need exists for us to see abusive parents as monsters with no hope for treatment. These natural inclinations are acted upon by taking punitive action in severe cases, and by disbelief or no action in minor cases. The burden of protecting the child, when coupled with a fear of misdiagnosis and resulting parental anger, overwhelms many professionals. A vicious circle of underreporting, lack of coordination, and lack of treatment results.

8. The best way to *break into this circle* is to provide professionals with the opportunity to become involved in a successfully resolved case. Providing them with the guidance and support to develop interdependent roles in the resolution of a case is a place to begin. The best way to begin to like abusive parents is to get to know them. The only way to learn to trust other professionals is to sit down together and share common concerns.

In essence, the task force and coordinator are institutionalizing procedures for interagency and interdisciplinary management of cases with a built-in evaluation mechanism—the successful outcome of cases. Many communities have made a serious error in attempting to provide treatment in child abuse and neglect by providing only one component of the program. As that component becomes successful, others in the community become resentful and a resurgence of jealousy occurs. The eventual loss of commitment and initiative by the successful group develops from a frustration in failing to gain cooperation from others. An effective program requires the synchronized development of each component.

The program coordinator is essential to the long term success of any child abuse and neglect endeavor. The job must be secure and those on the board committed to this concept. The coordinator must not have to spend large portions of time seeking new funding to keep the job viable. While new money is helpful (see below), the position itself should be permanent.

### Board of Directors

The program coordinator, like an executive director of a large corporation, cannot work in a vacuum. Coordination point 4 (see Figs. 13–1 or 13–5) must have a firm and lasting base from which to operate—i.e., a board of directors. The program coordinator, then becomes the staff person(s) for this board. The makeup of the board will vary somewhat from community to community. There are some fundamental guidelines that should be considered as this group is formulated.

1. Key people within the community must be members. Those who hold influential positions, e.g., the director of personnel for the juvenile court, the head of personnel for the school system, director or board members of mental health and public health, heads of key private agencies, and so forth.
2. While the front line workers must have access to the board via the program coordinator or their own agency director, they themselves should not be on the board. If they are on the board care must be taken not to deal with nitty gritty, day-to-day issues; rather, basic problems must be considered.
3. Influential lay people should be members of the board—a director of a local bank, head of a large business firm, representative from local pastors group, and so forth.
4. Women must be well represented on the board. This must be given special consideration, since many of the positions mentioned above are held by men in some communities. At times, less influential but committed men and women accomplish more work than busy executives. Both groups need to be represented.
5. The board should have ready access to consultants who will meet with them regularly or on an ad hoc basis. They may need, from time to time, advice from a physician, lawyer, accountant, grant writer, facilitator, psychiatrist, and others.

The board must meet monthly on schedule for sufficient time to conduct its business. The chairman, elected by this group, conducts the meeting from a predistributed agenda, developed by the chairman and the program coordinator. These should be serious and formal sessions, but open to informal discussion when appropriate. Most of informal discussions and problem solving should occur at the committee level, with reports at the monthly board meeting.

The major functions of the board are to (1) help develop and maintain a coordinated community program; (2) develop plans for new and innovative endeavors; (3) seek and find necessary funding for the program to operate and distribute equitably; (4) encourage and advise local people in their endeavors in the area of abuse and neglect, supporting their programs whenever feasible; and (5) assist in problem resolution among agencies. The board does this through its staff people—program coordinator, case coordinator, and others. At no time should the board or its component members set up competitive programs in the areas of diagnosis or treatment; their function is community coordination and programming.

Special note should be taken that this board does not *run* the individual components; each have their own administrative structure. This is a difficult task, but unless it is achieved successfully, the result will be a return to or an entrenchment into our present unidiscipline, "you-don't-trust-me-and-I-won't-trust-you" approach. (To go from trust development to a smoothly functioning board will probably take two to four years, if all goes reasonably well.) Emphasis must be given to the fact that the purpose of a community program is to build coordination and concern; an isolated and autonomous group runs counter to this endeavor.

The question of incorporation always arises and is a point that every community board will have to face eventually. There are certain major advantages and disadvantages which must be considered. Applying for funds certainly is easier if one is incorporated. On the other hand, certain legal obligations may make incorporation difficult. No firm answer can be given other than to encourage each board to give serious thought to the matter and seek appropriate legal council in the process.

One of the major spin-offs of the development of a board is the bringing together of key community people to resolve common problems. Little difficulty will be encountered seeing advantages of the mutual trust that is developed and the positive effect on many community service projects, other than child abuse and neglect. Children, families, and the community alike will benefit in many ways.

### Board Funding Options

The increased interest and funding availability for child abuse programs raises certain problems for a community board. Should they (1) raise money for component programs—e.g. hospital teams, parent aides, mental health agencies; or (2) raise money to administer certain programs themselves; or (3) raise money for others to use, keeping only enough to provide funds for the small staff of the board. Option three (administrative control only for their staff) has many advantages; it keeps the board from becoming administrators.

The coordinator's responsibility is program development and coordination. Administrative problems, such as staff selection and placement, and financial efficiency remain the territory of component agencies or institutions irrespective of their relationship to overall program goals. This is a definite advantage to coordinators since their role is often perceived as threatening (i.e., suggesting changes, critical of existing procedures, etc.; and doling out professional rewards such as speaking engagements, newspaper articles for superior professional work). The additional threat of administrative control would add to the already difficult task of program development and coordination. Our current recommendation is that the board should administer only enough money for their own small staff. Additional efforts at fund raising should be directed to the helping of its member agencies in finding funding for component services for abused and neglected families.

## THE PROCESS OF DEVELOPING A PROGRAM

Many community programs begin through the efforts of a small group of front line doers who become unhappy with what isn't happening in their community for the abused or neglected child and his or her family. After months of complaining and frustrations this small group finally seek each other out, for mutual therapy if nothing else. Eventually someone says, "Let's stop bitching and do something about this mess!" And so begins the task force.

### Where There's a Will . . .

There are several ways in which a community task force can develop a comprehensive, well coordinated child abuse and neglect program. First, they could, with great authority and sense of righteousness, hand out an article or report, wait for action, get mad when it doesn't occur, and disband. This will be termed the "moral" approach: if you are a good person (agency) and know "the truth," you will do the appropriate thing and all will listen. This approach is not recommended.

A second possibility is to write a grant to provide money for all involved, thereby assuring equal participation and cooperation. This can be termed the "don't do anything until we get money" or "the-kid-in-the-candy-store" approach. The results from this approach have been less than encouraging. We do not recommend this because the availability of funds *before* trust and clear purpose have been generated often leads to more intense fighting and competition. This is likened to getting an inheritance and being sought out by a long-lost relative. The bigger the inheritance, the more "relatives" appear.

A third approach is to delegate to a person or a committee the planning of a community program. This method sounds logical but runs into problems at the point of implementation, for the planners and implementers are often different people if not different groups or agencies. Few people (or agencies) like to be planned for; therefore, when the plans are laid out one suddenly discovers a great deal of resistance. We call this the "seemingly rational" approach and don't recommend it either.

In order to avoid being considered un-American and developing an unknown new approach, we suggest that the best method of organizing the community is the "stubborn plodder" approach, utilizing a combination of all the above methods: the combination of a little moral indignation, a little money, a few good committees, and a little muscle. The stubborn plodder approach will win out. A *"prime mover"* is mandatory, however; one with a "never-believe-a-no" personality.

Please note: enough knowledge is already available to plan the needed program for a community without an in-depth, time consuming assessment or survey of that community. The particular eccentricities of a given community can be included in the overall plan and should occur as an evolving process at the suggestions of local people, who will then have a part in the planning as their talents are being utilized. Don't let those not wanting to do anything delay the development of a program by the "let's-do-a-survey" routine.

The temptation to apply for funds and await their arrival before a program is developed must be avoided. Money coming to a nontrusting, unorganized community can be devastating. Too much money coming at any time can be detrimental. No money is equally as devastating.

### Step 1—Does a Prime Mover Need Charisma?

Many existing community programs have been developed through the sheer stamina and force of one or two charismatic individuals, people—professionals and nonprofessionals alike—who seem never to run out of energy or ideas. They also seem to be filled with wit and brilliance and are known for memorable statements or quotable epigraphs. Unfortunately, not all communities have such leaders, or, if they do, they already have causes other than child abuse. The purpose of this section is to give the rest of you some basic information and direction so that you too can develop a successful child abuse and neglect project. You *may not* become charismatic in the process but you *will have* created a program worthy of pride.

Your initial goal is to begin implementing components A, B, and C and the administrative structure for each. Initially, you will need a handful of people to do this work—five to ten is plenty. This group is best composed of a variety of disciplines and professional or nonprofessional status. The primary requirement is that they have time, or are willing to take time, for implementing work.

### Step 2—Legitimacy and Goal Setting

Goals and persons assigned to meet goals should be separated into the components mentioned earlier. Realizable goals need to be set in order to maintain momentum. The group as a whole should meet once a month to share progress and problems, and to gain support. It is especially important to expect everyone to work on at least one project; by dividing jobs into sections, you are creating a miniature model for implementation and expansion into your future community program. Everyone must work on a task. The problems of the community and child abuse and neglect are so complex that it is very easy to slip into a monthly "pity party" and accomplish nothing. Setting time limits helps to avoid this problem.

Suggested specific objectives for subcommittees and their charge are as follows.

**A. Administrative Subcommittee.** This group should work on a name for the task force, as well as a method of publicizing their goals, purpose, and membership. They can also be responsible for arranging meeting time, place, lunch, etc. They will keep track of component goals, lead the monthly meetings, and find new members as needed. If funding is eventually considered as one goal, they can begin the process of grant writing and seeking local funds. Staff members, as needed, would be provided by the member agencies.

**B. Diagnostic Subcommittee.** This group must establish a multidisciplinary structure for a child protection team (the beginnings of component A). This can be done in two ways. One way is to provide medical, legal, and psychiatric consultation to protective service workers through the purchase of service or (initially) through voluntary services. A second way is to initiate a hospital team composed of a protective service worker, social worker, nurse, physician, and psychologist. In both options the multidisciplinary group members should provide some direct services, gathering data to better assess case materials and reviewing findings on a regularly scheduled basis in a two-hour meeting.

The job of this task force is to sell the idea, and to be present to provide support and smooth out problems as they arise. A common mistake is having these groups deal only with difficult cases. Difficult cases are trying to everyone and do not build trust or hope; rather, they foster existing frustrations. The idea is to learn as you do, and you learn as much from successes as you do from failures.

Initially, you need to determine which option, community or hospital team, will be easiest to start, although eventually (especially if in a community over 500,000) both programs should be established. Do not be concerned over small gains; you are selling a concept. Once sold, and the benefits realized for a small group, the program and its participants will sell itself. Start with one physician and two protective service workers, or just one protective service worker and one hospital social worker. Start where you can and then expand as you go.

**C. Treatment Subcommittee.** Programs mentioned in the description of this component (B) require the selection of which treament programs are most feasible in a given community. Parent aides and Parents Anonymous are easiest to begin with because they require little new money.

1. *Parent Aides*—Your first task is to find a sponsoring agency and a supervisor. We have used such diverse agencies as the YWCA and Catholic Social Services. It doesn't matter who it is, so long as they're willing to support the program. The supervisor must be a professional, generally a social worker or psychologist. Once these are established, work with the supervisor to set up recruiting mechanisms, funding, publicity, etc. After a few aides are found and assigned, the supervisor must meet with the group of eight to ten aides every week as well as be available in-between-times for problem solving. Aides can initially be volunteers, with salaries or at least expense reimbursement available as the program grows. The task force (and/or program coordinator) will want to meet regularly with the aides and their supervisor to offer support and links to other programs. As this program develops, consulting services through a protective worker, psychologist, doctor, etc., will be necessary. Remember, aides can be very valuable if provided with supervision and frequent case reviews. However, if left on their own, they become discouraged and overinvolved. They may give up or begin to think they are the only treatment personnel for a family.

2. *Parents Anonymous*—These groups, not unique in child abuse treatment, need to remain as autonomous as possible. Initially, appeals to social

work associations, or agency personnel, should identify a professional sponsor. Once a sponsor is located, advertising for members is necessary. This can be done in two ways: through direct referral from agency contacts, and through the public media—TV, radio, newspapers, direct mail, etc. In order to use public media, a phone number should be available for potential members to call. Volunteers may be used for these purposes, or an existing crisis phone service. Once one group is established, the task force and/or coordinator should hold monthly meetings with the sponsor and others aiding volunteers or parent leaders to maintain contact, momentum, and to provide support and resolve problems such as obtaining babysitters, toys, reading material, publicity, fund raising, new sponsors, meeting places, etc. Again, once a group is begun, the chances for more groups escalates. Help from the national organization can provide many brochures and pamphlets (see address given earlier).

3. *Group Therapy*—Various forms of group therapy are appropriate. Finding co-therapists to provide the service and obtaining referrals is the job of the task force. Once begun, ongoing support and working through of co-ordination problems becomes the goal.

4. *Individual Therapy*—This is perhaps the most difficult task. This service requires the commitment of both agencies and individuals. The problems are: long waiting lists, little outreach available; ongoing case reviews (every two months) are rarely done, and therapists willing and able to work in this area are hard to locate.

5. *Other Programs*— The task force must plod along by meeting with agency supervisors and staff. It will continue to be a problem until agencies see a role for themselves in treating abuse and neglect and making the necessary "official" changes in policies to allow effective treatment to occur. Treatment options that require new allocations of funds, such as crisis nurseries, should not be pursued until you've found a source of funds. These types of projects usually require new sources of funds and, unless available, will only cause unnecessary headaches.

**D. Education Subcommittee.** The role of this task force is discussed above under component C. They should provide the training needed for workers in components A and B plus those in related community services. Finding volunteers through a local university, community college, or mental health center is helpful. Publicity for your activities on occasion should be kept separate and handled by the administrative component. The reason for this separation of responsibilities is that it's quite difficult to spend part of your time patting others on the back, and then have to pat yourself on the back, also. It's too easy to go overboard either way if one committee has both responsibilities.

### Step 3—Bush Beating and Implementation

All subcommittees need to begin implementing the goals set in Step 2. These tasks require many contacts for every one taker—five agencies contacted before one buys the idea of a parent aide program. Even though this process at times seems futile and hopeless, takers will eventually be found. In addition, the four seemingly lost contacts may well be takers for other programs in the plan. Community education is occurring in the process. Even though these contacts did not buy at this time, when they see that your program is working in other areas, you may be pleasantly surprised to hear from them a few months later in the form of an inquiry as to what they might contribute.

It is most important that all three components begin at the same time and continue at approximately the same rate. This is the reason behind dividing responsibilities. As an example, it will probably take from six months to a year for each component to be established. If it takes six months to establish a hospital team, and six months to establish educational resources for the team, the team is not going to wait six months more for their training. If the child protection team is more effectively identifying cases only to find no treatment resources available, and the parents are being sent to jail, they will surely begin to doubt the purpose of their efforts.

### Step 4—Hold Your Breath and
### Take Antidepressants

Essentially, the work in Steps 1, 2, and 3 has done very little to affect the management of abuse and neglect cases. Instead, a *system* has been established that will produce more effective diagnosis and treatment for these families. Goals have been set, ideas sold, and followers found. During Step 4, then, supportive work must be continued. Stand back and hope that participants will continue doing what they've been asked to do—not because someone has asked them, but because they think it's a good idea. In addition, they will begin coming up with their own ideas, *telling* you instead of *asking* you. One must be comfortable when someone in the community gets your idea and thinks it is his/hers.

This stage can be compared with adolescence in family development, and may well be accompanied by rule testing and so forth. And just as parents do, you must be willing to allow certain independence and have confidence that you have prepared them well in Steps 1, 2, and 3 for mature behavior.

Although this is a great day for the community, it is often a very trying time for the organizers. Many self-doubts, which were supressed earlier as one jumped into beating the bushes, now surface when less aggressive behavior is required. The fact that you really haven't improved anything for more than a handful of abused children adds a feeling of low self-worth. Unfortunately, there is very little you can do to make yourself feel better and you must just wait it out. The temptation to make radical changes or decisions is present, but you'll probably resist it, as you should. A party, vacation, or a trip to another community to see their problems—or all three—might help provide perspective.

**Step 5—Success and Self-Righteousness**

After your concepts and programs have been shown to be successful and are supported, the community will want to expand the programming efforts. In fact the nontakers will even begin to approach you as to what they might contribute. At this stage it's very easy to resent new interest and newcomers who haven't experienced the struggles, to feel that they are jumping on the bandwagon which you have created. A common approach on their part is to question the group's competence and to express a desire to learn how it's *really* done from the *real* experts in Denver, Boston, San Francisco. This can become a disaster and cause a split that could create two or more child abuse projects in the same locale. Now is the time to suggest that an out-of-town "big wig" come to your community and say all those things you've been saying all along. This will make you look good, and your program will be off and running.

Since your overall goal is coordination, trust building, and cooperation, the visitor may help you attain these goals. There may be specific agencies or hospitals, which you may feel need to be included in your program and which thus far have not been enthusiastic about the prospect. The strength gained from surviving Step 4 and the visiting big wig may help reinforce your previous method of persuasion, "forceful tactfulness," and persistent pursuit. Retain your confidence and remember: you got this far through the use of tact—don't abandon it in the face of success. It's still a very valuable tool and will be required in the years to come in order to maintain interagency and interdisciplinary cooperation.

All this effort will begin to show results in accomplishments, better case management, earlier diagnoses, and real treatment successes. Congratulations!! The learning you've had to do to get to this point will provide you with the skills for future planning and programming. Who knows, you may even stumble upon knowledge or techniques which "we experts" have not thought of. Glad to have you aboard!! Now you should go out of town and be a big wig visitor yourself.

## APPENDIX A
## SUGGESTED TRAINING PROGRAM IN CHILD ABUSE AND NEGLECT

### Content Listing and Instructional Method

| *Teaching Method* | I. **Legal Aspects** |
|---|---|
| | A. Knowledge of *your* state's law—children's code and mandatory reporting |
| Precourse: | 1. Definitions—abuse and neglect, child, investigators |
| Reading | 2. Those mandated to report |
| Discussion group | 3. Penalty for failure to report |

4. Immunity for reporters
5. Abrogation of privileged communications
6. Central registry
7. X-rays and color photographs
8. Required procedures for those mandated to receive reports
9. Protective custody
10. Guardian ad litem

| | |
|---|---|
| Lecture<br>Videotape<br>Simulation<br>and/or role playing<br><br>Court situation | B. Case preparation—gathering evidence, presentation of evidence<br>1. Intake interview<br>2. Medical reports—pathology/ruling out other explanations<br>3. Social report<br>4. Psychiatric evaluation parents/child: when and how?<br>5. Psychiatric development, child<br>6. Central registry—each jurisdiction<br>7. Lay vs. expert testimony<br>8. Temporary custody, adjudicational, dispositional hearings<br>9. Beyond a reasonable doubt vs. preponderance of evidence<br>10. Alternative avenues into the court—guardian ad litem<br>11. Basis for appeal, to which court?<br>12. Conflicting theories—child's best interests vs. keeping family unit intact. |
| Provide list of<br>suggestions<br><br>Discussion groups | C. How to find an attorney—qualifications and where<br>1. Civil, corporate and criminal vs. juvenile law<br>2. Time required for preparation<br>3. Multidisciplinary knowledge<br>4. Tax deductible time—large law firm<br>5. Law schools<br>6. Local bar association |
| Provide list of<br>"how to's"<br><br>Discussion groups | D. How to change the law—needs and who<br>1. What is present law?<br>2. What is needed?<br>3. Who is qualified and willing to do it:<br>   a. Law schools<br>   b. Child advocacy groups |

c. Bar association (family division)
d. Legislation (Colorado dealt with this before)
e. Organizations
f. Medical societies

*Teaching Methods*  **II. Making a Diagnosis**

A. What information to get

Lecture
*Videotapes
Discussion groups

1. Observational skills
   a. Behavior of child—age appropriate
   b. Child-parent interaction
   c. Is child different—real or perceived
   d. Physical findings
   e. Developmental status
   f. Growth status

2. Medical assessment—above plus

Precourse:
Cassettes,
Manual Cassettes
Slides

   a. Does history explain physical findings
   b. Complete pediatric history and physical
   c. Laboratory findings
   d. X-ray findings

Videotapes

3. Psychosocial—is potential to abuse or neglect present?
   a. Parents' rearing
   b. Parents' self-image
   c. Use of others
   d. Helpfulness of spouse
   e. What are children, in general, for
   f. Does child in question meet expectations
   g. Do sibs meet expectations

B. How to gather the data

Discussion groups
Videotapes—stop/
start
Simulation on video
Role playing
Sensitivity sessions

1. What to do on a home visit
2. The interview
3. Introduction of helpers and data gatherers
4. Self-image of helper (see section III)
5. In what order should data be gathered

C. What to do with data gathered (i.e., how safe is the home?)

Lecture
Videotapes–stop/start
Hold own conference,
   i.e., on role playing

1. Objectivity
2. Judgment
3. Correlation
4. Weighing data
5. Setting—conference

6. Individual roles of participants
7. Need for sharing information
8. List of problems
9. Delegation of responsibility

*Training Method* **III. Attitudes**

    A.  Interpersonal skills

Empathy training
   vignettes

       1. Communication
       2. Empathy
       3. Interviewing

Sensitivity sessions
Case study

    B.  Positive characteristics—self
       1. Flexibility

Personal testimony

       2. Open—nonjudgmental
       3. High frustration tolerance

1 to 1 sessions

       4. High self-esteem
       5. Trusting
       6. Tenacity
       7. Optimistic
       8. Nondefensive

    C.  Personal needs
       1. Of staff
       2. Of parents
       3. Of child

    D.  Negative characteristics
       1. Prejudice against parents or children
       2. Racial conflicts
       3. Fanatic beliefs

**IV. Treatment**

Orientation
  lecture

    A.  What-specific modalities
       1. Indications and contradicitions
       2. Knowledge of psychodynamics, i.e., where modalities work
       3. Limitations
       4. Interactions of various modalities on one another
       5. Short term and crisis oriented
       6. Long term
       7. Total family plan

Precourse Cassette
  Manual

Videotapes–stop/start

Critical incident
(positive/negative
Discussion groups
Case presentations

B.  By whom–characteristics of individual (helper and
agency, see IIIA 1-3, IIIB 1-8 under Attitudes, plus):
1.  Sex, age and race of therapist
2.  Not role oriented
3.  Trained to do job–general training and specific
experience
4.  Not rule dependent

*Training Methods*  **V.  Community Programs–Development**

Precourse
  Cassette Manual

Group discussion

Role playing

A.  Components
1.  Diagnostic
2.  Treatment
3.  Educational and Training
a.  public relations
b.  specialty people
1.  In-service
2.  Outside resources
c.  Parent education (parenting)
d.  public
4.  Evaluation
a.  program
b.  specific modalities
c.  people individually
5.  Research

(Note: outside of
Center resource
needed here)

B.  Administrative–structure
1.  How to write grants and get money
2.  Problems after money received
3.  Difference between program coordination vs.
case coordination
4.  Board of directors and advisory committee
5.  Full time administrative staff

C.  Multidisciplinary approach
1.  Importance
2.  How to find lawyer, doctor, psychologist,
or psychiatrist
3.  Difference between case and program
consultant
4.  Definition of roles
5.  Overlap of roles

D. Process for change
1. Teaching trust
2. Identifying an administrative structure
3. Existing services

## APPENDIX B

## PROGRAM COORDINATOR'S
## POSITION DESCRIPTION

### Basic Function

Stimulate, support, coordinate, and allow to mature the multidisciplinary and multiagency approach to the prevention and treatment of child abuse and neglect.

### Dimensions

The coordinator shall be responsible for relating to multiagency personnel and volunteers to enlist and support their effective participation in meeting the objectives of the child abuse center. It shall further be the coordinator's responsibility to supervise and direct the activities of additional staff members of the center. The coordinator shall relate to the board of directors the current status of programming efforts, and obtain their input for methods of advancing programming goals.

### Nature and Scope

The coordinator shall be responsible for stimulating, supporting, coordinating, and institutionalizing three program areas: *first,* the development of multidisciplinary diagnostic teams in the hospitals and community; *second,* the development of effective and sufficient treatment options in addition to the development of regular treatment team meetings in order to coordinate treatment; *third,* the development of education workshops, seminars, etc., for use with community personnel. Since the coordinator will be involved with all the agencies and disciplines involved in case management, the responsibility for uncovering and mediating interagency and interdisciplinary conflicts, duplication, etc., will be an additional responsibility.

The role of the coordinator is such that he or she provides no direct service in any of the three areas of diagnosis, treatment, or education. The coordinator's main task is to find and encourage others to perform these tasks. As various components become successful, use of participants to educate others is highly recommended. Maintenance of one family requiring direct social work service is, however, recommended in order to keep sight of the nature of child abuse.

The above mentioned responsibilities will be directed primarily at the early identification of and treatment of actual instances of abuse and neglect. As this process becomes more efficient, the coordinator will need to initiate and coordinate efforts aimed at prevention. This includes identification of high risk parents and the provision of supports and "parenting" education for these same parents and/or potential parents.

The board of directors will need to be in approval of and set major goals and objectives for the program—i.e., diagnostic teams, prevention, statewide coordination, and so forth. The coordinator in turn shall be responsible for devising methods whereby the implementation will proceed most effectively. Since implementation requires community support as well as involvement, it will be important that neither coordinator nor board become rigid in setting predetermined plans for implementation. Existing resource use requires that opportunities for involvement need to be examined and utilized when available. Therefore, formal approval for such decisions as where diagnostic teams meet or where a parent aide program is established are inappropriate. The responsibility of the coordinator is to research these possibilities in the community. The board members need to provide input and direction to this research. Informed support by board members for various programs and goals is required in order to legitimize the programming efforts.

### Knowledge and Skills Required

The coordinator shall possess a bachelor's degree in one of the helping or communication professions. Work experience and/or advanced degrees are required in the field of child abuse and neglect, communication, or community organization. Professional and personal skill in the areas of setting short and long term goals, discovering and utilizing resources, finding and maintaining supporters, uncovering and resolution of conflict, as well as methods of avoiding conflict and providing direction and support to various disciplines and agencies. Although the coordinator shall provide assistance and direction in the area of fund raising, the final responsibility for this shall fall to the board of directors.

### Principal Accountabilities

Job performance shall be judged by assessing the degree of coordinator involvement and evidence of trust established with community resources. Stages of implementation shall be evaluated as to their relevance to the attainment of long range objectives. The final evaluation shall include evidence of coordination, effective case management, and effective component program operation—i.e., diagnostic, treatment, education, and prevention projects.

※ Chapter Fourteen

# Perspectives on Child
# Maltreatment in the Military

John K. Miller

## INTRODUCTION

There is little difference to the victim of child abuse or neglect whether his parent is a civilian or a member of the uniformed services. The blood, bruises, and broken bones present the same clinical picture in any emergency room. Likewise, the principles of good child protection apply equally in the military services and civilian life. These two propositions, though briefly stated, are fundamental to any discussion of child abuse and neglect in the uniformed services. The purpose of this chapter is not to focus upon the common denominators of "maltreatment syndromes" in the military and civilian sectors, but rather to address those matters that are unique to military life and have impact upon child neglect and abuse in it. The goal is to provide the reader with a better understanding of military life style, child protection programs, treatment resources, legal implications, and other management perspectives. Such an understanding should facilitate working with the child protective case in the military community.

These matters are not important only to those who have primary responsibility for providing human delivery services to the Armed Forces; large segments of the civilian field also encounter the military family in their daily work and life. Military families live in civilian communities, their children attend civilian schools, and under the provisions of the Civilian Health and Medical Program of the Uniformed Service (CHAMPUS), they use civilian medical, social, and mental health resources. A relative may learn of a serviceman's family chaos two thousand miles away and seek advice from a local welfare office, a clergyman, or a Red Cross worker.

For many of these civilians the uniformed services seem a mysterious and unusual life, different from mainstream America. In some respects they are right; in others their judgments are based upon stereotypes and misperceptions that don't always fit reality. The television series M*A*S*H is not really a typical picture of Army medical care, though many Army medical personnel are as dedicated to saving patients as "Trapper" and "Hawkeye". One does not have to be a sadist to be a sergeant, and senior line commanders more frequently resemble civilian business executives than John Wayne leading his troops up the hill.

For the average civilian, military life is often equated with aggression and violence. This may be one reason why the first question posed a military child protective worker by his civilian counterpart is usually, "Is child abuse worse in the military than in civilian life?" The same question does not seem to be asked as much about whether it is worse among blacks, Orientals, Mexican-Americans, bankers, firemen—or television writers, who produce more violence in one year than most service personnel see in a career.

One civilian study aimed at assessing potential for child maltreatment among parents awarded 10 points "high risk" for merely being in the uniformed services.[1] Clerical workers and housewives were rated as "low risks" because of the nonviolent nature of their profession. Such a built-in bias demonstrates a lack of awareness about the broad complexities of military life, and it overlooks the clinical experience of most practitioners that the highest risk group for abuse or maltreatment in the United States is the "harassed parent" who vent their frustrations on their children.

What is required of the practitioner, then, is neither a denial nor a generalization about the impact of military life upon those service families who are suspected of, or found, to be mistreating their children. Objective evaluation and management with due consideration to all elements of the situation is the appropriate course. Whatever seems to be bad in civilian life often seems to be worse if it occurs in military life. Race riots in Germany among American troops seem worse than race riots in Watts among civilians; drug abuse at a military base worse than drug abuse in the city nearby; and child abuse by a marine worse than child abuse by a civilian.

No one really knows whether child maltreatment is more or less prevalent in the uniformed services than it is in civilian life. There are theoretical reasons and even some rudimentary evidence to indicate it might be greater.[2] There are equally sound theoretical reasons and some hard data to imply that it is no more of a problem for the armed services than it is for the average civilian community. The Department of Defense can be reasonably criticized for not knowing the answer to this question. It has now been nine years since every state passed a child protection law, and data gathering about morbidity and mortality is a common occurrence. Federal monies have been allocated through the Department of Health, Education, and Welfare for national clearinghouses on child maltreatment and other information gathering programs.[3] It is paradox that the uniformed services—federal entities—are not a part of these federally sponsored data collection systems.

The armed services are not immune from child abuse and neglect. There is no reason why they should be: they draw their personnel from civilian life, where it is an endemic problem. The central problem, then, is not whether there is more or less child maltreatment in the uniformed services, but rather that it exists to a degree where it deserves reasonable attention in the Pentagon.

Like those whom they serve to protect, child protection programs in the military services have sometimes been the victims of neglect. The reasons for this are complex, but in an oversimplification it may be speculated that although no one in the higher echelons of the defense establishment is opposed to good child protection, its importance in maintaining a national defense posture has not been viewed as critical. Clearly these programs have not received the attention given to drug abuse, alcoholism, and equal opportunity endeavors, all of which have more direct impact upon active duty troops and military effectiveness.

For the civilian practitioner who deals with child abuse and neglect, the issue of military effectiveness in relation to child maltreatment may seem irrelevant, but it is not to those who make a career of military life. In order to better understand this perspective and the factors that affect child abuse and neglect in the armed services, it is necessary to have some familiarity with what life is like in the military forces.

## MILITARY LIFE STYLE

Like related human beings, the "sister services" may have a kinship, but each also has its unique personality and characteristics. No one can fully define the patterns of any one military branch, let alone the collective traits of all of them. What is offered, then, is an attempt to present commonly shared values of the uniformed services with emphasis upon those aspects that are different from civilian life. Later on, these matters will be addressed as to their importance in child protection issues, but the reader can also reach independent conclusions about their impact.

Military life is deeply rooted in bureaucratic organization and a hierarchy of authority. The lines of authority in military society are more clearly defined than in civilian life and are reflected in rank, which is visibly shown on uniforms and in other ways. The armed services have only advertised themselves as protectors of democracy, not as models of it; thus it is ironic that in some cases they have actually been more democratic than the civilian sector. Military bases and posts may be the only segment of American society where, even if prejudice has not been eliminated, military family housing is at least completely racially integrated. "Segregation" occurs by rank on posts, but this does not always mean the best housing goes to the highest rank. Senior enlisted personnel may have better housing than junior officers. Theoretically—and often practically—anyone with the ability should be able to climb the ladder of success.

If one believes that in a democracy all citizens have an equal right to good medical care, then the uniformed services are probably the only place in the American scene when it occurs. Unlike most cities and states, military communities have no "unemployment" problem and everyone at least has the dignity of a job. This is no guarantee that everyone works or that there is no poverty. Though pay (including benefits) is generally good for those who have received some promotions—and is better than several years ago—there still remain some junior enlisted personnel with families who find their federal jobs entitle them to federal food stamps because they fall beneath the federal poverty levels.[4] In contrast with nearly every civilian community there are few ultra rich, and they keep quiet about their family inheritances.

The federal credit union and the finance officers replace the civilian bankers; the staff judge advocate and his military attorneys are the corporation lawyers, district attorneys, legal aid societies, and Perry Masons of military life. The police chief is the local provost marshall; the city building inspector is the safety officer. Physicians are not only "doctors" they are MCs (medical corps) and captains, majors, and colonels. The local supermarket and department store on a military base are not owned by the commissary and exchange officers. Clergymen come in three brands, Protestant, Catholic, and Jewish, and they are all cross-trained. The local travel agent is the transportation officer, who also takes care of the moving company's business. The housing officer fills in for a dozen real estate agents, but he only rents. School principals are school principals, unless they operate a military school for troops, where they are Commandants. Directing all these people is not the mayor or city manager, but the post commander.

Together all these people make up the "town fathers" and they have one thing in common: they are salaried employees who can realize no personal financial profit from their individual and collective enterprises. The base is a total community in nearly every respect, and operating as it does there is very little of the "politics" one sees in civilian government. Knowing the right people is helpful in order to get a matter considered, but this is more to grease the gears of the bureaucracy than to gain political favor. Since leaders are not appointed or elected, it is not essential that they hold favor with the citizenry so long as they can command its respect. Leaders tend to be conservative in outlook, but they rarely acknowledge to what political party they belong in order to preclude any accusation of interference or influence in civil political matters.

This community is comprised of a large number of young personnel, most of whom live in barracks on the military installation; a large number of married personnel and their families also living on the base; and usually an equal or larger number of military families who reside in the nearby civilian community (regardless of how big or small it is). Bridging both the military and civilian communities is an increasing number of retired military families who on the surface seem to have the best of both worlds.

Service personnel can be categorized in several ways such as rank, branch of service, or type of duty within each branch (i.e., infantryman, tanker, doctor, etc.). One way of looking at them for purposes of this discussion is the young new enlistee (two or less years of service) and the career military family (lifers). This will be discussed in more detail later, for it is a significant factor in child protection considerations. Suffice to say that not all the new young troops living in the barracks are single, and in fact this military community crosses state boundaries to the furthest point where a young military wife and her children may be located. These boundaries stretch around the world to a service man stationed in Korea or Germany whose family lives next to the gates of the post back in the United States.

Though members may hold different views, certain values tend to exist more in military life than the civilian sector. Patriotism and loyalty to country is expected and respected more. That is what it's all about, and even those who do not verbalize it still seem to feel it. When the flag goes down at retreat, everyone is expected to stop and respect it. There is a higher regard for discipline than might be seen in some segments of civilian life. Since it has high value, it also has strong sanctions against violations. Another high value area is that of sacrifice. This is true not just for military personnel, but also for family members. Military life style involves a twenty-four hour way of life as opposed to segmented life frequently seen in civilian experience. Families are expected to move anywhere and everywhere at any time, whether this involves uprooting children from school and friends, personal inconvenience, or other disruptions in life.

Those who seem to make it successfully through these stress periods appear to regard the experiences as opportunities for travel, bold new adventures, escape from boredom, a chance to meet new friends and see new places. Those who don't, interpret the event as intrusion into their privacy, separation from friends, and traumatic torture invoked by a heartless bureaucracy which could care less about families and personal life. Most people feel a little of both, but all of them recognize that sacrifice is involved, and playing "ain't it awful what they did to us" is a favorite pastime in the military.

Military families expect in exchange for their sacrifices some degree of reciprocity in terms of benefits. They get these, and much more than they realize or appreciate, so some of the sacrifice may not be bad; but unfortunately the sheet really never balances out for many. Nevertheless, the government does provide a comprehensive range of services and supports for its armed forces and their families. These range from free aspirin to expensive medical care at little or no cost to the family. As rank and tenure increase, some of the benefits also increase in terms of better housing and status in the community. This emerges from an old concept "rank has its privileges", R.H.I.P. And of course, privileges carry responsibilities.

Command responsibility as defined in military life is more inclusive than that normally expected in civilian life. A civilian manager is responsible for his employees and the quality of their performance at work only. A military manager is responsible for those under his command totally. This concept is based in long military tradition that a commander in war must be responsible for the health, morale, welfare, training, discipline, and performance of his troops. While military personnel carry individual and personal responsibility, their commander also carries responsibility for them.

This has specific and broad implications for those working with the military child protective case. If a civilian seriously injures or kills his child, his supervisor or boss may have no more of a reaction than anyone else who knows the man. The mayor of the town may only read about it and ask the police chief what happened. If a soldier commits the same act, his immediate commander will likely be on the scene in minutes, desperately trying to get the story together, determining what he should do, what went wrong, and what he will tell the "old man" (his commander). If a fatality or a particularly macabre incident occurs, the post commander may well be called in the middle of the night. In a few minutes a rather sizable task force of military police, command personnel, first sergeants, chaplains, physicians, investigators, and attorneys may be on the scene. If a deviant soldier has had a prior history of abuse, assault, incarceration, wife beating, or other symptoms of instability, and the commander is aware of them, the unit leader may be in for some rigorous questioning as to why he did not take preventive action to avoid this incident.

The concept of command responsibility transcends formal military structure and carries into family life as well. While military commanders have no direct command authority over family members, they clearly have influence in family lives. They are expected to assist families. If a soldier beats up his wife it is a command problem; if the wife beats up the soldier it is also a command problem. Since the soldier may be absent from duty because of injuries, or the incident may imply a breakdown of peace and order on post, it becomes a matter of command concern. If a teenager in a family commits an act of delinquency or misconduct everyone knows that his father will be held responsible and the commander may become involved. Some children are well enough versed in this code that they use it—if not consciously, at least indirectly—to get a negligent father's attention to their difficulties.

Women vary in calling domestic matters to a commander's attention. Some wives overuse commanders in domestic problems, while others will never let anyone known what is going on for fear of disciplinary action against the husband, possible reductions in pay, restrictions, and so forth. The unit leader walks a tight rope between invasion of privacy and meeting command responsibility. Credit companies are rather notorious for giving loans to young servicemen with precarious credit ratings, fully aware that if the serviceman is late or defaults on the loan, pressure can be exerted through the commander for action. Usually the letter to the officer reminds him that this soldier's nonpayment reflects poorly upon the Army as well as the individual soldier. If the wife made the bill, the letter still goes to the commander.

Central to all military life is one theme . . . the mission. The mission overrides all other considerations. It may be to win an engagement in war, it may be to train for war, it may be to feed the troops, or it may be to provide medical care. Programs not directly related to military mission accomplishment are incorporated not because they are desirable or a routine part of normal community life; they become justified by how they relate to military effectiveness and mission accomplishment. Medical services are offered to family members not because families are there or need care, but because such services help to "conserve the fighting strength" (the Army medical service motto). They do this by promoting health in the family, improving the service member's morale, and offering incentives for career retention. In fact they do just that. In spite of the CHAMPUS program, which offers families the option of using civilian medical resources at low cost, military medical facilities remain heavily used by those who seem to feel better being taken care of in their own system.

If a service person with family problems is seeing a marriage counselor, his ability to get off duty for an appointment will be decided to some extent upon the question of mission. Military personnel do not "accrue sick leave" as do many civilians; they seek permission to be absent from the unit (but on duty). If the commander or First Sergeant deems their presence in the unit more vital to the mission than a visit to the marriage counselor the request may be denied. In fact this rarely happens because the commander is also aware that a visit to a physician or marriage counselor may also be important to the mission. He does not want to be accused of interfering with the health and welfare of his troops.

Such issues rarely arise about a brief absence, but become more complex when the matter involves a permanent reassignment of the sponsor. Often the situation is one where the military member is overseas on a "hardship" tour when his family encounters difficulties in the United States. A civilian agency, physician, or clergyman recommends he be reassigned nearby until the problems can be worked out. All the branches of the service have provisions for doing this, but the criteria are specific and sometimes difficult to meet. The regulations differ among the major branches, but they generally require it be demonstrated that (1) a problem exists, (2) only the service person's presence can alleviate this problem, and (3) the problem can be resolved in a year or so in order that it will not reoccur.

If the latter situation cannot be demonstrated, the service member may be discharged from the service for hardship reasons. This is a serious event for those who have several years invested in a military career. The armed forces face a dilemma in these cases: they cannot require only those members who have no problems (or at least do not complain about them) to serve in unaccompanied tour areas, while families with chronic long term problems remain in protected assignments together. On the other hand, morale would be destroyed if a member could not get back home when needed. It would affect not only his morale, but that of all those around him, who would realize that if serious trouble happened to someone else it could also happen to them.

One solution to the problem has been to provide community supports around the family so that they are assisted without always having to bring the spouse back. These are extensive and include a few selected bases where families can live while spouses are overseas, counseling and medical services in the military, as well as the CHAMPUS program. Once again the issue of mission is the justification for these programs. Since mission is a primary consideration in all military life, emphasis tends to be placed upon active duty service personnel more than on family members. The military leader of a large military installation will view himself as military commander more than as a "mayor" or city manager. Community management will be conducted by his staff of military and civilian personnel who also handle military matters.

This system may be more efficient than a civil government system in many respects, because decisions can be made without regard to political or pressure group influences. Where it falls short is in the area of citizen input and broad community considerations, which are not in the experiential background of most military leaders. Intramural sports programs for active duty personnel may receive proportionally more attention than playgrounds for children. Day care centers will usually be housed in buildings cast off from military mission requirements. Adult mental hygiene clinics will be better staffed than child guidance clinics, if they exist at all. And while military community life offers nearly every community support available in civilian life, it occasionally finds it has blind spots that simply have not been considered.

In the previously mentioned list of community functions it should be noted that no military branch has entertained the idea that it might indeed need some kind of welfare department. These services are provided instead by a loosely organized system of chaplains, Army Emergency Relief, American Red Cross, military social workers, and health nurses. There are no juvenile courts on military installations and these problems are considered to be command problems, to be handled between the military police, the unit leader and post commander, the family, and sometimes a federal magistrate or the FBI. Sometimes there are juvenile disciplinary or control boards, but their powers are advisory. The problems of these blind spots becomes more apparent in the child protective area.

If military life poses so many problems, why do people remain in it? The answer is that it also offers many distinct advantages aside from the more obvious fringe benefits. One of them is a strong sense of belonging to a community. Both formal and informal codes exist among military families that reinforce a sense of belonging to a large international "primary group." This is especially true of career personnel, who are often provided sponsors (another service member and his family) to assist them in making the transitions to a new assignment. They may be international travelers, but they can move around the world without ever leaving the "group." Like early pioneers they cross the country, jumping from one military installation to the next, resupplying and exploring. They have a friend in every state, and their homes are reflections of their wanderings around the world.

For those who reside on a military post there may be a stronger sense of security and "community" than in the neighboring civilian city. The military police may be younger and less experienced than the city policeman, but they drive by the house more frequently. Notices in the mail box telling one to cut the grass may be irritating, but the neighborhood looks better. There may be objections to excessive "coffee clutches" in the housing area, but that is easier to control than not knowing the neighbors at all. The kids can play on the parade field and they can walk to the nearby youth activities programs. All in all, it is not a bad life. If it isn't good right now it might get better, for as the saying goes, "Your best military assignment was your last one and the next one."

Military families are normally well supported and that's why they remain in military life. At the same time there is a subtle and constant awareness that they are receiving these benefits more as privileges than rights. From a commander's viewpoint they are a necessary (and even desirable) logistical burden, but nevertheless a burden. As one Army officer put it, "Why do you think we call them 'dependents'?" The military family marches to a different drummer from their civilian counterpart and they hear two theme songs: one is, "the military takes care of its own," and the other is "if the Army wanted you to have a wife it would have issued you one." Since the music will probably not change, they must learn some steps most civilians never know. How well they make it is largely dependent upon their ability to do their own dance without losing step to the cadence created by the system.

## CHILD MALTREATMENT IN THE ARMED SERVICES

Little research has been done on maltreatment in the armed services, but that which has been conducted indicates there is probably not much difference between military and civilian child maltreatment in terms either of underlying causative factors or clinical manifestations. Differences probably do exist, however, in those elements that either precipitate or prevent the "high risk" family in crossing the line from being potential to actual maltreating parents. A reassignment, payroll mixup, disciplinary infraction, field training exercise, or similar event can tip the scales for a family living in a precarious social adjustment. These factors alone do not cause child abuse, but they may set the stage for it.

Less recognized by the general public are those elements of military life that may prevent the high risk family from becoming abusers and neglecters. A major asset in military life is the quality health care that is available and inexpensive to the consumer regardless of rank or income. This provides not only better case finding, but also better coordination among health care personnel. A steady pay check and a job for the man who was unemployed in civilian life may make a difference also. The concept of command responsibility for the welfare of the troops may not always be 100 percent effective, but it does promote community involvement.

The most vulnerable population in military society for child maltreatment is the young enlisted family who has been in the service less than two or three years. From this group come those "high risk" families frequently seen in civilian life which are characterized by immaturity, inexperience, lack of social skills, and inability to cope with life's problems. Since military entrance standards reject applicants with severe mental disturbances, antisocial traits, drug abuse problems, and marked mental retardation, some screening does occur. There is no assurance, however, that the spouse may not have such problems, and so the screening system is not perfect. This group is the most vulnerable because it is the largest of the younger population in the military services. It is the population most likely to have young children. In addition, it is the group which is most likely to have the least education and experience in life. The uniformed services attract and recruit young people who have not yet developed specific life goals, but are still in that phase between adolescence and adult maturity. Commissioned officers are largely selected from those who have already gone through this transition.

Compounding this vulnerability are two other factors. One is that the young service family is removed from their civilian extended family and community, thus putting them in a totally new and different society at a time when they are least prepared for it. The other factor is that, in contrast with higher ranking or more tenured military personnel, they are not provided all the military benefits others receive. Their pay is not only lower, but they also do not receive the family and moving expenses of senior personnel. Military housing is frequently limited or absent for the young married enlistees. The principal reason such military benefits are not provided them is probably related to the costs involved in supporting such a number of personnel, but it may also be related to long standing perception that young servicemen should not be married. That pattern has changed since World War II, but remnants of the "Brown Shoe Army" still remain in military culture that preclude fully recognizing that enlistment certificates do not erase marriage certificates.

Large private industry would not expect employees to move their families anywhere in the world at their own expense, but this is what is asked of the new enlistee who is married. Because the young enlistee has to make his own arrangements to bring his family to his new assignment, and because he draws less pay, he frequently finds it necessary to request advance or partial payment of his salary. Each time he does this the possibility of administrative errors increase. The military pay system is overly complicated, with a large variety of allotments and special allowances. Tampering with it can sometimes result in weeks or months of incorrect pay checks. The young couple may compound the problem by poor financial management, but sometimes they are the victims of clerical inaccuracies or bureaucratic red tape.

Whether their own families would or could provide either counsel or financial assistance, the young family finds themselves removed from them, and they are reluctant to seek outside help. They have borrowed money to buy tires for the car and to rent a trailer to get them and their limited personal goods to their next assignment. Upon arrival at the post, they find they cannot get post housing, rents are high outside, and they settle for the minimum facilities they can get. They do not know the military system well, and if they encounter problems they are hesitant to seek out a sergeant or commander for help. Such a series of events culminates in a crisis environment conducive to child neglect and abuse. The family is either almost totally isolated in a trailer park or small, rundown apartment, or they may have a few friends in the same area with the same problems. If they do not already have a child, they soon will, for if there is any family planning done, it is with the recognition that the costs of pregnancy and delivery will not have to be borne while one is in the service. For the lonely young wife whose husband is often gone on maneuvers, guard duty, and other extra military details, the house would seem less lonely with a child. In other words, the baby is expected to meet her needs—and that is one of the prime manifestations of the potential maltreating mother. There is little awareness of the financial and emotional costs the baby will represent to this family until it is too late.

For the young enlisted member's family who choose to remain "back at home" the situation is often not much better. There may be some extended family around to help out, but normally wives find subtle, and not so subtle pressures from both the relatives and the husband to join him. Loneliness becomes intense, and there is a constant awareness that if at all possible the wife should join her husband on this assignment because the next one may be some place where she is not allowed to go. For these "high risk" families there is also sometimes an unspoken suspicion about the fidelity of the other spouse during protracted separations.

One solution to the financial problems is for the wife to begin working. Since she often lacks specific skills, she may end up as a waitress in a fast food chain, or a bar. She may try for evening hours so that her husband will be home to look after the child(ren) and she can have access to the car. Many manage this way but there is always the problem of what to do with the child(ren) when the husband goes out for night maneuvers. Additionally, the husband is not very effective over the long run in pulling eight hours of military duty only to come home, change diapers, and put up with screaming babies while the wife flirts with other young men at the local pizza parlor. It is an ideal setup for abuse by the young military father, who sees the child as the cause of all his troubles.

It would be easy to surmise that such a life might be typical of most young enlisted families, but patterns differ and only a few are child maltreaters. What makes the difference seems to be the same things that make the difference in civilian life. If couples have some maturity, goal directed behavior, family supports (even from two thousand miles away), trust in each other, and enough appropriate aggressiveness to face their problems, they generally cope successfully. Luck may also play a part. It helps if they get associated with another couple who is succeeding and can provide some role models for them. If they can seek out the numerous inexpensive military recreational resources, they may find outlets from boredom and isolation. These include movies, craft shops, and sometimes discount tickets to civilian attractions. If they are associated with a military installation which has some recognition of their problems, there may be junior enlisted wife clubs (social and educational programs) and agencies such as the Army Community Service program, which will offer them either volunteer support from another Army wife or the chance to be a volunteer so they can get away from the house for a while and get involved with others. These programs normally provide free baby sitting during the hours of volunteer activity.

The major problem military services encounter with the young enlistee's family is getting them integrated into the military system. The command may desire to do so, but these families are often reluctant to "get involved." They enter the service (particularly the wife) with ambivalence about military life. As civilians the wife did not often find that her social network was intimately related to her husband's work. A branch of the armed services is a large organization. One hears that the military police are more strict than civilian police, the post is large, all the buildings look the same, everyone is saluting everyone else, identification cards have to be shown, and the total situation seems to be one built for "career personnel" and not the young service wife. She concludes that it is better to leave the military life to the husband, and except for a few of his friends who drop by, to stay away from everyone else.

In doing so she misses the commissary, where she can save 10 to 20 percent on groceries and instead shops at the nearest quick-serve grocery, where she pays an additional premium for the convenience. The family gets lost in the community where they have no social contacts and no way of making them. Isolated and lonely, this young mother with empty pocketbook and little food, in substandard housing, looks to her child, and curses the life that took her away from "home." For company she turns to day time TV serials where people have problems more interesting than her own. So engrossed, the scene is set for the next baby's cry, which is either unheard, or is responded to by an impulsive strike that drives him into a nearby open gas heater. The fragile balance has been disturbed and the family is no longer "making it."

If the young enlisted family is the most vulnerable, it is not the only military family where child maltreatment occurs. Abuse and neglect takes place wherever young children may be found. A large percentage of those cases that are reported come from middle enlisted grades also. Senior enlisted and senior officers account for less, but these are the populations which have older children. There is some incidence of maltreatment among young officers' families, but as in civilian society, the middle and upper middle service groups are less frequently reported. The most serious cases in this group often present as the "classic battered child." The parent may be borderline psychotic and go into a rage reaction. When the situation is reviewed, the signals of trouble are found to have been present, but have gone unrecognized or been covered up by the spouse and friends. The most common form of neglect in this group is probably leaving children unattended while the parents go to a movie, the officers' club, or visiting. In contrast with the young enlisted family, who may do the same thing because they can't afford a sitter, these neglecting parents are more blatantly irresponsible in child rearing practices because they can afford child care.

The incidence of child abuse as related to hard drug abuse is apparently much lower in the military community than it is in civilian life, but there is reason to be concerned about a high correlation between alcohol abuse and child maltreatment, especially in the older parents. Questions have also been raised about the relationship of authoritarian life style in the armed services and the incidence of child abuse. One hears of "sergeant's syndromes," "military syndromes," and similar descriptive phrases. The supposition is that military personnel who lead a highly disciplined life are apt to be overzealous and punitive towards their children. A study of the types of child maltreatment in a military society was done at William Beaumont Army Medical Center, El Paso, Texas.[5] The facility supports Fort Bliss, Texas, a large Army post similar to many in the United States. In this study 7 percent of the maltreatment cases represented "disciplinary abuse." This term was described by Delsordo[6] in his attempt to classify types of child abuse in a civilian population in Pennsylvania. His definition seems to describe the stereotype of the "military syndrome": the parent is "rigid and unfeeling . . . the homes were spotless . . . abuse was centered upon any child who broke the rules" and straps and sticks were used in place of hands. The parents were "upstanding citizens in the community." In his study of 80 civilian cases, twelve cases (15 percent) were classified as "disciplinary abuse." The tentative conclusion from these two very limited samples is that there is not much difference between civilian and military disciplinary abuse in either its morbidity or style.

The author's own observation about child rearing practices in the armed services is that they are not much different from those in civilian life. There may be more people who place higher value upon discipline and conformity in military family life, but that is not necessarily related to child maltreatment. Often these parents are very close to their children and compassionate with them. The children have traveled the world with their parents and have great trust in them. They accept the discipline without much question so long as it is fair and passed out to everyone on the same ground rules. Those who are overly regulated or unduly punished usually act-out in the same way the enlisted troops do: they fail in school, run away (go AWOL), or act-out directly. They end up more often in child guidance clinics than in child abuse programs, and if there is such a thing as a "military syndrome" it likely is seen more by the child psychiatrist than the pediatrician investigating suspected abuse.

The studies done at William Beaumont Army Medical Center (WBAMC) had a close interface with the Texas Department of Public Welfare child protection unit. Nearly every reported case of suspected or established child maltreatment in the El Paso–Fort Bliss military population (including retirees) was followed. Since its inception in 1967 the WBAMC program has considered about 400 cases. In 1971 the incident rate for all reported cases was 2.5 per 1,000 families per year. These figures have not changed dramatically for this military community since then. Initially it was believed that the military community was producing relatively more child maltreatment families than the civilian segment. In 1974 the Texas Department of Public Welfare initiated a large public information and case finding campaign regarding child maltreatment. In a one year period the civilian caseload increased threefold. While the military community in El Paso was also subject to this media effort, its rate increased about 50 percent, and if anything the military element is now underrepresented in child maltreatment reports.

Such a finding probably has little national or military significance. The uniformed services have no common reporting system except to measure the most severe "battered child syndromes." The WBAMC experience indicates this part of child abuse represents about 10 percent of a military child protective case load. Whatever data has been gathered about morbidity thus far has been informal and generally passed by word of mouth among those who work in such programs. Some military installations indicate rates four times greater than that at El Paso, while others have not yet discovered any significant problem. These latter groups usually do not have well established programs.

Since the child advocacy program began at Beaumont General Hospital, eleven military children have died in the El Paso community from possible neglect or abuse.[7] Only one or two of these were obvious battered children; the rest were deaths where at least some elements of maltreatment appeared to exist. Neglect was involved in six children's deaths and five involved abuse factors. Beyond the obvious conclusion that neglect is as serious a problem as abuse, is the fact that five of the six neglect fatalities involved families who were known to the child advocacy program prior to, or when, the child died. The program did not appear to be effective in preventing these deaths in spite of competent staff. Children died in homes while parents were absent or drowned in bathtubs without a parent to supervise them.

On the other hand, there were no deaths by abuse from any family who was in the program. All the abuse deaths occurred in families who had not been "reached." It is certain that at least three children's life were saved by the program. It is also likely that if the program had not existed nearly all of the eleven deaths would have been considered due to natural or accidental causes, without any implications of child maltreatment. In an informal study at this hospital for 1974 it was determined that child maltreatment was at least as significant a cause of death as all other diseases or true accidents among children at least 30 days of age.

If child maltreatment is a national problem for the United States it is an international one for the armed services. The military child protection worker is confronted not only with American families, who encounter severe cultural shock as they live in foreign countries, but must also deal with those foreign born wives of American servicemen who come to live in the United States. This is especially true in recent years with the bicultural marriage resulting from the United States military operations in Vietnam. Child maltreatment is frequently a symptom seen in those marriages that are not working out well, and often it is a most difficult problem in diagnosis and management. Frequently the wife has little command of English. Child rearing standards and patterns in the oriental culture are not only different from those of western society, but the mother has also lived in a war torn country and the scars of her experience are apparent. She has often lost all her cherished family ties. If the marriage is in the process of breaking up, serious question exists as to how the mother can survive in the American society alone, and return to her native land may not be possible or desired by her. Not infrequently the husband is a causative or contributing factor in the problem.

Such cases represent the ultimate in the "multiproblem family" and there are no easy answers to them. Generally the goal is to help the wife to achieve a degree of self-sufficiency. The methods commonly used are to reinforce the husband's responsibility in assisting in this task regardless of the outcome of the marriage, to provide the wife access to some wife of the same nationality who has adjusted successfully, and to help the wife acquire western skills and knowledge as quickly as possible. Education of staff working with these cases in the cultural implications is helpful, but sometimes difficult to find. Through all of this the issue of how well the children are doing must be paramount.

Many American military families going overseas encounter the same problem as the foreign born wife in the United States. They also have their culture shock, even if it may appear in less dramatic form. American military bases in overseas assignments may give the appearance of "American islands" but they are surrounded by a different environment. The American housing may be more crowded than in the United States and is influenced by the host country. For those who enjoy another style of life it is an excellent opportunity for travel and experience, but for those who are living a borderline adjustment it may be a terrifying and destructive event. While some resources often exist for assisting these families within the overseas American military community, these may be more limited than in the United States, and it is rare that the foreign government's resources can be readily used.

Often the only satisfactory solution is to return the family with severe problems to the United States. Essential in all such transfers is a referral to the receiving community, and a verification that they have made contact with the family. To do less may result in reinjury or death to the child victim, but it is sometimes left undone under the false assumption that once the family is back in the United States everything will work out all right. The overseas assignment did not cause the abuse or neglect, though it may have been a contributing factor. The family and the child deserve the right to continued protective services and the community to which they are going has a responsibility to provide them. How well the armed services do that is the next matter to be addressed.

## THE PRESENT STATUS OF CHILD ADVOCACY
## PROGRAMS IN THE UNIFORMED SERVICES

Child advocacy in the armed services has largely been a grass roots movement. Its proponents and supporters have emerged from military pediatricians, health nurses, and social workers, who have firsthand knowledge of the tragedies and complexities associated with child neglect and abuse. Where local command support has existed these workers have been able to develop policy, directives, and approaches, which although they have had varying degrees of success, have helped to point out that the child maltreatment is as endemic to military life as it is in civilian life. The strongest impetus has come from the Army, but the Air Force was the first major service to deliver a regulation and overall guidance to all its commands. To date, Navy and Marine programs exist only where local commands have initiated action.[a]

One reason for these program disparities, aside from the size of the service populations involved, may be that the Army has a greater number of military commissioned social work officers than do the other branches. Child welfare and protective services are rooted deeply in the social work profession. Though it was largely the pediatricians and public health nurses who "discovered" child maltreatment in the military services, it was often the social workers who knew how to organize child protective programs. From a tri-service perspective it is probably the pediatricians who represent the rallying point for child advocacy. It is well known that, up to now, while civilian physicians may have strongly supported child advocacy, they have not been frequent reporters of cases. Military physicians in contrast, and pediatricians especially, use child protection programs heavily wherever they exist. For whatever reasons, they do not seem as reluctant to report and refer suspected cases as remains the case in civilian medicine.

Many military child protection programs began as a result of some particularly dramatic or tragic case involving critical injury or death to a child. Usually the shock wave started in the emergency room, passed through the hospital, the military police, and ended up in the post or base command suite. The mayor of no city can rival a post commander who decides he wants something done. Whatever other solutions were proposed, the most effective was that a task force or study group be established to report back with recommendations. Usually this was the start of a child advocacy committee, or a child protection team, which is the basic model most military commands have used in addressing child maltreatment.

[a]Information about the November 1975 Army regulations can be obtained by writing to the Department of the Army and requesting Regulation No. 600-48.

These child protection committees are usually made up of key personnel in the military community who are most likely to have some contact with, or influence over, child abuse and neglect. Membership usually includes pediatricians, social workers, psychiatrists, nurses, Red Cross workers, military family service or Army Community Service workers, chaplains, lawyers, military police, and unit commanders. Often, representatives from local civilian child protection agencies will also sit on the military committee in liaison, consulting, and support roles. This provides the military community a tie with the civilian child protection field and insures a closer working association on those cases that involve military families who reside off post or are retired from the service.

The CPC committee approach differs somewhat from civilian life, where one agency such as the welfare department is the legally mandated child protection agency for the community. Such teams are sometimes used in large civilian medical centers, but they are not yet common for community programs. The military system has used them more because there is no welfare department in the military system and because the legal base for child protection in the uniformed services is extremely limited. A high degree of coordination and communication is thus required between agencies to manage a child protection case.

In 1971, Captain Benito Arellano[8], a social worker stationed at Fort Leonard Wood, Missouri, conducted a survey of all Army posts in the United States to determine what commands had child protection programs and how they were organized in order to improve his local programs of child protection. He determined that about two-thirds of all Army bases in the country had at least a written regulation aimed at managing child protective cases. The study indicated that different commands used different personnel to investigate and manage child maltreatment: one might use the military police, another a social worker or health nurse, and a third would use a commander.

At this time, nearly every Army post has developed some type of child protection program and the other military services are following a similar trend. While diversity in organization remains common, most are based on the child protection team approach. This diversity seems to be related to the question of how much child maltreatment is a command (or community) problem, and how much it should be managed as a "medicosocial" problem. It is both; but someone must be responsible for operating it. The civilian reader unfamiliar with military organization can compare this to whether, in the absence of child protection agency, such a program should be directed by the office of the city manager or the local public health department. The former concept insures community involvement and support; the latter emphasizes technical proficiency and scientific approach. The earlier Army programs tended to be more clinically focused, but the trend is now in the direction of command directed programs. Ideally there should be a marriage of these two concepts, somewhat analogous to the relationship of a hospital specialty clinic's relationship to a community's public health association, which supports it with educational and preventive programs.

The child protection team concept seems to have worked reasonably well in the military communities whenever it has received basic support and had skilled personnel available. In some respects it may work better than the usual "single agency" model in civilian communities, because it tends to broaden the treatment base by providing a multidisciplinary group to investigate, diagnose, and manage child protective cases. These teams have the potential for developing a high degree of morale and cooperation. The team also brings to bear increased community involvement in child abuse and neglect matters. It serves as an in-service training modality for team members and thus offers more staff available to handle cases. Since child abuse case management is known to be an emotional and intellectually draining experience for a single worker, the team concept can also offer individual staff support in the form of shared decisions, consultation, and morale boosting. It provides alternatives for entry and case management. Social workers or health nurses do not have to be the only ones who do all the initial evaluative work. The client may respond better to a pediatrician or a volunteer making the initial contact.

The child protection team concept has been used with success at William Beaumont Army Medical Center. Some of the team rules, which have evolved over the years, may have contributed to its success. Membership is limited to around ten to twelve, who are selected partially upon professional background but also upon personal interest and desire to serve on the team. For example, the team might lack a psychiatrist or an attorney for a period of time because one is not available who has an interest in serving on the committee. Consultation is still provided on request, for we believe voluntary participation is more important than having all professions represented at every meeting.

Committee members all have a clear understanding that each is expected to participate as necessary in direct work with an affected family. There are no "free advisors" or consultants who never do the leg work or "sweat the problems." Cases are often assigned on the basis of the credentials a team member may have with the client as opposed to his or her professional credentials. Every therapist is trained by and consulted by the team. The chairman is not the senior ranking officer or a specific professional, but is the individual who has the best credibility with the team in terms of technical competence and leadership.

A case cannot be closed without team consensus. This precludes precipitous closure by a team member whom, it is recognized, may have a natural desire to avoid discomfort in working with a client who does not want services. Someone must be on call at all times, but anyone can receive a complaint and initiate action. The team must meet at least once a month, even if there are no cases to discuss. The meeting can be devoted to education, a program review and followup, but team integrity and communication must be maintained. The purpose of the team is clinically and management oriented, with heavy emphasis upon professional decision making. Members are expected to read child protection literature and develop an appreciation of other professional team members' disciplines and viewpoints.

The team concept is most likely to break down when its membership lacks specific child protection skills and knowledge. This will occur when there is overrepresentation by persons who are expert in their own field, but possess little interest or information about child protection matters. Such problems can arise, not just with chaplains, law enforcement, legal, and other personnel, but also among social workers, pediatricians, and health nurses, who may mistakenly believe that their professional credentials include "prima facie" knowledge of child abuse and neglect. In the military services this may be reflected in the committee chairmanship's going automatically to the senior ranking person. In such a case the team may become more of a military staffing session.

Such a posture might be appropriate to preventive and community education areas, but it is not effective in case management problem solving. The minutes of case management meetings should have, for example, the same confidentiality as any other medical meetings, but sometimes the community-based child protection team ends up with the minutes being submitted to the post commander. He has a right and a need to know of some exceptional cases that may be of community significance, but it is not necessary to routinely pass information on each case. Invariably there is a "leak" or an overresponse, with the end result that families are reluctant to seek help from the team on a self-referral basis.

In the last few years the child advocacy team concept has become well enough established that an informal network has been developed among many military bases for referral and transfer of cases moving throughout the Army. These programs have not been as fully established in the Air Force and Navy or Marines, but the new Air Force regulation of 1976 will probably help in this respect. For the civilian who is attempting to make contact with child protective staff in the uniformed services, the primary resources are usually the base medical facility, the installation commander, American Red Cross, or (in the Army) the Army Community Service Agency. Since the child protection team may be located in different areas, depending upon the command, no single answer can be provided; but any of the above agencies can usually direct the request to the appropriate local contact. As of 1976 there may still be some military facilities that do not have child protection programs.

Grass roots program development may have its assets in the ability of local commands to be innovative and responsive to local needs, but it also has its deficits in lack of uniformity among commands and the potential for inadequate support throughout the military system. Further, line commanders frequently change, and unless established by orders of the Secretary of Defense, no uniform or permanent programs can exist. Clearly the military services have not yet decided that child abuse and neglect is a significant problem. Even though they are gradually issuing command directives, the questions of staffing, skill development, and provision of treatment services have not yet been addressed. Personnel who have in-depth knowledge about child maltreatment are scarce in the uniformed services, and one has to look a long way to find anyone whose full time job is child protection. While the military services do not have to "declare war" on child abuse, they should acknowledge more readily that it is an endemic social ill in their society, just as are venereal disease, drug and alcohol abuse, tuberculosis, rabies control, and discrimination between racial groups and sexes.

No formal military surveys have yet been done to determine morbidity or special military aspects of child maltreatment in the uniformed services. This is especially tragic when one considers that the armed services have a great deal to offer to the rest of the nation in the field of child protection. Their relatively well organized and closed societiew offer an excellent potential opportunity to approach this problem with much more effectiveness than can be possible in the average civilian community. They have more resources available, including high caliber social workers, health nurses, pediatricians, and other medical personnel working in a single health care system. They can mobilize a community to attack a problem more easily than the civilian sector can. As in other areas where they have elected, or been mandated, they can assume leadership and expertise that will have positive impact upon the country in terms of skills and treatment models.

Some movement has indeed begun in that direction, but at this point it is too early to say what the long term results will be. In 1975 two special research projects were awarded by the Department of Health, Education, and Welfare to study child maltreatment in the military services. One of them is based at Brook Army Medical Center in San Antonio, Texas. Entitled "Project Care," it will involve the Army, the Air Force, and the Texas State Department of Public Welfare. The second project is based at Fort Campbell, Kentucky, and is also related to the civilian welfare department that supports that post. Since these projects are just starting, it is too early to determine what roles they will play in developing overall military child advocacy programs.

The Army has assumed responsibility for development of a community education film on child abuse and neglect, and it should be released in 1976. The film should be equally valuable to civilian and military audiences. All the above projects involve joint civilian and military cooperative efforts, and this is the direction that will probably be most productive in the child maltreatment field, since it is neither a purely military or a civilian problem.

## CHILD PROTECTIVE LAW IN THE MILITARY— WHERE IS IT?

Nowhere is the interrelationship between civilian and military communities more crucial than in the area of military child maltreatment and the law. Civilian and military colleagues may debate the causes and cures of abuse and neglect in the armed services, but they can all agree that when it comes to the legal aspects of many of these cases we are all lost together.

If a single deficiency were selected that most severely handicaps child protection programs in the military services it is the lack of adequate legal supports. Concerned military leaders can develop programs at the local level even when they must use scarce resources to do so. But they cannot overcome legal deficiencies without twisting the law and sometimes even breaking it. There really is no justification for the military to fail to remedy these problems, for they have been advised of them through one channel or another over a period of the last several years. If they are lacking in that knowledge they have a body of law in the fifty states for reference; but it is fair to say that they are behind the times in this area of law.

The result is a tragic array of inconsistencies, confusions, and dilemmas which at times would be comic if they were not so serious in their consequences. On one Army post the military police assigned to "stake out" the home of parents who were suspected by the state protective agency of neglecting their children, watched as the parents carried the children out to the car in cardboard boxes and removed them from the post and the state. More than once state child welfare workers have been escorted off post by military policemen when the workers attempted to investigate a reported case of child maltreatment. In Kentucky, a civilian juvenile judge determined that he had no authority over persons who resided at the nearby military installation; in Texas, a similar judge determined exactly the opposite. The legal issues in both states were similar.

The legal problems do not arise in the cases of active and retired personnel who reside in civilian communities, since they are subject to the same laws as any civilian; but they can become quite complex for the child protective case where the family resides on a federal installation. The problem centers around the fact that many federal enclaves represent a "51st state" which, in effect, has not recognized that it needs the same legal process for child abuse and neglect management that is provided routinely in the other 50 states. For those who are opposed to federal intervention in state affairs it amounts to poetic justice in seeing the "kettle call the pot black."

The core problem revolves around the question of "concurrent" and "exclusive" jurisdiction. Concurrent jurisdiction involves a situation where the state and the federal installation share legal authority and responsibility over the federal enclave. A state policeman or military policeman can cite a traffic violator on a military base. In child protective cases presumably the state also has jurisdiction of the "on post" problem along with the federal government. But the real problems lie with those military bases which have "exclusive jurisdiction." Under original deeds and agreements, when these installations were created, the federal government was given "exclusive jurisdiction" over nearly all matters occurring on the base or post. Since this involves many of the older and larger military installations, it is no small problem. Here state law does not apply. Some military legal personnel are quick to point out that under the Assimilated Crimes Act the problem is resolved, because this law provides that whatever is a crime in the state may also be a crime in the federal reservation. That is only partially correct. The Assimilated Crimes Act pertains to criminal law, not to civil law, where most child protection matters correctly belong (at least in the judgment of all the state legislatures that put it there).

If the state has no control over these cases where exclusive jurisdiction exists, then the federal government must. That is correct—until one realizes that there *is* no federal law pertaining to child abuse and neglect. There may be law about assault and battery in both the Uniform Code of Military Justice (military law for active duty personnel) and other federal statutes, but it is doubtful that there is any definition of neglect in the laws that impact these federalized citizens. If such a law does exist, it has not been passed on effectively to the local military commands for guidance and information. Military personnel can be ordered to report child abuse, but there is no mandate for their wives to do so. Aside from the military police no one really has legal jurisdiction to investigate child mal-treatment, including state or federal child protection workers.

If a case were to be handled by the federal authorities in a manner similar to that in which most states handle it, some interesting gaps in services would be exposed. The matter would have to be taken to a federal magistrate or judge untrained in domestic and juvenile matters, who would soon learn that there were no federal foster homes or federal child protection staff in the military community to supervise the family and child. When it was suggested to one military attorney that the federal judge might remand the case to a state or county system which had the necessary facilities, the attorney was quick to point out that such action would be similar to the FBI's telling a state policeman that even if he didn't have the power he could go ahead and use the FBI's power to cross a state line.

The resultant impact these dilemmas have created is twofold. First, military authorities involved in child protection matters rely more heavily upon criminal law than is either required or desirable in most child protective cases. It is contrary to everything which has been learned in the last twenty years about child protection management. Military leaders have strong values of right and wrong, and when confronted with a classic battered child syndrome are not reluctant to criminally prosecute a military member. Their feelings may be understandable, but the paradox is that another soldier in the same command who lives off post may be receiving a different (and possibly more effective) type of treatment in the civilian community. Sometimes the desire for "justice" and punishment of the offender ends up with the opposite result: not only is the child victim denied justice in the sense of protection but defendants are able to avoid guilty findings by using technicalities in criminal law that could not be used in civil law. A side effect of this problem is that in the absence of civil child protective law, nothing may be done at all. In spite of the fact that child neglect may cause more deaths than child abuse, some may regard it as either "no crime" or at most a misdemeanor. The neglect case gets neglected.

The second major impact has been that local military bases—and to some extent higher echelons—have tried to resolve some of the problems by devel-oping regulations to implement child protective programs. The efforts have been valuable insofar as they can go, but they commonly do not address the basic legal problems because there is no law. For example, a regulation may establish a committee to manage and treat families who abuse or neglect their children. Such regulations cannot "order" a wife to take part in treatment with the same effect that a court order can. They cannot provide the rules under which children may be removed from one's home unless a "crime" has been committed. Military social workers and health nurses who make the home visits and investigate the reported cases are keenly aware that the military regulation lacks the sanctions and protections that their civilian counterparts in the nearby community have.

A military solution to this problem of lack of law is to force the maltreating family to move into the civilian community where they will be subject to civil law and child protection programs. This is a suggestion more commonly heard than practiced. Aside from the fact that it does not enhance the military's image in the civilian community, and that it creates more problems for the family who already has enough, one does not have to be an attorney to know that a judge is not likely to remove children unless it has been established that child neglect or abuse has occurred in his jurisdiction—especially when the evidence he hears pertains to alledged child maltreatment coming from a jurisdiction where there was no law. The case may have to be reestablished in civilian settings, which means possible reinjury and/or neglect to the children involved.

One of the lesser known considerations in these legal vacuums is that day care facilities for children on many military bases do not have to meet the standards of those in the civilian community. Most military day care facilities are sponsored and operated by civic groups or out of nonappropriated funds (special funds). They receive close fiscal audits, fire inspections, and other controls, but there are no licensing requirements comparable to those imposed upon civilian operations. They may be clean, sterile, and safe warehouses for children, but there is no assurance that they will be child development and social growth centers.

If Congress were to pass a law that simply states that in all matters of child protection, concurrent jurisdiction will exist on federal lands within the continental United States, many problems would be resolved. Interestingly, under status of forces agreements with some foreign countries where American military families reside, these families are subject to that country's laws. This is just one more inconsistency. A second course would be to adequately research the question of whether such a new law is even necessary. There are several examples where concurrent jurisdiction already exists, even on posts where it theoretically does not. Children born in federal hospitals, on federal land, receive state birth certificates. When they get killed by their parents on federal land they receive state death certificates. One cannot get a divorce on federal land, even if one resides there; this is done through county and state courts. People who marry in the base chapel get licenses from local governments. Now, if a state can decide if one was born, married, divorced, and died, there should be *some* precedence for the state to establish whether or not children are maltreated on federal land. Should the federal government decide that it does not want to relinquish exclusive jurisdiction, then it should develop a body of civil law that addresses these issues. While this is admittedly a larger task, it will be required if many of the problems are to be resolved.

## CONCLUSION

A pediatric social worker was asked to write a child abuse article for the army post newsletter which was mailed to military wives in the community. She observed that past copies had numerous recipes which were submitted and traded among the women. The following is her article.[9]

### Child Abuse Croquettes

From the Kitchen of
Susanne M. Wieder, ACSW

2  parents, inexperienced and slightly bruised
2  children, tender and under 4 years old
Assorted in-laws
1  small apartment with thin walls
A dash of privacy (optional)
Numerous bills of mixed size
5  letters of indebtedness (to the commander)
1  article 15 (minor disciplinary action)
7  days of isolation
1  batch of field training or TDY (temporary duty)
1  caring neighbor
1  fifth of alcohol or equal amount of beer
1  URI (upper respiratory infection)
4  trips to the emergency room
2  lost medical charts
1  aggravated hospital clerk
1  2-hour wait
1  teething, cranky baby
1  double dirty diaper
1  ½-hour constant crying
2  physicians
1  military policeman
1  social worker

Sift 2 inexperienced, slightly bruised parents and 2 tender young children with one small apartment with thin walls. Add a dash of privacy (optional) and assorted in-laws. Fold in numerous bills of mixed size and quickly add letters of indebtedness. Stir until one Article 15 develops. Set aside.

In separate bowl mix one upper respiratory infection with 4 trips to the emergency room. Separate 2 lost medical charts from one aggravated hospital clerk. Add one 2-hour wait.

Combine all above ingredients with one 7-day batch of field duty or TDY and an equal amount of isolation for the mother. Omit one caring neighbor. When mixture reaches a full boil, return husband from field and immediately add 1 fifth of alcohol or an equal amount of beer.

Soak one teething, cranky baby in one double dirty diaper and gradually add to the above mixture. Season with one-half hour of constant crying. Whip until stiff. Place ingredients in an 8 x 10 emergency room cubicle with two physicians, one military policeman, and one social worker. Bake until well done.

If these croquettes do not sound appetizing to you, help us change the ingredients. Child abuse does not occur because of any one of the problems listed above, but results when a combination of these stresses happen in a family. There are many resources available for families if we can help them take the first step by contacting either a pediatrician, health nurse, or social worker at the hospital. Each of us has the ability to help stop child abuse. It's our choice . . . and it's our children.

✳ Chapter Fifteen

# Managerial and Financial Aspects of Social Service Programs

George E. Kawamura
and
Claudia A. Carroll

## INTRODUCTION

This chapter, in spite of its title, is aimed at a much broader audience than the administrators and managers who are responsible for the planning and funding of community child protection programs. We would hope that, in addition to aiding administrators, the contents will be a resource tool for the lay community, interested professionals outside the social service system, and line protective service staff to use both in assessing the position of protective services in an agency or a community, and in demanding movement towards an adequate protective service system. Our hope is that this approach will serve as a catalyst to improve the quality of child protection programs through objective analysis and a process of meaningful communication rather than pure emotionalism.

Although there is still much to be learned about the treatment of children and parents in the area of child abuse and neglect, knowledge about the problem and the ability to deal with it has increased rapidly during the past few years. This technology goes far beyond the traditional model of protective services, which was useful some thirty years ago. Many service systems are still operating as if there were no change—or worse, as if the increasing awareness and recognition of the problem does not exist. This attitude is devastating to families in trouble.

The field of protective services has been plagued by buck passing and poorly defined responsibilities. Ultimate responsibility has to be vested in a single organizational structure. The traditional social service or protective service agency in a community is a logical choice and could carry out this function if the administrative process within the agency can be flexible enough to accommodate change, innovative enough to accept creative approaches, and aggressive enough to effectively advocate its commitment to child protective services. The backbone of a protective services system is the professional social worker. Equally clear is that without the full use of a multitude of other kinds of professional and lay staff and a full repertoire of resources, there will never be the adequate manpower and the variety of creative ideas to affect the problem.

Social service systems can adapt to the mandates of an effective child protecting program; however, two tasks need to be accomplished before this potential can be realized. First, there has to be an effort made to develop a means to achieve a manageable work load for protective services. A program budgeting and work load standard can result in a budget and a staffing pattern responsive to the needs of a child protection program. Achievement of this task will enable the system to realize several goals.

1. Protective service workers will not be under the constant pressure of unmanageable, chaotic case loads requiring them to jump from crisis to crisis. Manageable case loads permit for quality service.
2. A worker with a reasonable work load can find time for the activities such as resource development, community awareness efforts, staff development, training of others in the community and so on. These tasks provide much needed breaks from the intensive, emotionally draining day-to-day work with the difficult family situations seen in child abuse and neglect. This in itself will stem the high turnover rate in protective services, which is a deterrent to consistent, high level services. These innovative activities can also provide the worker with the recognition sorely needed, as the rewards in protective services work are small and slow to come.
3. The third gain is increased agency credibility. The most effective way of achieving this is a demonstrated commitment through a quality level of service delivery.

Once an agency begins the first small step of developing manageable work loads, the second task becomes immediately obvious; to construct an effective community outreach and treatment program. Consideration must be given to the entire range of existing resources and be willing to develop creative alternatives to the single-faceted, traditional social worker–client relationship model. The development and implementation of this broad range of services will move the system on to a phase that can be innovative and exciting.

### PROGRAM BUDGETING AND WORKLOAD STANDARDS—
### THE FIRST SMALL STEP

Any program, to be effective, must be translated into dollars. Without the vehicle of a budget, the best intentions and program planning cannot be moved from the conceptual state to the stage of implementation. A budget for any social services program must be seen as a means of communication rather than just a request for funding to "do good." A budget cannot be merely a sterile aggregate of figures but must communicate to the decision makers something about the components of the program and at least stimulate them enough to ask basic questions. This is critical, because we have concluded that many people in reviewing budget requests will merely skim any narrative related to the request. Their focus and primary point of reference becomes the budget breakdowns and related figures.

The responsibility of planning for funding for a critical program such as protective services requires a logical and understandable approach. The budgeting for child protective services advocated in this chapter is both basic and simple. A human services perspective, rather than a strict budget analyst point of view, is presented. This could be considered a layman's guide to protective services budgeting. Considering the fact that the decision makers are laymen themselves (i.e., legislators and other elected officials, the community at large, professional budget makers) in the area of child protective services, a direct and sensible method is mandatory.

The first step in budgeting is to evaluate current costs. The second is the evaluation of commitment to child protection in terms of budget allocation. The budget can communicate an inherent philosophical statement about the priority that the child protection program has in an agency and the community. The "state of the art" of cost analysis and budgeting in social services program, in many instances, is so primitive that even this first step of evaluating current position can be difficult. Social services agencies are usually multifunctional in nature. The ability to separate the cost of a protective service program from other functions such as adoption, adolescent services, programs for the aged, etc., can be a time consuming task. Many agencies have subsumed a multitude of functions under the meaningless heading of "social service" or "administrative costs" and expect others to understand the components of the system in every program area.

A program budgeting system in the social services must be developed that enables each program to be identified, costed out, and evaluated. Without this beginning step, true costs are unknown, and comparisons cannot be made or priorities set. One cannot even talk intelligently about the programs or make appropriate trade-offs. A budget that subsumes and levels vital functions such as protective services is a sham. A program such as protective services must be visible so that it can be scrutinized by the community at large. The community, by direct input and via their elected officials, must set priorities for public social services. Given the opportunity, the public response to protective services programs can be a viable source of support.

In order to be able to budget protective services soundly there must be sanction and support at a variety of levels, both within and outside the agency. The community must view protective services to families as a community problem that should be adequately addressed by a variety of community agencies. Support from local social service departments, health department, court, mental health center, law enforcement, physicians, and so forth, is essential. Building this type of community approach to child abuse and neglect takes considerable time. More important, it requires trust among the professional agencies based upon an attitude of shared responsibility.

As local departments of social services become more involved with Title XX and the task of setting service priorities, it will be crucial that protective services be identified among the top priorities as indicated by citizen, professional, and agency support. This goal can be approached through community education around such areas as (1) identification of the magnitude of the problem of child abuse and neglect in the local community, (2) the cost of these services currently being provided, and (3) services that need to be developed to combat the problem and their projected cost. On a broader spectrum there must be an awareness of the problem and issues by a variety of others—local county commissioners, the state department of social services, the legislators.

In order to proceed with the concept of program budgeting, strict working definitions of the programs within the agency must be developed. Budgeting then can follow. Here are several examples of program definitions for protective service programs. The first is a narrative statement and the second in a more detailed outline form.

1. **Narrative Format—Program for Child Protection**
   This program serves all families who are referred to the agency in which the identified problem is determined to be alleged or actual child abuse or neglect. This would include situations in which a child under age 18 is abandoned, homeless, physically neglected, or lacking in proper parental supervision; in which a child is in danger of physical or mental abuse; and/or in which a child has suffered actual inflicted injury and/ or sexual molestation. The goal of this program is to protect children whose physical and/or mental health and well-being are in jeopardy and to assist parents in bringing about positive changes in parenting and in preserving the family unit.[a]

2. **Outline Format—Program for Child Protection**
   A. *Target Group*
      All families in which a child under age 18 is abandoned, homeless, or lacking in parental guidance or supervision; in which a child is malnourished, has suffered inflicted injury and/or sexual abuse; in which a child is in danger of physical or emotional abuse.

---

[a]The points reviewed in both the narrative and the outline raise significant points regarding the difference between the responsibility for long range care and the responsibility for acute care and crisis intervention. A difference exists. This editor's view is that acute care protective service workers *cannot* be responsible for long term care. (These issues are discussed in more detail in Chapter Thirteen)—R.E.H.

B.  *Goal*

To protect children whose physical and/or mental health and well-being are in jeopardy and to assist parents in bringing about positive changes in parenting and in preserving the family unit.

C.  *Defined Problem Areas – Barriers to Goal Achievement*
   1.  Inflicted injury
   2.  Sexual abuse
   3.  Malnourishment, failure to thrive
   4.  Abandonment, lack of guardian
   5.  Lack of parental guidance and/or supervision
   6.  Child unduly confined
   7.  Withholding of medical care
   8.  Child is not wanted
   9.  Exploitation
   10.  Parent mentally ill or mentally retarded
   11.  Parent overwhelmed by economic stress, too many children, etc.

D.  *Goal Oriented Activities*
   1.  Evaluating the effect of neglect or abuse for child and parents; determining whether or not child can safely remain at home.
      a.  Exploring alleged abuse(s) or neglect with referral sources, relatives, and neighbors.
      b.  Conferring with physicians, psychiatrists, using psychological data and educational records to assist in decision making.
      c.  Counselling with parents about the reality of the neglect or abuse; their awareness of responsibility and need for change; their planning for the child's immediate future as well as their own.
   2.  Filing petitions in juvenile court when parents are not available or when parents are not responsive on a voluntary basis and the child requires protection. This action may be taken by the department, local law enforcement agency, or by others.
      a.  Consulting with attorney to assure protection of both the child's and parents' legal rights.
      b.  Advising parents of their right to legal counsel.
   3.  Providing or arranging for any needed remedial therapy required by the child.
   4.  Services to keep the child in the parental home.
      a.  Counselling and treatment with parents about their wish to be parents and ways of providing adequate care and guidance for children.
      b.  Providing or arranging for other services which will insure protection and adequate care for the child (homemaker service, day care, medical care, crisis nursery, etc.)
   5.  Temporary substitute care for children who cannot remain in parental home because of physical danger, family disorganization, or child's problem behavior.

a. Planning with parents, selecting and arranging for child's sub-stitute care with relatives or friends, in the department's foster boarding home, specialized group home, in residential treat-ment facilities, in institutions.

b. Conferring and counselling with foster parents about child's progress, adjustment, visits with parents, planning for child's future.

c. Counselling and planning with parents about conditions for child's return home and ways of providing adequate care and guidance for children.

d. Follow up and supervision of all children returned to parental home to insure continued safety of the child and to insure solidification of gains for both child and parents through pre-vious counselling.[b]

The thought that is invested in the definition of programs is well worth the effort, as the proper delineation of programs serves as the foundation to the process of costing out and arriving at a concept of program budgeting. We have found that the outline form of program definition has two distinct advantages. First, it is more readable and thus more understandable, and second, it is a good tool to help identify the program components and related costs.

Reaching the initial goal of assessment of current budget position requires defining the components of a social service program according to previously structured definitions in terms of cost factors. Such factors include: (1) differen-tial personnel needs—professional line staff, supervisors, homemakers, lay therapists, case aides, clerical staff, legal staff, consultants, and related expenses such as travel, fringe benefits, etc.; (2) purchased services—shelter/receiving homes, foster homes, residential treatment, day care, and other special needs purchases, payments, etc.; and (3) overhead—indirect and administrative costs such as staff training, the proportionate share of general operating expenses, and proportionate cost of administrative staff whose functions are not totally alloca-ted to one program area. Those general areas of program costs that exist in any agency must be included, in addition to any cost factors that have impact on the total service program and that are unique to the particular system—such as grants or other special program expenses, an emergency pager system, hot lines, and support of nontraditional treatment methods such as a lay therapy program.

An example of the format developed at the Adams County Department of Social Services in Colorado to analyze social service costs is given in Appendix A of this chapter. The cost analysis for protective services, the total social services program in the agency, and various comparisons between the program areas within the agency are included. As can be seen by this format, a multifunctional agency must go through this process for each program area within the agency

[b]See footnote a.

structure. If not done, there is no basis for comparison. The subtotals for each component service program must equal the overall agency budget for social service programs.

As personnel are costed out, the importance of knowing both the cost of staff and the exact number of staff allocated to each function within a program becomes clear. To complete this process of gathering basic data, one must proceed to get an accurate case count for each of the program areas. The classification of cases into these program areas must follow the definitions that were developed, describing the discrete program functions of the agency. In many agencies with multiple functions, some cases may present a combination of problems; but in dealing with case classification, determining a primary focus for the case and assigning this to a particular program area is much easier.

In summary, the following material must be gathered:

1. Program definitions.
2. Cost components of each program.
3. Cost of each of these components.
4. A total cost for the entire social service program.
5. Exact number of positions allocated to each program function.
6. An accurate case count as to number of families being served in each program area.

With the accumulation of these data, programs can be put into perspective, evaluated, and compared. Information such as comparisons of expenditures, allocation of staff, costs per case, and average monthly case loads can be communicated intelligently. The position and priority given to the child protection program can, for example, now be clearly seen and articulated. What is seen may or may not confirm the subjective observations about individual program costs.

Even with the information at hand, the position may still be static. Now that "where we are" is known, the next logical progression is the questions of "Is the present position adequate?" "Where should we be going?" "What should we be asking for?" An adequate response to these questions must be available to move a budget from a static position to a moving force, responsive to program needs. One of the first steps is adequate case loads. Unless a credible work load standard for protective service workers is established, the quality of services that are delivered to protect children and to rehabilitate families will continue to decline or stagnate. Without a work load standard to drive a staffing pattern and a budget, the future for outstanding child protection programs is virtually nonexistent. Good programs that presently exist will crumble from the sheer weight of added cases.

The issue of work load standard poses the question, "How much time does a protective service worker have and what is a reasonable work load within that allocated time frame to insure the delivery of quality services?" The critical variable for any professional or lay person involved in treating the problem of child abuse and neglect is *time*. The tasks and activities that are necessary to carry out the responsibilities related to the job of child protective services can be defined, categorized, and standardized for the purpose of developing average time values on cases. These variables will depend on the nature and intensity of a case situation. Through a combination of analytical methods such as task analyses, time studies, and objective professional judgments, agreement can be reached on how much time is needed to provide adequate, quality services to a protective services case situation.

This developmental phase of setting workload standards is not an easy task. A multitude of variables must be taken into consideration and compromises and decisions must be made. Caseload profiles should be assessed. These are made up of cases in varying stages, some requiring maximum contact, some moderate contact, and others minimal contact. Families move between these stages. During the intake and evaluation phase, a heavy commitment of time is required. Situations in which a child is placed outside the home situation require more time because of issues such as working with the child separately, visitation, and work with foster parents as well as natural parents. Court cases require additional time for legal consultation and court hearings. Involvement of other community agencies and resources, which is a necessity in a majority of protective service cases, takes more time to coordinate and keep up a flow of good communication.

In writing and assessing work load profiles, a distinction must be made between acute crisis intervention and long term therapy. The impossibility of a given worker or section of the department of social services to do both well has already been emphasized (see Chapter Thirteen). And yet, the department of social services has a long term responsibility. At some point during the case assessment a point is reached when a logical and smooth transition to the long term treatment/coordination group (also within the department of social services) can and should be made. Program budgeting will make the delineation of these responsibilities much clearer.

When all these varied activities are seen as valid and necessary, the next step is to begin the process of assigning time values to this inventory of required tasks. Realizing that some work has been done in this area in various parts of the country, we must begin to pull all available data together and fill the gaps that exist. The wheel doesn't have to be completely rediscovered.

The preliminary calculations to reach a workload standard must first define the blocks of time available to a protective service worker for direct services to families and direct case-related collateral contacts. These calculations could be approached in the following manner:

2,080 — **number** of hours available in 52 weeks based on a 40-hour week

less 270 — the average number of hours (estimated at 6 weeks per year) annual leave time and holidays leaving 1,810 — gross hours available for service delivery

    less 500 — number of hours utilized for general agency activities such as staff meetings, resource development, supervisory conferences, staff development, travel, paper work, form filling, required reportings, etc. (estimated at 1 "free" week every 4 weeks[c])

totalling 1,310 — net hours available for direct client and collateral contact

Assuming that the above figures are an accurate reflection of reality, the conclusion can be reached that a single protective services worker in an agency has approximately 1,310 hours in a year to devote to direct service delivery. Considering all the variables involved in a typical case load, how many families can be served at any one point? Begin with the following estimate: The range of the time requirements for protective service cases, after the intake stage, can be from 1 hour to 10, plus hours of worker time in direct services in any one month. During the intake phase, a case can consume anywhere from a minimum of 2 hours to a maximum of 15 hours in a week's time.

All the tasks and activities related to intake and ongoing treatment of protective service cases can be classified and average time values assigned. This becomes an extensive process of task analysis, requiring some type of time study. Objective professional judgment and concensus must also be used. The conclusions that were reached in Adams County have been a combination of a careful analysis of what has been done in other states, such as Utah, studies of social service activities, and professional judgments from within and without the social services arena.

Our conclusions bring us to a point of a beginning work load standard. Considering all the previously mentioned variables and the profiles of protective services case loads, we have determined that a minimally acceptable average time requirement for a protective service case would be approximately 5 hours per month or a total of 60 hours per year for each family. The development of a work load standard then becomes a process of mathematical calculation. Dividing the 60 hours required per case into the available inventory of 1310 hours for each worker, we see that one worker cannot adequately handle any more than 22 family situations in protective services at any one point in time.

To develop an agency staffing pattern, one must know the total protective service case load and multiply the number of families by 60 and then divide by 1310 figure to arrive at where you should be in relationship to the standard. A standard, if it can be objectively developed, defended and sold, becomes the basis for program funding because there is now a mechanism to drive your budget according to work load. This may sound like the end of a process but it is only the basic beginnings of a modern, comprehensive protective services system in a community. Following the process described here will establish one facet of a program to address a problem that requires many more alternatives.

[c]A "free" week means no new cases that week.

## TOWARDS A COMPREHENSIVE COMMUNITY
## CHILD PROTECTION PROGRAM

The initial requirement of the transition from the single option treatment model for child abuse and neglect to a true multidisciplinary approach is a philosophical change. This change must take place within the social services agency at every level. Social services must move from a closed, defensive posture to an open system that encourages detailed scrutiny and input to develop. An open system strives to develop policies, practices, and procedures to protect children, not to act as a barrier to protect itself.

A basic tenet of the open system is the concept of trust. So many social services organizations are in a defensive posture because they do not have a positive self-image due to their perception of lack of community trust. A destructive cycle is thus developed. An agency that feels distrusted becomes more inwardly oriented to protect itself from attack; this tends to reinforce distrust. To break this cycle of distrust, the agency must learn to trust rather than see all outside systems as potential attackers. Given the ability to trust, coupled with a demonstration of a commitment to a quality program of child protection by responsive services, then an open, accessible system will begin to turn around the image of a social service agency in any community.

An open system also mandates involvement. A commitment to an interdisciplinary approach necessitates the full utilization of all community resources. These should always include the legal, law enforcement, and court system; the schools; community mental health, medical, and public health resources; and any private agencies that may exist. Agreements and strong alliances must be developed between these agencies and the social services agency to effect any movement towards an adequate child protection program.

In many communities this means that the dysfunctional "turf battles" have to be overcome in order to reach a point of meaningful interagency communication, cooperation, and trust. This requires not only an attitudinal change on the part of the social service agency, but also a parallel change in the other community agencies. The most effective beginning to this process of change is the realization that child abuse and neglect is a problem shared by the entire community, not the problem of any single agency.

Quality legal representation is an essential component of any child protection program. The size and case load of an agency would determine the need for the amount of attorney time that would be required. Any community or county approaching 100,000 population needs a full time attorney in the area of protective services. Any attorney in this field must be accessible to staff and housed within the agency. He would represent the interests of that agency. The selection process is critical. The attorney must have knowledge of and interest in family law and protective services in addition to being comfortable working with other disciplines outside the legal system. He or she should have the ability to trust other professionals and be able to balance legal issues with treatment concerns. All that is said for the attorney who works with the department is equally true for *staff* pediatricians and psychologists.

The full utilization of agency resources such as day care and homemakers for protective services must be considered. Day care is an underutilized alternative to foster care in child protection. The use of day care takes planning, development, and training of day care staff and facilities to meet the special needs of these children. In many cases, appropriate day care can provide the proper adjunct to a case situation with the least disruption to a family. The potential for treatment oriented day care is largely untapped. The use of well trained homemakers can also provide another alternative in the treatment plan that can have effective outcomes in terms of the parenting and household management skills that so many of these abusive and neglecting parents need.

The development of specialized foster homes for abused and neglected children also requires sophisticated planning and a concentrated effort. The treatment needs of children require that these foster parents have the training to handle these usually difficult children and to see themselves as an integral part of the treatment plan. This requires thinking about the development of training programs for foster parents as well as incentives for the foster parents to pursue training.

Consultation and staff development is vitally important for protective service staff. This type of work requires the constant reinforcement, stimulation, and support of learning activities. The upgrading of skills and the opportunity to share problems and points of view will enhance the ability of workers to make the day to day decisions that are required.

From this point, we can and must proceed to encourage, plan, and develop the other alternatives and structure a model that will begin to resemble the modern, comprehensive community child protective system. The components would include (1) multidisciplinary review teams who have the sanction to effect necessary changes, (2) an increased awareness of the treatment needs of children as well as parents and resources for child therapy, (3) a strong emphasis on the value of a lay therapy program, (4) the encouragement and support of self-help groups such as Parents Anonymous, and (5) the development of an adequate crisis nursery system to handle the emergent placements and as a source of immediate relief for potentially abusive parents.

The agency must also support or develop 24-hour, 7-day, hot line referral systems and the means to respond to crisis situations by the use of such devices as electronic pagers and support staff to respond to calls for help. Strong working agreements, in contractual form, with both public and private agencies strengthens the protective service program and broadens the alternatives to families for treatment.

In addition, any agency can and should pursue all the alternatives of grant funding to demonstrate innovative methods and approaches to the problem. (See chapter thirteen for a discussion of interrelationship of community programs.) All these components have some costs and must be considered in the budget of some organizational structure. How they are planned, managed, and coordinated will differ from community to community, but the task can be accomplished if the concept of the open system of protective services to children is nurtured and sustained.

## CONCLUSION

The planning, functional development, and funding of a coordinated service to protect the lives and safety of children, and to rehabilitate and treat families in which child abuse and neglect occur, is a responsibility that cannot be taken lightly. In these times, when the competition for the limited human services dollar is at its peak, the critical area of child protective services must not be short-changed because of a lack of good planning, valid data to communicate the needs, or the lack of commitment by uncaring administrators.

Program Cost Analysis  (Adams Co., Colorado, Pop.: 200,000)

Program Title:   Child Protective Services                                     FY 1975

| I.  Personnel[1] | Dollar Expenditures | FTE # |
|---|---|---|
| Staff—Intake Function | $   70,718 | 6.36 |
| Fringe Benefits—Intake Function | 7,099 | |
| Travel Expenses—Intake Function | 3,723 | |
| Staff—Ongoing Treatment | $  240,009 | 22.02 |
| Fringe Benefits—Ongoing Treatment | 24,044 | |
| Travel Expenses—Ongoing Treatment | 12,567 | |
| Homemaker Staff | $     6,779 | .94 |
| Fringe Benefits—Homemaker Staff | 829 | |
| Travel Expenses—Homemaker Staff | 557 | |
| Community Service Aides | $     1,428 | 1.33 |
| Fringe Benefits—Aides | 35 | |
| Travel Expenses—Aides | 193 | |
| Clerical Staff | $   15,496 | 2.20 |
| Fringe Benefits—Clerical Staff | 1,917 | |

| | | |
|---|---|---|
| Consultants | $   3,240 | |
| Total | $ 388,634 | 32.85 |

## II. Purchased Services

| | | |
|---|---|---|
| Shelter/Receiving Homes | $     4,812 | |
| Foster Homes | 162,292 | |
| Group Homes | –0– | |
| Residential Child Care Facilities | 137,225 | |
| Day Care | 175,200 | |
| Independent Living | –0– | |
| Social Services Payments[2] | 3,458 | |
| Less Recoveries and Support[3] | $   14,049 | |
| Total | $ 468,938 | |

## III. Administrative Expenses

| | | |
|---|---|---|
| Overhead and Indirect Costs[4] | $   47,124 | |
| Administration[5] | 44,874 | 2.28 |
| Total | $   91,998 | 2.28 |

## IV. Other Program Costs[6]

| | | |
|---|---|---|
| Grants | $ 146,234 | 14.70 |
| General Assistance | 3,603 | |
| Total | $ 149,837 | 14.70 |

## V. Summary

| Staff in Program | Agency FTE # | Grant FTE # | Total FTE # |
|---|---|---|---|
| Social Services | 30.66 | 10.00 | 40.66 |
| Homemaker | .94 | | .94 |
| Aides | 1.33 | 1.00 | 2.33 |
| Lay Positions | | 2.70 | 2.70 |
| Clerical | 2.20 | 1.00 | 3.20 |
| Total | 35.13 | 14.70 | 49.83 |

| | | |
|---|---|---|
| Total Program Costs (Grant Excluded) | $ | 953,173 |
| Total Program Costs (Grant Included) | | 1,099,407 |
| | | |
| Cost Per Case (Grant Excluded)[7] | $ | |
| Cost Per Case (Grant Included) | | |
| | | |
| Monthly Cost Per Case (Grant Excluded)[8] | $ | 144.86 |
| Monthly Cost Per Case (Grant Included) | | 163.74 |
| | | |
| Average Caseload During FY 75[9] | | 584 |
| | | |
| Number of Families Served During FY | | |
| | | |
| Number of Children Served During FY | | |
| | | |
| Projected Average Caseload for FY [10] | | |

Program Cost Analysis

Program Title:   Social Services Total                    FY 1975

| | Dollar Expenditures | FTE # |
|---|---|---|
| I.   Personnel[1] | | |
| | | |
| Staff—Intake Function | $ 222,281 | 19.91 |
| Fringe Benefits—Intake Function | 22,355 | |
| Travel Expenses—Intake Function | 11,756 | |
| | | |
| Staff—Ongoing Treatment | $ 665,413 | 61.59 |
| Fringe Benefits—Ongoing Treatment | 66,617 | |
| Travel Expenses—Ongoing Treatment | 34,783 | |
| | | |
| Homemaker Staff | $ 58,605 | 7.90 |
| Fringe Benefits—Homemaker Staff | 7,064 | |
| Travel Expenses—Homemaker Staff | 4,682 | |
| | | |
| Community Service Aides | $ 2,347 | 2.10 |
| Fringe Benefits—Aides | 56 | |
| Travel Expenses—Aides | 305 | |
| | | |
| Clerical Staff | $ 90,383 | 13.40 |

| | | |
|---|---|---|
| Fringe Benefits—Clerical Staff | 11,427 | |
| Consultants | $ 3,240 | |
| Total | $1,201,314 | 104.90 |

II. Purchased Services

| | | |
|---|---|---|
| Shelter/Receiving Homes | $ 22,822 | |
| Foster Homes | 286,230 | |
| Group Homes | 175,334 | |
| Residential Child Care Facilities | 611,927 | |
| Day Care | 874,719 | |
| Independent Living | 26,918 | |
| Social Services Payments[2] | 12,808 | |
| Less Recoveries and Support[3] | $ 58,539 | |
| Total | $1,952,219 | |

III. Administrative Expenses

| | | |
|---|---|---|
| Overhead and Indirect Costs[4] | $ 149,362 | |
| Administration[5] | 139,630 | 6.60 |
| Total | $ 288,992 | 6.60 |

IV. Other Program Costs[6]

| | | |
|---|---|---|
| Grants | $ 146,234 | 14.70 |
| General Assistance | 26,550 | |
| Total | $ 172,784 | 14.70 |

V. Summary

| Staff in Program | Agency FTE # | Grant FTE # | Total FTE # |
|---|---|---|---|
| Social Services | 88.10 | 10.00 | 98.10 |
| Homemaker | 7.90 | | 7.90 |
| Aides | 2.10 | 1.00 | 3.10 |
| Lay Positions | | 2.70 | 2.70 |
| Clerical | 13.40 | 1.00 | 14.40 |
| Total | 111.50 | 14.70 | 126.20 |

| | |
|---|---|
| Total Program Costs (Grant Excluded) | $ 3,469,075 |
| Total Program Costs (Granted Included) | 3,615,309 |
| | |
| Cost Per Case (Grant Excluded)[7] | $ |
| Cost Per Case (Grant Included) | |
| | |
| Monthly Cost Per Case (Grant Excluded)[8] | $ 103.00 |
| Monthly Cost Per Case (Grant Included) | 107.54 |
| | |
| Average Caseload During FY 75[9] | 2,762 |
| | |
| Number of Families Served During FY | |
| | |
| Number of Children Served During FY | |
| | |
| Projected Average Caseload for FY [10] | |

Program Cost Analysis

Comparison of Expenditures in Program Areas

| Program Area | Percentage of Total Social Services Budget (FY 75) |
|---|---|
| Adult Living Services | 5.0% |
| Adult Protective Services | 2.3% |
| Family Living Services | 8.3% |
| Youth Services | 28.8% |
| Child Protective Services | 27.4% |
| Adoptive and Relinquishment Services | 3.7% |
| Community and Agency Resource Planning, Development, and Coordination | 2.9% |
| Informational and Referral Services | 0.8% |
| Day Care Only Services | 20.8% |
| | 100.0% |

Grant monies are excluded from this chart.

Program Cost Analysis

Monthly Costs per Case, by Type of Case

| Program Area | Average Cost Per Case Per Month[1] |
|---|---|
| Adult Living Services | $  36.00 |
| Adult Protective Services | 55.74 |
| Family Living Services | 49.68 |
| Youth Services | 276.54 |
| Child Protective Services | 144.86 |
| Adoptive and Relinquishment Services | 80.69 |
| Informational and Referral Services | 10.50 |
| Day Care Only Services | 114.55 |

1. These figures are based upon the 9-month period October, 1974, through June, 1975. Grant monies are excluded from this chart.

Program Cost Analysis

Number of Staff Positions, by Program Area

| Program Area | Total ACDSS FTE # (FY 75) |
|---|---|
| Adult Living Services | 12.51 |
| Adult Protective Services | 6.78 |
| Family Living Services | 15.76 |
| Youth Services | 18.48 |
| Child Protective Services | 35.13 |
| Adoptive and Relinquishment Services | 7.80 |
| Community and Agency Resource Planning, Development, and Coordination | 7.23 |
| Informational and Referral Services | 1.80 |
| Day Care Only | 6.01 |
| | 111.50 |

Grant staff is excluded from this chart.

FTE = Full-time Equivalents
FY = Fiscal Year

✳ **Part V**

# The Family and the Law

# ✳ Introduction

"A Delicate Balance of Rights." We are beginning to consider that a balance ought to exist. Brian Fraser's review of the history of children's rights is enlightening and provides a better understanding of why the rights of children continue to be overlooked.

One of our local juvenile judges commented on the religious exclusion clause in the new Michigan reporting law. "Children are citizens. Their right for life supersedes their parents' rights to believe." To which we can only say, "Amen!"

The two chapters in this section are complementary. Fraser assesses the problem with great completeness, and Delaney is doing something about it. Judge Delaney recently told us that there were 225 abuse and neglect petitions filed in his court last year (in a community of 300,000 population). Using his humane and therapeutic approach he facilitated the development of a long term treatment plan without using the formal adversary court hearing in 221 of the 225 cases.

To this some cry, "Foul! Due process has been overlooked!" To which Judge Delaney comments, "I'm looking for the truth and this is the best way I know of getting it." When one looks at his approach carefully, the rights of parents and children in his court are, indeed, balanced.

Ray E. Helfer
C. Henry Kempe

✳  Chapter Sixteen

# The Child and His Parents:
# A Delicate Balance of Rights

Brian G. Fraser

As far as I know, masonry is older than carpentry, which goes clear back to the Bible times. Stone masonry goes way before Bible times; the pyramids of Egypt; things of that sort. Anybody that starts to build anything, stone, rock, or brick, starts on the northeast corner, because when they built King Solomon's temple, they started on the northeast corner. To this day, look at your courthouse, your big public buildings, you look at the cornerstone, when it was created, what year, it will be on the northeast corner. If I was going to build a septic tank, I would start on the northeast corner. Superstition, I guess.

Studs Terkel, *Working*
("Preface III, The Mason")

That is an unusual quote to begin a chapter entitled "The Child and His Parents: A Delicate Balance of Rights," but perhaps it is an appropriate quote. The parent-child relationship is a historical continuum, rooted in ancient cultures. Many of the concepts, principles, and doctrines that govern the child's relationship to his legal guardians bear a striking resemblance to the stone mason's cornerstone. Both find their origins in antiquity. Both have been passed along from father to son, from one generation to the next, and from one era to the next. And today, both are bestowed with that respect we reserve for our most endearing superstitions.

This chapter is not concerned with the rights of *a* child nor the rights of *an* adult. It is a chapter that deals with the status of individual family members and the parent-child relationship.

315

## THE HAMMURABI CODE

Written in approximately 2150 B.C. the Code of Hammurabi[1] is considered to be mankind's earliest comprehensive set of statutory enactments. In reality, the Code is a compilation of earlier Babylonian common law. Hammurabi, the first king of united Babylonia, requested that the priesthood transcribe the common law into a written, standardized form. Although transcribed and partially written by the priesthood, the Code shows little evidence of any religious influence; it is civil in nature.

Thirty sections of the Hammurabi Code refer specifically to the parent-child relationship. Like all other sections of the Code, they are harsh but just. Children, by the very nature of their existence, owed a duty of respect to their parents. If this duty of respect was paid, the parent owed a reciprocal duty to provide the child with minimum care and treatment. If the child's duty of respect was violated, the parent owed the child nothing. These reciprocal duties only pertained when the father had accepted the child as his own. As an indication of acceptance, the father would blow into the child's face, imparting a soul, and giving the child his own name or the name of a family ancestor. Until the child had been accepted by the father, the child had no status in the family and no status as an individual. Infanticide of unwanted children or children with birth defects was a common practice.

The Hammurabi Code was the first set of standardized statutes to define the parent-child relationship as a proprietary interest. It is a concept that has had a remarkably healthy lifespan of over 3,000 years. Under the Code, a father who had contracted a debt was free to give his child (or his wife) as payment for that debt. Unlike slavery, however, the child was returned to his father at the completion of three years' service. If one man stole another man's child, he was considered a thief and was put to death. A man who purchased articles from another man's child was also considered a thief and was put to death. And, if a home builder constructed a house that later collapsed and killed the owner's child, the home builder's child was put to death (an exceptionally good consumer guarantee). The child, in simple terms, was an economic unit which could be sold or exchanged freely.

If a child violated his duty of respect to his father, his status reverted to that of slave (i.e., to property) or a nonfamily member. A child who struck his father had both hands cut off. A child who showed a lack of respect for his parents was punished by the removal of both eyes and his tongue. The Hammurabi Code established the father as the sovereign of a familial power: it adopted infanticide as an accepted practice; and it defined a parent-child relationship as a proprietary interest. These concepts were adopted in varying degrees in statutory systems that followed the decline of the Babylonian Empire.

## THE HEBREW CODE

The exact date of the Hebrew Code[2] is uncertain, but is believed to date from around 800 B.C. Unlike the Babylonian Code, the Hebrew Code is predominantly religious in nature, conceived and written by priests. Although the Hebrew Code is less concise and less complete than the Babylonian Code, which preceded it, there are remarkable similarities. Specifically, it upheld the adoption of infanticide as an accepted practice, the father as the familial sovereign, the child's absolute duty of respect to his parents, and the concept of the parent-child relationship as a proprietary interest.

*Exodus 21:7*—A man may sell his daughter as a slave, but she may go free [unlike a slave] after six years.

*Exodus 21:15*—Whosoever strikes his mother or his father shall be put to death.

*Exodus 21:16*—A kidnapper shall be put to death.

*Exodus 21:17*—Whosoever curses his mother or his father shall be put to death.

*Exodus 21:28–32*—If an ox gores a child and the ox's owner knows the ox's dangerous tendencies, the owner shall be put to death. [Another excellent example of product liability.] If a slave is gored, the ox's owner must pay the slave's owner 30 shekels of silver.

The Hebrew Code, like the Roman law that followed it, did not recognize the doctrine of majority. A parent's proprietary interest in his child and the parent-child relationship continued long into a child's maturity. Like personal property, ownership of the chattel did not cease with the completion of some arbitrary period of time. The parent-child relationship remained fixed, until a child's father died.

## GREEK LAW

Greek law[3] cannot be spoken of as any one set of fixed statutes. In many aspects, the Greek law was repressive and as cruel as the Babylonian and Hebrew laws that preceded it. In other aspects, it was unique. As Greek civilization evolved, the treatment of children became more enlightened and indubitably more benevolent. As Greece died, however, so did its benevolent attitudes toward children.

At the inception of Greek civilization, infanticide of unwanted children, deformed children, or children of "inferior parents" was an accepted practice. Like the Babylonian Code, before the child was accepted into the family and given status as a family member, the father must formally accept the child. In Athens, a ceremony known as the Amphidroma was performed five days after the child's birth. As an affirmative indication of the father's acceptance, the newborn was carried around the ancestral hearth and was named. Infanticide before that ceremony was completed was tacitly accepted. As Greek civilization evolved, the father's unilateral right to take his child's life was abolished. In its place, the father was given the right to physically chastise the child, but not to take his life. A father who took his child's life was punished with three years in exile.

During the formative years of Greece, a father, like a father in Babylonia, was free to pledge his son or daughter as payment for a debt. Solon, however, limited this practice in later years to unchaste daughters. Unlike the child under Babylonian law and Hebrew law, the child under Greek law was eventually viewed as a distinct person (extraneous) from his father. As a distinct person, a child could acquire and hold property through gift or inheritance, a concept that would later be adopted in the English Common Law. Although that property might be administered by the child's father during infancy, the child's father could be held accountable for its preservation.

Orphans under Greek law were accorded special preference. Once a child was adopted, the adoptive parents were held accountable for the child's well-being. As a separate person, the adopted child could hold his guardian responsible for ill treatment and could sue for damages. This remedy for damages remained viable even after the child reached maturity and the parent-child relationship was severed.

## THE ROMAN LAW

Rome was founded in 1753 B.C. The Digest and the Institutes written during the rule of Justinian (527 A.D.–565 A.D.) marked the end of the Roman Empire. Roman law,[4] however, had a profound effect on the early English Common Law. Portions were adopted into the English Statutory Law and many of the principles, concepts, and doctrines spilled over into the American statutory system.

During the 1300-year period that marked the Roman Empire, there developed an elaborate code of law, initially barbaric, increasingly complex, and at times humane. The dominant feature of the Roman law, was the unilateral, almost unlimited right of the father *(patria potestas)*. Although officially limited to Roman citizens, the Peregrens (noncitizens and commoners) practiced the tenets of patria potestas as regularly as did the citizens. The Roman family consisted of all direct male descendants (including their wives and unmarried children) of the common living male ancestor. The oldest living common male ancestor, the *paterfamilias,* was the family head and the undisputed leader. All persons within the family *(filiifamilias)* were directly responsible to the pater and were members of the same potestas. When a daughter was married, she passed out of her father's *potestas* and into the *potestas* of her new husband. Like the Babylonian and Hebrew codes, the power of the *pater* did not terminate when the child matured and became an adult. It continued until the *paterfamilias* died.

Although specifically outlawed, the *paterfamilias* retained his unilateral power to put to death any child who was deformed, any child who was unwanted, or any child who had offended his parents. The *paterfamilias* retained the power to sell (or to offer for debt) any person within his *potestas.* Although the direct sale of adults was prohibited in 27 B.C. and the sale of children was prohibited in 565 A.D., the power of the *paterfamilias* and the practice remained. Exceedingly more oppressive than the Babylonian or the Greek law, the Roman law did not permit the child to revert to the father after the passage of some arbitrary period of time.

Once the sale or the exchange was completed, total ownership vested in the buyer. All of the property and all of the earnings of the *filii familias* belonged to the *paterfamilias.* And, reciprocally, the *paterfamilias* exercised total control over all property. Because the *paterfamilias* exercised this total control, he was responsible, in turn, for all acts committed by persons within his *potestas.* Thus, any injury inflicted by a child was viewed as an injury inflicted by the *paterfamilias.* The *paterfamilias* could pay the wronged party a sum of cash or he could forfeit the child in payment.

*Patria potestas* was the heart of an entire complex system of interfamilial relationships. It was not a simple concept that just expressed the relationship of a father to his children. The concept of *patria potestas* and the Roman's respect for the family and the judgment of the *paterfamilias* simply overwhelmed the dicta of various emperors. Although numerous acts (selling the children, infanticide, etc.) were legislatively declared immoral or illegal, the practice continued.

Perhaps the explanation for the strength and tenacity of *patria potestas* was the fact that it was more than a set of rules. It expressed the prevailing social mores.

> The reason which caused the Romans to accept and to uphold the *patria potestas* to maintain it with singular tenacity against the influence of other systems with which they came into contact, must have been the profound impression of family unity, the conviction that every family was, and of right ought to be one body, with one will and executive.[5]

The concepts of family unit and family sanctity did not die with the collapse of the Roman Empire. Their influence is seen today in American courts, in American statutes, and in basic American philosophy.

## THE VISIGOTHIC CODE

The Visigothic kingdom[6] occupied an interesting, transitory position between the fall of the Roman Empire and the beginning of feudal Europe in the Middle Ages. Born at the fall of the Roman Empire in 476 A.D. and exercising dominance over western Europe until 711 A.D., the Visigothic kingdom was an amalgam of Roman, Germanic, and newly emerging Christian influences. This amalgam produced a surprisingly enlightened and humane society noted for its high regard for and humane treatment of children.

The primary emphasis of the Visigothic Code was on the duties of the parent, not the powers of the parent—a striking contrast to the Roman concept of *patria potestas.* Abortion and infanticide were punishable by blinding or by execution of the offender. A blow to a pregnant woman causing a miscarriage resulted in a severe fine. The sale, donation, or pledging of a child in return for a debt was specifically forbidden. A parent was free to contract with a third party to raise his child, but if the parent faulted in his contractual obligations (i.e., failed to pay the foster parent), he was enslaved.

Children, in return, were expected to honor their parents. The parent had the authority to utilize reasonable physical punishment in the raising of his children, but it was not permitted to cross the threshold of reasonableness. In stark contrast to the Babylonian, Hebrew, and Romanic laws, a child who struck his parent (or who was disobedient) could be disinherited but could not be executed unilaterally by his parent. Children were extended a statutory share of the family property on the death of one or both parents, and an orphan's property was protected by the appointment of a guardian, who was ultimately responsible for the preservation of all inherited property.

The concept that children had statutory rights to life, the concept that children did indeed have rights of their own, and the diminution of the concept that the child was an economic unit to be bought, sold, or pledged, were outstanding exceptions in an otherwise bleak history of prefeudal Europe.

## EARLY ENGLISH LAW

English Common Law,[7] the precursor to modern English law, can be dated as post 1300 A.D. Prior to the death of Edward I, in 1307, English law was in a period of flux. The Norman invasion of England in 1066 brought with it a strong influence of continental (and in a large part Roman) civil law. In the areas of property and family law, continental theories and concepts were imported in toto.

Early English law is remarkably similar to Roman law. There was a limited right to sell a man's son or daughter in times of poverty. Infanticide was practiced and condoned if perpetrated within a few days of birth; and the father exercised the right of custody and control over all his offspring and his heir apparent (should they differ).

Unlike Rome, however, England never adopted the concept of *patria potestas*. Children, in fact, were emancipated from parental control at the age of majority (usually at the age of twenty-one). A child had the right to own property before the age of majority. If a child were under the age of twenty-one, the father acted as the child's guardian in relation to that property. In the latter part of the twelfth century and during the thirteenth century, children did have legal rights as persons. They could sue and be sued. A child could bring an action against his custodian for a mismanagement of money or a mismanagement of property that belonged to him.

Court action was initiated by a court appointed "next friend" or an action was defended by a court appointed "guardian ad litem." In many cases the court neither appointed a "next friend" nor "guardian ad litem." It rather assumed itself a total responsibility for the protection of the child's interest. The motive may have been benevolent, but the result was not. The court may have sought to protect the child's interest, but by not appointing a "next friend" or a "guardian ad litem" it denied the child the right of independent respresentation—a fatal mistake that still flourishes today.

## ENGLISH LAW AFTER THE THIRTEENTH CENTURY

"Guardianship" in pre-thirteenth century England (and after) was invoked in cases when the child had inherited property or would inherit property. It was not invoked on behalf of poor children who had no access to property. There was no benevolent motive lurking behind the concept of guardianship. Guardianship was used more often to benefit the guardian than to preserve the property for the child's benefit. The guardian held the property "for the use" of the child, and the child held the fee, but the guardian absorbed all profits and all interests that accrued in the property until the child reached majority. In many cases the guardian married his wards to one of his own daughters or sold the right of marriage to some third person. It was not until 1259 that the English sovereignty enacted a law that converted the guardian's profitable rights during his ward's infancy into a trust for the benefit of the child.[8]

In feudal England the ownership and control of land was of a primary importance and concern to the crown. It was around the issue of land, its transfer and its disposal, that the doctrine of *parens patriae*[9] *first emerged. Translated literally, parens patriae* means, "father of his country." It was a doctrine that developed in case law, grew in scope, and eventually proved to have a tremendous effect on the parent-child relationship. In 1696 (193 years after the English sovereignty attempted to protect a minor's interest in inherited land) a minor child, through his mother, brought a bill of accounting against the child's guardian. In part, the court stated

> An infant may . . . call his guardian to account, even during his minority; if a stranger enters and receives the profits of an infant's estate, he shall in consideration of this court, be looked upon as a trustee, for the infant and the like.[10]

Twenty-five years later, in the case of *Beaufort vs. Berty,*[11] the English court ruled that it could intervene on behalf of a child when it felt that a guardian of an educational trust would not serve the child in absence of court regulation. One hundred years later, in the case of *Wellesley vs. Beaufort,*[12] the court noted that it could only intervene on behalf of the child if property were involved, ". . . this court has not the means of acting, except where it has the property to act upon." In 1828, in the case of *Wellesley vs. Wellesley,*[13] the English court firmly cemented the relationship of the child to parent and the State. The parent's right, it noted, emanated from the crown (the State).

The relationship between the parent and the child was a trust. The right was endowed by the crown as a trust because it was assumed that the parent would discharge faithfully on behalf of his child. If the trust were not faithfully discharged, it would be incumbent upon the crown to intervene and to protect the child's interest. And finally, in the case of *In Re Spence,*[14] the court ruled that intervention was proper even though there was no property involved in the dispute. The doctrine of *parens patriae* simply interjected a third party into conflict between the child and his parents: the State. The State would act as a guarantor of the trust.

What originally began as discretionary authority by the court to intervene in disputes involving property grew to become an affirmative duty to intervene when a child's rights were jeopardized. While the court would intervene to protect a child's interests, it did not provide the child with a vehicle to present his grievances to the court, nor did it guarantee the child the right of independent representation.

### Work Laws and the Poor

The sixteenth century marked a period of economic stress and transition for England. During this period the number of poor increased dramatically. At an ever increasing rate, children from poor families turned to begging for survival. The private English charities, which had previously cared for unwanted poor children, buckled under the increase. Beginning in 1535, the English parliament attempted to deal with starving parents and starving children by putting them to work.[15] The "Elizabethan Poor Laws,"[16] enacted in 1601, provided England with its first comprehensive program for poor relief. Children whose parents could no longer provide for them were put directly to work or were apprenticed.[17] Many of the children who were separated from their parents were apprenticed into the English Merchant Marine, and beginning in 1617, thousands of other children were sent directly to the American colonies to work.

It has been suggested that the passage and the enactment of the Elizabethan Poor Laws rested upon three assumptions:

1. A family's financial inability to provide for its children was sufficient grounds to separate the child and his parents.
2. Once a child was separated from his parents, he became, for all practical purposes, a ward of the state, and that ward became a financial burden to the state. By putting the child to work (apprenticing him), the child assumed a portion of that cost. Economically this was a most advantageous system for providing for the poor.
3. While only poor children were separated from their parents, the motive behind this move was benevolent. The system provided clothing, food, and housing, and taught children a trade, something they otherwise would not receive.

The Elizabethan Poor Laws may have been thought to be benevolent and economically feasible, but they were an abject failure. By the mid sixteenth century, the Poor Laws were laid to rest and in their place the English government enacted workhouses for children.

With the advent of the Industrial Revolution in England (1760), children of the poor became an increasingly important element in private industry. Too young to articulate their needs, too young to petition the courts, and largely unrepresented in government, children provided industry with an easily trainable, extremely cheap, and quite durable (5 years of age and up, 14 hours a day, seven days a week) work force. The "Pauper Apprentice System" was so badly abused, and children so cruelly and inhumanely treated, that the English parliament outlawed the Pauper Apprentice System with the passage of the "Factory Acts" in the early 1800s.

The Factory Acts applied only to poor children who had been separated from their parents; they did not apply to young children who were still living with their own parents. Since a parent was entitled to his child's earnings, it became increasingly popular for the parents to put their children to work in factories. Parents simply exercised their proprietary rights, contracted out their children to industry, and collected their wages. The void in the work force created by the Factory Acts was quickly filled by individual parents collecting their child's wages. The Babylonian, Greek, and Roman concept that children were economic units to be manipulated by their owners flourished again in nineteenth century England.

### Infanticide

Infanticide was specifically prohibited in England. Nevertheless, it retained a certain amount of viability. As late as the nineteenth century, 80 percent of the illegitimate children put out to nurse in London died, for many nurses took the children, killed them, and continued to collect the nursing fees. In England a newborn child could be insured for about one pound sterling. If the child was killed by his parents, or given to a third party and killed, the insurance premium netted a profit of between three and five pounds sterling. The insurance scheme was referred to as the "Burial Club." Earlier societies had predicated the practice of infanticide on the basis that a child was unwanted, was deformed, or had wronged his parents. In England, the practice was predicated on the basis of profit.

Like earlier socioeconomic systems, the English practiced infanticide and defined the parent-child relationship in terms of a proprietary interest. Unlike earlier socioeconomic legal systems, the English began to view the child as a distinct person. In an effort to define the parent-child relationship more specifically, and to insure that certain rights of a minor were protected, a third party was introduced through the doctrine of *parens patriae:* the state.

## AMERICAN LAW

There is little doubt that the treatment of children in America grew out of the English social and economic environment (beginning with the importation of children from England under the Elizabethan Poor Laws). The pattern of child treatment and the parent-child relationship closely paralleled that in England: involuntary separation of children from parents who could not support them, and apprenticeship. As in England, children who were not separated from their parents for financial reasons, were put to work by their parents for financial purposes. Children were characterized as economic units, used to satisfy a debt, to offset financial burdens to a state, and to generate income.

Initially, American courts offered little protection for children who were cruelly treated by their parents. In fact, in 1628, the colony of Massachusetts adopted and enacted into law the "Stubborn Child Act," seemingly a descendant of the ancient Babylonian, Greek, and Roman laws.

> A stubborn or rebellious son of sufficient years of understanding; viz 16, who will not obey the voice of his mother or his father, and that when they have chastened him will not harken unto them . . . such a person shall be put to death.[18]

There were some reported cases where American courts took active measures to protect a child's safety, but these were exceptions, not the rule.[19]

Finally, in 1874 the state, its citizens, and the court seemed to take active cognizance of the fact that a child did have the right of not being severely beaten and cruelly and inhumanely treated. It was the dramatic case of Maryellen[20] that signalled: (1) that children do have a right of not being cruelly and inhumanely treated; (2) the advent of and impetus for a number of privately funded charities whose task it was to protect children; and (3) the beginning of an era that would see every state adopt neglect statutes to protect children.

At the beginning of the 1900s, juvenile courts began to appear in states throughout America. Recognizing that problems concerning children were complex matrices of medicine, psychology, and sociology, as well as law, the juvenile courts took a different approach from the criminal courts that were currently in existence. Justified on the basis of *parens patriae,* the juvenile court gave its judges great flexibility in dealing with the problems of children. Functioning properly, it was hoped that the juvenile court would provide safety and offer treatment for the child, not exact retribution. As the concept of the juvenile court evolved, its jurisdiction fell into three rather broad areas: juvenile delinquency, status offenses (acts which if perpetrated by adults would not constitute crimes and would not be actionable), and neglect (broadly interpreted to include abuse as well).

## A DELICATE BALANCE OF RIGHTS

The basic mold of the parent-child relationship was struck over three thousand years ago. Aristotle theorized that children lacked the intellectual and emotional capacity for self-government. This intellectual and emotional capacity could be developed, but Aristotle felt that it must be fostered through a wise and mature adult whom the child respected: his father. Plato, although he agreed, noted that the raising of young children was a fundamental concern of the public and of society as a whole. Over the centuries the mold has been twisted and pulled, but it has remained basically unaltered.

The doctrine of parental absolutism that evolved during the Babylonian, Hebrew, Greek, and finally the Roman societies died a natural death. In its place, the concept of presumptive parental rights has arisen. Today, the parent-child relationship is characterized as a presumptive parental right: American society presumes that a child's parent(s) wants to act in the child's best interests. It furthermore presumes that a parent does act in his child's best interests. These presumptions are only overcome when the facts in a particular case dramatically indicate otherwise. The presumption of right rests with the parent.

History should have taught us, however, that these assumptions are not always correct. It is rather naive to believe that a child's interest and his parents' interests are always the same. They are not.

> One does not have to work in the juvenile court for long to learn in countless circumstances, the juvenile's rights and the interests are often in sharp variance with his parents'.[21]

American laws presume that parents want to act and do act in a child's interests. If there is any doubt, that doubt is resolved in favor of the parent. In certain strictly limited circumstances, the state, under the doctrine of *parens patriae* as a guarantor of the child's negative legal rights, may intervene. If there is any intervention, the state must show an immediate and pressing danger to the child or to the interests of the state. In short, the state must rebut the presumption of parental right.

The doctrine of *parens patriae,* originally conceived in England, was formally adopted by the American legal system. Noted specifically in 1839 in the case of *Ex Parte Crouse*[22] (". . . rights guaranteed to the parent are granted by the grace of the state. . ."), and specifically delineated in the case of the *Finley vs. Finley*[23] (. . . the responsibility to do what is best for the interests of the child), it became firmly entrenched in the case of *Prince vs. Massachusetts*[24] (. . .parents may make martyrs of themselves but they are not free to make martyrs of their children. . .).

Although the doctrine was roundly criticized in the *In Re Gault*[25] case as a vehicle used to deny due process in juvenile delinquency cases (". . . its meaning is murky and its historical credentials of dubious relevance . . ."), this was revived a year later by the same court in the case of *Ginzburg vs. the United States.*[26] There is little doubt that a state may intervene in the parent-child relationship, under the doctrine of *parens patriae,* to protect children from their own parents (abuse and neglect), to compel obedience of a child to his parents, and to compel a child's duties to the state (e.g., education). However, there is similarly little doubt that it is a difficult doctrine to invoke.

### Parental Rights
The doctrine is difficult to invoke because it must be utilized to overcome the presumption of parental right, a doctrine that has become firmly established in American law. The right of a parent to be free from state interference and to raise his child in the manner that he sees fit has been described as "a right which transcends property" (*Denton vs. Jones*[27]), as an "inalienable right" (*In Re Agor*[28]), as a "sacred right" (*In Re Hudson*[29]), as a "natural right" (*Anguis vs. Superior Court*[30]), and most recently as a right that has been established beyond debate as an American tradition (*Wisconsin vs. Yoder*[31]), and as a right that, even, has a constitutional basis.[32]

Parental rights are usually expressed generically as the rights of care, custody, and control. Care, custody, and control include the right to name the child, to instill religious and political beliefs, to educate, to grant or withhold health care, and to physically discipline. In equally simplistic terms, the child does have a number of negative legal rights. He has the right of not being totally denied an education. He has the right of not being neglected to the point that his life or his health is imminently threatened, and he has the right of not being physically chastised to the point that his physical well-being is endangered.

### Children's Rights
The child's rights are described as negative legal rights because they come into

being when parental behavior drops below some acceptable standard. Only after parents so grossly abuse their rights of care, custody, and control does the state intervene and delineate a child's rights. The child is not guaranteed—nor does he have an absolute right to—parental care that will provide him with adequate food, clothing, and shelter. The child does not have a right to medical and health care that will insure his future health. The child does not have the right to receive an education that will eventually prove beneficial to his own needs. The child is regularly denied due process (except in those cases falling within the scope of *In Re Gault*); he has no vehicle to address and petition the court; he has no access to his own advocate or his own spokesman; he may be prosecuted, persecuted, and confined for acts which, if committed by an adult, would not be actionable; and he is subject to punishment which has been declared as cruel and unusual if inflicted upon an adult.

American law views the child's interests and the parents' interests as one and the same. A parent is said to owe a duty of support to his child. A parent must provide his child with food, clothing, and shelter. If a parent fails to provide any food, clothing, or shelter, he violates his duty of care and support; and the child is then said to be neglected and the jurisdiction of the juvenile court may be invoked. The difficult issue to resolve, however, is not whether the child is entitled to any food, clothing, or shelter, but at what level?

### Care and Support

Some commentators have argued that a child is entitled to that standard of care and support that a "reasonably prudent man" would provide.[33] Others have argued that a child is only legally entitled to that care and support which represents the minimum, accepted community standard.[34] From a practical point of view, the latter opinion probably reflects more realistically that level of care to which a child is legally entitled. Courts seem to be extremely hesitant to intervene and to invoke the doctrine of *parens patriae* unless the level of care and support of a child falls below what the community views as being minimally acceptable. In any event, the possibility of intervention rests upon two assumptions: (1) that someone has identified and noted that the standard of care is below that which is accepted within the community; and (2) that somebody is willing to intervene.

Similar questions of standard surround the issue of needed medical and health care for children.[35] No person would debate the fact that a child is entitled to medical care which is necessary to preserve his life. Every state permits the delivery of needed medical treatment when a child's life is in imminent danger, either with or without parental permission.[36] When a parent fails to provide a child with the medical treatment that is necessary to preserve his life, that parent violates his duty of care and support, the child is said to be neglected, and the jurisdiction of the juvenile court may be invoked.

The issue is not so neatly resolved, however, when the child suffers from a medical or health impairment which in itself is not life threatening. Medical or health problems that involve a child's vision, hearing, speech, motor development, and emotional development obviously do not fall within that category of a life threatening condition. The end result may be just as permanent, the process just as debilitating and cruel, but the courts have yet to forge a standard that delineates between what is medical neglect and what is not medical neglect. In precise terms, there is no commonly accepted standard of health care for children. Some courts are willing to intervene when a child's health is threatened,[37] while other courts feel that this falls within its purview of parental prerogative and refuse to intervene.[38] Again, the possibility of intervention rests upon two assumptions: (1) that someone has identified the child and has noted that the standard of health care is beneath that which is minimally accepted by the community; and (2) that someone is willing to intervene.

It is axiomatic that there can be no intervention of any sort until the need is identified. But in many cases that is exactly the issue. Young children have no access to society as a whole. They have no access to the early identification of health and care needs. Too young to identify their own needs, too inarticulate to express their hurts, and unable to attract the attention of third parties, a child's access to needed health or medical care, to adequate food, clothing, and shelter, rests with the absolute discretion of his caretakers. This in turn rests on the assumption that a child's parents can identify their child's needs and will provide the necessary care and support. From the date that a child is born and leaves the hospital until the date that a child enters school, the identification of needs (at whatever standard) and the delivery of needed services rests solely with his parents.

Every American child from the age of six to sixteen is entitled to some form of education. Every state provides some framework for compulsory education.[39] The basis for such compulsory education is probably predicated upon the fact that education not only benefits the child, it benefits the state, and it is a state benefit that assures stability and growth. Although the right to an education may be based upon the state's interests, the courts have recognized the intrinsic value of education for a child. The Supreme Court in 1954 noted that, "in these days it is doubtful that any child may reasonably expect to succeed in life, if he is denied the opportunity of an education."[40]

While that may be true, it is the child's parent who decides the type and the quality of education that he will receive. Every parent has the right to choose a school he believes most closely represents his own values and his own ideology. The Supreme Court, in the case of *Pierce vs. The Society of Sisters,* declared that a parent could choose his child's own school; "to do otherwise would infringe upon the parents' rights to guide a child intellectually and religiously, a most substantial part of the freedom and the liberty of a parent."[41] A parent cannot, of course, totally dictate or control his child's school curriculum,[42] and each school must meet minimum state requirements. Nevertheless, while a child does have the right to receive an education, it is a right that is exercised by the parent on behalf of his child.

### Children and the Courts

Children have the rather dubious distinction of falling under the "benevolent jurisdiction" of the juvenile court for acts which, if committed by adults, would be permissible. Children who do not attend school, who are sexually promiscuous, who violate curfews, who run away, and who "cannot be controlled" by the parent, are all susceptible to the jurisdiction of the juvenile court.[43] The phrase "child in need of supervision" (CHINS) was originally intended to provide therapeutic intervention and treatment for children whose behavior was not socially acceptable.

In the past decade, the concept of CHINS has been increasingly used by parents to control behavior and to remove unwanted family members. That in itself may not have proved detrimental to the interests of the child. However, once a child was designated as a CHINS and removed from his home, there proved to be a lack of therapeutic milieus in which to place the child. At an ever increasing rate, the final dumping spot became the state's training school, the boys' home, or the correctional facility (a rather fancy name for a rather common facility—the jail). Until 1967, a child could be committed to a state training facility without the benefit of counsel, without the right of cross-examination, without the right to confront his accuser, without the right to notice, and without the right against self-incrimination.

The Supreme Court, in the *In Re Gault* case noted, "neither the Fourteenth Amendment nor the Bill of Rights is for adults alone."[44] In cases in which a child might be incarcerated, the court has said that a child does have the right to legal counsel, does have the right to receive adequate notice, does have the right to confront his accuser, does have the right of cross-examination, and does have the right against self-incrimination. In short, in those cases where a child's liberty might be deprived, he has the right of due process.

The *In Re Gault* case referred specifically to cases in which a child might be incarcerated; just how far these rights might be expanded in other areas has never been delineated. While it would seem to be axiomatic that a child should be represented in cases where his life is endangered as well as cases where his liberty is endangered, the right of independent representation in cases of neglect has not been specified by the federal courts.

## OVERVIEW AND CONCLUSIONS

The individual family is viewed in American Law as the basic social unit. It has retained its viability because of the sense of tradition that seems to be inherent in American culture; because it has proved to be flexible, able to change with the times and social mores; and because no one has developed a better system for raising children and insuring that their basic psychological and emotional needs are met.

The individual family unit provides for the basic needs of the child. It instills values, fertilizes religious and political beliefs, and provides a vehicle to develop in a child the knowledge, education, and experience that will enable him to become a productive citizen. In the vast majority of cases, the family unit does function very adequately. In the vast majority of cases, parents do act in the best interests of their child. In some cases, however, the family unit does not function properly, and parents do not act in their child's best interests. In 1972, 141,000 cases of neglect were filed in the juvenile court.[45] In 1975, the estimate is that between 665,000 and 1,675,000 children were abused, sexually molested, or seriously neglected.[46]

The doctrine of parental absolutism that characterized the parent-child relationship in ancient Babylonia, Greece, and Rome died a natural death. Infanticide is no longer condoned—although many Americans would argue that the line of demarcation between infanticide and abortion is negligible. Children are no longer regarded as economic units to be bought, sold, exchanged, or used to guarantee a debt. Today, the parent-child relationship is legally severed when a child reaches majority. And today children in certain circumstances are viewed as distinct persons from their parents, with certain legal rights—negative legal rights to be sure, but legal rights nevertheless.

The parent-child relationship today is still viewed as a presumptive right. An American parent can raise his child in any manner he sees fit, and we assume that that manner is acceptable, if not correct. Only when a parent so badly abuses his child's rights to care, custody, and control that the child's life or health is seriously threatened, or a valid state interest is seriously threatened, will American society intervene. And intervention is only successful to the extent that the presumption of parental right is overcome.

While many of the absolute doctrines that characterized the Babylonian, Hebrew, Greek, and Romanic legal systems have passed away, much of the philosophy that underlies those doctrines remains. The child may no longer be regarded as an economic unit, but the parent's interests in the parent-child relationship are still characterized as proprietary in nature: the rights of children are exercised by the parent.[47] A child may exercise these rights when he is legally emancipated[48] from his parents or when he reaches the age of majority. But the age of majority is 18 to 21, and at that point the child becomes, for all legal purposes, an adult.

Interestingly enough, the age of majority used to be fifteen. However, in feudal England, as warfare became more sophisticated, and his armor became heavier, the status shifted from the completion of fourteen years' service to completion of twenty years.[49] The age of majority is simply a concept that developed over 1500 years ago, that was passed along from father to son, from generation to generation, and was finally incorporated into the American legal system. In fact, American law has paid very little attention to the fact that a child can develop physically, emotionally, and psychologically well before the arbitrary age of majority. Denying duties and responsibilities to a child may prove just as deleterious to his or her development as giving all young children the duties and responsibilities commensurate with an adult.

American courts seem to have tacitly recognized the parents' proprietary interest in their child. At an ever increasing rate, the juvenile courts are utilizing foster homes as dumping grounds for abused and neglected children. The assumption seems to be that all parents can be treated, it just takes a certain amount of time. The rather sad fact is that some parents can never be treated successfully. Nevertheless, the child remains in foster care, patiently waiting for successful treatment for his parents and for the development of a safe and stable home environment. Courts have simply refused to recognize that children are on one time schedule and that parents are on quite another.[50] Children would seem to have a very real interest in not living in a number of foreign foster homes waiting for their parents' lives to become stabilized. The preservation of a family integrity is certainly a benevolent motive, but there comes a point at which the child's interests should simply outweigh the parents' proprietary interest.

No one would suggest, of course, that the parent-child relationship today is the same as it was 3,000 years ago. It is not. There have been changes, and the changes have been good. Some impetus for change has been generated by a genuine desire to see the child as an individual with his own legal rights, and some impetus for change has been generated as a result of economic realities. Under either the result is exactly the same: there is some standard of care that every child must receive. When that standard of care is not met, either through parental misfeasance, parental malfeasance, or parental nonfeasance, the state may intervene.

Every state has available to it a mechanism to provide legal intervention when that standard is not met,[51] and every state identifies some agency (protective services, social services, social and rehabilitative services, and so on) that is mandated to intervene when the child's level of care has slipped beneath that accepted minimum standard. The fact that every state requires some form of affirmative action once a child's care slips beneath that standard assumes that those children and that standard can be identified. That, in many cases, proves to be an erroneous assumption. All children who are abused, who are neglected, or who are deprived of the necessities of life are not identified. And until there is some form of identification, there can be no form of intervention. America, unlike many other countries, has not yet adopted a vehicle to identify young · children who are in danger.

Preschool children in America have no guaranteed access to society. A number of European countries have adopted a form of the "child health visitor," which guarantees to the child this right. These countries have simply recognized that a child's health care is most important during the child's formative years. A child health visitor is a person who has been trained to identify health needs, and developmental and emotional lags in young children. The health visitor examines all children at regular intervals, regardless of the parents' financial status. The purpose of the program and the visits is to provide the child with a vehicle to society, to identify health needs, and to provide the family with access to community health programs.

Under either the humanitarian theory (children are persons with certain inherent rights) or the economic theory (it's cheaper to correct now than to correct later), such a program is feasible and advisable in America. Perhaps at no point in one's life is health more important than during one's youth. The damage and the scars that are left with young children who do not receive adequate care are scars that they will bear for the rest of their lives. And it is society as a whole which must eventually bear the burden. If America truly does guarantee to its youngest citizens a minimum standard of care, then it would seem to be incumbent upon Americans to identify those children who fall beneath that standard.

In Babylonia, Rome, and England, children were provided with independent representation in issues involving property. In some respects things have not changed much in the past 3,000 years. Children are *guaranteed* independent representation only in those cases where they may be incarcerated. In cases involving property in the probate court or the estate court, children are *usually* represented by their own attorney. A few states are slowly beginning to recognize that the parents' interests and the child's interests are not always the same. Some states now provide independent representation for children in divorce proceedings, and in custody suits. A few states now provide the abused child with a guardian ad litem in cases of child abuse that are heard by the juvenile court.[a]

The fact that a child is guaranteed independent representation in cases where his liberty may be at stake and in disputes involving property is reassuring. It is not reassuring to note that a child's health or life may be adversely affected without independent representation. It is, in fact, rather ludicrous to suggest that a child should be afforded independent representation in cases where his liberty is threatened, but denied independent representation in cases where his life is threatened.

When the American Constitution was originally drafted, the belief was that oppression could only be prevented if all interests were equally represented. Every competent adult is guaranteed two very basic rights: the right to vote and the right to emigrate. The right to vote is a tool to be used to appoint responsive judges, responsive legislators, and responsive executives. The assumption is that

---

[a]The recent enactment of P.L. 93-247 by the federal government requires that a state provide for the independent representative a guardian ad litem in cases that proceed into the juvenile court.

once a judge, legislator, or an executive is elected, he will reflect the will of the people who elected him. If he does not reflect the will of the people, he may be removed at the next election. If an American adult does not believe that his elected officials represent his interests, and that their personal philosophies are abhorrent to his own personal ideology, he is free to emigrate. Neither of these rights is guaranteed to an American child. He is not represented at the judicial, legislative, or the executive level. There may be judges, legislators, and executives who are sensitive to the needs and the interests of the child, but in the final analysis, elected officials represent those persons and those interests which can return them to office—i.e., the franchised adult.

There is no doubt that the child's interests and the interests of the franchised adult are not always the same. Similarly, there is little doubt that the child is not adequately represented (or even represented minimally for that matter) at the judicial and at the legislative level. A child's interests lie in better and more extensive educational programs, better and more adequate health care, future city planning and zoning, independent representation, and so forth. The American child who emigrates from an oppressive and a dangerous home environment or an unresponsive school is simply picked up under the jurisdiction of the juvenile court, is returned to his home, or is placed in a state training school.

This is not to say that the doctrine of presumptive parental rights is a bad doctrine. It is not. This is not to say that the state should intervene in all aspects of family life. It should not. This is not to say that all children should be franchised and have the unilateral right to leave home. They should not. What *is* being said is that the parent-child relationship and the stone mason's cornerstone have certain similarities. The problem, of course, is that a blind adherence to tradition and superstition in laying of a cornerstone can cause no harm. The blind adherence to superstition and tradition in areas of human development and interpersonal relationships can, however, have devastating results.

Perhaps the time has finally come to recognize that a child's interests and a parent's interests may be different. Perhaps the realization is dawning that parents do not always act in a child's best interests, that some parents will never be good parents, and that they should never have originally become parents. Perhaps it is time to recognize that children do not belong to their parents; they belong to themselves, in trust of their parents.

## Chapter Seventeen

# New Concepts
# of the Family Court

James J. Delaney

## INTRODUCTION

All of society, from the smallest unit, the family, to a nation, shares
a common need: the regulation of human behavior. This is the purpose of the law. Those rules of conduct for members within the
family, in their relation to each other, are largely matters for the family itself to
decide: where they will live, what they eat, the occupation they follow, their
assignment of tasks within the family, their forms of recreation. But the rights of
family members and the family's relation to other families—i.e., to society—is a
matter for all families collectively to determine.

These regulations, which we often call "family law," are concerned with
marriage and its dissolution; and with the rights and obligations marriage creates;
of parents' relation to children and children's rights and duties toward parents;
of the family's relation to society and society's relation to the family. Inherent
in family law is the delicate balance between what is exclusively a matter within
the family and what is of concern to society. This is a balance that must be
constantly adjusted, within a changing and increasingly complex society, by
both the legislative and judicial branches of government. It is for the law makers
to determine these rules of conduct; the court is the legal mechanism for inter-
preting and enforcing them. This court may be called the family court, the
juvenile court or it may be a juvenile and family division within a court of
general jurisdiction.

## FAMILY LAW IS FOR PEOPLE

As Newton observed of inanimate objects, the law tends to remain at rest. It is

*335*

highly traditional, presumably aloof and impersonal, seldom innovative. This is not a matter of judicial indifference, nor is it lack of concern for people, as much as an effort to obtain and maintain objectivity. Yet this detachment, untempered by reason and a personal commitment, may defeat the very purpose of the law; which is to achieve the greatest good for the greatest number.

In no part of the legal structure is this more apparent than in family law. No court has a greater responsibility and a clearer legislative mandate to make the law work for and serve people than the family court. The Uniform Dissolution of Marriage Act states its underlying purposes as:

> To promote the amicable settlement of disputes that have arisen between parties to a marriage;
> To mitigate the potential harm to the spouses and their children caused by the process of legal dissolution of marriage; and
> To make the law of legal dissolution . . . more effective . . . by making an irretrievable breakdown of the marriage . . . the sole basis for its dissolution.

The Legislative Guide for Drafting Family and Juvenile Court Acts, published by the Office of Child Development, states the purposes of such acts:

> a) To preserve the unity of the family whenever possible and to provide for the care, protection and wholesome mental and physical development of children coming within the provisions of this act; . . .
> b) Consistent with the protection of the public interest, to remove from children committing delinquent acts the consequences of criminal behavior, and to substitute wherefor a program of supervision, care and rehabilitation; . . .
> c) To achieve the foregoing purposes in a family environment whenever possible, separating the child from his parents only when necessary for his welfare or in the interests of public safety; . . .
> d) To provide judicial procedures through which the provisions of this Act are executed and enforced and in which the parties are assured a fair hearing and their constitutional and other legal rights recognized and enforced.

Thus, if the legislative pronouncements are to be achieved, those limitations that demand detachment of other branches of the court system cannot be aptly applied to the family court in family matters.

## THE COURT—TWO CONCEPTS

What, then, is a family court? How does it differ, if it does, from other components of the judicial system? There are two basic concepts of a family court. One is a separate court with jurisdiction limited to family law: marriage, dissolution, support, maintenance, child custody, juvenile delinquency, child abuse and neglect and similar matters. This is generally a legislative product, established for populous areas, with specific qualifications for judges and with a separate method for their selection. The other concept of a family court is as a part of a court of general jurisdiction, with a division or department devoted to family law.

Both concepts have some advantages, and some drawbacks. On the positive side, the family court is a specialized forum, staffed by judges who serve there by choice and who have developed expertise in this branch of the law. The less apparent disadvantages are these: A family court can be justified only by a sufficient volume of work to warrant a full time specialized court. This factor limits the family court to large cities and populous communities. Sparsely settled areas have a different court system and different standards, resulting in unequal or disparate treatment.

Any special court, separated from the rest of the judicial system, tends to become narrow and introspective. Because of its isolation, it seldom receives its fair share of funds or judicial manpower. The family court lacks flexibility, since family court judges can handle only family court matters. Judges in other courts with spare time cannot be shifted into the family court, nor can family court judges obtain relief from the monotony of a single form of work by occasionally presiding over other matters.

The court of general jurisdiction has some distinct advantages over the special courts. As the state trial court of highest jurisdiction, its judges enjoy a prestige (whether warranted or not) not accorded courts of limited jurisdiction. As the court which serves the greatest number of people, and the forum in which most lawyers practice, the court has the attention of the legislature and the public and is generally better staffed and equipped. Because these judges receive higher salaries than those in courts of limited jurisdiction, they are frequently better qualified and generally enjoy a more equitable division of work.

In multijudge courts of general jurisdiction, special divisions are usually established: a criminal division, a family division, and general civil divisions. Since all branches or divisions are a part of the same court, judges, although they do specialize, may be reassigned temporarily to other divisions to relieve overloads. Thus they have the opportunity of broadening their experience and viewpoint. The general trend today, and one that seems to serve the family best, is toward including family court jurisdiction in the highest trial court, away from a multiplicity of special courts of limited jurisdiction.

## THE COURT'S PURPOSE

Whatever the court structure may be, whether a juvenile court, a separate family court, or a general trial court exercising juvenile and family jurisdiction, its name and composition is less important than its purpose. In the area of family law the

court's true role is to define and protect the rights—and enforce the responsibilities—of the parent, of the child, and of the community. There is fairly uniform agreement that such family matters as marriage, divorce, paternity, child
support, and custody should be regulated by law. There is far less agreement—
and, until recently, considerably less concern—over the rights of children.

Child abuse and serious neglect are often thought of solely as medical or
sociological problems. For this reason the role of the law as a therapeutic factor
may be minimized or overlooked completely. Both disciplines tend to think of
"law" in terms of criminal prosecution. Too often their view of the court is
based not on objective evaluation, but subjectively, on the viewer's own experience, responding to a traffic ticket or as a juror or witness. This is akin to
judging the medical profession from the observation of an emergency ward in a
large hospital, or the efficiency of a social service agency from the confusion and
the often calculated indifference of the agency's intake process. This limited
perspective, usually self-induced, may incline most of the medical and social
service professionals to avoid the court, which not only deprives them of a
valuable resource in treating abuse and neglect, but more important, may deny
the child, and the parents as well, the very considerable assistance and protection the law affords.

## THE LAW—A MOVING FORCE

The law is not just applicable to individuals, to protecting their rights, to enforcing their obligations; it is equally applicable to the constructive uses of
formulating public opinion, of eliciting community support to create resources,
mandate services, reform outmoded practices, set standards, and establish priorities. This is graphically illustrated by what has been done to create awareness
of child abuse, to update laws, and to create resources when the law is brought
to bear on the subject.

For a hundred years or more, social service agencies have worked to combat
maltreatment of children. These efforts have met with only modest success,
largely because abuse and neglect have been seen as social ills, to be solved solely
by social workers. The social service profession in the past has prided itself on its
competence to deal singlehandedly with these matters, to exclude other disciplines. It is their proud boast that in no more than 10 percent of the cases it is
necessary to invoke the law; a goal not to be acclaimed.

The problems of child abuse and neglect are not the special responsibility or
preserve of any one profession or discipline. It is far more than the individual
problem of one child or one parent or one family; it is a matter of universal
concern. Equally obvious should be the fact that every incident of child abuse or
serious neglect involves basic legal rights and duties of the parents, of the child,
and of the community; and that a program for identification and alleviation of
such behavior must therefore be one under law. The family court must be more
involved, not only at the case level, but also in modifying and formulating
community and state policy.

## RIGHTS AND OBLIGATIONS

The role of the law, in the context of child abuse and neglect, must be considered and understood in the light of the basic concept of human rights.

### Parents

First, parental rights must be acknowledged. These are the right of a parent to rear his children, free of undue interference from the state; to have his children with him; to enjoy their love and companionship, a right to their services and even, in old age or disability, to their support. These rights need little exposition. They have been defined, stressed, and legally protected by English Common Law and by the law of this country for five hundred years.

### Children

Less well understood and often ignored, are the equally fundamental rights of children, rights which are not derived from, nor conferred by their parents, but accrue to them as free human beings, from constitutional guarantees. Because the child has little capacity to assert these rights—and because they are often obscured by overemphasis of those of the parent—the child is frequently treated as a nonperson or chattel. In too many instances the physician, noting physical abuse of a child, decides to ignore this invasion of the child's right to adequate care and protection. The social worker who, with the concurrence or even at the request of a parent, "voluntarily" places a child in an institution or other non-family setting, recognizes the parental prerogative of deciding on the care of the child but may completely overlook the child's right to a secure home. The protective service worker who allows abuse or neglect to continue in the optimistic expectation that the parent can be changed, may be respecting the right of the parent but may totally deny the child's right to protection. (For a more detailed discussion, see Chapter Sixteen.)

### The Community

Finally, the community has a vital stake in preserving and protecting the rights of children and of seeing that the obligations of both parent and child are fulfilled. Each child who goes into adulthood handicapped by a remediable mental or physical defect, uncorrected because of parental ignorance, indifference, or any other cause, may well prove a burden to society. Children deprived of education, socially maladjusted or otherwise handicapped, create and perpetuate the major social problems of poverty, alcoholism, drug abuse, criminal conduct, and frequently repeat the cycle of abuse and neglect of their own children.

## CHILD PROTECTION—A TEAM EFFORT

Child abuse and neglect is a legal as well as medical and social concern. Any effective program for dealing with this problem must be one under law; the court must be a full partner in such effort. This is not a matter of election or choice by the behavioral specialist, by the medical profession, by the police, by the court, by anyone else. It is so mandated by constitutional requirements and statutory definition.

Since community programs for combatting abuse and neglect require the efforts of a number of disciplines, these programs will be no better than their weakest component. The community, then, must be concerned not only with the quality of medical care, child protection, and supportive services to families, but with the legal assistance the child and family receive, with the availability of the court, and with its capacity to meet their needs.

The effectiveness of the court in dealing with abuse and neglect is often determined by the extent to which it is used. Court structure, manpower, and availability are usually based on the needs of the community as determined by use. The criminal and general civil divisions of the court, being in constant demand, receive high judicial priority. They are usually better staffed, with the most competent, best trained judges, who are given time to perform their duties and receive frequent ongoing judicial training and education. Branches of the law which are little used by the lawyers and the public, or which handle the less important legal issues (traffic offenses, petty crimes, small claims), often considered "judicial junk," are afforded a low priority. Sometimes included in this category are juvenile and family matters.

Because of these out of balance priorities, it seems perfectly acceptable, to the bench, the bar, and the public, for a judge in the civil division to spend a leisurely two weeks trying a run of the mill civil dispute between two litigants, but to demand that a judge in the domestic relations court dispose of 30 or 40 cases a day. It is established practice to extend an accused felon every possible judicial safeguard: a public defender, free transcripts, investigative services, unlimited use of the court's time in preliminary hearings, motions and trial to jury, appeals and post conviction remedies. To expect a judge in the juvenile division in this same period of time to hear and dispose of perhaps a hundred matters is common practice. The community cannot and must not accept this lopsided priority system.

The paradox of the juvenile justice system is that it is underused or improperly used because it is frequently unable to respond to the needs of the community. Yet it is less capable of responding because it *is* underused. This is especially true in the field of child abuse and neglect, where the social service and medical professions have made a fetish of keeping cases away from the juvenile court. It is not surprising, then, that this underuse of law has not only failed to develop strong courts that should be at the leading edge of child protection, but has actually created the illusion that such need is minimal.

## BUILDING A STRONG ABUSE AND
## NEGLECT PROGRAM

Every community needs certain basic components to deal effectively with child abuse and neglect. These include:

1. Laws that define the rights and responsibilities of the child, the parent and the community.
2. A visible, simple reporting system which encourages detection.
3. Prompt investigation coupled with constructive action.
4. A legal system readily accessible to parent and child alike.
5. Backup resources to provide care for children in protective custody (shelter facilities, foster homes, group homes, treatment centers); to offer therapeutic services to abusive or neglectful families (legal assistance, marriage and other counselling, psychiatric care, nurseries, day care centers, homemaking services, lay therapists, etc.)

While we are concerned here principally with trends in the family court, the court itself is not a separate, independent entity; it must be seen as part of the community's total approach to abuse and neglect. Hence, the laws that cover abuse and neglect, the reporting system, the investigation of reports and the resources available all relate to—and at least to some degree determine the efficiency of—the family court.

### Statutes

Of course the mere passage of a law does not insure its immediate acceptance and observance. Many new laws, or reenactment and updating of old ones, invite challenges to constitutionality, to interpretation, to application. This is certainly true in the area of child abuse and neglect. Although most states have had statutes that would have protected children had they been used, they have been little observed or applied. Except for extreme incidents which goad the courts into action, most communities have been content to leave the application of those laws to the medical and social service professionals. Strong emphasis on parental rights and the "sanctity of the home" concept have barred legal intrusion into child rearing practices. Until a decade or so ago, the major portion of child protective work was provided on a voluntary basis, only with consent of the parent, with little or no recognition of the child's legal right to protection.

### Reporting

Obviously, a community cannot deal with child abuse unless it is known. Hence reporting is fundamental to case finding. A reporting system is something more than a statutory requirement; it is more than a telephone number, a telephone receptionist. It is, rather, a community attitude, one that makes abuse and neglect a concern of everyone, yet rewards the reporter and family by a positive response, which both protects the child and helps the parents.

There are a few fundamentals to good reporting. Reports should be made to a nonthreatening source, usually the protective service unit of the public social service agency. Mandatory reporting to the police connotes criminal or punitive response rather than a civil and therapeutic one. It is not necessarily true, of course, that the police will so react, but it is an assumption made by many. Obviously, some abuse and neglect is serious enough to invoke the criminal law, but the social service agency should be trusted to pass on to the police those cases that appear to be criminal in nature. If early reporting is encouraged and prompt intervention occurs, few cases will reach criminal proportions.

Reports should be encouraged, not only from the professionals mandated to do so, but from any segment of the community. When a case of child abuse or serious neglect occurs in any community it is generally known to someone outside the family, be it a neighbor, a relative, or physician. That such persons do not report their observations is due to several factors: a reluctance to become involved; anxiety that the parent may be arrested or exposed to public censure; concern that the reporter's observations are faulty, yet may be the cause of the child's removal from the parent. Three of the more obvious sources of observations (and thus early identification and reporting) are relatives, friends, or neighbors; the schools; and the medical profession. Following are suggestions for encouraging reports from these sources.

**Relatives and Other Observers.** Relatives, friends, neighbors—even casual observers—are important sources of reporting abuse and neglect, but they require special encouragement. The reporter should not be required to identify himself if he does not wish to do so. A competent protective service worker investigating the report can generally identify "crank" or spite calls from those that are genuine. Assurance needs to be given that the reporter will remain anonymous, that the child will be protected, and, where possible, the parents helped.

**Schools.** Although school personnel are generally mandated to report suspected abuse or neglect, the requirement is widely disregarded. Teachers, administrators, even school social workers and nurses, are reluctant to identify abuse and neglect. There are seldom clear-cut channels for reporting and the extent of the school's involvement is uncertain. Yet few professions are more genuinely concerned about children. The schools' failure to report suspected cases is due in large part to lack of understanding of results to be expected.

A variety of methods can be developed to encourage school reporting. Each individual school can create a small committee or team to assess suspected abuse, thus diffusing responsibility. A report and request for investigation should be directed to the public welfare agency's protective service unit. If verified, the complaint can usually be handled in a professional and helpful manner.

When schools learn that referrals are handled promptly and therapeutically, they will soon be willing to share responsibility for dealing with these problems.

**The Medical Profession.** No group has done more to create public awareness of child abuse than the medical profession. Yet most of the leadership is coming from a small segment, usually physicians who staff the larger public and private hospitals. Despite statutory requirements for reporting abuse—often coupled with criminal sanctions for failure to do so—a substantial number of physicians and other medical personnel, both in private practice and even in public health work, do not identify child abuse as such, or simply do not report it.

This failure to report abuse arises from several factors. Probably the most common is an uncertainty as to what will happen to the parent and child, a basic distrust of the system. This is especially true where reports must be made to the police, a procedure that implies criminal action against the parent. Physicians are usually loath to involve patients in anything that will worsen their situation. A second cause is uncertainty as to whether the observed injury is actually abuse. Physicians with limited exposure to this phenomenon are reluctant to label many child injuries as "abuse." A third impediment to reporting is the physician's desire to avoid legal involvement, especially appearance in court.

These difficulties can be obviated by (1) allowing the physician to report to the protective service unit rather than to the police (an alternative to this is reporting to a physician-consultant to the protective service unit); (2) demonstrating to the medical profession that the response to a report is constructive and therapeutic, that the child receives protection and the parents are afforded help; (3) making it clear that the physician, in allowing abuse to go unreported, may invite further and more serious injury, resulting in permanent damage to the child, loss of parental rights, and possible criminal prosecution of the parents; and (4) that a failure to diagnose, treat, and report child abuse may well be a form of medical malpractice (sometimes not covered by traditional malpractice insurance) with resulting civil liability.

### Investigation

Reporting is of little value unless followed by prompt, competent assessment. Invitation to make reports, without adequate followup, is disillusioning and undermines respect for and confidence in the legal, medical, and social service systems. Investigation of reports and abuse requires two elements: (1) an understanding and reasonable agreement by the community agencies as to what constitutes abuse and neglect; and (2) sufficient trained protective service workers to make prompt, efficient, and objective inquiry.

**Definitions.** One of the most vexing problems is a proper description, both legal and practical, of what does constitute abuse and neglect. Until there is reasonable agreement among the various components, there will be a diversity of goals, which will render the community's efforts less effective. Does abuse have to be defined by the number or severity of bruises, contusions, fractures; their length, depth, or frequency? Does someone have to witness the act of abuse? Does a child have to be in imminent danger to justify legal intervention? How can abuse be proved; do the parents, or one of them, have to be identified as the abuser? Where does legitimate parental discipline stop and abuse begin? Should traditional or cultural factors in child rearing be considered?

And what is neglect: an untidy home? lazy or indigent parents? those who abuse alcohol or other drugs? who quarrel and separate and reconcile and reunite? whose children are poorly clothed, who are not washed or groomed to acceptable standards; who do not attend school regularly; who do not receive periodic medical and dental checkups?

The answer is both simple and complex. The more one tries to define abuse and neglect in precise terms, to describe the circumstances or conditions, the more confused and limited the definitions become. The alternative is a broad, generalized definition. The concept of child abuse and neglect is very much akin to the concept of negligence, a subject with which lawyers and judges have dealt for four hundred years. One dictionary defines negligence as failure to exercise the care that the circumstances justly demand.

This same simple concept is equally applicable to child abuse and nelgect; each is a failure to provide the child with the care the circumstances demand. It is broad enough to take in all forms of child maltreatment, whether willful or not; whether physical or emotional, whether acts of omission or commission, whether affecting the body or the spirit, or both. In this light, physical abuse and various forms of neglect (malnourishment, emotional trauma, and the like) appear as they are, a continuum of a child's mistreatment, ranging from the grossest, most obvious physical injury to subtle, intangible emotional deprivation. Thus every case of seeming abuse or neglect must be determined on its facts; the age and physical and mental condition of the child; the act or omission, or combination of both; the reasons therefor and whether an isolated occurrence or repetitive; and the impact on the child.

Because determining abuse or neglect is both a question of fact and of law, the court is an essential part of the child protective process. No medical professional nor behaviorial scientist should hesitate to expose his observations and conclusions to legal scrutiny. In most cases, if he is competent and has done his work well, the court will provide legal confirmation and will, additionally, provide him with the legal protection and the very considerable support often needed to deal effectively with such problems.

**Protective Services.** Every community, if it hopes to safeguard children, must have a protective service staff or unit, one of sufficient size to offer immediate service. Abuse and neglect is not a nine-to-five occurrence. Response to reports should not be a casual matter, to be worked into a social service department's routine. If children are really to be protected, if early intervention is the objective, a competent social worker must be available twenty-four hours a day, seven days a week. This means that some designated person be available for after-hours, emergency investigation and service to children.

The term "protective services" means different things to different people. In the context of child abuse and neglect it should encompass at least these minimum capabilities.

1. A general knowledge of elements of abuse and neglect; the signs to look for; the questions that should be asked; when to seek help in identification; the criteria for removing a child from parental care to place in protective custody.
2. Familiarity with and the ability to invoke the community resources available to aid in dealing with problems of abuse and neglect.
3. Sufficient training and experience to work without supervision and to make independent judgments.
4. An understanding of the rudiments of the rules of evidence so that observations may be used if legal intervention is needed.

Whether the protective services worker should be used only for investigation, identification, and early protection of the child or should also be an ongoing caseworker with the same family is a matter of agency policy. Generally, the investigative worker can do a more objective job if not required to work thereafter with that family; conversely, the ongoing worker can establish a better relationship with the client if not involved in the initial identification.

**The Police**. Often overlooked as a valuable resource in early evaluation of abuse and neglect cases is the local police officer. The police are frequent observers of family disruptions that produce child abuse and neglect: marital quarrels, drunkenness, or other drug abuse; evictions, desertion, nonsupport, and so on. Usually the police have no real remedy for such conduct. Settling family disputes is a thankless, frustrating experience. They welcome the chance to involve social services, to refer the problem to an agency equipped to deal with such matters. A close working relationship between police and social services is, therefore, important.

Those who believe the police are insensitive to the medical and social implications of abuse and neglect should be reminded that police officers generally act, and react, according to the expectations of the community. If they are viewed as aggressively punitive, they probably will be. If given credit for the empathy and concern most officers have for others, and their wish to be of maximum service to their community, with even limited training they can convert their observations of destructive family conduct into constructive action by teamwork with the protective service unit.

### Legal Aspects of Abuse and Neglect

If a report of abuse or neglect is verified, what is next? Who is responsible for protecting the child? Who should help the parents? What happens if the parents refuse help? When should a child be removed from the home? Who decides on such action? How is a child placed in protective custody—only with consent of the parents, or by mandate of law? If a child is in protective custody, how long should this continue? When should an abused or neglected child be returned to the parents; and who decides? When should a matter of abuse or neglect be referred to the court? Which cases should be handled informally; which should require official action? And who makes this decision?

These are the hard questions that daily confront the protective service worker and others in the child care field. If an actual or hypothetical case raising these issues were posed to a dozen professionals dealing with abuse and neglect, there would be many different answers. Each would be largely subjective, depending on that person's perception of his role, his or her own competence, and prior experiences. There would be few reliable, objective criteria with universal application that could be used alike by the physician, nurse, social worker, police officer, school teacher or administrator. Each, if acting alone, would be guided by his or her own perception of role and responsibility, of assessment of the needs of the child, of concept of the law and concern for parental rights. These views are usually based on personal experience of the effectiveness of various community resources. It is indeed unfortunate that the fate of many abused and neglected children depend upon such tenuous grounds.

The one universal common denominator for dealing with these questions is the law. If we remember that simple definition of abuse or neglect—the failure to provide that care which the circumstances justly demand—then every case of suspected or actual abuse or neglect becomes an issue of fact, the ultimate determination of which is for a court. But fact finding is not an end in itself; it is merely the doorway through which intervention on behalf of the child and into the lives of the parents may legally proceed. The truly important issue is what must be done to protect the child, to correct the abusive or neglectful conduct, and to prevent its recurrence—all within limits that respect the legal rights and responsibilities of the child and of the parents.

### A Social-Medical-Legal Issue

Every case, then, of abuse or neglect, if intervention is warranted at all, becomes a mixture of legal and social, or legal, social, and medical issues. That legal aspects of dealing with abuse and neglect are often minimized or totally ignored does not alter the fact that they exist. In nearly every case basic rights of child and parent are at issue. If this concept is correct, then a new dimension must be introduced into most child protective services: the intelligent, constructive use of law. The outmoded cliches that the law is used only as a last resort, only in matters of gross physical abuse, and only in 5 to 10 percent of the cases, have no modern validity. Rather, the law should be invoked in *every* case where the rights and responsibilities of the child, the parent, and the community are involved.

This positive use of law does not mean, of course, that every case must result in a court contest. It does not necessarily even mean the filing of formal pleadings or the taking of evidence. What is meant is that the protective services be so conducted that basic rights are observed and protected, that obligations are met. Occasionally this may be accomplished by the protective service worker without legal assistance; more often it cannot be.

## THE COURT AS A FULL PARTNER IN COMBATTING ABUSE AND NEGLECT

Parents who abuse or neglect children to the degree that requires intervention are seldom amenable to gentle persuasion. Their unreasonable expectations of children, preoccupations with self, marital discord, or other deep-seated problems are seldom solved by the mere offer of help and guidance. The firm mandate of a court is often required to gain their attention and to create an atmosphere in which the needed service will be accepted.

Where the social worker or physician can only cajole or seek to persuade, the court can demand. Where the child is in danger, the protective service worker is powerless to protect without the support of the law. When needed resources for the abused or neglected child or the parents are unavailable, these can be created only by mandate of law. When it becomes evident that parents cannot or will not meet the needs of a child, and it appears the child should have permanent parent substitutes, only the law can free the child for adoptive placement. The decisions that must be reached by physicians, social workers, or other professionals, when exposed to scrutiny of the legal process and reinforced by a judicial order or decree, are more readily implemented, have the built-in safeguards of shared decision making, and afford almost total protection against a claim of professional error or malpractice.

The thoughtful sorting out and balancing of rights and responsibilities afforded by the judicial process is far more likely to insure fair treatment to all than the unilateral decision of one professional. Hence, in almost every case, and at nearly every stage of identification and treatment of abuse and neglect, the intelligent use of the law will make the effort more effective. The ability to invoke the law constructively on behalf of abused and neglected children and their troubled parents is an essential ingredient of the protective service worker's training and a measure of competence.

To whatever degree the courts have failed, or have been unable to respond to the legal aspects of child abuse and neglect, the problem is remediable. There are basic components of an effective legal system that must be developed consciously and systematically. These components, their elements and methods of development, are discussed here. This development will not occur by ignoring or bypassing the court, but by using it and forcing it to improve. These are the components of an effective legal system.

### The Protective Services Attorney

Physicians and social workers are seldom well versed in the use of law. Giving legal advice, determining what are or are not legal issues, evaluating evidence, and the use of the court are all functions of a lawyer. Therefore, if a protective service agency is to use the law properly, it must have competent legal advice, not just occasionally but in virtually every case that comes to its attention. This in turn means a legal specialist who understands not only family law and how to use the courts, but one who also knows and respects the functions, the capabilities, and the limitations of the social worker and other behavioral scientists. In short, he or she must be the social service agency's lawyer, an advocate for the protective service worker, one who provides legal sanction for their efforts and whose priorities are theirs, not his.

A fundamental weakness of the legal aspects of most child protective systems is the lack of a competent legal advisor to those who deal with child abuse and neglect. In most instances such agencies and their staff must rely on an attorney furnished by the state or other political subdivision. This person is usually one who shares this duty with many others which may be more to his liking. He or she may have little knowledge or experience in the field of protective services. Insensitive to the needs of those he serves, performing a task not sought and accepted only as a means to a more desirable assignment, such a "pool" lawyer is seldom adequate for the important role of counseling the protective service worker.

Because most case workers are not knowledgeable in the gathering of legal evidence, the indifferent lawyer may reject those cases most in need of his attention, brushing them aside with such remarks as: "This won't stand up in court" or "The judge won't go for this kind of case." The "pool" lawyer, when a case is filed, often appears in court without having assessed the evidence, without interviewing witnesses, without having learned the facts of the case—sometimes even without a knowledge of the law. With inept preparation, and applying traditional adversary procedures, the merits of the case—the true problems of family disfunction—seldom come to light, resulting in a dismissal. It should be evident then that the intelligent, constructive use of law involves, not only an understanding of the legal process, and of when and how to invoke the law, but the ability to function in the legal system—to be able to get into court and to stay there.

No protective service agency can function efficiently without its *own* lawyer. Every agency budget should build in such a position. Competent legal service is just as important as the case worker, the casework supervisor, the business manager, the director or any other component of the system. This lawyer should be one selected by the agency, paid by the agency, responsible to the agency. As in any client-attorney relationship, the client should be able to direct the kind of service expected. While the attorney may advise for or against a certain course of action, the ultimate choice should be with the client, not the attorney. If the attorney is dissatisfied with such choice he may terminate the client-attorney relationship, but he should not be free to continue to represent the agency and reject its wishes; his priorities must be those of his client. If the agency is dissatisfied with the legal services it receives, it should be free, as is any client, to terminate the services of its attorney and hire another. These principles apply whether the agency lawyer is employed full time or works on an as-needed fee basis.

The social service attorney has a variety of duties in addition to actual court appearances. He or she should be readily available to protective service workers for consultation and advice, and for training in the gathering of legally competent evidence; should assess all cases for legal implications; and should determine which cases should be referred to court, and which cases might more properly be assessed by an interdisciplinary team. The attorney should have ready access to the court for the filing and prompt hearing of cases filed, for emergency orders, for protective custody or medical care, and for informal reference of cases. He or she should represent the agency in every court appearance, including routine reviews. As one responsible for the rights of both child and parents, this attorney should also review the agency's progress on all cases where custody has been removed for the parent to be certain that all possible progress is made toward reuniting the child and parent.

In those cases where parents show no inclination to regain custody of a child, the attorney should see that steps are taken to free the child for adoptive placement. He or she should be responsible for insuring, also, that children awaiting adoption receive attention for early placement. Finally, the attorney should insure that the acts and doings of the agency personnel are proper under law and, where necessary, are supported by court order or mandate. Any protective service agency which has legal counsel who performs these duties will have a more effective program. To whatever degree any of these functions are absent, the agency's efficiency will thereby be diminished.

### The Parents' Attorney

In all abuse or neglect proceedings, parents have a right to be represented by counsel. They should also have the right to forego this right if intelligently made. When parents are indigent, the court should appoint counsel, if requested. Appointment, whether requested or not, would seem mandatory in every proceeding where termination of parental rights is at issue.

### The Child's Attorney

Many states now require in abuse and neglect cases that the court appoint an attorney to represent the child. Even where not mandated, prudent judges make such appointments anyway. The attorney is usually called a "guardian ad litem" (attorney for the particular litigation in question as contrasted with guardianship of the child's person or property). The duties, or concept of responsibility, of such guardian may vary considerably from court to court and from one person to another. Traditionally, the guardian ad litem is not an advocate; his or her duties are largely perfunctory: to examine the pleadings and other material in the file and to ascertain that proceedings that affect the child are legally correct.

In a child abuse or neglect case, the child needs more than a technician to insure legal precision; he needs an advocate. It should therefore be the duty of the appointed attorney to see that the child is fully represented; that he is insured the right to a secure home, preferably with his parents if they can and will meet his needs; or with a surrogate family if his own fail or refuse to provide such care.

To a casual observer it may appear that an attorney who represents the parents will also represent the best interests of the child; that the parents and child have a community of interest. While this may be true generally, in abuse and neglect cases the opposite is usually the case. Neither is the attorney for the protective service agency necessarily the child's advocate. In fact, in most abuse and neglect cases, the rights of the child, the rights of the parents, and the rights of the community are all in conflict. Since the protective service agency represents the community, its attorney is primarily the attorney for the people. He or she cannot, therefore, represent either the child or the parent. The parents' attorney perceives his first duty as to them; to secure the dismissal of the petition, to regain custody of a child, to do that which the parents want him to do. Thus neither attorney may truly represent the child; if he receives adequate representation from either, it is merely incidental to the attorney's other duties.

Because of the traditional role of the guardian ad litem (that of a legal technician), an attorney appointed for the child in an abuse or neglect case may imply a similar role—that of a passive observer and advisor. This is not the case. This attorney is an advocate *for* the child; is the child's attorney in every sense. To this end, the term "guardian ad litem" probably should be eliminated and the word "attorney" substituted. A child's attorney in an abuse or neglect case has a special trust, a unique obligation. Where the child is an infant or of tender years, as is often the case, he can be of no help to his attorney in the preparation or presentation of his case. Thus the attorney has the additional burden not only of knowing the law, but of ascertaining facts—about the parents, about the child, from the protective service worker, from physicians, from relatives.

Few attorneys who offer to accept court appointments are prepared for, or paid for, their demanding role. Legislatures, the legal profession, court administrators, even most judges other than those in the family court do not understand the exacting duties of the child's attorney in such matters. It is highly important, therefore, that the judge set the standards for such service; that he make clear, in advance, what is expected of any attorney who accepts appointment to represent a child in an abuse or neglect matter. He or she must be fully familiar with the law relating to abuse and neglect, and to the numerous appellate court decisions on the subject. He or she must be prepared to make an extensive factual investigation as to the causes, nature, extent, and effect of any abuse or neglect suffered by the child. He or she must know the basic literature on the subject, as well as the social, medical, emotional, and psychological implications, in order to assess with any degree of certainty what will be in the child's future interest. And yet despite these demanding requirements, this attorney will receive a miserably inadequate fee. This must no longer be accepted.

Few lawyers, understanding the demands of such appointments, will volunteer to accept such service. Yet there are enough lawyers who, out of their concern for children and out of a sense of responsibility to their community, will provide the court with sufficient attorneys to meet this need. Any judge can locate such lawyers, by canvassing the family law section of the local bar association, by an appeal to the law schools, and to the larger law firms whose pro bono services provide high quality legal representation free or at modest costs.

## THE JUDICIAL PROCESS

### Criteria for Court Referral

What are the criteria for referring abuse and neglect cases to court? The first rule should be, "When in doubt, refer the case. Let the court help decide whether it is or is not an appropriate referral."

### Protective Custody Hearing

A referral to court should always be made if a child is taken into protective custody. When a child is removed from parental care, either as an emergency measure by a police officer (or other person authorized by statute), or by an ex parte court order (an order entered on application of the protective service agency and without a notice to the parent), the court should afford the parents a hearing to determine need for further custody. It should be held within a limited time, usually 48 to 72 hours. If not established by statute or court rule, this practice can be set up by agreement between the court and the protective service agency.

At such "detention" hearing, only enough information is needed to establish the reason for protective custody and, if the recommendation is for continued protection, the justification. A hearing of this nature is akin to the "probable cause" hearing in a criminal proceeding. Usually, hearsay evidence, in oral or written form, may be used. If insufficient information is available within the set time limit, the hearing can be continued for a reasonable time.

### Advisement Hearing

When a petition alleging child abuse or neglect is filed, the court sets a return date and issues notice or a summons to the parents to appear at that time. This initial proceeding, usually called an "advisement" hearing, is intended to acquaint the parents with the nature of the case, reasons for filing, their right to counsel and to possible appointed counsel and determines whether the statements of the petition are admitted or denied.

If the petition is denied, the matter is continued for a pretrial conference. If admitted, the court may enter a "consent decree," based on the admission, or may merely continue the petition to another date if the court believes that it is not necessary to take official jurisdiction. If the petition is admitted or if the statements are not disputed, the case is then continued for "disposition." Experience shows that about half the cases are disposed of at the advisement hearing, either by a consent decree or by agreement to continue the case with the cooperation and consent of the parents. If the petition is to be contested, the court should appoint a lawyer to represent the child.

### Pretrial Conference

At a pretrial conference, the social services attorney will be expected to have a pretrial statement prepared, stating what is to be proved and listing the witnesses who may be called, together with a resumé of the evidence each will offer. If there are written statements, reports, pictures, or other forms of exhibits that will be used at trial, these are identified and, to whatever extent possible, their admissibility agreed upon. The respondent parents will also disclose their witnesses and such defenses as they expect to assert.

At the pretrial conference, experience shows that about three-fourths of the seemingly contested matters are disposed of by some form of consent decree. The attorneys may "plea bargain" or negotiate as to grounds upon which the court takes jurisdiction. For example, the parents may admit to serious marital problems that adversely affect their children, but deny physical abuse. Such qualified admission is generally acceptable to everyone, since the object is to acquire jurisdiction, the precise grounds being immaterial.

Using this experience, out of every 100 petitions filed, half will be disposed of at the advisement hearing before a pretrial conference. Of the remaining 50, three-fourths, or about 35 will be settled at the pretrial conference. Of the remaining fifteen set for trial, five or more will be settled by agreement on or before the trial date. Thus, out of every 100 filings, probably no more than 10 percent will actually reach trial.

### Trial

Those few cases that actually reach the trial state are usually tried under the regular adversary process. It is this process that is so threatening to the social worker, physician, and parents. Actually, if represented by a competent attorney, and if the case is carefully prepared and the factual conditions warrant, the allegation of abuse or neglect can be readily proved. When poor results are obtained under the traditional adversary system, it is not so much the fault of the law, the rules of evidence, or the judge's rulings, but rather the poor preparation and incompetence of the attorney who presents the case.

## Dispositions

Although the court cannot proceed further until it has acquired jurisdiction, the truly important part of an abuse or neglect proceeding is the disposition. This dispositional hearing is usually scheduled three to four weeks after the child and parents are within the court's jurisdiction. At disposition, the agency charged with management of the case, usually the public social service agency, will be expected to present to the court and the parents a "case plan." This plan should include the following.

1. A concise statement of the abuse or neglect, its apparent duration, causes and effect on the child and family.
2. If the child is in protective custody, any plan contemplated for the child's return to the parents.
3. Conditions that the parents will be expected to meet. This should be as explicit as possible, stating the nature of the counseling, treatment or therapy the parent is to receive, by whom, how frequently, and for what period. Vague or imprecise statements such as "Is to seek psychiatric evaluation" and the like must be avoided. Arrangements for care, counseling, or other services should be made by the planner in advance.
4. A time schedule within which the plan will be expected to be fulfilled.
5. A schedule for periodic review by the court (one to three months intervals).
6. Where the child is out of the parents' custody, a plan for visitation.
7. Any other special conditions.

At the dispositional hearing, the case plan should be discussed fully with the parents. The court should consider any legitimate objections or request for modification. The parents' own routine, hours of work, available transportation, and similar matters, as well as the convenience and schedule of the case worker, all should be taken into account. Once the plan is agreed upon, the court should exact a commitment from the parents to support it and should make clear to them that their performance, and that of the agency offering services, will be reviewed periodically. If either the parent or the agency is dissatisfied with the program, or if a contingency arises, either may seek an earlier hearing.

## Review Hearings

At the periodic reviews, the court should assess progress and should modify the plan as needed. Parents who persistently do not keep appointments or otherwise fail to follow agreed-upon procedures should be cautioned that further refusal to abide by their commitments may result in termination of parental rights.

A verbatim record should be made of all proceedings, including review hearings. Such record makes clear the identified problems to be solved, the offer of services, the degree of cooperation from the parents, and what they have done to regain custody of children. In event parental rights must be severed, it provides the petitioner and the court with the supporting data by which such action may be justified. It precludes the usual contentions: "They never offered me any help" or "They never told me what they wanted me to do" or "I called and called and could never get an appointment."

### Bringing Case to Conclusion

While there are always notable exceptions, most abuse and neglect cases should be terminated within one year, either by the safe return of the child and a disengagement of the court and protective services, or by the termination of parental rights and permanent placement of the child. A court should never remove a child from parents and place in custody elsewhere without constant monitoring to insure that every reasonable effort is being made to return the child. This is a judicial obligation, which should never be delegated to a probation officer, a social worker, or any other person.

Because of the volume of cases, it is easy to allow a case to drift or remain unresolved unless a schedule is set and followed. Children in placement tend to get "lost." Marginally competent parents are often content to leave a child in placement indefinitely. They may enjoy periodic visits with the child without any of the personal or financial obligations of parenthood. The busy case worker tends to ignore those cases that do not demand attention. In this way a child is lost.

### RESOURCES

Any abuse-neglect program is only as effective as its components, one of which is the nature and extent of resources. Children cannot be protected and abusive parents cannot be helped by case work alone, or by medical treatment alone; other supportive services must also be available. These include crises nurseries, day care centers, individual and group foster homes, homemaker services, lay therapists, mental health and marriage counseling, and volunteer programs such as Parents Anonymous, to name a few. Few communities have the backup services needed, not only because funds are not available but because the money is spent for other things; and because child care and protection holds a low priority. The court has responsibility to help define community needs and obtain essential resources. This obligation includes identifying these needs and encouraging development, as well as the actual use of the law to mandate such services.

A great deal of "case" law—i.e., appellate court decisions—is currently appearing on the right to treatment. All over the country inadequate prisons, mental hospitals, nursing homes, and the like are being emptied by court edict because they do not meet minimum standards of humane care. New resources are being created in the same manner. One need only look at what the law has accomplished in extending suffrage, of protecting civil rights, of improved fair employment practices, to realize that these reforms originate with improved laws and their firm, constructive application by the courts.

While courts have the inherent power to mandate needed services, and generally have the respectful attention of the public, few judges use their very considerable authority and influence to gain these ends. It is, of course, easier to do nothing, to avoid this responsibility by saying "this isn't the court's job." In one sense this is perhaps true. Traditionally, courts are not expected to assume leadership roles. Rather, it is for the reformer, the civic activist, to identify needs and, when appropriate, to invoke the aid of the law to achieve their creation. But this must cease.

Regardless of how the law or the authority of the court is brought to bear on these issues—whether by the initiative of the judge or by the efforts of those who invoke the law and use the courts to achieve these ends—in every community which is meeting the human needs of its citizens, the court has usually been the leader or active participant in such effort.

## CONCLUSIONS

If the court of the future is to fill its true role of protecting abused and neglected children, it must be actively involved in community programs. The court of the future will probably continue to be, as it has been in the past, a reflection of community attitudes. If the law is to remain preoccupied with private civil disputes and prosecuting criminals, rather than improving the equality of community life, it will be no better in the years to come than it has been in the past.

If the court of the future is to be an active participant in community life, in improving the lot of children and families, it will have to be used far more extensively than previously. The medical and social service professionals must stop preempting to themselves the decisions which affect the legal rights of others. The phobic avoidance of the court must give way to its constructive use, for only by such use will the court structure itself to meet the needs of children and their families.

Finally, those who serve in the child abuse and neglect field must understand that the law cannot reconstruct itself to deal with them on their terms. If they are to invoke the aid of the court, they must do so in the same fashion as any other litigant, through a competent advocate who can translate their concerns into legal action.

## COMMENTARY ON JUDGE DELANEY'S CHAPTER

Donald N. Duquette

Judge Delaney's thoughtful article develops the philosophy and goals of a family court dealing with problems of child abuse and neglect in a way that probably most judges, lawyers, social workers, doctors who work within the current systems would agree with. A difficult problem, and one that remains to be answered throughout the country, is: how do we actualize that philosophy and realize those goals? The judge's comments stimulate some questions and observations about the interrelationship among the court and other elements of the child protection family treatment network. If we can scrutinize and describe those relationships, perhaps we will be a step closer to realizing the goals of the family court as Judge Delaney describes them.

Actually, its philosophy, goals, and ideals are part and parcel of a broad family treatment network that goes beyond the courthouse and includes protective service agencies, counselling centers, hospitals, parent aid programs, Parents Anonymous, schools, foster care agencies, foster homes, and the like. The court and legal process is an essential part of the protection and treatment network, just as social workers and mental health counselors are. But the court is just *one* part of the team of resources that constitute our society's response to child abuse and neglect. The question then becomes: What ought to be the role of the court in this child protection and family treatment network, and how should the court interface with the others, i.e., those working with the social agencies? Judge Delaney writes: "In the area of family law the court's true role is to define and protect the rights—and enforce the responsibilities—of the parent, of the child, and of the community."

A most fundamental and unique responsibility of the legal system is to act as a buffer between the individual and intrusions by the state. In the child abuse and neglect context, certain representatives of society as a whole such as social workers, physicians, police, etc., are attempting to intervene in and intrude upon strongly held and constitutionally protected rights of personal freedom and family privacy, without the willingness and voluntary consent of those persons affected. Legal process then is required when protection is needed for a child or treatment is needed to stabilize a dysfunctional family and the persons affected refuse to agree to protective measures or treatment programs on a voluntary basis. The coercive power of the state may need to be employed in such a case, but individual liberties of family members must be protected at every juncture.

Where competent adult persons freely consent to intervention of whatever kind, legal process, of course, is unnecessary. But when persons object to intervention, or when the "cooperation" of the families may be coerced and involuntarily given, the court's role is clear. It must act as protector of parents' liberty on one hand, and as protector of the child's interests and well-being on the other. After hearing the facts and balancing the competing interests, it is the court that decides whether coercive state intervention ought to be allowed. Once the question of human rights under law is resolved, the court's legal role should recede into the background. The court should remain involved only to monitor the progress of the treatment plan decided upon; and either dismiss the case, or terminate parental rights after a reasonable period of time and therapeutic effort has been spent.

Does the law as arbiter of human rights have a therapeutic role to play in abuse and neglect cases? Judge Delaney thinks so, and he advocates more frequent use of the court system. To many of us, the notion of the court as a positive force, as a therapeutic agent in family change, is foreign and hard to accept. We are too familiar with examples of the court system itself acting in a counterproductive and often destructive fashion. Despite court philosophies and enlightened judicial guidance, in the adversarial system suspicion supplants trust, tactics and strategy replace openness, competition supplants cooperativeness. The trauma of a court contest is exacerbated by the exceeding slow grinding of the wheels of justice. Court intervention may cause as much trauma and destruction as the initial family dysfunction that the child protection/family treatment network set out to alleviate.

In certain cases, it will be impossible to avoid or mute the trauma of the full court process. In many other cases, however, improved procedures and a greater understanding and cooperation between the legal and social/psychological elements of the child protection/family treatment network can accommodate both the ends of justice in protecting human rights and the ends of family rehabilitation and child protection. Judge Delaney provides good suggestions for achieving that goal. It is a formidable challenge for all of us concerned with abused and neglected children and their families.

Do the legal aspects of the child protection/family treatment network begin and end with filing a petition and formal adjudication? Clearly, they do not. Judge Delaney writes: "What is implied (by the positive use of law) is that the protective services be so conducted that basic rights are observed and protected, that obligations are met." Protective service workers and supervisors should recognize that their clients often attribute considerably more power and authority to them than they may actually possess; that the threat of court action is present in every protective service case, whether expressed or implied; and that clients may accede to protective services' demands or suggestions out of fear of protective services authority or fear of a court petition that may result in harsh consequences to them, such as loss of their children.

Add to these considerations the fact that protective service clients are often poor and powerless, and the risk of arbitrary social work action, of agency coercion, and of overreaching in violation of personal liberty and integrity looms large. How are the parents' and child's freedoms to be protected in this area, hidden as it is from the scrutiny of the public and of the courts? Shall procedural safeguards be established within the administrative structure of protective services to protect the privacy and personal liberties of clients? Or shall we rely on individual protective services workers to be respectful of personal liberties and clearly advise clients of their legal rights whenever coercion and involuntariness may exist?

The risk of agency overreaching and infringement of personal liberties clearly exists at the early intervention stage of the child protection/family treatment network. Because of that risk to personal liberty, some rule of law or some legal procedure may be required to protect personal rights and safeguard the constitutionally protected, fundamental right of family privacy. That rule of law or procedure need not be cumbersome or time consuming. Perhaps improvement of the juvenile (family) court system and its increased use by the child protection team, as Judge Delaney suggests, will accomplish these goals. Perhaps administrative procedures could be devised to smoothly, yet effectively, safeguard the personal integrity of potential clients. That some steps need be taken in this regard is clear. In Judge Delaney's words, the law must be sure that "basic rights are preserved and protected; that obligations are met."

✻ Part VI

# Early Recognition and Prevention of Potential Problems in Family Interaction

※ **Introduction**

The key to the problem of child abuse is early prediction and prevention. We are beginning the long and arduous task of answering the question: "Can the problem be identified early and prevention undertaken before child abuse and neglect occurs?" Several studies are currently being conducted in this country with financial support from the Office of Child Development, Department of Health, Education, and Welfare. These will begin to provide us with the answer to this question.

Chapter Eighteen reviews the basic issues about prediction. Any discussion of this topic without acknowledgement of the ethical issues, which are of significant importance to all of us working in this field, would be incomplete. The accessibility of women to helping professionals during the pregnancy and delivery period makes this an opportune time to try and identify those who may need help the most. Chapter Nineteen summarizes research studies which are based primarily on studies made during the perinatal period.

The final chapter brings the reader up to date on an eight-year endeavor to develop a reliable and valid prediction questionnaire. This instrument is being developed as a means to identify families who have the potential for problems with parent-child interaction. This is not an attempt to find preabusive parents only. Rather, the details of this chapter are presented to move us closer to the serious research that this field demands if progress in prediction and prevention is to occur.

C. Henry Kempe
Ray E. Helfer

✳ Chapter Eighteen

# Basic Issues
# Concerning Prediction

Ray E. Helfer

Unusual child rearing practices are manifested in a variety of ways. While the overt physical abuse (the battered child) and/or serious neglect to a child generate a good deal of public attention, there are thousands of children with behavior disorders, learning problems, hyperactivity, withdrawal, and the like, who are products of bizarre rearing patterns. All too often people assume that when the concept of early identification and prevention is mentioned, only those parents who may someday beat or seriously neglect one or more of their children are being identified. This is *not* the case. While these two manifestations of unusual child rearing practices are no doubt among the more severe outcomes of this problem, the scores of other manifestations, even though physically less harmful, are more common and may well be equally as devastating to the child and his or her family.

For a variety of reasons the ability to separate out a distinct group of parents (or future parents) who will *physically* abuse or serious neglect one or more of their children will probably never be possible.[a] What is available, however, is the ability to identify "at risk" parents or future parents who themselves had unfortunate childhood experiences that could manifest as unusual child rearing as they become parents. These rearing practices have every likelihood of producing children who eventually will present to helping professionals with a variety of

[a]At this stage of our understanding it would appear that to separate out potentially abusive or neglectful parents from those who fall into the more general high risk category will be most difficult. What is being determined by available screening methods is a parent or parents who may have a potential problem with parent-child interaction. How this problem eventually manifests itself depends upon a variety of circumstances, such as availability of a supporting spouse, financial stability, presence of an extended family, educational experiences, friendly neighbors, an easy-to-care-for child, and so forth.

Printed, in part, in the spring 1976 issue of *Pediatric Annals,* and reproduced here with their permission. Copyright, 1976 Insight Publishing Co., Inc.

problems, from behavior disorder or overt physical abuse to learning problems or delinquent adolescent behavior. Early identification programs seek to screen for those parents who are more likely to have problems with parent-child interaction than the general population. The prevention counterpart of these screening programs attempts to intervene with educational and training experiences, thereby modifying or eliminating the basic causes of unusual rearing practices that produce children with a variety of difficulties.

Putting the degree of this problem in perspective may be helpful. In 1974, Michigan recorded approximately 2,000 cases of suspected physical abuse. These resulted in formal reports made because of the child abuse reporting law. During the same time, Michigan recorded approximately 20,000 cases of suspected child neglect. Considering there are approximately two million children in that state, in one year, 1 percent of Michigan's children were suspected and reported to have been abused or neglected. If we add to this the number of cases that were not reported, as well as the siblings of those who were reported, this problem is truly one of epidemic proportions. Another example comes from Florida. In the year prior to October 1971, Florida reported less than 100 cases of suspected child abuse and neglect. In the fall of 1971, the Florida State Department of Social Services undertook a statewide public awareness campaign and provided the public with a toll-free number to call in cases of suspected child abuse and neglect. By February 1975 the state had received over 86,000 reports.

## A COMPARISON

Drawing an analogy with a "serious disease model" makes the history of child abuse and neglect a bit easier to understand. During the early and mid 1950s, children with cystic fibrosis presented to physicians with the most severe, morbid state of this disease. Growth was slow, lungs were infected, nutrition was poor, and death was imminent. As experience was gained and research progressed, this disease became better understood, and treatment became available to modify the problem and help these children. Early diagnostic methods were developed and the problem began to be recognized at a point when much of the irreversible pathology could be prevented. Methods are now being studied for intrauterine diagnosis, which offers still another approach for control of this disease. Not only have the last twenty years provided a better understanding of the early recognition, treatment, and possibly prevention of cystic fibrosis, but these years have permitted understanding and knowledge in more basic areas such as pulmonary physiology, pharmacology, microbiology, and genetics. Thus an in-depth study of a disease that originally presented in a severe, fatal form some twenty years ago has led not only to the improvement of the outlook but also to a better understanding of a whole host of other related problems.

Similar stories could be told for other disease entities—e.g., polio, cholera, diphtheria, and measles. The sequence of events is almost always the same.

Step 1. Presentation of the most serious form of a given disease.
Step 2. Nonspecific and supportive treatment programs are developed.
Step 3. Concurrent study and research into its causes takes place.
Step 4. Initiation of more *specific* treatment programs begin.
Step 5. Expansion of the concepts of this problem to related areas.
Step 6. Study and research in early identification and prevention.
Step 7. Initiation of screening and preventative programs.

This natural history is very similar in the area of child abuse and neglect. Step 1 occurred in the late 1950s and early 1960s with the recognition of the "battered child."[b] Step 2 began with the onset of intervention of child protection programs. Concurrently, intensive studies (step 3) developed to explain this problem, which had been with us for many years but for a variety of reasons had gone unrecognized.[1] Once a better understanding of the causes became known, then step 4, more specific treatment programs, could be initiated.[2] This natural history of child abuse and neglect seems to be somewhat bogged down at step 4. The implementation of what is known to be effective to help families who are abusive or neglectful requires the cooperation of a variety of professionals and disciplines. These individuals heretofore have had little contact with one another, resulting in poor understanding and communication and a general lack of trust that precluded easy and rapid development of cooperative, therapeutic endeavors (see Chapter Thirteen). While some communities are struggling with step 4 (and still others are stuck at step 2), steps 5 and 6 are taking place in a few areas of the country. In the minds of some, child abuse and neglect is no longer an entity unto itself, but is rather a severe manifestation of unusual child rearing practices that appears to be sweeping through the country in epidemic proportions.

Expansion of the concepts of child abuse and neglect (step 5) to include more of the "unusual child rearing iceberg," rather than just the tip which protrudes above the water, requires a deeper understanding of the effect of these unusual rearing practices on the child and his or her family. When one realizes that many children who should be experiencing the phenomenon of normal growth and development are subjected to less than acceptable rearing methods, it becomes apparent that an in-depth understanding of the phenomenon of early child development is necessary in order to fully comprehend the effects of these bizarre rearing practices on the developing child (see Chapter Three). Once this has been achieved, then step 7, the initiation of screening and preventative programs, can begin.

[b]In early 1960, Dr. C. Henry Kempe coined the term "the battered child" for the specific purpose of gaining the attention of the lethargic and complacent medical profession. It was first used as a title for a talk before the annual meeting of the American Academy of Pediatrics. This term has been effective and has served its purpose well.

## THE CONCEPT OF SCREENING

Frankenburg[3] has clarified the concepts of screening and established basic guidelines for those wishing to move into this field. These guidelines are appropriate whether or not one is screening for lead poisoning, sickle cell disease, or unusual child rearing practices. He identifies several areas of importance and provides us with some key definitions. He gives great emphasis to the need to assure that any screening method has both sensitivity and specificity. *Sensitivity* is the degree of accuracy of a screening test in correctly identifying high risk subjects. *Specificity* is the degree of accuracy of a screening test in correctly identifying low risk subjects. The guidelines set forth by Frankenburg must be strictly adhered to if a screening program is to be useful to any group in which there exists a potentially serious problem.

There must be certain further considerations. Is it ethical to delve into family and personal life to determine how parents or future parents are going to interact with their children? Do we have this right? Should the rights of some parents to remain uninvolved be paramount over the right of a child to be reared in a positive environment? Few question our "right" and responsibility to screen a pregnant woman for tuberculosis, high blood pressure or syphilis, but how about screening her for child rearing potential?

Leon Eisenberg has raised a fundamental question: Will the identification of potential behavioral problems result in the creation of that very same or similar problem? Is this, if you will, a type of self-fulfilling prophecy? "The behavior of man is not independent of the theories of human behavior that men adopt."[4]

These are difficult, but not unanswerable, problems. If one tries to establish an unusual child rearing screening program in a local hospital, these issues will be quick to surface, some with almost tidal wave velocity and emotionality. But considering the epidemic proportions of child abuse and neglect and the devastating effects that unusual rearing practices are having on our children and our society, some type of involvement must occur. Some will say everyone needs to learn parenting skills, no question about that. Certain parents, however, need skills to a greater degree, and sooner, than others. This group must be found early and helped with persistant positive pursuit.

Regardless of how we feel about the ethical issue, one critically important fact remains. The great majority of parents, irrespective of how they were reared, want to bring up their children in a manner that will have very positive results. The motivations are there; ways must be found to tap them. Our attempts to develop screening programs have been met with cautious concern. The process of getting such a program under way requires slow, deliberate plodding by quiet, tactful, pleasant plodders. Doors to administrative and medical staffs must be open so these plodders can come in and tread softly, always emphasizing the positive, helpful aspects of the program. Once the plodders are accepted, the program is under way.

Those who participate in a program of this type must not only be fully informed but also assured of confidentiality. The approach taken in our studies does both. Those who are screened receive a signed copy of the "Guarantee of Confidentiality and Informed Consent" form (Table 18–1), and we in turn keep their signed copy in our locked files. A mutual agreement is thereby developed. While this is not to be considered appropriate for all research in this area, it serves as a sample of an informed consent protocol that is mandatory in these kinds of research studies.

**Table 18–1.** Guarantee of Confidentiality and Informed Consent for Survey on Bringing Up Children

---

The past few years have seen considerable interest develop in how people are brought up and how they, in turn, bring up their children. This survey was developed to help answer some of the questions that have been raised in considering the variations in bringing up children.

Dr. Ray Helfer guarantees all responses will be confidential and your name and address will not be used except to contact you. Only a number will appear on the answer and *not* your name.

Ray E. Helfer, M.D.

I understand the above points and agree to voluntarily participate in this survey.

Witness _____     Signed _____

                                        Address _____
                                                        Street

                                        _____
                                        Town          State          Zip

                                        Phone _____

                                        Date _____

---

Survey developed and conducted by Ray E. Helfer, M.D., Michigan State University, College of Human Medicine; and Carol Schneider, Ph.D., University of Colorado.

## WHERE CAN HIGH RISK PARENTS (OR FUTURE PARENTS) BE FOUND?

The reader should keep in mind that the term "high risk" refers to parents who are likely to have some type of difficulty with parent-child interaction resulting in unusual child rearing practices. There is both direct and indirect evidence that parents who are "at risk" make up a fairly large percent of the population (Chapter Nineteen). Although parents who are likely to have problems in bringing up their children can be found literally everywhere, the implementation of an inexpensive, efficient screening program necessitates the identification of at least one or more places where these potentially high risk parents or future parents might be found in large numbers.

There are three times in the life of parents or future parents, when they are readily accessible for a mass screening and/or mass intervention program: first, during the future parents' school years, particularly at the junior and senior high school years; second, at the time when the pregnant woman comes in for pre-natal care or delivery at a hospital; and third, when parents bring their child to the school system at age five or six to begin the mandatory educational program. In regard to this last group, i.e., the family with 5–6-year-old children, the concept of developing an early recognition and prevention program for unusual rearing practices precludes the use of families whose children have already reached the age of five or six years. In other further discussions we will eliminate this source as a possible group for mass screening. While it is important to identify results of unusual rearing practices for "after-the-fact" family-directed services, this population is not suitable as a screening population.[c]

Children who are in elementary school and high school present an additional challenge because of their ready accessibility. The use of the school system to introduce parenting skills and child development content material is intriguing. While this idea is not unique, it clearly is a concept that has not yet gained the wide support it needs. Rather than develop a screening program for this age group, *all* children should be taught these skills, not just a select few. The precedents are there: driver education, for example, is clearly established in the curricula of a large number of educational programs.

Those who *are* most available to be screened are pregnant women coming for prenatal care to offices and clinics and subsequently to the hospital for delivery of their baby. This would seem to be the most accessible group for early screening. When parents are identified to be in the high risk category, they must be *offered* an intervention program to assist the mother, her baby, and mate with a learning experience to improve upon their child rearing capabilities.

An important ethical question must be raised at this point. Should we limit a screening program to just that group of pregnant women who are *most* accessible—i.e., those using the public hospitals and clinics? Categorically no! We have no good evidence that women who use private practitioners and hospitals have fewer problems with child rearing than those who are less well off finan-cially and use public facilities. Care must be taken to assess *all* populations in a screening program, even those hard to reach, before conclusions are drawn as to the likelihood that any given group should or should not be screened.

---

[c]By the time the child has reached the age of five and is ready for formal schooling, a good deal of child rearing has already taken place. It would seem likely that utilizing this period of time to screen out high risk families is much beyond the time when truly preventive programs could be helpful. This does not mean that families with rearing problems with their 5-year-old children should not be helped. These would be after-the-fact services rather than preventive services.

## HOW CAN THESE PARENTS OR FUTURE PARENTS BE IDENTIFIED?

While the understanding of the basic underlying causes of unusual rearing practices is being clarified,[5] the development of reliable and valid screening methods are still in an early stage. Research is progressing, and the preliminary results are encouraging. Eight years ago, attempts were begun to develop a child rearing questionnaire to assist in the screening and early identification of parents who may have problems interacting with their children. This questionnaire has now been revised. This 50-item instrument is currently being tested in field study to assess its reliability and validity as one method of screening (see Chapter Twenty).

Other screening assessment methods are also being studied. Detailed observations of mothers and babies in the delivery room are demonstrating behaviors that appear to correlate positively with potential problems in mother-child interaction (see Chapter Nineteen). Observations shortly after delivery of the mother and baby during an early feeding experience (Chapter Two), and the interaction of the father and the newborn baby during the first few days of life are providing key information that appears to correlate positively with high and low risk parenting skills.[6]

Other methods of identifying parents with potential child rearing problems have been adopted throughout the years even though they are less well documented. For example, teenage, addicted, and/or incarcerated parents are seen as being high risk by many groups (and some state laws). Subjective reactions of nurses, doctors, and others in delivery rooms, hospitals, and clinics all tend to identify parents with potential parenting problems. The interest and concern in each of these areas will be helpful to both the child and his or her parents, and hopefully our attempts to single out a high risk group will result in a positive intervention experience for the family. The goal must be to improve family life and child rearing practices prior to the development of serious, often irreversible problems for both the child and family.

### WHAT CAN BE DONE TO HELP?

Any discussion of preventive services will necessarily have to be speculative, since only minimal experience is available. It is encouraging to note, however, that not only has this preventive approach been effective in other fields and disciplines, but the experience with after-the-fact services in helping abusive and neglectful parents is now extensive and the results have been most encouraging.

One major obstacle in establishing preventative programs is that the service system that is charged with after-the-fact services for child abuse and neglect (departments of social services) has little precedent for early intervention. Unlike fire prevention, driver education, and public health programs, social services are usually mandated to wait for something to happen before services can be offered. This plus their tradition of servicing only poor people makes it unfair to expect departments of social services around the country to be leaders in the screening and prevention of child abuse and neglect. They do not have the staff, the experience, nor the funding to proceed in this area.

From the theoretical point of view, what programs should be expected to work? The basic therapeutic approaches that are effective in the after-the-fact treatment of child abuse and neglect are at least a place to start. Only experience and evaluation will determine what modifications will be required and the expansions that will be necessary. The basic approaches include the following.

1. A family planning program.
2. A skills and content learning experience in parenting and early child development.
3. A vigorous approach to teach trust of others, to improve one's self-image and the skills of developing friendships.
4. A joint therapeutic approach to help the parents better understand, accept, and support one another.
5. An extensive program to provide the children with age-related early childhood experiences both in the home and community.
6. Teaching methods of problem solving, crisis prevention, and resolution.

Since departments of social services around the country cannot be expected to provide this preventive approach, where then can we turn? These tasks must be picked up by others. Several options exist; some or all should be available in every community.

1. The school system must be convinced, pressured, or even coerced to initiate parenting and early child development courses and skill learning experiences for every elementary, junior, and senior high school student. If preschool programs (nursery school and day care) were associated in some way with the public school system, then a natural laboratory experience would be readily available for these students. This plus classroom work should be readily available for these students, thereby making a significant advance in the present dearth of educational experiences in parenting in the public school system.

2. The same public school system must add parenting and early child development programs to its *adult education* program. If we can justify basket weaving, speed reading, and cabinet making in adult education, surely we can justify child rearing courses and experiences.

3. Hospitals must expand their prenatal education program beyond the handicraft skills that are now being taught to include parenting skills. These

courses must also extend *beyond* delivery for several months, in order to provide a continuing experience for the new parents.

4. Likewise, hospitals must not only allow, but encourage, fathers in the delivery room, as well as permitting and encouraging both parents to have early *physical* contact with their baby within a few minutes after delivery. This contact should continue throughout the hospitalization with frequent supervised mother-father-baby interactions in the hospital room, and, if the baby cannot leave the nursery for some reason, the parents must be allowed to participate in the child's care in the nursery or intensive care unit.

5. Hospitals must make available mother-baby helpers to work with every mother and newborn to help them establish a positive bonding or attachment while the mother and baby are hospitalized. These helpers could be either volunteers or hired personnel. Regardless of how it is resolved, a program to augment mother-baby bonding cannot be left to the chance that the busy nursing personnel will have the time to spend with the mother and her baby. A specific person needs to be delegated this task for each family.

6. Home visiting and calls to the home should occur at frequent intervals after the discharge of the mother and baby. This could be done by specially trained volunteers.

7. We must expand mental health services, group practices in pediatrics or family practice, private social service agencies, and schools to provide courses in child rearing.

8. A network of home extension services (the old Ag Extension Program) has moved into nutrition. There is no reason why child rearing and parenting skills cannot be appended to this group of capable and existing workers.

The reader will be able to add many other options available within his or her own community. The cost of implementing any of these programs would be minimal compared to the yield—particularly if the group provided these services has been identified through the screening programs as those most in need.

An ethical question is raised when one considers if these instructional programs are to be voluntary or mandatory. Little can be gained by "forcing" someone to learn something. If the screening assessment clearly indicates that a high risk situation is present, then a variety of efforts must be made to work with the parents to help them better understand the need to improve their parenting skills.

Finally, who might be helped by these programs? Clearly all parents and their children. Some will need more help than others—i.e., those who fall into the high risk group of parents identified in the screening programs. These may be the most resistant, reluctant, and frightened group. Reaching them will be difficult but not impossible with *persistant, positive pursuit.*

## COMMENTARY TO CHAPTER EIGHTEEN

Because of the many ethical questions that arise in any program for early identification and prevention of unusual child rearing practices, the author asked the group on medical ethics at Michigan State University to comment on this paper. Their critique is included below. The issues that are raised must be given every consideration as we move forward in our endeavors to help these children and their families—R.E.H.

## ETHICAL ISSUES IN EARLY IDENTIFICATION AND PREVENTION OF UNUSUAL CHILD REARING PRACTICES

### Howard Brody and Betty Gaiss

Since child abuse causes a staggering amount of injury and death each year, while less severe forms of abnormal parent-child interactions add to the toll of human misery, the beneficial results that would be gained from an effective detection and prevention program are clear. On the other hand, a screening and intervention program such as that urged by Dr. Helfer raises a number of significant ethical issues. Two questions are basic: first, do these ethical issues pose an insurmountable obstacle to such a program; second, if not, how can the ethical problems encountered be minimized? In this brief discussion, only the major issues will be listed; a few of these will be discussed.

Attention should be given to the problems associated with the term "unusual rearing practices." Parents who intentionally use bilingual conversation in the home so that the child will learn a foreign language at an early age are "unusual," but this child rearing practice may in no way be pathological. We will assume that a definition of "unusual" can be given to suit Helfer's intent.

Helfer's advocacy of a screening-intervention program depends on two assumptions: first, that a high degree of correlation between observational methods and/or testing instruments and the actual characteristics that determine a parent to be high risk can be developed through research; and second, that it is possible to design and implement a parenting skills training program that allows parents to identify their own values and to raise their children according to these values. If prediction methods are not valid and reliable, and training programs are not flexible and individually developed, the ethical problems increase tremendously. In order to get to what we see as other major issues, we will assume Helfer to be correct in his optimism on these two points.

The remaining ethical issues can then be outlined as follows.

1. A balance must be achieved among the rights of all parties involved, including the child, the parents, and society at large.
2. Major distinctions must be observed between after-the-fact and before-the-fact intervention, as well as between those services to a patient who comes to a health worker as compared to mass, public distribution of services. What is appropriate in one case may not be appropriate in the other.
3. Both parts of the program—i.e., the screening for and the training of high risk parents—must be designated either as mandatory ("routine") or as voluntary, and the inherent problems with each taken into consideration.
4. For any voluntary part of the program, a proper mode of consent and guarantees, including disclosure of all necessary information about the nature of the program, must be designed.
5. Elements of the program that might have a coercive influence on parents must be identified and minimized.
6. Since a few parents inevitably will be mistakenly labeled as high risk through *many* false positive test results, the emotional impact of such labeling must be minimized.

A number of models seem to suggest the validity of screening for abnormal parent-child interaction tendencies. Whether these programs are voluntary or mandatory is another issue. The analogy with community genetic screening programs is appropriate. Many have recommended that such programs be voluntary wherever possible.[A1] On the other hand, many states mandate routine screening of newborns for PKU. Serious criticism has developed in the case of XYY chromosome screening, where routine testing of newborns was done to detect a trait thought to be related to later abnormal behavior.[A2] In some screening programs, including the one under discussion, those who are most at risk may be the last to admit the need for assistance. In these situations, a voluntary screening program might have a low yield.

An analogy that seems to favor a mandatory screening program is the routine testing of all patients admitted to hospitals for venereal disease. While individual patients might refuse if consent were required, it is generally assumed that the public health benefits outweigh the minor loss of personal rights. Even granting this, it may not be applicable to the child rearing case. First, while high risk traits in the parents will affect another party (the child), such traits are not comparable to communicable diseases in posing a direct threat to the public welfare. Second, the option of carrying out tests on a routine basis without individual consent is not an inherent right of the medical profession, but is a privilege that may be exercised only so long as society raises no objection.

If a patient goes to a doctor for a backache, the doctor detects high blood pressure and begins treating the patient for this condition, the doctor is praised for practicing good preventive medicine. Most of us, given the choice as patients, would prefer this comprehensive approach rather than one that simply treated the backache and looked no further. The reaction of most people may be different if the doctor proposed to test for, and treat, not something that is universally recognized as a disease, but rather something that has been considered outside the area of medical involvement. Society jealously guards how one chooses to bring up one's children as part of one's personal life. The ethical problem is compounded if the doctor, not content to test patients who voluntarily come to his office, goes out into the streets to test the public at large.[A3] At issue is whether the doctor is treating disease or is imposing "treatment" that is regarded as a violation of personal freedoms.

Still, a mandatory screening-intervention program would be justified if concern over the rights of parents is overridden by the need to protect the more essential rights of the child. Certainly one such right is the right to be free from physical harm; once such harm is documented by abuse or neglect, a court will take custody of the child away from the parents. If a test could be developed that could accurately predict abuse or neglect specifically, instead of the entire spectrum of "unusual child rearing practices," preventive intervention to protect the child would be justified on similar grounds; but Helfer explains the apparent impossibility of developing such a test.

Can one reasonably suppose that there is a similar right of the child to be free from psychological harm that would in turn justify a mandatory screening program for "unusual child rearing practices" across the board? Certain deleterious psychological environments can be as destructive to the individual as some types of physical abuse. The problem of deciding what is to be classified as "psychological harm" is very difficult. There are actually two problems here. "Experts" may be able to formulate clear and easily applicable criteria for such "harm," but the public at large might refuse to accept these criteria. On the other hand, there might be criteria that meet with wide popular acceptance, but that, upon careful analysis, turn out to have no rational basis. Where either or both of these sources of disagreement are present, trying to justify a mandatory screening program on the basis of a posited "right to be free from psychological harm" raises more ethical issues than it solves. To take what might seem an extreme example, some might insist that television news be censored to eliminate any content that might be "psychologically harmful" to children.

For these reasons, one might come to the same conclusion about mandatory screening for "unusual child rearing practices" as others have come to with regard to genetic screening—that the increased yield of positive test results is not worth the infringement on individual liberties, and as a consequence the erosion of public trust in the health professionals involved. This suggests that every attempt (such as community education programs) that can be used to increase the yield of a voluntary program ought to be considered before a mandatory program is implemented. Similar concerns would move one to opt for a voluntary intervention component of the program. Intervention consists of training in parenting skills. An additional concern is that parents will find it hard to develop optimal learning motivation if they are pressured to attend the classes.

For any program to have the appropriate personal safeguards, informed consent ought to be obtained from participants; Helfer's consent form, which is intended for research purposes, is inadequate for a fully implemented program. Adequate disclosure of information should include the aims of the program and the fact that if parents show high risk scores on screening, there will be followup contact to encourage them to accept the training program. Parents should also be informed of the possibility of false positive or false negative test results where these risks are known. The psychological harm to those parents who are incorrectly labeled as high risk due to testing error is a major negative factor that may never be completely eliminated. This can be minimized to a degree by keeping the screening and training programs as free from moralistic overtones as possible, and by stressing in the community education programs the fact that high risk parents are generally in their position due to their own upbringing rather than through any fault of their own. (This, in turn, may decrease motivation for change by appearing to relieve parents of responsibility for their actions. Possibly the use of the phrase "degree of parenting potential" may be more appropriate than "high risk" or "low risk" parents.)

Another potentially serious problem must be mentioned. Laws are now being rewritten to mandate reporting of any suspected child abuse or neglect, even where no firm evidence exists. Law enforcement authorities might seek to subpoena the results of the screening test. Overzealous program workers might use the threat of court action to coerce the high risk parents to consent to the training program. The program must be designed with such possibilities in mind so that safeguards can be provided. Emphasis must be given to the fact the *screening* for a problem does not definitively *diagnose* that problem.

While we have emphasized voluntary programs because of the difficulties seen with mandatory programs, one argument in favor of mandatory intervention has been neglected. One can argue that the widely held social beliefs in the rights of parents to maintain more or less exclusive control over their child raising methods are themselves anachronistic and deleterious. Parenting is a learned skill, one may argue, and a person ought to be required to demonstrate a minimal level of that skill by a suitable method before he is allowed control over the life of another human being.

There is some merit to this line of argument; an advocate of intervention for "unusual child rearing practices" might want to take this position and provoke a full scale public debate over parental rights and responsibilities. Another approach would be to implement "routine" screening of parents who present to the health care system for other reasons, with as little public notice as possible; this would probably only postpone the day of accounting. Finally, one could opt for a voluntary approach with emphasis on the public education component. This alone might prove adequate in the long run. If not, the research and data generated by such a program would no doubt provide a stronger case for a mandatory program at some future date.

Chapter 19

# Perinatal Assessment
# of Mother-Baby Interaction

Jane Gray, Christy Cutler, Janet Dean, C. Henry Kempe

The perinatal period affords a unique opportunity to assess the mother and her baby for potential problems with their ongoing interaction. Not only are they readily available for these observations to be made (see Chapter Eighteen), but also the mother and her baby are experiencing stage 6 and 7 of their attachment (see Chapter Two). Unless careful observations are made and recorded during this period a rather large number of future problems will be missed. Emphasis must be given to the fact that these are problems that are manifest in a variety of ways, overt abuse and neglect being two of the most severe (but by no means the only) demonstration of a serious dysfunction in mother-baby interaction.

The material discussed here summarizes those assessments that can and should be made during the three critical phases of the perinatal period—i.e., late prenatal, labor and delivery, and early postnatal. The discussion will include many factors which may indicate a questionable start for the mother-infant pair. No single factor, rather varying combinations and the family's degree of emphasis on them, is important. The observer must take into account the parents' ages, culture, education, affect and the significance of their feelings. These factors should be assessed at several stages of the perinatal period. At the end of this chapter a brief summary of a recently completed research study is presented. This study utilized several of the techniques discussed and is published in detail elsewhere.[1]

## THE PRENATAL OBSERVATIONS

The prenatal clinic setting is most often the medical staff's first contact with the prospective parent. Throughout pregnancy, staff will have the opportunity to

*377*

view the many stressful changes that future parents undergo while preparing for the arrival of their baby. For this reason the prenatal period is an ideal time to begin the collection of an information base, which will be augmented during labor, delivery, and the neonatal period. This knowledge base may help determine whether or not individuals might have the potential for abnormal parenting. The two top priority tasks throughout the entire pregnancy and perinatal phase are the collecting and relaying of pertinent data to personnel who in the future could be involved with the family. This provision of specific information can then help staff more readily empathize with the parents' own unique situation.

Prenatal settings, in comparison with labor and delivery and post partum, may at times offer a more low keyed atmosphere where the collection process can begin through observation, interviews, and interactions with staff. Important information can most easily be obtained in casual, informal conversation, rather than during a rapid-fire question-and-answer interview. Emphasis should be placed on the awareness of strengths within the family as well as risk factors. The documentation of positive factors can enable those responsible for followup services to further develop and utilize these strengths (see Table 19–1).

**Table 19–1.** Positive Family Circumstances

1. Parents see likable attributes in baby; see baby as separate individual.
2. Baby is healthy and not too disruptive to parents' life style.
3. Either parent can rescue the child or relieve one another in a crisis.
4. Marriage is stable.
5. Parents have a good friend or relative to turn to, a sound "need meeting" system.
6. Parents exhibit coping abilities—i.e., capacity to plan and understand need for adjustments because of new baby.
7. Mother's intelligence and health good.
8. Parents had helpful role models when growing up.
9. Parents can have fun together and with personal interests or hobbies.
10. Birth control planned; baby planned or wanted.
11. Father has stable job. Have own home and stable living conditions.
12. Father supportive to mother and involved in care of baby.

While the gathering of factual material can occur during most of the pregnancy, our experience indicates that the best time to record attitudes and behavior is during the third trimester. The greater physical burden of the unborn child is beginning to create an imminent situation. The reality of birth, especially once quickening has occurred, is increasingly more difficult to deny. Most parents at this stage start making realistic plans for the baby's arrival by selecting possible names, buying items for care, and in general by directing much of their energy to the anticipation of birth. Parents who continue to deny the inevitability of the birth and make little attempt at preparation should create concern among the staff.

Parents who possess the most potential for abnormal parenting are those who display extremes of behavior. These may be individuals who can be easily identified prenatally as chronic defaulters or ones who come in quite often for minor or nonexistent complaints. Attendance, therefore, can be a useful measure of a mother's involvement with her pregnancy. The very population that we need to help are the most often inaccessible, untrusting, uncommunicative, and overly passive—i.e., the people most easily overlooked in a busy medical setting. One way to alleviate this problem is to provide the patient with the opportunity for an alliance with one supportive staff person. One step in this direction is a program in which nurses are assigned prenatally to patients as a part of a team and who are on call for the labor and delivery, providing continuity of care.[2]

The parents' reasons for wanting a child, their concept of the unborn child, and their degree of preference for a particular sex are all significant issues. Understanding why a particular sex is desired and how rigid this expectation might be is helpful. The mother who "always wanted a little boy because she has never had anyone to rely on," should alert the staff. In these situations, the unrealistically high expectations for a newborn to immediately step into the role of caretaker and begin to fulfill the parents' needs will often bring parents such as these to the breaking point when they realize that the infant cannot possibly meet these expectations.

Observing the interaction between the mother and the individual who brings her to the clinic or office will help in assessing the type of supports systems available to her. Observing the mother who brings her own mother to appointments and how she relates to this person will be one way of assessing the type of supports she has available to her. She may be accompanied by a spouse, neighbor, a close friend, or she may come alone. Gaining an awareness of how reliable and available her friends really are for her, and if she in turn has the ability or inclination to call upon them, is of primary importance.

Parents have a great tendency to raise their children the way they themselves were raised. Understanding the parents' own background yields invaluable knowledge as to how they might react to the child rearing experience. They may report instances of having been severely disciplined or neglected, or they may fantasize ideal parenting at great variance with reality. Harsh treatment may not be perceived as being out of the ordinary. Their self-image is often low, and in fact, they may feel that they deserved everything they received. This type of upbringing is most often observed as the kind of behavior that prevents patients from seeking help or even asking necessary questions.

Another area that nursing and medical staff often have the opportunity to observe is the relationship between the mother and father. Couples will be starting to make important decisions regarding finances, housing, and other matters such as the naming of the baby. How they work through these decisions and how they organize their own lives to avert crises can be valuable material to the alert staff. If parents are constantly in crisis over decisions, the arrival of the baby will only accentuate the problems. The decision as to whether to have a baby, abort a pregnancy, or keep the baby are all most important and difficult; what is especially important are the reasons upon which these decisions were based.

The specific risk situations mentioned are designed to help staff communicate more effectively their concerns to other personnel who will have future contact with the family (see Table 19–2). Too often information is relayed on a vague level—i.e., "this lady is just weird"—which makes it very difficult to know just how to work with the parent. Once specific behaviors are referred to in terms of actions, verbalizations, or omissions, the message to other staff will be clear and will enable them to follow through more carefully. For example, nurses and other staff could keep separate index cards upon which they record observations and pertinent factual material to be passed on. They might also devise a stamp for the hospital chart indicating further important information was available on the family. Regardless of the particular method devised for the collection and relaying of this data, the important point is that it be done. The direct communication of family strengths and risk factors documented during the prenatal phase should occur before delivery takes place, and should be considered just as important as the relaying of critical medical information.

## LABOR AND DELIVERY OBSERVATIONS

Labor and delivery is a critical, sensitive period because of the intense emotions, the realization of the final physical process of birth, the fatigue, and the general stress of being in a hospital setting. All these factors combine to place an expectant mother in an extremely vulnerable, open, and often beautifully honest situation. Parents who are well prepared, mutually supportive, and reasonably cooperative can approach labor and delivery under good control. On the other hand, when parents are frightened, ill prepared, and fail to be mutually supportive, the woman may lose control during labor and delivery. When this loss of control occurs, she must depend on the support from those around her. She may feel isolated from persons to whom she is close, relying only on her self and the nurses and doctors who are there to help her give birth. This mandates that her labor and delivery be handled with the utmost sensitivity and caring on the part of the staff involved. Observations and assessments are made and recorded during this critical period. Staff attitudes and verbalizations can have a profound positive—or negative—effect on the parents' reactions and early attachment process.

The first interactions between a parent and infant are crucial determinants of the "binding in," bonding, or early claiming process. Most parents interact for the first time with their newborn in the delivery room. Each individual parent is on his or her own timetable and will be comfortable with differing levels of interaction at this point. The comments of everyone involved, the noises and sounds of the environment, and the comfort of the surroundings all have varying effects on this early claiming process.

**Table 19–2.** High Risk Signals in the Prenatal Clinic Setting

A high risk situation is not just any *one* of the items listed below, but rather varying combinations of these signs, the family's degree of emphasis on them, and their inflexibility to changes. The interviewer must take into consideration the patient's age, culture, and education; combined with observations of her affect and the significance of her feelings. Many of these signs can be assessed interchangeably throughout the entire perinatal period, but are listed in this order because they are found most commonly at these times.

A. Overconcern with the unborn baby's sex.
  1. Reasons why a certain sex is so important—i.e., to fill the mother's needs.
  2. The mother's need to please the father with the baby's sex.
  3. The quality and rigidity of these needs.

B. Expressed high expectations for the baby.
  1. Overconcern with the baby's physical and developmental progress, his behavior and discipline.
  2. The parents' need to have control over his actions and reactions.
  3. Is this child wanted in order to fulfill unmet needs in parents' lives?

C. Is this child going to be one too many?
  1. Is there adequate spacing between this child and the next older child?
  2. During the pregnancy has there been evidence of a disintegrating relationship with the older child(ren), i.e., physical or emotional abuse for the first time?

D. Evidence of the mother's desire to deny the pregnancy.
  1. Unwillingness to gain weight.
  2. Refusing to talk about the pregnancy in a manner commensurate with the reality of the situation.
  3. Not wearing maternity clothes when it would be appropriate.
  4. No plans made for baby's nursery, layette, etc., in the home.

E. Great depression over the pregnancy.
  1. Date of onset of depression to this pregnancy.
  2. Report of sleep disturbance that cannot be related to the physical aspects of pregnancy.
  3. Attempted suicide.
  4. Dropping out socially.
  5. Bland affect.

F. Did either parent formerly ever seriously consider an abortion?
  1. Why didn't they go through with it?
  2. Did they passively delay a decision until medically therapeutic abortion was not feasible?

G. Did the parents ever seriously consider relinquishment?
  1. Why did they change their minds?
  2. The reality and quality expressed in the change of decision.

H. Who does the mother turn to for support?
  1. How reliable and helpful are they to her?
  2. Who accompanies the mother to the clinic?
  3. Are any community agencies involved in a supportive way?

I. Is the mother very alone and/or frightened?
  1. Is this just because of lack of education or understanding of pregnancy and delivery?
  2. Is she overly concerned about the physical changes during pregnancy, labor and delivery.
  3. Do careful explanation, prenatal classes, etc., dissipate these fears?

**Table 19-2.** (Continued)

---

    4. The mother tends to keep the focus of the interview on her fears and needs rather than any anticipation, excitement, or joy projected onto the new baby.

J. Because of I, the mother has many unscheduled visits to the prenatal clinic or the emergency room.

    1. With exaggerated physical complaints that cannot be substantiated on physical examination or by laboratory tests.

    2. Multiple psychosomatic complaints.

    3. An overdependence on the doctor or nurse.

K. What are the patient's living arrangements?

    1. Are the physical accommodations adequate?

    2. Do they have a telephone?

    3. Is transportation available?

    4. Are there friends or relatives nearby?

L. The parents can't talk freely on the above topics and avoid eye contact.

M. What can you find out about the parents' backgrounds?

    1. Did they grow up in a foster home?

    2. Were they shuffled from one relative to another?

    3. What type of discipline was used? (They may not see this as abusive.)

    4. Do they plan to raise their children the way their parents raised them?

---

Pertinent information should be relayed to the labor and delivery staff from prenatal care, to allow them to gain perspective on why certain behaviors occur. Such knowledge allows the hospital staff to modify their behavior to meet the situation by exploring and understanding their own preconceived ideas and prejudices, as well as feelings toward the particular parents involved. For example, knowing that a particular mother has had three previous children die early in life can explain why, upon delivery of the fourth, she is extremely hesitant, or even refuses, to begin a claiming process with this infant, and has no name picked out. In another situation, knowing that a patient's husband refused to be with her in labor and delivery, that she had wanted a child of the opposite sex, and that she herself had been abandoned as a child, would be important in understanding why she was extremely depressed and cried during delivery.

The realization that labor and delivery room personnel can influence such a critical event in people's lives can be somewhat anxiety producing. An important point to keep in mind, however, is that this influence is most intense with those parents whose own strengths are minimal and who are very susceptible to outside influence. In these cases, this "shared difficult experience" can in fact establish some lines of trust between parents and willing staff, which can then be used to facilitate the transition to postpartum staff and continued followup if necessary. Even though the labor and delivery experience may become habitual and routine for the staff, this is a critically sensitive time for all families, especially these vulnerable families. Direct observations of labor and delivery are recorded in many hospitals by the OB-GYN nurses. Notations can be made on a concise, simple form, asking three questions (see Table 19–3): (1) How does the mother LOOK? (2) What does the mother SAY? (3) What does the mother DO?

**Table 19-3.** High Risk Signals in the Delivery Room

---

A. Written form with baby's chart concerning parents' reactions at birth.
1.  How does the mother LOOK?
2.  What does the mother SAY?
3.  What does the mother DO?

B. The following phrases may help in the organization of information regarding observations for the above-mentioned form.
1.  Does the parent appear sad, happy, apathetic, disappointed, angry, exhausted, frightened, ambivalent?
2.  Does the parent talk to the baby, talk to spouse, use baby's name, establish eye contact, touch, cuddle, examine?
3.  Does the spouse, friend, relative offer support, criticism, rejection, ambivalence?

C. If this interaction seems dubious, further evaluation should be initiated.

D. Concerning reactions at delivery include:
1.  Lack of interest in the baby, ambivalence, passive reaction.
2.  Keeps the focus of attention on herself.
3.  Unwillingness or refusal to hold the baby, even when offered.
4.  Hostility directed toward father, who put her "through all this."
5.  Inappropriate verbalizations, glances directed at the baby, with definite hostility expressed.
6.  Disparaging remarks about the baby's sex or physical characteristics.
7.  Disappointment over sex or other physical characteristics of the child.

---

Observations that might indicate a positive verbal interaction would involve the parents speaking of him/her in affectionate terms, commenting on the beauty of the child, or at least realistically of the infant's physical characteristics. Positive non-verbal clues include the mother turning to look at the baby, reaching out to him/her, being excited by or smiling at the baby's first cry. When the baby is offered to her, she holds the baby closely, may kiss and hug him/her, tries to establish the "en-face" position, and expresses interest in exploring the newborn.

The risk factors present at this time are generally centered around the concept of rejection. This rejection may be active or passive, verbal or non-verbal, ambivalent or total. It may be apparent in the very blatant sense as when a mother refuses eye contact with her infant, says nothing, looks away, and will not touch or examine the newborn. Or, this rejection may be more subtle, as in a mother who wanted a male baby, gives birth to a female, and instantaneously changes her plans for breastfeeding to bottle feeding. Openly hostile remarks may be made as in the case of the mother who remarked upon seeing her new baby, "He looks so much like his father, it's sickening. He looks like an ape."[3] An interchange between parents, inability to allow attention to be focused on the baby, repulsion, apathy, disappointment, etc., can all be clues to possible problems and merit further evaluation. Information and observations are most useful when specifically organized around basic questions which will help to clearly express the more blatant reactions and to define the less obvious reactions more precisely.

The unwanted pregnancy does not always result in the unwanted child, nor does the wanted pregnancy always result in the wanted child. Pregnancy and the reaction to the child must *both* be evaluated to gain a complete impression. There must be a consideration of the character and length of a woman's labor, her fatigue, the degree of pain or discomfort, the amount and timing of any medications, and any disorientation associated with delivery itself.

During the time we spent making delivery room observations, a number of changes were taking place in staff attitudes and procedure. On the procedural level, changes included mother's hands being freed to touch and examine her newborn, babies being given to parents to hold in the delivery room, and babies being allowed to accompany their parents into the recovery room. These new practices had been evolving for some time within the unit, but were perhaps catalyzed by the self-observation available through videotaping being done in the delivery rooms.[3] Direct feedback was given to staff regarding the reliability of their observations and the effect that this assessment had on the provision of followup care for families. Information regarding the family's need for followup services provided tangible evidence of the importance of making and relaying to postpartum obstetrics and nursery staffs the observations made during labor and delivery.

### POSTPARTUM OBSERVATIONS

The postpartum period offers the unique opportunity to observe the mother-infant pair as the mother begins to assume the responsibility for her infant's care. The recent and commendable advances in newborn care have given us greater opportunities for meaningful observations. Modern rooming-in units allow maximum accessibility of the mother to the infant, and allow the hospital staff to assess the mother/child interaction.

The job description of the personnel who collect the data base (both by interview and observation) is not nearly as important as that the designated staff member or social worker have a warm, empathetic, understanding personality. Young mothers seem to relate more easily and effectively to personnel with a medical orientation (physician, R.N., paramedical personnel, or nurse's aide) rather than to a social worker, whom the young mothers tend to view as being more threatening.

Several short, casual contacts with a new mother may be more productive than one longer interview. This is true for several reasons, among them that the mother is often physically tired in the immediate postpartum period and a prolonged interview may exhaust her and leave her limited resources unavailable to the interviewer. In addition, mothers most likely to be at risk for abnormal parenting practices are also often untrusting, and several interviews in which promises to return are kept will help to build trust and rapport.

Data gathered in a casual manner can be obtained by using the baby as an opening for conversation. New mothers often talk freely of their experience in pregnancy and delivery, which can then lead the conversation into the more emotional aspects of the mother's hopes and expectations as well as her doubts about her own and her husband's ability to fulfill the responsibilities of parenthood. Some feel that one contributing factor in the development of postpartum depression is the fear of not being able to parent. Certainly a supportive hospital worker can set the stage for helping a mother accept added services, as a positive means to increase her parenting potential.

On an interactional level, one of the easiest aspects to document is how often the baby is in the room with the mother. In an increasing number of hospitals, mothers (and fathers) can hold the baby in the delivery room, have their newborn with them in the recovery room, and have the opportunity to be with the child in a rooming-in situation. In addition to the documentation as to how often mother and baby are together, notation should be made whether or not the mother comes to the nursery and requests the baby or if the mother and baby are together because of the nurses' initiative. When mother and baby are together, the level of contact needs to be recorded—i.e., is the child left in his or her bassinet or does the mother hold and care for the child?

As the mother with normal parenting potential becomes acquainted with her baby she begins to take charge of "child crafting" procedures, including diapering and feeding. She becomes more comfortable and self-assured as hospitalization progresses. In working with young primigravidas an emphasis on educational aspects of parenting is of immeasurable benefit. As a mother gains confidence, she begins to anticipate the baby's needs and becomes more in tune with her child. She shows increasing skill with diapering and feeding and begins to initiate these tasks as the need arises, rather than waiting for prompting from the nursery staff. A lack of experience in young primigravidas will require support and education, but should not be confused with risk for parenting potential.

Mothers with difficulty assuming a maternal role (rather than solely in child crafting skills) tend to view their babies as too demanding or as deliberately interrupting the parents' life style with their demands. The mother who appears to be having difficulty attaching to her baby sees both feeding and diapering as messy and repulsive. Frequently she will not ask for help (nor can she easily make use of suggestions given spontaneously), but will instead tend to ignore the child, almost in an effort to protect herself from a situation that is unpleasant to her.

Another area that is extremely difficult for mothers who are having trouble interacting with their baby is the aspect of crying (see Discussion in Commentary). Many mothers with interactional difficulties have problems in handling a baby's crying. They often say it makes them feel helpless, hopeless, or like crying themselves. They sometimes feel the child is crying on purpose. These mothers do not have the personal resources that are necessary to quiet a fussy baby.

Besides watching a new mother take physical care of her baby, listening how she talks to and about her baby is important. Does she call the baby by name, rather than "it"? Mothers without parenting problems will attempt to get the baby's attention by using his or her name and will talk or coo to the baby in an effort to stimulate reaction. The mother with difficulty relating to the baby may make negative remarks about the child and be demanding, disparaging, or even openly hostile. It is also valuable to watch the mother's affect during these verbal exchanges, because while some interchanges sound negative in content, the mother is actually expressing her pride in this way: "He's so fat!" or "She eats like a pig!" In spite of the wording, these verbalizations can actually be very positive and are often accompanied by smiles. Throughout a conversation with a baby, a mother with normal interactional potential makes a usually unconscious but continued effort to establish and maintain eye-to-eye contact with the baby. This behavior is rarely seen in mothers who are having interactional difficulties (see Chapter Two).

Since the mother and baby are a "captive audience" during their postpartum confinement, a valuable opportunity is available to assess the family's support system at a time when it should be in operation. The most important aspect is the father's relationship to the mother and the baby; how he begins to assume his new role, and how he supports his wife in assuming her new role. This is a time to see the rest of the family: both sets of grandparents, other relatives, and maybe even the parents' friends who visit the mother and child in the hospital. These people should not only be supportive and helpful but also encourage the young parents to grow in their new role and in their interactional abilities with the baby. If the "friends" are critical of the parents' efforts or attempt to take over for the parents, this must be noted, for support systems will assume a new importance as the family is discharged from the hospital.

In the immediate postdischarge period the physician, nurse, health visitor, and public health nurse are in important positions to assess developing relationships and to provide positive support. They are also often the ones to whom "cries for help" are first made. Cries for help can take the form of multiple telephone calls or visits to medical personnel, especially about complaints that seem very minor. A very worrisome feature is a mother who has complaints about the child that cannot be verified by physical examination or laboratory testing. These contacts are usually an effort to get the helping professional to focus on the parent and his or her inability to cope with the situation.

During the early visits for well child care, a mother with normal parenting potential is constantly hovering over her child, holding, cuddling, soothing, and attending to his needs. She finds something positive for herself in the child's growth and development. On the other hand, a mother who is having difficulty relating to her infant may relinquish the care of her baby to the office or clinic staff. She does not undress, hold, or comfort the baby. She may leave him lying alone on the examination table with little apparent regard for his safety or comfort. She may also try to focus the medical personnel's attention on herself; this, again, can be viewed as her cry for help (see Table 19–4).

Throughout the perinatal period, warm, supportive medical personnel can begin to establish a helping relationship with the family. As rapport and trust develop, these medical personnel can serve as lifelines to parents with difficulties. And as lifelines, they can also be available to facilitate any referrals for extra services that may be necessary to help this family use its positive elements to form a better parent-child relationship.

The type of extra services for families with potential for abnormal parenting will need to be organized on an outreach basis. Responsibility should be taken to insure the family of continuity of medical care, and, whenever possible, to designate one person to be in charge of this continuity. This person could be a physician, allied health professional, public health nurse, health visitor, or lay worker. The relative ability of a family to begin to trust those who will be doing followup will determine how much liaison work and time must be spent in helping them make a link with these services.

Some ideas that might be useful for opening up lines of communication are:

1. Direct contact between parent and follow-up personnel before leaving hospital.
2. Telephone call to family within days of discharge.
3. First return visit to take place within the first two weeks after discharge.
4. Several 24 hour telephone numbers given to families, one of which should be someone in charge of some aspect of direct care for the family.
5. One 24 hour telephone number might be the postpartum unit. This is an effective source of help especially if coupled with a log book, in which pertinent data have been recorded.

## SUMMARY OF RESEARCH STUDY

Research in the area of identification and followup of those who might have potential for abnormal parenting is being done in several areas throughout the country. One such study was completed by the authors.

Utilizing an interview, a questionnaire, and labor, delivery, and postpartum observations, a sample of 100 mothers was identified as "high risk for abnormal parenting practices." These mothers were randomly divided into a high risk intervene group (N=50) and a high risk non-intervene group (N=50). In all 100 families our concern regarding the risk for abnormal parenting was shared with physicians and visiting nurses. The intervene group received comprehensive pediatric followup by a single physician, a health visitor, and/or public health nurse

**Table 19-4.** High Risk Signals in the Postpartum Period (On Postpartum Ward and in Well Baby Clinic)

---

A. Does the family remain disappointed over sex of baby?

B. What is the child's name?
 1. Who is he named for/after?
 2. Who picked the name?
 3. When was the name picked?
 4. Is the name used when talking to or about the baby?

C. What was/is the husband's and/or family's reaction to the new baby?
 1. Are they supportive?
 2. Are they critical?
 3. Do they attempt to take over and control the situation?
 4. Is the husband jealous of the baby's drain on the mother's time and energy?

D. What kind of support, other than family, is the mother receiving?

E. Are their sibling rivalry problems? Does she think there will be any? How does she plan to handle them? Or does she deny that a new baby will change existing family relationships?

F. Is the mother bothered by the baby's crying?
 1. How does it make her feel? Angry? Inadequate? Like crying herself?

G. Feedings
 1. Does the mother view the baby as too demanding in his needs to eat?
 2. Does she ignore the demands?
 3. Is she repulsed by his messiness, i.e., spitting up?
 4. Is she repulsed by his sucking noises?

H. How does the mother view changing diapers?
 1. Is she repulsed by the messiness, smells, etc.?

I. Are the expectations of the child developmentally far beyond his or her capabilities?

J. Mother's control or lack of control over the situation
 1. Does she get involved and take control over baby's needs and what's going to happen (waiting room and during exam interaction)
 2. Does she relinquish control to the doctor, nurse, etc. (undressing, holding, allowing child to express fears, etc.?)

K. Can the mother express that she is having fun with the baby?
 1. Can she view him as a separate individual?
 2. Can attention be focused on him and she see something positive in that for herself?

L. Can she establish and maintain eye-to-eye, direct contact, en face position, with the baby?

M. How does she talk with the baby?

N. Are her verbalizations about the child usually negative?

O. When the child cries, does she, or can she, comfort him?

---

**Table 19-4.** (Continued)

---

P. Does she have complaints about the child that cannot be verified?
   1. Multiple emergency calls for very minor complaints, not major issues.
   2. Calling all the time for small problems, things that to you seem unimportant, but could be very major for her.
   3. The baby does things "on purpose" just to aggravate the parents.
   4. In your presence the mother describes a characteristic you can't verify—e.g., baby cries continually.
   5. Tells you essentially unbelievable stories about the baby—e.g., has not breathed, is turning colors for the past 30 minutes and now seems fine.

Q. Manipulation of those working with the family: pitting nurse against lay therapist, doctor against social worker, through complaints and stories. Miscommunicating information, etc.

---

in the home. The nonintervene group merely received routine care. A group of 50 mothers who also delivered during the same time period, and who were assessed as low risk in terms of abnormal parenting practices, served as controls. The results were as follows.

1. A high risk group was successfully identified on the basis of perinatal screening procedures; these children had significantly different parenting practices from the low risk (control) group.
2. Five children in the high risk nonintervene group required hospitalization for treatment of serious injuries thought to be secondary to abnormal parenting practices, as contrasted to no such hospitalizations in the high risk intervene and low risk control groups.
3. Labor, delivery, and nursery observations provided the most accurate predictive information.

Perinatal assessment and early, consistent intervention with families identified as high risk for abnormal parenting practices significantly improves the infants' chances of escaping serious physical injury.

Of additional interest is the fact that more cases of suspected abuse were identified in the high risk intervene group. These cases were all in an early phase without serious injury. The close observations and followup of this high risk intervene group provided an opportunity to identify abuse much earlier than in the high risk nonintervene group.

## COMMENTARY

The editors asked Dr. Ann Wilson to write a brief commentary on this chapter giving emphasis to the "Role and Capabilities of the Infant" as this baby becomes involved in the interaction process. Her comments are given below.

For many years behavioral scientists and physicians suggested that babies were unable to perceive their surrounding world as anything more than a mass of confusion. In the last ten years there has been a great deal of interest in changing this concept of a newborn's capabilities. Research findings are now showing, with increasing clarity, that newborns come into the world able to see, hear, smell, and taste. They are also able to discriminate stimuli with each of these sensory modalities. Such findings are probably no surprise to mothers who, by intimately knowing their babies, have long been able to sense how very competent an infant is from the time of his birth.

An infant is not only endowed with remarkable sensory capabilities, but with perceptual capacities refined to enable him to orient to his mother. Such innate abilities provide the means of establishing a relationship between a parent and child. Research studies have most carefully examined the capacity of a newborn to respond to visual and auditory stimulation. Striking evidence has been provided that some infants two hours following delivery, and all infants twenty-four hours following delivery, can make visual pursuit movements.[1] Although a newborn's ability to focus his eyes upon an object is initially limited, he can best accommodate his vision at a focal distance of about eight inches away from himself, the usual distance of his mother's face during a feeding.

Eye-to-eye contact between mother and baby has been noted by many as playing an especially important role in mediating the nature of a caregiving relationship. In a longitudinal study of maternal attachment, mothers were reported as indicating how eye contact with their infants enhanced their positive feelings for their babies.[2] In assessing a newborn's innate capabilities, visual fixation and following are the only naturalistic neonatal reflexes which do not drop out in time; and, that by two months following birth these responses will have reached their full maturity. An infant is born with an amazing visual capability.

The newborn's auditory responsivity has also been demonstrated to be functional from the time of birth. Wolff[1] has observed that from birth onwards an infant will respond to sound by turning toward the source of the stimuli and by attenuating diffuse motor activity. Aside from these perceptual abilities, newborns come into the world with other inborn responses, which are patterned to enable newborns to maintain proximity with their mothers. Rooting, sucking, grasping, crying, and postural adjustments to being held are all functional in facilitating closeness between them and their caregivers.

Newborn perceptual competencies and behavioral organization together provide an infant with the capability to orient and accommodate to his environment and to those who give him care. To protect himself from being bombarded with visual, auditory, and other sensory stimuli, a newborn has innate mechanisms that serve to limit the stimulation he encounters in his environment. Studies that have investigated newborn selective attention provide intriguing evidence that newborns prefer both visual and auditory stimuli that have inherent characteristics of the human face and voice. These findings indicate that represented in the selective behavior of infants is a genetic bias to respond to stimuli having potential social and survival value to them.

As active seekers of socially significant stimulation, infants are most certainly not the passive recipients of care they were at one time considered to be. Even as newborns, infants initiate social interaction by eye-to-eye contact, smile, cry, and coo and present unique styles of behavior to those who care for them. Mothers and nursery nurses have always been aware of the unique nature of every newborn. Infants are characteristically individual and their differences affect their emerging relationship with their parents, the care they receive, and their subsequent development. The very active role an infant plays in initiating social interaction has been clearly illustrated in a study which showed that four-fifths of the interaction taking place with an infant and his mother in the first month of life is initiated by the infant.[3] Indeed, the gratification that both the mother and the infant receive from these interactions will influence the nature of their ensuing relationship.

Klaus,[4] in describing the difficulties parents have in becoming attached to their premature infants, has stated that "you can't love a dishrag." Preemies, who typically are more flacid, irritable, and have fewer episodes of alert wakefulness than full term newborns, have little with which to reciprocate the parental care given to them. Many mothers need positive reinforcement in order to enhance a beginning relationship. Epidemiological studies investigating the perinatal histories of children who have been abused[5] and who fail to thrive[6] indicate that a disproportionate number of these children were premature at birth. This finding can, in part, be interpreted to reflect how deficits in these children's early behavior can later become manifest in a very disturbed parent-child relationship.

Though comparisons of premature and full term newborns provide clear evidence of how infant behavior can differentially affect parental caregiving, individual differences of "normal" full term newborns are also of importance. Innate differences in newborn behavior can most certainly be significant in setting the stage of the future parent-child relationship. Korner[7] has singled out high level of arousal as a feature of a newborn's behavioral repertoire which is most salient in affecting the caregiving relationship. Her work has shown clear, significant differences in the duration of waking activity. Frequency in shift of state of consciousness, and the frequency of global diffuse motions are apparent in newborn behavior. Korner surmises that wakefulness and a high degree of restlessness most probably evoke more frequent interaction between a newborn and mother than does quiet sleepiness.

The role of the infant's remarkable visual competency has been recognized as being functional in eliciting maternal care. Reliable differences exist among newborns in how frequently they spontaneously alert.[8] To mothers, an infant's alert visual behavior provides opportunities for playful interaction, which serves to help build a positive foundation for a mutually rewarding social relationship. In addition to an infant's overall level of arousal (which will determine how alert or irritable a baby will be), how readily he can be soothed is also important in understanding the ease with which the parent and child can begin to relate to one another.

Chess[9] clearly recognized a child's temperament as playing an important role in determining his potential for developing behavior disorders. Her work differentiated attributes in infants during their first five weeks of life and identified patterns of temperament likely to make a child vulnerable to damaging interaction with the environment. Children whom she had identified as being at greatest risk for developing behavior disorders are irregular in biological functions, have predominantly negative responses to new stimuli, are slow to adapt to environmental change, and have a high frequency of negative mood expressions and intense reactions.

These research findings, which show how behavioral characteristics and temperamental dispositions vary in the very young child, provide an understanding of how neonatal problems can be compounded early in life with inappropriate interaction with the physical and social environment. Brazelton,[10] a pediatrician, reported how physiological factors are involved in eliciting maternal behavior and developed a rating scale to assess neonatal behavior. The Neonatal Behavioral Assessment Scale[11] evaluates both the infant's use of state to maintain control of his reactions to environmental stimuli and the infant's response to various kinds of stimulation. Focusing on assessing these behaviors, the scale evaluates those interactive capabilities that will most significantly affect those who care for the newborn. By identifying these capabilities, a mother can be supported in her effort to reinforce pleasurable interaction.

Both the objective quality of an infant's behavior and the maternal perception of the behavior will be important in affecting the ongoing relationship. In a longitudinal study Broussard and Hartner[12] have found that newborns perceived by their mothers as "not as good as" the average baby were independently evaluated at four years of age as needing therapeutic intervention. The study findings have been interpreted by the authors to indicate that either innate pathological behavioral characteristics can be detected by a mother early in a newborn's behavior, or that a mother's early perceptions become manifest in a self-fulfilling prophecy. In either case, maternal perceptions can be considered as an important variable related to an infant's future development.

The mother-infant relationship represents a dynamic complex of behaviors. The very delicate balance between a mother and child has been described as a fit,[13] an interactive mesh,[10] an intricate ballet,[14] and as an interactive spiral.[15] Implicit in each of these descriptions is an understanding that the baby as well as the mother plays an important role in making their relationship either harmonic or dissonant. The recognition of the newborn's perceptual competencies and innate behavioral responses, which are biased to promote social interaction, has prompted recent interest in understanding how a newborn will actively relate to those who care for him. Such information can be helpfully used by those who care for new mothers and their infants.

## Chapter Twenty

# A Predictive
# Screening Questionnaire
# for Potential Problems in
# Mother-Child Interaction

Carol Schneider, James K. Hoffmeister,
and Ray E. Helfer

## INTRODUCTION

In 1972 Schneider, Helfer, and Pollack[1] published an account of the
preliminary results from their questionnaire, which was originally
designed to predict abuse potential. The material presented in this
chapter represents an update on those results, based on the administration of
this instrument to 500 additional women. As we use this questionnaire it is becoming increasingly apparent that about 20 percent of this population of parents
have child rearing attitudes and experiences that are so similar to known abusers
as to make them indistinguishable from abusers on any dimension except the
absence of documented abuse. That each of these parents will physically abuse
or neglect their children is unlikely. However, we consider that we may be identifying a group of parents who have markedly deviant attitudes and perceptions
about child rearing. The unusual rearing practices these parents condone, if
actually practiced, have every likelihood of producing children with a wide variety of problems ranging from physical abuse to behavior disorders, learning
problems, or delinquency.

Our early identification program is aimed at identifying those parents who are
more likely to have problems with parent-child interaction than is the general
population. Support for this position is found in the study by Grey (see previous
chapter), who identified 25 percent of their population as "at risk" because they
have attitudes or past experiences or condoned rearing practices similar to
those characteristic of abusers. In following up half of this large group, they

The authors would like to pay tribute and their respects to Carl Pollock, M.D., who was
so instrumental and helpful in the early development of this work. Carl died in December
1975.

found that while actual physical abuse was rare (possibly because of their inter-vention), milder emotional neglect or abuse was all too frequent. These children had developmental deficits in language, cognition, and perception to a far greater extent than the children of the nonrisk parents.

Our questionnaire was given to the parents in that study, although it was used as a criterion for assignment to risk. The results contained in this chapter are based on comparing the responses of this high risk sample of parents with a known low risk sample. Emphasis must be given to the fact that all the data on this questionnaire has been gathered from *mothers*. While the present revised form of the questionnaire can be used for fathers, no data has yet been gathered. We will also present the first reliability data available on this questionnaire. The methodology section is highly technical, as there have been many requests by researchers for an exposition of the techniques used to analyze the question-naire.

## METHODOLOGY

### Selection of Sample

From 1970 to 1974 the 74-item predictive questionnaire was given to 500 mothers in Colorado and Michigan. The mothers were from varying ethnic and socioeconomic backgrounds and ranged in age from 16 to 35 years. The ques-tionnaires were answered while the mothers were in a doctor's office, a prenatal clinic, or a hospital after delivery. The data from this larger group of women was used to develop the measures described subsequently in this chapter.

Among the 500 mothers, 267 fell into one of several subgroups, who were of particular interest with respect to validating the questionnaire. The first group was made up of 14 mothers who were identified child abusers. The second group was made up of 67 women who were designated as having a high potential for child abuse on the basis of past history, prenatal interviews, and observations of mother-child interactions. A third group of mothers was formed from data col-lected from women described by their physicians as "model mothers." Eighty-six mothers were included in this group. A fourth group of 100 mothers in-cluded those in whom a review of the history suggested they would have little likelihood of being abusive with their children.

Two hundred sixty-seven women were assigned. These four groups were labeled, respectively: Known Abusers, High Potential, Best Moms, and Low Potential. Data from these four groups were used to provide information regard-ing the extent to which the predictive questionnaire measures could be used to identify mothers who were likely to use unusual child rearing practices. The Known Abusers and the High Potential mothers were treated for analysis purposes as high risk. The Best Moms and the Low Potential mothers were simi-larly treated as low risk. Finally, 92 expectant mothers enrolled in a childbirth education class in San Diego, California, were asked to respond to the ques-tionnaire on two different occasions approximately two weeks apart. These data were used to provide an initial estimate of the stability (reliability) of the measures across a short time interval.

### Development of the Predictive Questionnaire

The predictive questionnaire used here was in its third revision.[2] The questions contained in this form were based on interviews with abusive parents, non-abusive parents, and a study of case and research literature from throughout the United States and England and the results of earlier studies in this area.

**Statistical Procedures.** The primary statistical procedure used to develop measures from the predictive questionnaire was cluster analysis,[2] which provides an efficient, computerized procedure for identifying patterns of responses in a set of data. A given pattern (cluster) is indicated when a subset of questions has a high degree of correlation between the various questions of that subset and low to moderate correlation between those questions and the remaining questions in the total set of data.

**Computing Cluster Scores.** Convergence analysis[3] was used to compute scores for each person on each of the predictive measures. This computerized procedure ensures that scores are computed for a person on a measure only if the responses to the various questions making up that measure are reasonably consistent. When the responses are reasonably consistent, only those that converge on or about a point on the response scale are used to compute a score. This process is designed to minimize the effect on data of such factors as person-item interaction, carelessness, and misunderstanding. Convergence analysis was presumed to be of particular interest in this effort because of its ability to identify inconsistency in answers to common questions. One of the more pervasive characteristics of persons known to be abusive is their inconsistent manner of describing situations leading up to and associated with the expression of unusual ways of child rearing. We found it intriguing that the degree of inconsistency in responses to the questions was one of the better ways to separate our high risk group from the low risk group. The use of convergence analysis not only provides the opportunity to determine the extent to which this inconsistency was manifested in test patterns, but also identifies consistency when it does occur.

**Data Analysis.** ,Three statistical procedures were used to illuminate trends in the data: (1) frequency distributions of the responses on the various measures, (2) Pearson correlations between the measures both at one point and across time, and (3) one-way analyses of variance. Results were not assumed to be significant for reporting purposes here unless they had a probability of occurrence due to chance of 1 in 1,000 or less.

### RESULTS

The cluster analysis of the predictive questionnaire yielded six clusters, which accounted for 90 percent of the mean square of the raw correlation matrix. These clusters were called Problems with Mother (PWM), I'm No Damn Good (IM), Isolation (ISO), Child Expectations—A (CEA), Child Expectations—B (CEB), and Depression/Crisis (DEP). Sample items making up these measures are displayed in Table 20–1. All items included in these measures had an oblique factor coefficient of at least .50 with their respective cluster. Responses to these questions were combined in such a manner that a high score would indicate (theoretically, at least) that a person would be likely to manifest unusual child rearing practices.

**Table 20–1.** Sample of Items Included in Predictive Questionnaire Measures

---

| *Sample Item* |
|---|
| **CLUSTER I: *Problems with Mother (PWM)*** |
| My mother and I have always gotten along well. |
| The main thing I remember from childhood is the love and warm affection my parents showed me. |
| **CLUSTER II: *I'm No Damn Good (IM)*** |
| No one has ever really listened to me. |
| I am always being criticized by other people. |
| I have never really felt loved. |
| **CLUSTER III: *Isolation (ISO)*** |
| I am close to other people. |
| I am always good to other people. |
| I am very well liked by everyone. |
| **CLUSTER IV: *Child Expectations—A (CEA)*** |
| Children should know even before the age of 2 years what parents want them to do. |
| Children need to be taught before the age of 2 to respect and obey their parents. |
| **CLUSTER V: *Child Expectations—B (CEB)*** |
| I never become angry with my child (ren). |
| My child (ren) is (are) always good. |
| Most children should walk well by 9 or 10 months of age. |
| **CLUSTER VI: *Depression/Crisis (DEP)*** |
| I am afraid of many things. |
| Often when my baby cries, I don't know what to do about it. |
| Sometimes I just feel like running away. |

---

## Additional Measures

Because there was some uncertainty regarding the usefulness of the cluster measures, two other types of measures were included in this research. The first was based mainly on the clinical impressions of Dr. Ray Helfer. Based on these experiences, 18 questions were combined into what was called the "Gut" score

(GUT). As indicated in Table 20–2, many of these items are included in the various measures derived from the cluster analysis. However, the thrust of this effort was to pool the responses to this set of questions, even though, in a number of cases, the correlations between these questions was close to 0.0. The responses to the questions making up the GUT score were combined so that a high score would indicate, at least theoretically, a tendency to manifest unusual child rearing practices.

**Table 20–2.** Sample of Items Used to Compute the Gut and the Discriminant Measures

| *Sample Item* |
| --- |
| *Gut Score (GUT)* |
| Children should know even before the age of 2 years what parents want them to do. |
| As a child I often felt no one paid much attention to what I wanted or needed. |
| Often when my baby cries, I don't know what to do about it. |
| When I was a child my parents used severe physical punishment on me or one of my siblings. |
| *Discriminant Items (DIS)* |
| When I was a child my parents used severe physical punishment on me or one of my siblings. |
| At least one of my parents didn't really listen to me or understand my feelings. |
| It is extremely important for me to have my children behave well even when they are infants. |

One additional score was also generated from some of the questions included in the predictive questionnaire. This score was based on previous efforts to use a discriminant analysis technique to select items that might be useful for predicting to the manifestation of unusual child rearing practices.[4] This measure was called the Discriminant Score (DIS). Table 20–2 also displays sample questions used to compute this score.

As with the other measures described above, the responses to the questions included in the Discriminant Score were combined so that a high score would be likely to indicate the use of unusual child rearing practices. Since the average interitem correlation of this set of questions was close to 0.0, the convergence analysis procedures were not used to compute this score, for under such conditions, half of all the scores computed would have to be inconsistent. Consequently, a simple average of the responses to these questions was used as the score on this measure. Table 20–3 displays the correlations between these eight measures.

**Table 20–3.** Correlations of Predictive Questionnaire Measures

|      | PWM     | IM    | ISO   | CEA  | CEB  | DEP  | GUT  |
|------|---------|-------|-------|------|------|------|------|
| IM   | .28[a]  |       |       |      |      |      |      |
| ISO  | .25     | −.04  |       |      |      |      |      |
| CEA  | .00     | .18   | −.07  |      |      |      |      |
| CEB  | .10     | .39   | −.06  | .34  |      |      |      |
| DEP  | .23     | .38   | .26   | .09  | .26  |      |      |
| GUT  | .72     | .93   | .41   | .16  | .43  | .32  |      |
| DIS  | .45     | .66   | .04   | .11  | .34  | .18  | .60  |

[a]Minimum number of cases is 95.

Frequency distributions were computed for each of the measures across the 267 persons of particular interest in this study. Table 20–4 displays this information. As indicated, a considerable number of mothers responded inconsistently on IM, CEB, and GUT. No numerical scores were computed for these mothers on these measures, or others to which they responded inconsistently. As indicated earlier, the Discriminant Score was not computed by the method of Convergence Analysis since the degree of relationship between the items assigned to this measure tended to 0.00.

As indicated in Table 20–5, significant differences were observed between the low and high risk with seven of the eight measures. One of the critical concerns expressed in regard to the development of predictive information was that such measures must both be "sensitive" and "specific"—that is, the measure must predict to persons or situations that are known (or presumed) to be likely to manifest a characteristic. But at the same time, the measure must also correctly predict to persons who do not (or are not presumed to be likely to) manifest this same characteristic. Therefore, the seven predictive questionnaire measures that significantly differentiated between the two risk groups identified in this research were reexamined in terms of their sensitivity and their specificity.

The degree of overlap between the low and high risk groups on PWM, CEA, and DEP was so great that even though there were statistically significant differences between them, it was not possible to find a separation point in the scores that provided both a high degree of sensitivity and a high degree of specificity. Consequently, their usefulness for prediction purposes seemed questionable and no further analyses were done on these variables. However, four of the predictive measures appeared to have considerable potential for differentiating between these groups. Table 20–6 displays the percent of persons correctly predicted to belong to the low or high risk groups of mothers as a function of their scores on the four measures. As indicated in Table 20–6, the degree of sensitivity (predicting high risk) varied from 21 to 63 percent,

**Table 20-4.** Distribution of 267 Mothers on the Predictive Questionnaire Measures

|  | PWM | IM | ISO | CEA | CEB | DEP | GUT | DIS |
|---|---|---|---|---|---|---|---|---|
| 1.00–2.99 (Low) | 57[a] | 86 | 61 | 24 | 50 | 38 | 91 | 24 |
| 3.00–4.99 (Moderate) | 10 | 6 | 26 | 22 | 46 | 39 | 5 | 76 |
| 5.00–7.00 (High) | 33 | 8 | 13 | 54 | 4 | 23 | 4 | 0 |
| Mean | 3.18 | 1.87 | 2.84 | 4.35 | 2.75 | 3.58 | 1.79 | 3.33 |
| Std. Dev. | 2.15[b] | 1.44 | 1.34 | 1.90 | 1.32 | 1.65 | 1.14 | .49 |
| Number of Subjects | 260[b] | 200 | 231 | 257 | 185 | 209 | 149 | 265 |
| Percent Inconsistent | 1 | 25 | 12 | 0 | 25 | 16 | 44 | 0 |
| Homogeneity Ratio[c] | .67 | .42 | .34 | .33 | .25 | .29 | .23 | .01 |

[a]Percent of mothers having a score in this range.

[b]The total number of subjects was 267. The differences in the number of subjects for whom scores were available varied from 267 due to missing data or to the fact that they responded inconsistently to the items making up a given measure.

[c]This statistic is included so as to indicate the average intercorrelation of the items combined to provide a score on a given measure.[5]

**Table 20-5.** Means, Standard Deviations, Number of Cases and F Ratios for Low and High Risk Groups on the Predictive Questionnaire Measures

| Group | | Low Risk | High Risk | F Ratio | Df |
|---|---|---|---|---|---|
| PWM | Mean | 2.77 | 4.14 | 24.29 | 1/258 |
| | Std. Dev. | 1.91 | 2.39 | | |
| | N | 181 | 79 | | |
| IM | Mean | 1.47 | 3.60 | 97.32 | 1/198 |
| | Std. Dev. | .87 | 2.09 | | |
| | N | 163 | 37 | | |
| CEA | Mean | 4.00 | 5.12 | 20.30 | 1/255 |
| | Std. Dev. | 1.95 | 1.53 | | |
| | N | 178 | 79 | | |
| CEB | Mean | 2.36 | 3.57 | 40.83 | 1/183 |
| | Std. Dev. | 1.18 | 1.25 | | |
| | N | 126 | 59 | | |
| DEP | Mean | 4.30 | 3.29 | 17.17 | 1/207 |
| | Std. Dev. | 1.58 | 1.60 | | |
| | N | 60 | 149 | | |
| GUT | Mean | 1.48 | 3.43 | 96.66 | 1/147 |
| | Std. Dev. | .42 | 2.03 | | |
| | N | 125 | 24 | | |
| DIS | Mean | 3.17 | 3.70 | 87.62 | 1/263 |
| | Std. Dev. | .39 | .51 | | |
| | N | 185 | 80 | | |

depending upon the measure, while the degree of specificity (predicting low risk) varied similarly from 45 to 84 percent.

As indicated earlier, the high risk group included 14 mothers who had a history of child abuse, and the low risk group included 86 mothers whose child rearing practices were judged to be exemplary. Since these two subgroups of mothers provided potentially the worst and best cases for predictive purposes,

**Table 20-6.** Percent of Mothers Correctly Predicted to Belong to the High or Low Risk Groups in Terms of Their Scores on *IM, CEB, GUT,* or *DIS*

| Group | High Risk | Low Risk |
|---|---|---|
| IM | 22 | 84 |
| CEB | 57 | 45 |
| GUT | 15 | 67 |
| DIS | 63 | 77 |

they were examined separately. Table 20–7 displays the percent of these two groups of mothers correctly predicted from their scores on the four measures. As indicated, except for the Discriminant score, the degree of sensitivity is still marginal. However, the degree of specificity is high across all four measures. This situation is made clearer when the type of response pattern (consistent or inconsistent) is examined.

**Table 20–7.** Percent of Mothers Correctly Predicted to Belong to the Known Abusive and Best Moms Groups as a Function of Their Scores on *IM, CEB, GUT,* or *DIS*

| Group | Known Abusers | Best Moms |
|---|---|---|
| IM | 21 | 88 |
| CEB | 50 | 74 |
| GUT | 14 | 72 |
| DIS | 86 | 73 |

Convergence analysis requires that persons respond reasonably consistently to most of the questions presumed to measure a given variable. And, as was indicated in Table 20–4, from one-fourth to nearly one-half of the mothers responded inconsistently on IM, CEB, or the GUT scores. It was discussed earlier (Chapter Six) that inconsistency is one of the characteristics of mothers who are known to have a history of unusual child rearing patterns. The data were therefore examined to determine the extent to which those who answered inconsistently on the IM, CEB, or GUT measures were included in the high or the low risk groups. Table 20–8 displays this information. As indicated, mothers included in the high risk group were from two to four times more likely to respond inconsistently on the GUT or IM measures than were their counterparts in the low risk group.

**Table 20–8.** Percent of High and Low Risk Mothers Who Responded Inconsistently on *IM, CEB,* or *GUT*

| Group | High Risk | Low Risk |
|---|---|---|
| IM | 54 | 12 |
| CEB | 20 | 26 |
| GUT | 70 | 32 |

The response patterns for the Known Abusers and the Best Moms were similarly examined. Table 20–9 displays this information. As indicated, mothers included in the Known Abusers group were three to eight times more likely to respond inconsistently on the IM or the GUT measures than were their counterparts in the Best Moms group.

Tables 20–8 and 20–9 clearly indicate that a pattern of response inconsistency was strongly associated with a mother being included in the high risk group. However, it was also just as clear that such a pattern was dependent upon the measure to which the mother was responding. Since both the scores on a particular measure and the type of response pattern appeared to be strongly related to the risk grouping, further analyses were done to determine the extent of sensitivity and specificity when both were taken into consideration.

**Table 20–9.** Percent of Known Abusers and Best Moms Who Responded Inconsistently on *IM, CEB,* or *GUT*

| Group | Known Abusers | Best Moms |
|-------|---------------|-----------|
| IM    | 64            | 8         |
| CEB   | 21            | 21        |
| GUT   | 64            | 29        |

Table 20–10 displays the results of these analyses for the high and low risk groups. Table 20–11 displays this same information for the mothers included in the Known Abusers and the Best Moms groups. As indicated in Table 20–11, the degree of sensitivity and specificity, while dependent somewhat on the measure, is quite high. That is, the extent of correct prediction for either group varies from seven out of ten to nearly nine out of ten, depending upon the measure. When compared to the Discriminant score (Table 20–6), both sensitivity and specificity are considerably greater for the IM measure than for the Discriminant score when both the score and the type of response pattern are used to make a prediction from the IM measure. And, this situation is similar when the

**Table 20–10.** Percent of Mothers Correctly Predicted to Belong to the High and Low Risk Groups as a Function Both of Their Numerical Score and the Type of Response Pattern Observed on *IM, CEB,* and *GUT*

| Group | High Risk | Low Risk |
|-------|-----------|----------|
| IM    | 77        | 84       |
| CEB   | 77        | 45       |
| GUT   | 85        | 67       |

**Table 20-11.** Percent of Mothers Correctly Predicted to Belong to the Known Abusers or Best Moms Groups Both as a Function of Their Numerical Scores and the Type of Response Pattern Observed on *IM, CEB* and *GUT*

| Group | Known Abusers | Best Moms |
|-------|--------------|-----------|
| IM | 86 | 88 |
| CEB | 71 | 74 |
| GUT | 79 | 72 |

Discriminant scores for Known Abusers and Best Moms are compared to their numerical scores and type of response pattern on IM. Table 20–12 displays this information.

**Table 20–12.** Percent of Persons Correctly Predicted as a Function of the Type of Response Pattern and/or the Measure

| | High Risk | | Low Risk | |
|---|---|---|---|---|
| | Known Abusers | Total Group | Best Moms | Total Group |
| IM[a] | 86 | 77 | 88 | 84 |
| DIS[b] | 86 | 63 | 73 | 77 |

[a]Prediction based both on the numerical score *and* the type of response distribution.
[b]Prediction based only on the numerical score.

### Stability of the Predictive Measures

As indicated earlier, test-retest data were available for 92 mothers. Since only four of the predictive questionnaire measures appeared to be useful for indicating a potential to use unusual child rearing practices, stability (reliability) information was computed only for these four measures. Convergence analysis was again used to compute the scores on IM, CEB, and GUT. And, a simple average was used to compute the score on DIS. Table 20–13 displays the test-retest correlations for IM, CEB, GUT, and DIS.

**Table 20–13.** Pearson Correlations Between the Test and Retest Scores on *IM, CEB, GUT,* and *DIS*

| | IM | CEB | GUT | DIS |
|---|-----|-----|-----|-----|
| Pearson Correlation | .60 | .75 | .83 | .70 |
| N | 57 | 56 | 34 | 89 |

As indicated in Table 20–14, the stability of the scores across a short interval of time is fairly high, except for IM. Table 20–14 also indicates that approximately the same percentage of mothers responded inconsistently in this sample as was observed in the original groups of mothers described earlier in this chapter. The test-retest data were further examined, therefore, in order to determine the extent to which the types of response patterns were similar across this time period.

**Table 20–14.** Percent of persons having the same or different type of Response Pattern or Score Across Time

| Response Pattern or Score | IM | CEB | GUT | DIS |
|---|---|---|---|---|
| Scores in the same range at both test periods | 57 | 49 | 33 | 79 |
| Scores were high on one test and low on the other test | 5 | 15 | 1 | 22 |
| Response patterns were inconsistent at both test periods | 14 | 7 | 26 | |
| Response pattern was consistent at one time and inconsistent at the other time | 24 | 29 | 40 | |
| Total scores or responses patterns table across time | 71 | 56 | 59 | 78 |
| Total scores or response patterns different across time | 29 | 44 | 41 | 22 |

Since the cutting points developed earlier for making a prediction about whether a mother was likely to be in a high rather than a low risk group seemed to be fairly successful, they were also used on the test-retest scores. Consequently, four types of test-retest response patterns were possible: (1) the test-retest scores were in the same range at both testing periods—i.e., both above or both below the cutting point; (2) the scores were not in the same range on both tests—i.e., one was above and one was below the cutting point; (3) the response patterns were inconsistent on both tests; and (4) one response pattern was consistent and one was inconsistent. Table 20–14 displays the results of this analysis. As indicated, the extent of stability of the scores on IM, CEB, GUT or DIS across a two-week interval for this group of mothers ranges from 56 to 78 percent.

## DISCUSSION

It is clear that there are large and significant differences in questionnaire responses between groups of parents designated as low risk for having problems in relating to their children and those designated as high risk. Those who are independently assessed to be doing well with their children can be identified as low risk by their questionnaire responses in nearly nine out of ten cases. Those who are independently judged as having difficulty or as potentially having problems relating to their children can be identified as high risk in better than eight out of ten cases. Current scoring procedures can identify all the known child abusers.

The current results corroborate our early findings that high risk parents are distinguished from low risk in part by the extreme variability of their answers to questions in several attitude areas. Our predictive accuracy is increased considerably when we take variability (inconsistency) as well as magnitude of scores into account. Reliability is still too low to be acceptable as a clinical tool, however. This is possibly related to our method of analyzing this statistic. Using "degree/risk" rather than actual answers to questions may produce more acceptable results. This is, after all, what is really being sought—i.e., consistency in determining degree of risk. Further assessments of reliability are under way.

It is encouraging that the face validity built into the instrument continues to be substantiated by the clusters that developed in these analyses. The six major identified clusters cover problems with parents, problems with self-esteem, isolation, expectations of children, and reactions to crisis. These clusters all show large differences between high risk and low risk in the direction predicted by observations made on the psychodynamics of abuse in the mid sixties.

In assessing prediction in individual cases, it is no surprise that the single best predictive cluster is the one indicating problems with self-esteem (IM, I'm no damn good). In order to love oneself, one has to first be loved, approved of, and nurtured by parent figures. Lacking this parenting, the high risk parent cannot develop high self-esteem. Most crucial for the problem of prevention, the high risk parents cannot give the love, approval, and nurturance to their own children that would allow these children to develop their own high self-esteem. Research in progress in Denver[3] shows that abusive parents have significantly lower self-esteem than parents who comprise a normal sample. Intervention programs must consider self-esteem problems.

It is likewise no surprise that the single best item for discriminating the known abuser from those high risk parents who are not known to have abused is "When I was a child my parents used severe physical punishment on me."[4] This seems to validate the observations that the selection of the unusual child rearing practice of physically abusing a child requires prior experience with a severely punitive parent model. While these results do not say that every abused child will become an abusive parent, we can be more certain that most abusive parents have had prior experiences with child abuse and that prevention of child abuse in the present is likely to contribute to prevention in the future.

Our experiences with the questionnaire seem to lend the support of data to the theoretical observation made about these parents. We are currently continuing to gather data with the questionnaire.[a] Based on results presented here, a questionnaire with 50 items is now being used. Emphasis must be given to the fact that this questionnaire *appears* to be capable of separating groups of women who are at high and low risk in their capabilities of rearing their children. There should be a clear understanding by any who wish to use this questionnaire that it has not been fully validated, nor has its reliability been completely assessed. We have a reasonable amount of data to indicate that it is a valid instrument, but to date we are uncertain as to how many "false negative" and "false positive" answers will be picked up by this form of screening. Cross-validation studies are in process to answer this question.

This clearly indicates the need for further research. It would appear that many parents have the potential to rear their children in an unusual way, and yet few apparently come to the attention of those who are providing help to these families. The presence of a very special child and a family crisis seems to be necessary to precipitate the abusive act or unusual rearing practice. We feel that many families have varying "degrees of potential" to bring their children up in an unusual way, and that this may be precipitated only on the occasion when a particular crisis persists. This instrument must, therefore, be considered *only* as a screening device which, hopefully, can identify those families who are in need of further evaluation, followup, and help during the first few years of a new child's life within this atmosphere.

The need for further research on the questionnaire to assist in developing data to ascertain the true reliability and validity of the instrument, coupled with the many requests from programs to use the questionnaire in specific research endeavors, have resulted in our decision to allow this questionnaire to be shared—on controlled basis—with a number of individuals during an extensive field study. Hopefully this field trial will benefit those who are involved in gathering their data, as it certainly will benefit us in our continued efforts to develop a dependable screening method.

## USES OF THE QUESTIONNAIRE

In assessing the possible uses of this questionnaire, which does appear to have capability of identifying high risk families, four areas come to mind.

1. It should be helpful in assisting those individuals working directly with families who may be abusive and/or neglectful of their children, in gathering necessary data to augment their diagnostic impressions about the family in question. Impressions of those working with the family, and possibly even

---

[a]A field study is in progress and funded by the Office of Child Development, HEW. Some ten researchers across the country are making use of the questionnaire in their projects.

confession on the part of the parents, would assist us in developing data to measure the validity of the instrument.

2. The possible predictive capabilities of the questionnaire might be used in a carefully controlled research study to identify families who should be followed over a long period of time and observations made as to the methods of rearing employed by these parents. These families would more than likely be a part of another research study carried out by an individual, and the questionnaire could serve as an adjunct to the data gathered for the specific research that was being undertaken.

3. The possibility of using the questionnaire as a pre- and posttest instrument for students who are taking a course on child rearing techniques is an intriguing thought. It might be possible to ask students to answer the questions as if they were a parent of an abused child in a pretest. This could be followed up in a posttest to determine whether or not there were any significant changes in the student's perception of those parents having difficulty with their children.

4. Whether or not the questionnaire would be helpful for the purpose of determining the "success or failure" of a treatment program for families who are known to have difficulty with their children is still unknown at this time.

## LIMITATIONS OF THE QUESTIONNAIRE

This predictive questionnaire must not be considered, as yet, to be a valid instrument, and must be used only as a *research tool or a screening instrument.* Until further research is completed, definitive decisions about a given family should not be based solely on the results of the questionnaire. Although it was originally used only for women—and seems at this point to have its greatest usefulness in young mothers or mothers-to-be—it is hoped that further study will expand the usefulness of this questionnaire to fathers as well.

# ✳ References

**CHAPTER ONE**

1. Upham, T.C. *Elements of Mental Philosophy.* New York: Harper and Bros., 1852.
2. Steele, B.F. "Violence in our Society." *The Pharos of Alpha Omego Alpha* 33, No. 2 (April 1970): 42–48.
3. Daniels, D.N., Gilula, M.F., and Ochberg, F.M. (Eds.). *Violence and the Struggle for Existence.* Boston: Little, Brown, 1970.
4. Kelley, C.M., Director, Federal Bureau of Investigation. *Uniform Crime Reports for the United States.* Washington, D.C.: U.S. Government Printing Office, 1973.
5. FBI, *Law Enforcement Bulletin,* January 1963.
6. Bohannan, Paul. "Patterns of Murder and Suicide." In Bohannan, P. (Ed.), *African Homicide and Suicide.* Princeton: Princeton University Press, 1960.
7. Wolfgang, M.E. "Who Kills Whom." *Psychology Today* (October 1969).
8. Bard, M. "The Study and Modification of Intra-Familial Violence." In Singer, J. (Ed.), *The Control of Aggression and Violence.* New York: Academic Press, 1971, pp. 149–164.
9. Cannon, W.B. *Bodily Changes in Pain, Hunger, Fear and Rage.* New York: D. Appleton, 1925.
10. Conner, R.L., and Levine, S. "Hormonal Influences on Aggressive Behavior." In Garratini, S. and Sigg, E.B. (Eds.), *Aggressive Behavior.* New York: John Wiley, 1969.
11. Mark, V. and Ervin, F. *Violence and the Brain.* New York: Harper and Row, 1970.
12. Price, W.H. and Whatmore, P.B. "Behavior Disorders and Pattern of Crime

Among XYY Males Identified at a Maximum Security Hospital." *Brit. Med. J.* 1:533, 1967.

13. Gardner, L.I. and Neu, R.L. "Evidence Linking an Extra Y Chromosome to Sociopathic Behavior." *Arch. Gen. Psychiat.* 26:220–222, 1972.

14. Telfer, M.A., Baker, D., Clark, G.R., and Richardson, C.E. "Incidence of Gross Chromosomal Errors Among Tall Criminal American Males." *Science* 159:1249–1250, 1968.

15. Walzer, S., and Gerald, P. S. "Social Class and Frequency of XYY and XXY." *Science* 190:1228–1229, 1975.

16. Chiswick Women's Aid and the Problem of Battered Women, Anonymous Report. London, 1973.

17. Steinmetz, S.K. and Straus, M.A. "General Introduction: Social Myth and Social System in the Study of Intra-Family Violence." In Steinmetz, S. and Straus, M. (Eds.), *Violence in the Family.* New York: Dodd, Mead, 1974.

18. Straus, M. A. "Cultural and Social Organizational Influences on Violence Between Family Members. In Prince, R. and Barried, D. (Eds.), *Configurations: Biological and Cultural Factors in Sexuality and Family Life.* New York: D.C. Heath Lexington Books, 1974.

19. Gelles, R. J. "Child Abuse as Psychopathology: A Sociological Critique and Reformulation." *Amer. J. Orthopsychiat.* 43:611–621, 1973.

20. Erikson, E.H. "Identity and the Life Cycle."*Psychological Issues* I:1, 1959.

21. Mead, M. *Male and Female.* New York: William Morrow, 1949.

22. Brown, C. *Manchild in the Promised Land.* New York: Macmillan, 1965.

23. Gil, D.G. "Violence Against Children." *J. of Marriage and the Family* 33 (November 1971): 644–648.

24. Morton, Arthur. Personal communication, 1975.

25. Steele, B. and Pollock, C. "A Psychiatric Study of Parents Who Abuse Infants and Small Children." In Helfer, R. and Kempe, C.H. (Eds.), *The Battered Child.* Chicago: University of Chicago Press, 1968.

26. Steele, B.F. "Parental Abuse of Infants and Small Children." In Anthony, E.J. and Benedek, T. (Eds.), *Parenthood: Its Psychology and Psychopathology.* Boston: Little, Brown, 1970.

27. Benedek, T. "Adaptation to Reality in Early Infancy." *Psychoanal. Quart.* 7:200–215, 1938.

28. Erikson, E. *Childhood and Society.* New York: W.W. Norton, 1950.

29. Benedek, T. "Parenthood as a Developmental Phase: A Contribution to the Libido Theory." *J. Amer. Psychoanal. Ass.* 7:389–417, 1959.

30. Kramer, N. *From the Tablets of Sumer.* Indian Hills, Colo.: The Falcon's Wing Press, 1956.

31. Mercurio, J.A. *Caning: Educational Rite and Tradition.* Syracuse, N.Y.: Syracuse University Press, 1972.

32. Hunt, D. *Parents and Children in History: The Psychology of Family Life in Early Modern France.* New York: Basic Books, 1970.

33. Kohlberg, L. "Development of Moral Character and Moral Ideology." In Hoffman, M.L. and Hoffman, L.W. (Eds.), Review of Child Development Research. New York: Russel Sage Foundation, 1964.

34. Sears, R.R., Maccoby, E.E., and Levin, H. *Patterns of Child Rearing.* New York: Harper and Row, 1957.

35. Aichorn, A. *Wayward Youth.* New York: Viking Press, 1935 edition.

36. Bender, L. and Curran, F.J. "Children and Adolescents Who Kill." *J. Crim. Psychopath.* 1:297, 1940.

37. Bender, L. "Psychopathic Behavior Disorders in Children." In Lindner, R.M. and Seliger, R.V. (Eds), *Handbook of Correctional Psychology.* New York: Philosophical Library, 1947.

38. Bender, L. "What are the Influential Factors that Predispose the Youth of Our Society to Delinquency and Crime?" In Cohen, F.J. (Ed.), *Youth and Crime.* New York: International University Press, 1957.

39. Glueck, S. and Glueck, E. *Unraveling Juvenile Delinquency.* Cambridge Mass.: Harvard University Press, 1950.

40. Weston, James. Personal communication, 1970.

41. Hopkins, J. Personal communication (to be published).

42. Alafro, J. "Report of New York State Assembly Select Committee on Child Aubse." *Child Protection Report.* Vol. II, No. 1. Washington, D.C., January 1, 1976.

43. Johnson, A.M. and Szurek, S.A. "The Genesis of Antisocial Acting Out in Children and Adults." *Psychoanal. Quart.* 21:323, 1952.

44. King. C.H. "The Ego and the Integration of Violence in Homicidal Youth." *Amer. J. Orthopsychiat.* 45:134–145, 1975.

45. Martin, H., Beezley, P., Conway, E., and Kempe, C.H. "The Development of Abused Children." *Advances in Pediatrics* 21:25–73, 1974.

46. Russell, D.H. "A Study of Juvenile Murderers." *J. Offender Therapy* 9:55–86, 1965.

47. Easson W.M. and Steinhilber, R.M. "Murderous Aggression by Children and Adolescents." *Arch. Gen. Psychiat.* 4:1–9, 1961.

48. Duncan, G.M., Frazier, S.H., Litin, E.M., Johnson, A.M., and Barron, A.J. "Etiological Factors in First-Degree Murder." *J.A.M.A.* 168:1755–1758, 1958.

49. Satten, J., Menninger, K., Rosen, I., and Mayman, M. "Murder Without Apparent Motive: A Study in Personality Disorganization." *Amer. J. Psychiat.* 117:48–53, 1960.

50. Tanay, E. "Psychiatric Study of Homocide." *Amer. J. Psychiat.* 125:1252–1258, 1969.

51. Curtis, G.C. "Violence Breeds Violence—Perhaps?" *Amer. J. Psychiat.* 120:386–387, 1963.

52. Silver, L.B., Dublin, C.C., and Lourie, R.S. "Does Violence Breed Violence? Contributions from a Study of the Child Abuse Syndrome." *Amer. J. Psychiat.* 126:404–407, 1969.

53. Mead, M. "Cultural Factors in the Cause and Prevention of Pathological Homicide." *Bull. Menninger Clin.* 28:11–22, 1964.

## CHAPTER TWO

1. Bowlby, J. "The Nature of the Child's Tie to His Mother." *International Journal of Psychoanalysis* 39:350–373, 1958.

2. Spitz, R. "Hospitalism: An Inquiry into the Genesis of Psychiatric Conditions in Early Childhood." *The Psychoanalytic Study of the Child* I:53–74, 1945.

3. Meier, G.W. "Maternal Behavior of Feral and Laboratory-Rear Monkeys Following the Surgical Delivery of Their Infants." *Nature* 206: 492–493, 1965.

4. Sackett, G.P. and Ruppenthal, G.C. *The Effect of the Infant on Its Caregiver.* Lewis, M. and Rosenblum, L. (Eds.). New York: John Wiley, 1974.

5. Brazelton, T.B. "The Early Mother-Infant Adjustment." *Pediatrics* 32:931–938, 1963.

6. Caplan, G. *Emotional Implications of Pregnancy and Influences on Family Relationships in the Healthy Child.* Cambridge, Mass.: Harvard University Press, 1960.

7. Bibring, G.L., Dwyer, T.F., Huntington, D.S., and Valenstein, A.F.: A study of the Psychological Processes in Pregnancy and of the Earliest Mother-Child Relationship. I. Some Propositions and Comments. Psychoanalytic Study of the Child. 16:9–27, 1961.

8. Lynch, M.A. "Ill-Health and Child Abuse." *The Lancet* Aug. 16, 1975.

9. Newton, N. and Newton, M. Mothers' Reactions to Their Newborn Babies." *J.A.M.A.* 181:206–211, 1962.

10. Lang, R. Personal communication, 1974.

11. Kennel, J.H., Jerauld, R., Wolfe, H., Chesler, D., Kreger, N.C., McAlpine, W., Steffa, M., and Klaus, M.H. "Maternal Behavior One Year after Early and Extended Post-Partum Contact." *Developmental Medicine and Child Neuroloty* 16:172–179, 1974.

12. Ringler, N.M., Kennel, J.H., Jarvella, R., Navojosky, B.J., and Klaus, M.H. "Mother-to-Child Speech at 2 Years—Effect of Early Postnatal Contact." *Behavioral Pediatrics* 86:141–144, 1975.

13. Lind, J. Personal communication, 1973.

14. McBryde, A. "Compulsory Rooming-in in the Ward and Private Service at Duke Hospital." *J.A.M.A.* 45(a):625, 1951.

15. Greenberg, M., Rosenberg, I. and Lind, J. "First Mothers Rooming-In with Their Newborns: Its Impact Upon the Mother." *American Journal of Orthopsychiatry* 43:783–788, 1973.

16. Robson, K. The Role of Eye-to-Eye Contact in Maternal-Infant Attachment." *Journal of Child Psychology and Psychiatry* 8:13–25, 1967.

17. Lang, R. *Birth Book.* Ben Lomond, California: Genesis Press, 1972.

18. Desmond, M.M., Rudolph, A.J., and Phitaksphraiwan, P. "The Transitional Care Nursery: A Mechanism of a Preventative Medicine." *Pediatric Clinics of North America* 13:651–668, 1966.

19. Brazelton, T.B., School, M. and Rabey, J. "Visual Responses in the Newborn." *Pediatrics* 37:284–290, 1966.

20. Leifer, A., Leiderman, P., Barnett, C. and Williams, J. "Effects of Mother-Infant Separation on Maternal Attachment Behavior." *Child Development* 43: 1203–1218, 1972.

21. Parke, R. "Family Interaction in the Newborn Period: Some Findings, Some Observations, and Some Unresolved Issues." In Riegal, K. and Meachm, J. (Eds.) *Proceedings of the International Society of Behavior Development,* 1974.

22. Ambuel, J.P., Harris, B. "Failure to Thrive: A Study of Failure to Grow in Height and Weight." *Ohio State Medical Journal* (October): 997–1011, 1963.

23. Shaheen, E., Alexander, D., Truskowsky, M. and Barbero, G. "Failure to Thrive—a Retrospective Profile." *Clinical Pediatrics* 7:225, 1968.

24. Evans, S., Reinhart, J., and Succop, P. "A Study of 45 Children and Their Families." *Journal of the American Academy of Child Psychology* 11:440–454, 1972.

25. Elmer, E. and Gregg, D. "Developmental Characteristics of Abused Children." *Pediatrics* 40:596, 1967.

26. Skinner, A. and Castle, R. "Seventy-Eight Battered Children: A Retrospective Study." *Report by the National Society for the Prevention of Cruelty to Children,* London 1969.

27. Klein, M. and Stern, L. "Low Birth Weight and the Battered Child Syndrome." *American Journal of Diseases of Children* 122:15, 1971.

28. Oliver, J.E., Cox, J., Taylor, A., and Baldwin, J. "Severely Ill-Treated Young Children in North-East Wiltshire." *Research Report #4,* Oxford University Unit of Clinical Epidemiology, 1974.

29. Barnett, C.R., Grobstein, R., and Seashore, M. Personal communication, 1970.

30. Solnit, A.J. and Stark, M.H. "Mourning and the Birth of a Defective Child." *Psychoanalytic Study of the Child* 16:523–537, 1961.

31. Bloom, B. "Definitional Concepts of the Crisis Concept." *Journal of Consulting Psychology* 27:42, 1963.

32. Rappoport, L. "The State of Crisis: Some Theoretical Considerations." In Parad, H.H. (Ed.), *Crisis Intervention.* New York: Family Service Association, 1965.

33. Roskies, E. *Abnormality and Normality: The Mothering of Thalidomide Children.* New York: Cornell University Press, 1972.

34. Drotar, D., Baskiewitz, A., Irvin, N., Kennell, J., and Klaus, M. "The Adaptation of Parents to the Birth of an Infant with a Congenital Malformation: A Hypothetical Model." *Pediatrics* 56:710, 1975.

35. Bibring, G. "Some Considerations of the Psychological Process in Pregnancy." *Psychoanalytic Study of the Child* 14:113, 1959.

## CHAPTER THREE

1. Freiberg, S. *The Magic Years.* New York: Charles Scribner, 1959.

2. Loomis, W.G. "Management of Children's Emotional Reactions to Severe Body Damage (Burns)" *Clin Pediatrics* 9(6):362–367, 1970.

3. Spitz, R. "Hospitalism." *Psychoanalytic Study of the Child* 2:113–117, 1946.

4. Bowlby, J. *Separation, Anxiety and Anger.* Travistock Institute, 1973.

5. Illingworth, R.S. and Lister, J. "Critical or Sensitive Period, with Special Reference to Certain Feeding Problems in Infants and Children." *J. Pediat.* 65:839–848, 1964.

6. Chase, H.P. and Martin, H.P. "Undernutrition and Child Development." *N.Eng.J.M.* 282:933–939, 1970.

7. Elmer, E. and Gregg, G. "Developmental Characteristics of Abused Children." *Pediatrics* 40(4):596–602, 1967.

8. Peterson, K. "Contributions to an Abused Child's Unlovability; Failure in the Developmental Tasks and in the Mastery of Trauma" M.S.W. thesis. *Smith College Studies in Social Work,* 44(1):24–25, 1973.

9. Cohen, M. "A Warning to Conscientious Mothers." *Today's Health* (February 1974):22–61.

10. Brackbill, Y. "Cumulative Effects of Continuous Stimulation on Arousal Level in Infants." *Child Development* 42:17–26, 1971.

11. Tronick, E., et al. "Mother-Infant Face-to-Face Interaction." For publication in Gosh, S. (Ed.), *Biology and Language* (in press).

12. Fullerton, D.T. "Infantile Rumination: Case Report." *Arch. Gen. Psychiat.* 9:593–600, 1963.

13. Luckey, R.E., Watson, C.M., and Musick, J.K. "Aversive Conditioning as Means of Inhibiting Vomiting and Rumination." *Am. J. Ment. Deficiency* 73:139–142, 1968.

14. Menking, M., et al. "Rumination: Near-Fatal Psychiatric Disease of Infancy." *N. Eng. J. M.* 280:802–804, 1969.

15. Filippi, R. and Rousey, C.L. "Delay in Onset of Talking: Symptom of Interpersonal Disturbance." *J. Am. Acad. Child Psychiat.* 7:316–328, 1968.

16. Kenny, T.J., et al. "Characteristics of Children Referred Because of Hyperactivity." *J. Pediatrics* 79:618–622, 1971.

17. Condon, W.S. and Sander, L.W. "Neonate Movement Is Synchronized with Adult Speech: Interactional Participation and Language Acquisition." *Science* 183:99–103.

18. Montagu, A. *Touching: The Human Significance of the Skin.* New York: Columbia University Press, 1971.

19. Helfer, R. "Making the Diagnosis of Child Abuse and Neglect." *Pediatric Basic* 10, 1974.

20. Pavlov, I.P. "Conditioned reflexes: *An Investigation of the Physiological Activity of the Cerebral Cortex (trans.).* London: Oxford University Press, 1927.

21. Watson, J.B. and Raynor, R. "Conditioned Emotional Reactions." *Journal of Experimental Psychology* 3:1–4, 1920.

22. Jones, M.C. "A Laboratory Study of Fear: The Case of Peter." *Pedagogical Seminary* 31:308–315, 1924.

23. Jones, M.C. Albert, P., and Watson, B. *American Psychologist* 29:581–583, 1974.

24. Harlow, H.F., Harlow, M.K., and Suomi, S.J. "From Thought to Therapy: Lessons from a Private Laboratory." *American Scientist* 59:538–549, 1971.

25. Maurer, A., *Corporal Punishment American Psychologist* 29:614–626, 1974.

26. Spinetta, J.J. and Rigler, D. "The Child-Abusing Parent: A Psychological Review." *Psychological Bulletin* 77:296–304, 1972.

27. Fraiberg, S., Adelson, E., and Shapiro, V. "Ghosts in the Nursery: A Psychoanalytic Approach to the Problems of Impaired Infant-Mother Relationships. *Journal of Child Psychiatry* 14:387–421, 1975.

28. Bandura, A. and Walters, R. *Social Learning and Personality Development.* New York: Holt, Rinehart, and Winston, 1963.

29. Dollard, J., Doob, L.W., Miller, N.E., Mowrer, O.H., and Sears, R.R. *Frustration and Agression.* New Haven: Yale University Press, 1939.

30. Bandura, A., Ross, D., and Ross, S.A. "Imitation of Film-Mediated Aggressive Models." *Journal of Abnormal and Social Psychology* 66:3–11, 1963.

31. Fontana, V.J. "Further Reflections on Maltreatment of Children." *New York State Journal of Medicine* 68:2214–2215, 1968.

32. Melnick, B. and Hurley, J.R. Distinctive Personality Attributes of Child-Abusing Mothers." *Journal of Consulting and Clinical Psychology* 33:746–749, 1969.

33. Harlow, H.F., Harlow, M.K., and Suomi, S.J. "From Thought to Therapy: Lessons from a Private Laboratory." *American Scientist* 59:538–549, 1971.

34. Bell, R.Q. "A reinterpretation of the Direction of Effects in Studies of Socialization." *Psychological Review* 75:81–95, 1968.

35. Mandler, G. "Parent and Child in the Development of the Oedipus Complex." *The Journal of Nervous and Mental Disease* 136:227–235, 1963.

36. Galdston, R. "Observations on Children Who Have Been Physically Abused and Their Parents." *American Journal of Psychiatry* 122:440–443, 1965.

37. Provence, S. and Ritvo, S. "Deprivation in Institutional Infants." *Psychoanalytic Study of the Child* 16:189–205, 1961.

38. Brazelton, T.B. *Infants and Mothers, Differences in Development.* Delacorte Press/Seymour Lawrence, 1972.

39. Temmes, K. "Personality Development of a Battered Child" Unpublished paper presented at Reiss Davis Child Study Center, Los Angeles, 1973.

40. Steckler, G. "Autoplastic and Alloplastic Behavior: How the Parent Manipulates Input." In *Issues in Human Development* Vaughan, C. (Ed.), National Institute Child Health and Human Development. U.S. Government Printing Office, Washington, D.C.: 1967.

41. Tronick, W., Adamson, L., Wise, S., Als, H., and Brazelton, T.B. "Infant Emotions in Normal and Purtubated Interactions." Presented at meeting of Society for Research in Child Development, April 11, 1975, Denver, Colorado.

42. Lewis, M., "Mother-Infant Interaction and Cognitive Development: A Motivational Construct," *Issues in Human Development.* Vaughn V. NICHD. U.S. Government Printing Office, Washington, D.C.: 1967.

43. Maier, S.F., Seligman, M.F.P., and Solomon, R.L., "Pavlovian Fear Conditioning and Learned Helplessness" in Campbell, B.A. and Church, R.M. (Eds.), *Punishment and Agressive Behavior* New York: Appleton-Century-Croft, 1969, pp. 229–342.

## CHAPTER FOUR

1. Lynch, M.A. "Ill-Health and Child Abuse." *Lancet* 2:317–319, 1975.
2. Erickson, E. (title of chapter??) (p. 168). In Tanner, J.M. and Inhelder, B. (Eds.), *Discussions on Child Development.* Vol. III. London: Tavistock Publications, 1955.
3. Ounsted, C., Essay on Developmental Medicine, *Psychiatric Aspects of Medical Practice.* Mandelbrote, B., and Gelder, M.G. (Eds.), London: Staples Press, 1972, p. 130.
4. Pollock, C. and Steele, B. (what is chapter title?) (p. 10). In Kempe, C.H. and Helfer, R.E. (Eds.), *A Therapeutic Approach to the Parents in Helping the Battered Child and His Family.* Philadelphia: Lippincott, 1972.
5. Gray, J.A. "Drug Effects on Fear and Frustration." In Iverson, L., Iverson, S., and Snyder, S. (Eds.), *Handbook of Psychopharmacology.* New York: Plenum Press. In press.
6. Lynch, M.A. "Abused Children and Their Siblings." In Martin, H. (Ed.), *The Child Who Is Abused.* In press.
7. Ounsted, C. "Some Aspects of Seizure Disorders" (p. 371). In Gairdner, D. and Hull, D. (Eds.), *Recent Advances in Pediatrics.* London: Churchill, 1971.
8. Bernard, C. *Introduction à l'Etude de la Médicine Experimentale.* Paris: J.B. Balliere et Fils, 1895.
9. Bertalanffy, L. *General Systems Theory.* London: Penguin Press, 1968.

## CHAPTER FIVE

1. Silverman, F.N. "Radiological Aspects of the Battered Child Syndrome" In Helfer, R.E. and Kempe, C.H. (Eds.), *The Battered Child.* 2d. ed. Chicago: Univ. of Chicago Press, 1973.
2. Cameron, J.M. and Rae, L.J. *Atlas of the Battered Child Syndrome.* New York: Churchill Livingstone, 1975.

## CHAPTER SEVEN

1. Levy, I. "Marriage Preliminaries." *Jewish Marriage* 3:36, 1967.
2. Frazer, J.G. In Gaster, T.H. (Ed.), *The New Golden Bough.* New York: Criterion Books, 1959.
3. Sidler, M. *On the Universality of the Incest Taboo.* Stuttgart: Enke, 1971.
4. Norton, R., Feldman, C., and Tafoya, D. "Risk Parameters Across Types of Secrets." *J. of Counselling Psychol.* 21:450–454, 1974.
5. Weinberg S. *Incest Behavior.* New York: Citadel Press, 1955.
6. Stoenner, H.: *Child Sexual Abuse Seen Growing in the United States.* Denver: American Humane Assoc., 1972.
7. Eaton, A. and Vastbinder, E. "The Sexually Molested Child: A Plan for Management." *Clin. Peds.* 8:438–441, 1969.
8. Apfelberg, B., Sugar, C., and Pfeffer, A. "A Psychiatric Study of 250 Sex Offenders." *Am. J. Psychiat.* 100:565, 1944.

9. Lukianowicz, M. "Incest: I. Paternal incest: II. Other types." *Brit. J. Psychiat.* 120:301–313, 1972.

10. Parker, G. "Incest." *Med. J. of Australia* 1:488–490, 1974.

11. Riemer, S. "A Research note on Incest." *Amer. J. Sociol.* 45: 554, 1940.

12. Sarles, R. "Incest." *Ped. Cl. of North America* 22:3, 633–642, 1975.

13. Williams, J. and Hall, J. "The Neglect of Incest: A Criminologist's View." *Medicine, Science, and the Law* 14:64–67, 1974.

14. Schonfelder, T. "Sexual Trauma in Childhood and Its Consequences." *Oraxis der Psychotherapie* 15:12–20, 1970.

15. Takagi, S. "Sexual Development of Mentally Retarded People and Discipline." *Psychiatrica et Neurologica Paediatrica Japonica* 13:29–34, 1973.

16. Swanson, D. "Adult Sexual Abuse of Children." *Diseases of the Nervous System* 29:677–683, 1968.

17. Weiner, I. "On Incest: A Survey." *Excerpta Criminilogica* 4:137, 1964.

18. Bender, L. and Blau, A. "A Reaction of Children to Sexual Relations with Adults." *Am. J. Orthopsychiat.* 7:500, 1937.

19. Cavallin, H. "Incestuous Fathers: A Clinical Report." *Am. J. Psychiat.* 122:1132, 1962.

20. Devroye, A. "Incest: Bibliographical Review." *Acta Psychiatrica Belgica* 73:661–712, 1973.

21. Ramussen, A. "The Importance of Sexual Attacks on Children less than 14 Years of Age for the Development of Mental Diseases and Character Anomalies." *Acta Psychiat. Neurol.* 9:351, 1934.

**Other Readings**

Berman, L. and Jensen D. "Father-Daughter Interactions and the Sexual Development of the Adopted Girl." *Psychotherapy: Theory, Research and Practice* 10:253–255, 1973.

Bethscheider, J., John, L., Young, J., Morris, P., and Hayes, D. *A Study of Father-Daughter Incest in Harris County Child Welfare Unit.* Sam Houston State Univ., Huntsville, Texas, 131 pgs. 1971.

Brown, W. "Sex Offenders and Their Psychiatric Treatment." *Howard Journal of Penology and Crime Prevention* 13:113–121, 1971.

Cormier, B., Kennedy, M., and Kennedy, S. "Psychodynamics of Father-Daughter Incest." *Canad. Psychiat. Assoc. J.* 7:203, 1962.

Easson, W. "Special Sexual Problems of the Adopted Adolescent." *Medical Aspects of Human Sexuality* 7:92–103, 1973.

Fox, J. "Sibling Incest." *Brit. J. Sociol.* 13:128, 1962.

Friedman, S. "Conversion Symptoms in Adolescents." *Ped. Clin. No. Amer.* 20:873, 1973.

Frosch, J. and Bromberg, W. "The Sex Offender—A Psychiatric Study." *Am. J. Orthopsychiat.* 9:761, 1939.

Gebhard, P. *Sex Offenders* New York: Harper and Row, 1965.

Glaser, K. "Masked Depression in Children and Adolescents." *Am. J. Psychother.* 21:565, 1967.

Gordon, L. "Incest as Revenge Against the pre-Oedipal Mother." *Psychoanalytic Review* 284, 1955.

Gowell, E. "Implications of the Incest Taboo for Nursing Practice." *Journal of Psychiatric Nursing* 11:13–19, 1973.

Guttmacher, M. *Sex Offenses.* New York: W.W. Norton, 1951.

Henderson, D. "Incest: A Synthesis of Data." *Canadian Psychiatric Assoc. Journal* 17:299–313, 1972.

Kaufman, I., Peck, A., and Taguiri, C. "The Family Constellation and Overt Incestuous Relations Between Father and Daughter. *Am. J. Orthopsychiat.* 24:266, 1954.

Kaplan, S. and Poznanski, E. "Child Psychiatric Patients Who Share a Bed with a Patient." *J. of Am. Acad. Child Psychiatry* 13:344–356, 1974.

Kunter, M. "Socioanthropological Aspects of Father-Daughter Incest." *Offentliche Gesundheitswesen* 34:48–51, 1972.

Levine, S. "Family Relationship Systems: A Theoretical Framework for Understanding Father-Daughter Incest. *Smith College Studies in Social Work* 45:58–59, 1974.

Lichtenberg, J. and Lichtenberg, C. "Eugene O'Neill and Falling in Love." *Psychoanalytic Quarterly* 41:63–89, 1972.

McCord, J. "Etiological Factors in Alcoholism: Family and Personal Characteristics." *Quarterly Journal of Studies on Alcohol* 33:1020–1027, 1972.

McKerrow, W. "Protecting the Sexually Abused Child." American Humane Society Symposium, Denver, 1973.

Nedoma, K. and Pandelickova, J. "Incest Pedophiliac Delinquency." *Ceskoslevenska Psychiatrie* 65, 224–229, 1969.

Papertian, G. "The Rubicon Complex: Incest in Ancient Civilizations." *Borderlands of Psychiatry* 15:116–124, 1972.

Pirnay-Dufrasne, R. "Incestuous Relationships in a Large Family." *Acta Psychiatrica Belgica* 73:713–724, 1973.

Schachter, M. and Cotte, S. "A Medical-Psychological and Social Study of Incest from a Pedopsychiatric Point of View. *Acta Paedopsychiatr.* 27:139, 1960.

Schultz, L. "The Child Sex Victim: Social, Psychological, and Legal Perspectives. *Child Welfare* 52:147–157, 1973.

Sloane, P. and Karpinski, E. "Effects of Incest Upon the Participants." *Amer. J. Orthopsychiat.* 12:666, 1952.

Szabo, D. "Problems of Sociocultural Socialization and Integration—A Contribution to the Etiology of Incest. *Canad. Psychiat. Assoc. J.* 7:235, 1962.

Tormes, Y. *Child Victims of Incest.* Denver: American Humane Assoc., 19??.

Tuteur, W. "Further Observations of Incestuous Fathers." *Psychiatric Annals* 2:9, 77, 1972.

Van Gijseghem, H. "Father-Daughter Incest." *Vie Medicale au Canada Francais* 4:263–270, 1975.

Virkkunen, M. "Incest Offenses and Alcoholism." *Medicine, Science, and the Law* 14:124–128, 1974.

Wahl, C. The Psychodynamics of Consummated Maternal Incest." *Arch. Gen. Psychiat.* 3:188, 1960.

Wimnik, H. and Magal, V. "Role of Incest in Family Structure." *Israel Annals of Psychiatry and Related Disciplines* 6:2, 173–189, 1968.

## CHAPTER EIGHT

1. Mead, M. "Incest." *International Encyclopedia of the Social Sciences.* New York: Crowell, Collier and Macmillan, 1968.
2. Caprio, F.S. and D.R. Brenner. *Sexual Behavior: Psycho-Legal Aspects.* New York: The Citadel Press, 1961.
3. Kling, G. *Sexual Behavior and The Law.* New York: Bernard Geis Associates, 1965.
4. De Francis, V. "Protecting the Child Victim of Sex Crimes Committed by Adults." *Federal Probation* (September 15–20) 1971.
5. Weinberg, S.K. *Incest Behavior.* New York: Citadel Press, 1955.
6. Master, R. *Patterns of Incest: Psycho-Social Study.* New York: Julian Press, 1963.
7. Besharov, D. J. "Building a Community Response to Child Abuse and Maltreatment." *Children Today* (September-October): 2–4, 1975.
8. Sgroi, S. M. "Sexual Molestation of Children." *Children Today* (May-June): 18–21, 1975.
9. James, Jennifer. Private communications.
10. Baisden, M.J. *The World of Rosaphrenia: The Sexual Psychology of the Female.* Calif.: Allied Research Society, Sacramento, 1971.
11. Baisden, M.J. Unpublished data.
12. Benward, Jean and J. Densen-Gerber. *Incest as a Causative Factor in Anti-Social Behavior: An Exploratory Study.* New York: Odyssey Institute, 1975.
13. Weinberg, op. cit.
14. Satir, V. *Conjoint Family Therapy.* Palo Alto, Calif.: Science and Behavior Books, 1967.
15. Assagioli, R. *Psychosynthesis.* New York: Hobbs, Dorman, 1965.
16. *Ibid.*
17. Chaudhuri, H. *Integral Yoga.* San Francisco: California Institute of Asian Studies, 1970.
18. Perls, F.S., Hefferline, R.F., and Paul Goodman. *Gestalt Therapy.* New York: Julian Press, 1951.
19. Giarretto, H. and A. Einfield. "The Self-Actualization of Educators." In Marcia Perlstein, (Ed.), *Flowers Can Even Bloom in Schools.* Sunnyvale, Calif.: Westinghouse Learning Press, 1974.
20. *Op. cit.*
21. *Op. cit.*

## CHAPTER TEN

1. Martin H.P. (Ed.). *The Abused Child: A Multidisciplinary Approach to Developmental Issues and Treatment.* Cambridge, Mass.: Ballinger, 1976.
2. Martin, H.P., Beezley, P., Conway, E.F., and Kempe, C.H. "The Development of Abused Children." *Advances in Pediatrics* 21:25–73, 1974.
3. Elmer, E. and Gregg, G.S. "Developmental Characteristics of Abused Children." *Pediatrics* 40:596–602, 1967.
4. Birrell, R.G. and Birrell, J.H.W. "The Maltreatment Syndrome in Children: A Hospital Survey." *Med. J. Aust.* 2:1023–1029, 1968.

5. Lynch, M.A. "Ill-Health and Child Abuse," *Lancet* 2:317–319, 1975.

6. Martin, H.P. and Beezley, P. "Prevention and the Consequences of Child Abuse." *Journal of Operational Psychiatry* VI:68–77, 1974.

7. Goldstein, J., Freud, A., and Solnit, A.J. *Beyond the Best Interests of the Child.* New York: Free Press, 1973.


## CHAPTER ELEVEN

1. Ounsted, C. Lindsay, J., and Norman, R. "Biological Factors in Temporal Lobe Epilepsy." *Clinics in Developmental Medicine* 22:119–121, 1966 (Spastics International Publications. London: Heinemann).

2. Lynch, M.A., Steinberg D., and Ounsted, C. "Family Unit in a Children's Psychiatric Hospital." *Brit. Med. J.* 2:127–129, 1975.

3. Lynch, M.A. "Ill-Health and Child Abuse." *Lancet* 2:317–319, 1975.

4. Ounsted, C., Oppenheimer, R., and Lindsay, J. "Aspects of Bonding Failure." *Dev. Med. Child Neurol.* 16:446–456, 1974.

5. Lynch, M.A. "Abused Children and Their Siblings." In Martin, H. (Ed.) *The Child Who Is Abused.* In press.

6. Lynch, M.A., Lindsay, J., and Ounsted, C. "Tranquillisers Causing Agression." *Brit. Med. J.* 1:266, 1975.

7. Gray, J.A. "Drug Effects on Fear and Frustration." In *Handbook of Psychopharmacology.* Iverson, L., Iverson, S., and Snyder, S. (Eds.). New York: Plenum Press. In press.

8. Erikson, E. *Discussions on Child Development.* Tanner, J.M. and Inhelder, B. (Eds.). London: Tavistock Publications, 1955, pp. 168–215.


## CHAPTER TWELVE

1. Kempe, C.H. and Helfer, R.E. (Eds.). *Helping the Battered Child and His Family.* Philadelphia: Lippincott, 1972.

2. Tracy, James J. & Clark, Elizabeth H. "Treatment for Child Abusers" *Social Work,* May 1974, 338–342.

3. Holland, Cornelius J. "An Interview Guide for Behavioral Counseling with Parents." *Behavior Therapy* 1:70–79, 1970.

4. Birnbrauer, J.S., Peterson, C.R., and Solnick, J.V. "The Design and Interpretation of Studies of Single Subjects." *American Journal of Mental Deficiency* 79, 191–203, 1974.

5. Slater, P.E. *The Pursuit of Loneliness: American Culture at Breaking Point.* Harmondsworth, England: The Penguin Press, 1971.

6. Newson, J. and Newson, E. "Cultural Aspects of Childrearing in the English-Speaking World." In Richards, M.P.M. (Ed.), *The Integration of a Child Into a Social World.* Cambridge: Cambridge University Press, 1974.

7. Gil, David G. "Unraveling Child Abuse." *American Journal of Orthopsychiatry* 45 (3):346, 1975.

8. Aveling, M. Personal communication, 1975.

9. Gorky, M. *My Childhood*. Harmondsworth, England: Penguin Books, 1966.

10. Patterson, G.R. "A Basis for Identifying Stimuli Which Control Behaviors in Natural Settings." *Child Development* 45:900–911, 1974.

11. Musil, J. "Socio-Economic Goals for New Residential Development." *Planning and Administration* 1(1):7–16, 1974.

12. Newman, O. "Defensible Space." *The Listener,* 7 March 1974.

13. Sanson-Fisher, R. & Stotter, K. "Necessary Steps in Designing a Successful Contract." *Australian Social Work,* 28,(4): 21–28, 1975.

14. Lawick-Goodall, J. "The Behavior of Free Living Chimpanzees in the Gombe Stream Reserve." *Animal Behavior* Monog. 1:165–311, 1968.

15. Luria, A.R. *The Role of Speech in the Regulation of Normal and Abnormal Behaviors*. London: Pergamon Press, 1961.

16. La Fontaine. "The North Wind and The Sun." (Illus. Wildsmith, B.) A Fable by La Fontaine. London: Oxford University Press, 1964.

17. Kimmel, H.D. and Kimmel, E. "An Instrumental Conditioning Method for the Treatment of Enuresis." *J. Beh. Ther. & Exp. Psychiat.* 1:121–123, 1970.

18. Foxx, R.M. and Azrin, H. "Dry Pants": A Rapid Method of Toilet Training. *Behavior Research and Therapy* 11 (4):435–442, 1973.

19. Bean, S. "The Parents' Centre Project: A Multi-Service Approach to the Prevention of Child Abuse." *Child Welfare* L (5):277–282, 1971.

20. Court, J. and Kerr, A. "The Battered Child Syndrome—A Preventable Disease?" *Nursing Times* June 10, 1971.

21. Richards, M.P.M. *The Integration of a Child Into a Social World*. Cambridge: Cambridge University Press, 1974.

22. Ilg, F. and Ames, L.B. *Child Behaviour*. London: Hamish Hamilton, 1955.

23. Doll, E.A. *The Vineland Social Maturity Scale*.

24. Gesell, A. *The First 5 Years of Life*. London: Menthuen, 1950.

25. Lewis, M. and Rosenblum, L.A. (Eds.). *The Effect of the Infant on Its Caregiver*. New York: John Wiley, 1974.

26. Rutter, M. *Maternal Deprivation Reassessed*. Harmondsworth, England: Penguin Education, 1972.

27. Prechtl, H.F.R. The Mother-Child Interaction in Babies With Minimal Brain Damage. In Foss, B. (Ed.), *Determinants of Infant Behavior II*. London: Menthuen, 1963.

28. Robertson, J. "Mother-Infant Interaction from Birth to 12 Months: Two Case Studies." In Foss, B.M. (Ed.), *Determinants of Infant Behaviour III*. London: Menthuen, 1965.

29. Blurton-Jones, N.G. "Ethology & Early Socialisation." In Richards, M. (Ed.), *The Integration of a Child into a Social World*. Cambridge: Cambridge University Press, 1974.

30. Brazelton, T.B., Koslowski, B. and Main, M. "The Origins of Reciprocity: The Early Mother-Infant Interaction." In Lewis, M. and Rosenblum, L.A. (Eds.), *The Effect of the Infant on Its Caregiver*. New York: John Wiley, 1974.

31. Schaffer, H.R. and Emerson, P.E. "The Effects of Experimentally Administered Stimulation on Development Quotient of Infants." *Brit. J. Soc. Clin. Psychol.* 7:61–67, 1968.

32. Barton, S.S. and Blank, M. "Soviet Research on Speech and Language: An American Perspective." *Early Child Development & Care* 1:3–14, 1971.

33. Oswin, M. *The Empty Hours.* Harmondsworth, England: Penguin Books, 1971.

34. Sayegh, Y. and Dennis, W. "The Effect of Supplementary Experience Upon the Behavioral Development of Infants in Institutions." *Child Development* 36:81–90, 1965.

35. Rheingold, H. "The Effect of Environmental Stimulation Upon Social and Exploratory Behaviour in the Human Infant." In Foss, B.M. (Ed.), *Determinants of Infant Behaviour.* London, Menthuen, 1961.

36. Brossard, M. and Decarie, T. "Effects of Three Kinds of Perceptual and Social Stimulation on the Development of Institutionalized Infants." *Early Child Development & Care* 1:111–130, 1971.

37. Elardo, R., Bradley, R., and Caldwell, B.M. "The Relation of Infants' Home Environments to Mental Test Performance from 6 to 36 Months: A Longitudinal Analysis." *Child Development* 46:71–76, 1975.

## CHAPTER FOURTEEN

1. Haberland, John A., Ph.D., "Psychological Test Results of Parents of Battered Children," Orange County Medical Center, Orange, Calif.

2. Wichlacz, C.R. et al. "Characteristics and Management of Child Abuse in the U.S. Army-Europe." *Clinical Pediatrics* 14 (6):545, 1975.

3. Public Law 93–247, 93rd Congress, S.1191, January 31, 1974.

4. Saunders, D.N. "Poverty in the Army," *Social Service Review* (December 1969).

5. Miller, J.K. "The Maltreatment Syndrome in the Military Community." Presented to Current Trends in Army Social Work Conference, August 1972. William Beaumont Army Medical Center, El Paso, Texas.

6. Delsordo, J.D. "Protective Casework for Abused Children." *Children* 10: (Nov.-Dec.), 1963.

7. Miller, J.K. "Red, White and Bruised, The Maltreatment Syndrome in the Army." Presented to the American Medical Association Meeting, June 1974, William Beaumont Army Medical Center, El Paso, Texas.

8. Arellano, B., "Systems of Handling Abuse/Neglect, Child Protective Services: A Survey of Selected CONUS Installations." Fort Leonard Wood, Mo., 1970.

9. Wieder, S.M. "Child Abuse Croquettes." *Army Community Service Bulletin,* Headquarters, U.S. Army Air Defense Center and Fort Bliss, Fort Bliss, Texas, April 1975.

## CHAPTER SIXTEEN

1. Edwards and Chilperic. *The Hammurabi Code.* London: Kennikat Press, 1904.

2. The Hebrew Code may be found in the Old Testament of the *Bible,* in Exodus, Chapters XX to XXIII.

3. Jowett, *The Dialogues of Plato*. New York: Random House, 1898; Jones, *Law and Legal Theory of the Greeks*, Oxford Clarendon Press, 1956.

4. Buckland. *Textbook of Roman Law from Agustus to Justinian*, 3rd ed., Stein, Cambridge: Cambridge University Press, 1963.

5. Ali Hamid. *Outlines of Roman Law*. New Delhi, 1952, p. 89.

6. King, *Law & Society in the Visogothic Kingdom*. Cambridge: Cambridge University Press, 1972.

7. Pollock, Nathanel, *History of English Law*. Cambridge: Cambridge University Press, 1968.

8. In 1503 Henry VIII established a court of wards to protect the estate of minors and to regulate the sale of wardships.

9. Cogan, "Juvenile Law, Before and After the Entrance of Parens Patriae," *South Carolina Law Journal*, 22:147 (1970).

10. *Falkland v. Bertie*, 2 Vern 333, 23 Eng. Rep. 814 (Ch. 1696).

11. *Duke of Beaufort v. Berty*, 1 P.Wms. 702, 24 Eng. Rep. 579 (Ch. 1721).

12. *Wellesley v. Beaufort*, 38 Eng. Rep. 236 (Ch. 1827).

13. *Wellesley v. Wellesley*, 4 Eng. Rep. 1078 (H.L. 1828).

14. *In Re Spence*, 41 Eng. Rep. 937 (Ch. 1847).

15. 37 Hen. 8, C. 25 (1535).

16. 43 Eliz. 1, C.2 (1601).

17. From an excellent article describing this period of England and America and the development of the doctrine of neglect, see Areen, "Intervention Between Parent and Child: A Re-appraisal of the States Role in Child Abuse and Neglect Cases." *Georgetown Law Journal* 63:887, 1975.

18. N. Shurtleff, *Records of the Governor and Company of the Mass Bay Colony in New England* (1628–1686). The stubborn child law (minus its penalties) is still in effect today: Mass. Gen. Laws Ann. Ch. 272 353 (1958). See Sidman, "Mass. Stubborn Child Law: Law and Order in the Home." *F.L. Quart.* 6:33, 1972.

19. *Johnson v. State*, 21 Tenn. 183 (1841); *State v. Jones*, 95 N.C. 465 (1886).

20. The Maryellen case is noted and discussed in *The Battered Child*, Kempe and Helfer ed., University of Chicago Press, 2nd ed. 1974. Chapter 1, History of Child Abuse and Neglect: Radbill author.

21. *In Re Clark*, 21 Ohio, Op. 2d 86$_3$ at 87, 185 N.E. 2d 128 at 130 (1962).

22. *Ex Porte Grouse*, 4 Whort. 9, Pa. 1839.

23. *Finley v. Finley*, 240 N.Y. 429, 148 N.E. 624 (1925).

24. *Prince v. Massachusetts*, 321–U.S.1 (1967).

25. *In Re Gault*, 387 U.S.1 (1967).

26. *Ginsburg v. United States*, 390 U.S. 629 (1968).

27. *Denton v. Jones*, 107 Kansas 729, 193 Pa. 307 (1920).

28. *In Re Agor*, 10 C.D. 49 (1878).

29. *In Re Hudson*, 13 Wash. 2d 673, 126 Ped 765 (1942).

30. *Anguis v. Superior Court*, 6 Ariz. App. 68, 429 P. 2d 702 (1967).

31. *Wisconsin v. Yoder*, 406 U.S. 205 at 232 (1972).

32. "The integrity of the family unit has found protection in the Due Process Clause of 14th Amendment." *Stanley v. Illinois*, 405 U.S. 645 at 651 (1972).

33. Gil, D., Legal Nature of Neglect, N.P.P.A.J. 6:1 (1960).

34. Paulsen, M. "The Delinquency, Neglect & Dependency Jurisdiction of the Juvenile Court. In Rosenheim, M. (Ed.) *Justice for the Child* 1962.

35. From a rather definitive discussion of the medical rights of a minor. See Fraser, "A Pediatric Bill of Rights." *South Texas Law Journal* 16 (3): 245–308, 1975.

36. See Fraser *ibid.*, p. 264; see *State v. Perricone,* 37 at J. 463, 181 Ariz. 751 (1962).

37. *In Re Carstairs,* 115 N.Y. S 2d 314 (Don. Rel. 1952); *In Re Rotkowitz,* 175 Misc. 948, 25 N.Y. 2d 624 (Don. Rel. 1949).

38. *In Re Hudson,* 127 Ped. 675 (Wash. 1942) In Re Weiferth, 309 N.Y. 80, 127 N.E. 2d 820 (1955).

39. *State v. Bailey,* 157 Ind. 324, 61 W.E. 730 (1901) - parent could be presented for *not* sending the child to school.

40. *Brown v. Board* of Education: 347 U.S. 483 (1954).

41. *Pierce v. Society of Sisters,* 268 U.S. 510 at 518 (1925) brought by parents and the K.K.K.

42. The Supreme Court in 1925 struck down a suit which would have prohibited the teaching of German. *Meyer v. Nebraska,* 262 U.S. 390 (1925).

43. From an excellent discussion of the Juvenile Court and its procedures. See: Besharov, Juvenile Justice Advocacy: Practice in an Unique Court, Practicing Law Institute, (1974).

44. *In re Gault,* 387 U.S., at 1967.

45. U.S. Department of Health, Education and Welfare, Juvenile Court Statistics 14, Table 11 (1972).

46. Light. "Abused and Neglected Children in America: A Study of Alternative Policies." *Harvard Ed. Ref.* 43: 556 at 557, 1973.

47. There are some exceptions; see Fraser at note 34.

48. From a discussion of emancipation. See Katz. "Emancipating Our Children." *Fam. Lay Quart* 7:215, 1973.

49. From an interesting discussion of the legal matricies of majority. See Jones. "The Age of Majority." *Am. J. Leg. History* 4:22, 1966.

50. Goldstein, Freed, and Solnit, *Beyond the Best Interests of the Child.* New York: Macmillan, 1973, Chapter III.

51. Areen, note 17.

## CHAPTER EIGHTEEN

1. Reference at this point should be made to the book entitled *The Battered Child,* edited by Ray E. Helfer, M.D. and C. Henry Kempe, M.D., University of Chicago Press, first edition 1968, second edition 1974.

2. The reader is referred to the book, *Helping the Battered Child and His Family,* edited by C. Henry Kempe, M.D. and Ray E. Helfer, M.D. Philadelphia: Lippincott, 1972.

3. The material on screening is covered in "Pediatric Screening" by William Frankenburg, M.D., *Advances in Pediatrics,* Vol. 20, pp 149–175, 1973.

4. The reference to Leon Eisenberg is found in "On Humanizing of Human Nature." *Impact of Science on Society* 23:213–223, 1973.

5. Reference is made at this point to two articles in the Gerber Company Publication, *Pediatric BASICS*. "Making the Diagnosis of Child Abuse and Neglect" and "Therapeutic Approaches," which appeared in January 1974 and November 1974 respectively. In addition to these works, the Office of Child Development has published a manual entitled "Diagnostic Process and Treatment Programs," which contains an overview of some of these basic points. This manual can be obtained by writing to the Office of Child Development. Department of Health, Education and Welfare, P.O. Box 1181, Washington, D.C. 20013.

6. Dr. Ross Parke at Fels Research Institute is one of the few researchers doing work in fathering. His work would indicate that fathers react to newborns much like mothers, and that fathers truly have been underestimated in their capability of providing positive experiences for newborn infants. Refer to *The Developing Individual in the Changing World*, edited by K. Riegal and J. Meacham. Vol. II, The Hague, Mouton 1975.

## CHAPTER EIGHTEEN COMMENTARY

A1. Institute of Society, Ethics, and the Life Sciences—Research Group on Ethical, Social, and Legal Issues in Genetic Counseling and Genetic Engineering. "Ethical and Social Issues in Screening for Genetic Disease." *New Eng. J. Med.* 286: 1129, 1972.

A2. Culliton, B.J. "Patients' Rights: Harvard Is Site of Battle Over X and Y Chromosomes." *Science* 186: 715, 1974. (This research project has since been stopped.)

A3. Further discussion of ethical issues in mass screening programs in general may be found in Chapter 14 of Brody, H. *Ethical Decisions in Medicine*. Boston: Little, Brown. 1976.

## CHAPTER NINETEEN

1. Gray, J. Cutler, C., Dean, J., and Kempe, C.H. "Prediction and Prevention of Child Abuse," *J.A.M.A.* (submitted 1976).

2. Kowalski, K. "On-Call Staffing." *American Journal of Nursing.* October 1973.

3. Dean, J. and Cutler, C. "Mother-Infant Interaction." National Center for the Prevention and Treatment of Child Abuse and Neglect, Department of Pediatrics, University of Colorado Medical Center, Denver. Videotape, 1973.

## CHAPTER NINETEEN COMMENTARY

1. Wolff, P.H. *The Causes, Controls and Organization of Behavior in the Neonate*. New York: International Universities Press, 1966.

2. Robson, K. and Moss, H.A. "Pattern and Determinants of Maternal Attachment." *Pediatrics* 77:976–985, 1970.

3. Moss, H.A. and Robson, J.S. "Maternal Influences in Early Social Visual Behavior." *Child Development* 39:401–403, 1968.

4. Klaus, M. *Maternal Attachment*. Presentation given to College of Human Medicine, Michigan State University, April 1974.

5. Klein, M. and Stern, E. "Low Birthweight and the Battered Child Syndrome." *American Journal of Diseases of Children* 122:15–18, 1971.

6. Shaheen, E., Alexander, D., Truskowsky, M., and Barbero, G.J. "Failure to Thrive—A Retrospective Profile." *Clinical Pediatrics* 7:255–261, 1968.

7. Korner, A., "The Effect of the Infant's State, Level of Arousal, Sex and Ontogenetic Stage On the Caregiver." In Lewis, M. and Rosenblum, L. (Eds.). *The Effect of the Infant on Its Caregiver,* New York: John Wiley, 1974.

8. Korner, A. "Visual Alertness in Neonates: Individual Differences and Their Correlates." *Perceptual and Motor Skills* 31:67–78, 1970.

9. Chess, S. "Temperament and Children at Risk." In Anthony, E., and Koupernik, C. (Eds.). *The Child In His Family.* Vol. 1. New York: Wiley Interscience, 1970.

10. Brazelton, T.B. "Psychophysiological Reaction in the Neonate." *Journal of Pediatrics* 58:513–518, 1961.

11. Brazelton, T.B. *Neonatal Behavioral Assessment Scale.* Philadelphia: J.B. Lippincott, 1973.

12. Broussard, E. and Hartner, M. "Further Considerations Regarding Maternal Perception of the Firstborn. In Hellmuth, J. (Ed.). *Exceptional Infant.* (Vol. 2). New York: Brunner/Mazel, 1971.

13. Escalona, S. *The Roots of Individuality.* Chicago: Aldine, 1968.

14. Spitz, R. *The First Year of Life.* New York: International Universities Press, 1965.

15. Ainsworth, M. and Bell, S. "Some Contemporary Patterns of Mother-Infant Interaction in the Feeding Situation." In Ambrose, A. (Ed.). *Stimulation in Early Infancy.* London: Academic Press, 1969.

## CHAPTER TWENTY

1. Schneider, C., Helfer, R.E., and Pollock, C. "The Predictive Questionnaire: A Preliminary Report." In Kempe, C.H. and Helfer, R.E. *Helping the Battered Child and His Family.* Philadelphia: Lippincott, 1972.

2. Tryon, R.C. and Bailey, D.E. *Cluster Analysis.* New York: McGraw-Hill, 1970.

3. Hoffmeister, J.K. From Self-Esteem Questionnaire Analysis. Personal Communication. Boulder, Colo.: Test Analysis and Development Corporation, 1975.

4. Wachtel, J. and Anderson, S. "A Discriminant Analysis of Known Child-Batterers and Assumed Non-Batterers." Unpublished paper, University of Colorado, Department of Psychology, Boulder, Colo., 1974.

5. Scott, W.A. and Wertheimer, M. *Introduction to Psychological Research.* New York: John Wiley, 1962.

# Index

427

# ✳ Contributors

Helen Alexander, M.S.W.
Coordinator, Circle House
National Center for Prevention and Treatment of Child Abuse and Neglect
Denver, Colorado

---

Patricia Beezley, M.S.W.
Instructor, Department of Pediatrics
Assistant Director, National Center for Prevention and
Treatment of Child Abuse and Neglect
Denver, Colorado

---

Howard Brody, M.D.
Departments of Human Development and Philosophy
Michigan State University, East Lansing, Michigan

---

Claudia A. Carroll, M.S.W.
Clinical Social Worker, Child Protection Team
Department of Pediatrics, University of Colorado School of Medicine
Denver, Colorado

---

Christy Cutler
Research Associate, Department of Pediatrics
University of Colorado School of Medicine
Denver, Colorado

---

Janet Dean
Research Associate, Department of Pediatrics
University of Colorado School of Medicine
Denver, Colorado

---

James Delaney
Judge, 17th Judicial District, Juvenile and Family Division
Hall of Justice
Brighton, Colorado

---

Donald Duquette, J.D.
Assistant Professor, Department of Human Development
Michigan State University, East Lansing, Michigan

---

Brian Fraser, J.D.
Executive Director, National Committee for the Prevention of Child Abuse
Suite 510, 111 East Wacker Drive, Chicago, Illinois

---

Sister Betty Gaiss, O.P.
Graduate Assistant, Department of Human Development
Michigan State University, East Lansing, Michigan

---

Henry Giarretto
Director, Child Sexual Abuse Treatment Program
840 Guadalupe Parkway, San Jose, California

Jane Gray, M.D.
Assistant Clinical Professor, Department of Pediatrics
University of Colorado School of Medicine
Denver, Colorado

---

Candace A. Grosz
Coordinator, Child Protection Team
Department of Pediatrics, University of Colorado Medical Center
Denver, Colorado

---

Ray E. Helfer, M.D.
Professor, Department of Human Development
Michigan State University, East Lansing, Michigan

---

James Hoffmeister, Ph.D.
President, Test Analysis and Development Corporation
Boulder, Colorado

---

Margaret Jeffery
Clinical Psychologist, Child Life Protection Unit
Department for Community Welfare
Perth, Western Australia

---

George Kawamura, M.S.W.
Supervisor of Social Services, Adams County Department of Social Services
Commerce City, Colorado

---

C. Henry Kempe, M.D.
Professor of Pediatrics and Microbiology
Director, The National Center for the Prevention and
Treatment of Child Abuse and Neglect
Department of Pediatrics, University of Colorado Medical Center
Denver, Colorado

Ruth Kempe, M.D.
Assistant Professor of Psychiatry, University of Colorado Medical Center
The National Center for the Prevention and
Treatment of Child Abuse and Neglect
Denver, Colorado

---

John Kennell, M.D.
Professor, Department of Pediatrics
Case Western Reserve University School of Medicine
Cleveland, Ohio

---

Marshall Klaus, M.D.
Professor, Department of Pediatrics
Case Western Reserve University School of Medicine
Cleveland, Ohio

---

Margaret Lynch, M.D.
University of Oxford
Park Hospital for Children
Oxford, United Kingdom

---

Harold Martin, M.D.
Associate Professor, Department of Pediatrics
Assistant Director, JFK Child Development Center
University of Colorado Medical Center
Denver, Colorado

---

John McKinney, Ph.D.
Professor, Departments of Human Development and Psychology
Michigan State University, East Lansing, Michigan

John K. Miller, M.A.
Regional Director of Social Services
Texas Department of Public Welfare
El Paso, Texas

———————————

Christopher Ounsted, M.D.
University of Oxford
Park Hospital for Children
Oxford, United Kingdom

———————————

Leo Roberge, M.D.
Assistant Professor, Division of Child and Adolescent Psychiatry
State University of New York, Upstate Medical Center
Syracuse, New York

———————————

Marshall D. Schechter, M.D.
Professor and Director, Division of Child and Adolescent Psychiatry
State University of New York, Upstate Medical Center
Syracuse, New York

———————————

Rebecca Schmidt, M.A.
Program Specialist, Division of Protective Services
Michigan Department of Social Services
Lansing, Michigan

———————————

Barton D. Schmitt, M.D.
Associate Professor, Department of Pediatrics
Medical Director, Pediatric Outpatient Department
University of Colorado Medical Center
Denver, Colorado

Carol Schneider, Ph.D.
Assistant Professor, Department of Psychology
University of Colorado
Boulder, Colorado

---

Brandt Steele, M.D.
Professor, Department of Psychiatry
University of Colorado Medical Center
Denver, Colorado

---

Diana Voos, B.S.
Research Assistant, Department of Pediatrics
Case Western Reserve University School of Medicine
Cleveland, Ohio

---

Ann Wilson, Ph.D.
Postdoctoral Fellow, Child Development Project
University of Michigan Medical Center
Ann Arbor, Michigan

---